THE POST-IMPRESSIONISTS

THE
POST-
IMPRESSIONISTS

A RETROSPECTIVE

Edited by Martha Kapos

BEAUX ARTS
EDITIONS

For Andrea and Peter

ISBN 0-88363-963-7

This book was produced by Elisabeth Ingles, London, for Hugh Lauter Levin Associates, Inc.

Designer Robert Updegraff.
Typeset by Wyvern Typesetting Ltd, Bristol, UK.
Printed in China.

The excerpts in this book are reproduced by kind permission of the copyright owners and publishers, as follows:

Robert Rey, *La Renaissance du Sentiment Classique dans la Peinture Française à la Fin du XIXe Siècle*, Les Beaux-Arts, Éditions d'Étude et de Documents, Paris 1931. By permission of Archives Wildenstein Institute, Paris.

Norma Broude (ed. and trans.), *Seurat in Perspective*, Prentice Hall, 1978. By permission of Norma Broude.

Joan Ungersma Halperin, *Félix Fénéon, Aesthete and Anarchist in Fin-de-Siècle Paris*, Yale, 1988. Reprinted with permission from Yale University Press, New Haven and London.

John Rewald, *Georges Seurat*, Albin Michel, Paris 1948. French edition © Éditions Albin Michel.

Paul Gauguin, *Lettres à sa Femme et à ses Amis*, ed. Maurice Malingue, 1946. Reprinted by permission of Éditions Bernard Grasset, Paris.

Cézanne: Letters, ed. John Rewald, trans. George and Elsie Hill, 1976. By permission of the Assigns and Successors of Bruno Cassirer Ltd, Oxford.

William Rubin, ed., *Cézanne: The Late Work*. The Museum of Modern Art, New York, 1977. By permission.

Herschel B. Chipp et al (ed.), *Theories of Modern Art: A Source Book by Artists and Critics*. © 1968 The Regents of the University of California.

The Complete Letters of Vincent van Gogh, ed. V. W. van Gogh, 1958. Reprinted with permission of Thames and Hudson Ltd, London.

J.-K. Huysmans, *Against Nature (À Rebours)*, trans. Robert Baldick. Penguin Classics. © Estate of Robert Baldick, 1959.

Judith Wechsler (ed.), *Cézanne in Perspective*, © Prentice Hall, 1975. Reprinted with permission of the publisher, Prentice Hall/A division of Simon & Schuster, Englewood Cliffs, N.J.

Virginia Woolf, *Roger Fry: A Biography*, 1940. With acknowledgements to the Estate of the author and Hogarth Press (Random House UK).

Jack Flam, *Matisse on Art*, 1973. By permission of Phaidon Press Ltd, London.

John Berger, *The Moment of Cubism and Other Essays*, 1969. By permission of the author.

Rainer Maria Rilke, *Letters on Cézanne*, ed. Clara Rilke, 1907. With acknowledgements to the Estate of the author and Jonathan Cape (Random House UK).

Alfred H. Barr, *Picasso, 50 Years of His Art*, trans. Myfanwy Evans. © Museum of Modern Art, New York, 1946.

Maurice Merleau-Ponty, *Sense and Non-Sense*. Trans. with preface by Hubert L. Dreyfus and Patricia Allen Dreyfus, 1964. With acknowledgements to Northwestern University Press, Illinois.

Clement Greenberg, *Art and Culture*, 1961. © Clement Greenberg 1961, reprinted by permission of Beacon Press, Boston, Mass.

Adrian Stokes, *Reflections on the Nude*, Tavistock Publications, 1967. Reprinted with permission of Routledge Ltd.

Bridget Riley, "The Artist's Eye: Seurat," 1991. By permission of *Modern Painters* magazine, London.

The Diaries of Paul Klee, ed. Felix Klee, 1965. By permission of Peter Owen Ltd, London.

Georges Bataille, "Van Gogh as Prometheus," 1937. © Editions Gallimard, 1937. English trans. © *October* Magazine, New York, 1986.

W. H. Auden, *Forewords and Afterwords*, ed. Edward Mendelson. By permission of Faber and Faber Ltd, London, and Random House, Inc., New York.

The Reach of Mind: Essays in Memory of Kurt Goldstein, ed. Marianne Simmel, 1968. © Springer Publishing Co. Inc., New York 10012.

John Rewald, *A History of Impressionism*, 1946, 1961. © the author.

Paul Signac, *D'Eugène Delacroix au Néo-Impressionnisme*, ed. Françoise Cachin, 1964. With acknowledgements to Éditions Hermann, Paris.

Sven Loevgren, *The Genesis of Modernism*, Indiana University Press, 1971. © Estate of the author.

Full information for each excerpt is given in the Bibliographical Index, page 10.

Jacket: Detail of *Orchard in Bloom with Poplars* by Vincent van Gogh. 1889. Bayerische Staatsgemäldesammlungen, Munich. See Colorplate 55.

CONTENTS

Post-Impressionism Defined

Matisse, Braque, and Bonnard

Twentieth-Century Views of Post-Impressionism

ACKNOWLEDGEMENTS

A book of this nature represents the culmination of a process, begun long before the work on the book itself, to which many colleagues and friends have contributed over the years. I am especially indebted to Nicholas Wadley, whose enthusiasm and freely-given help on matters, large and small, to do with this book have been sustaining and indispensable. Steven Bury, the head librarian at the Chelsea School of Art, London, and Liz Ward on his staff have provided unstinting support: I am particularly grateful to them. Financial assistance for research was provided by the Staff Research Fund at Chelsea and I wish to thank Colin Cina, Dean of Art, and Professor Toshio Watanabe, Director of Research, for making this possible. My warmest thanks are due to Judith Landry for work on the translations and particularly to Leon Vilaincour who came to our rescue by applying his imaginative scrutiny to particular obscurities. I am grateful to Sara Waterson for her determined pursuit of some stubbornly elusive pictures and to the editorial and design team with whom I have worked on this book, to Robert Updegraff, and particularly to Elisabeth Ingles whose sensitive and expert supervision of the project in all of its stages has made it a pleasurable and congenial collaboration. For valuable help and more than help I am again grateful to David Black. I also want to thank Ken Kiff who has contributed to the subject of this book with his support, criticism and constant example.

MARTHA KAPOS

Bibliographical Index

Full details of each source book are listed at the first reference, and in abbreviated form thereafter. Where a later edition has been used, the original publication date is given in parentheses. Translations of material previously unpublished in English are by Judith Landry.

p. 37 Linda Nochlin (ed.), *Impressionism and Post-Impressionism, Sources and Documents*, Prentice Hall, N.J. 1966, p. 60, from Notes of Louis Le Bail cited in and trans. J. Rewald, *The History of Impressionism* (1946), Museum of Modern Art, N.Y. 1961, p. 458.

p. 38 Lilla Cabot Perry, "Reminiscences of Claude Monet 1889–1909," *The American Magazine of Art*, XVIII, No.3, March 1927.

p. 39 Jules Laforgue, trans. Wm. J. Smith, "Impressionism: The Eye and the Poet," *Art News* LV, May 1956, pp. 43–5, 16–18, quoted in Nochlin, op. cit.

p. 48 Jules Huret, "Enquête sur L'Évolution Littéraire," Charpentier, Paris 1891, pp. 55–60, rep. in Mallarmé, *Oeuvres complètes*, ed. H. Mondor and G. Jean-Aubry, Gallimard, Paris 1945, pp. 869, 870.

p. 50 Georges Lecomte, "L'Art Contemporain," *La Revue Indépendante*, April 1892, No. 66.

p. 52 Marcel Proust, *By Way of Sainte-Beuve*, trans. Sylvia Townsend Warner, Chatto and Windus, London 1958, pp. 266–8.

p. 54 Pierre Francastel, *L'Impressionnisme*, Paris 1937, pp. 138, 143–7.

p. 57 *Lettres de Gauguin à sa Femme et à ses Amis*, ed. Maurice Malingue, Édns Bernard Grasset, Paris 1946, pp. 44–7.

p. 58 *Camille Pissarro: Letters to Lucien*, ed. J. Rewald, Routledge, London and Paul Appel, N.Y. (1943) 1980, pp. 377–8.

p. 59 *Pissarro: Letters*, op. cit., p. 276.

p. 59 *Cézanne: Letters*, ed. J. Rewald, trans. George and Elsie Hill, Bruno Cassirer, Oxford 1976, pp. 270–1, 296–9.

p. 61 Lawrence Gowing, "The Logic of Organized Sensations," *Cézanne: The Late Work*, ed. Wm. Rubin, Museum of Modern Art, N.Y., and New York Graphic Society, Boston 1977, pp. 61–2.

p. 71 Robert Rey, *La Renaissance du Sentiment Classique dans la Peinture Française à la Fin du XIXe Siècle*, Les Beaux-Arts, Édns d'Étude et de Documents, Paris 1931, pp. 95–6.

p. 72 *Pissarro: Letters*, op. cit., pp. 72–4.

p. 73 Félix Fénéon, "Eighth Impressionist Exhibition," *La Vogue*, June 7 and 15, 1886, quoted in Norma Broude (ed. and trans.), *Seurat in Perspective*, Prentice Hall, N.J. 1978, pp. 36–9.

p. 75 J.-K. Huysmans, "Chronicle of Art: The Independents," *La Revue Indépendante*, April 1887, quoted in Broude, op. cit., pp. 43–4.

p. 76 J. U. Halperin, *Félix Fénéon, Aesthete and Anarchist in Fin-de-Siècle Paris*, Yale, N.H. and London 1988, pp. 137–42.

p. 78 John Rewald, *Georges Seurat*, Albin Michel, Paris 1948, pp. 111–16.

p. 83 Paul Signac, *D'Eugène Delacroix au Néo-Impressionnisme*, ed. Françoise Cachin, Hermann, Paris 1964, pp. 89–101.

p. 85 V. W. van Gogh (ed.), *The Complete Letters of Vincent van Gogh*, Thames and Hudson, London, and New York Graphic Society, Boston 1958, III, No. 607.

p. 86 Maurice Denis, *Théories 1890–1910: Du Symbolisme et de Gauguin vers un nouvel ordre classique*, ed. L. Rouart and J. Watelin, Paris 1920, repr. in Herschel B. Chipp (ed.), *Theories of Modern Art: A Source Book by Artists and Critics*, University of California, Berkeley 1968, pp. 100–4.

p. 97 Paul Sérusier, *ABC de la Peinture, Correspondance* (1921), Floury, Paris 1950, pp. 39–42.

p. 99 Maurice Denis, *Théories*, op. cit., repr. in Chipp, op. cit., pp. 94–7.

p. 101 Paul Signac, *Journal Inédit*, ed. J. Rewald, in *Gazette des Beaux-Arts*, July–September 1949, pp. 101, 102, 107, 123–5.

p. 103 *Pissarro: Letters*, op. cit., p. 49.

p. 104 *Van Gogh Letters*, op. cit., III, No. B11.

p. 106 Jacques Daurelle, "Chez les Jeunes Peintres," *Écho de Paris*, December 28, 1891.

p. 109 Charles Morice, "Enquête sur les Tendances Actuelles des Arts Plastiques," *Mercure de France*, August 1 and 15, September 1, 1905.

p. 123 George Moore, *Reminiscences of the Impressionist Painters*, Maunsel, Dublin 1906, pp. 34–5.

p. 124 repr. in Nochlin, op. cit., pp. 103–4.

p. 125 Maurice Denis, *Théories*, op. cit., pp. 245–6.

p. 126 *Van Gogh Letters*, op. cit., III, Nos. 543, 544.

p. 129 *Lettres de Gauguin*, op. cit., No. XCI.

p. 131 Paul Gauguin, *Lettres à Odilon Redon*, ed. R. Bacou, Librairie José Corti, Paris 1960, pp. 193–4.

p. 132 J.-K. Huysmans, *Against Nature*, trans. Robert Baldick, Penguin, London 1959, pp. 194–7, 198–9.

p. 134 Henri Beauclair and Gabriel Vicaire, *Les Déliquescences, Poèmes Décadents d'Adoré Floupette*, Crès, Paris 1911, pp. 11–45.

p. 148 Jean Moréas, "Un Manifeste Littéraire: Le Symbolisme," *Le Figaro Littéraire*, September 18, 1886, pp. 31–5, 38–9.

p. 151 Gustave Kahn, "Réponse des Symbolistes," *L'Événement*, September 28, 1886.

p. 153 Téodor de Wyzewa, *Nos Maîtres, Études et Portraits Littéraires*, Librairie Académique Perrin, Paris 1895, pp. 11–55 (excerpts).

p. 167 J.-K. Huysmans, *Certains*, Tresse & Stock, Paris 1889, pp. 150–4.

p. 168 *Lettres d'Odilon Redon*, Librairie Nationale d'Art et d'Histoire G. van Oest, Paris and Brussels 1923, pp. 33–5.

p. 169 repr. in Chipp, op. cit., pp. 116–19.

p. 172 *Lettres de Gauguin*, op. cit.

p. 173 Sven Loevgren, *The Genesis of Modernism: Seurat, Gauguin, Van Gogh and French Symbolism in the 1880s*, Indiana University Press, 1971, pp. 144–5.

p. 174 *Lettres de Gauguin*, op. cit., No. CVI.

p. 175 G.-Albert Aurier, "Le Symbolisme en Peinture: Paul Gauguin," *Mercure de France*, March 1891.

p. 181 Alphonse Germain, "Théorie des Déformateurs: Exposé et Réfutation," *La Plume*, September 1, 1891.

p. 191 Paul Gauguin, "Armand Séguin," *Mercure de France*, February 1895.

p. 193 Maurice Denis, "À Propos de l'Exposition d'Armand Séguin," *La Plume*, March 1, 1895, repr. in *Théories*, op. cit., pp. 20–3.

p. 196 René Maurice, "Concernant Gauguin," *Nouvelle Revue de Bretagne*, Rennes, November–December 1953.

p. 199 Paul Gauguin, "Genesis of a Painting," *Cahier pour Aline*, 1893, Bibliothèque d'Art et d'Archéologie Fondation Jacques Doucet, Paris.

p. 200 André Fontainas, "Modern Art – Gauguin," *Mercure de France*, January 1899, repr. in J. Rewald, *Studies in Post-Impressionism*, London and N.Y. 1986, pp. 180–2.

p. 203 Paul Gauguin, Letter to Fontainas, March 1899, repr. in J. Rewald, *Studies in Post-Impressionism*, op. cit., pp. 182–4.

p. 206 Paul Gauguin, *Lettres à Daniel de Monfreid*, Crès, Paris 1918.

p. 216 *Van Gogh Letters*, op. cit., II, Nos. 309, 418.

p. 218 *Van Gogh Letters*, op. cit., III, No. B3.

p. 219 *Van Gogh Letters*, op. cit., III, Nos. 534, 535, 574.

p. 222 *Van Gogh Letters*, op. cit. IV, No. B21. Translation amended by the editor.

p. 223 G.-Albert Aurier, "Les Isolés: Vincent van Gogh," *Mercure de France*, January 1890.

p. 227 *Van Gogh Letters*, op. cit., III, Nos. 625, 626, 626a, W.20, 629.

p. 229 *Lettres de Vincent van Gogh à Émile Bernard*, Vollard, Paris 1911, Preface.

p. 245 Paul Gauguin, Letter to Émile Bernard, January 1891.

p. 245 Paul Gauguin, "Avant et Après," *Mercure de France*, October 1903, repr. Crès, Paris 1923.

p. 250 *Joachim Gasquet's Cézanne*, Paris 1921, trans. Christopher Pemberton, Introduction by Richard Shiff, Thames and Hudson, London 1991.

p. 252 repr. in Judith Wechsler (ed.), *Cézanne in Perspective*, Prentice Hall, N.J. 1975, pp. 39–45.

p. 258 *Cézanne: Letters*, op. cit., pp. 305–6, 316–17, 336–7.

p. 259 *Pissarro: Letters*, op. cit., pp. 275–6.

p. 269 R. P. Rivière and J. F. Schnerb, "L'Atelier de Cézanne," *La Grande Revue*, December 25, 1907, repr. L'Échoppe, Paris, 1991.

p. 274 "A New School," *Le Figaro*, September 14, 1891.

p. 274 Charles Merki, "Apologie pour la Peinture," *Mercure de France*, June 1893, pp. 141–4, 147–9.

p. 277 repr. in Nochlin, op. cit., pp. 104–7.

p. 280 Georges Lecomte, "Paul Cézanne," *La Revue d'Art*, December 9, 1899, pp. 81–7.

p. 284 Émile Bernard, "Reflexions à propos du Salon d'Automne," *La Rénovation Esthétique*, December 1907, pp. 59–66.

p. 296 Roger Fry and Desmond MacCarthy, Introduction to the catalogue "Manet and the Post-Impressionists," Grafton Galleries, London, November 8, 1910–January 15, 1911, pp. 7–12.

p. 299 Virginia Woolf, *Roger Fry: A Biography*, Hogarth Press, London (1940) 1969, pp. 152, 153–8.

p. 302 Desmond MacCarthy, "The Art-Quake of 1910," *The Listener*, February 1, 1945, pp. 123–4.

p. 304 Jack Flam, *Matisse on Art*, Phaidon, London, and Praeger, N.Y. 1973, p. 128.

p. 304 "The Persistence of Fauvism," *Minotaure*, October 15, 1936.

p. 306 *L'Art Vivant*, p. 55, repr. in Flam, op. cit.

p. 306 André Verdet, *Entretiens, Notes et Écrits sur la Peinture, Braque, Léger, Matisse, Picasso, XXe Siècle* 24, No. 18, February 1962, repr. Édns Galilée, Paris 1978, pp. 14, 18–19; *Chroniques du Jour, XXe Siècle*, Supplément au No. 18.

p. 308 Jacques Lassaigne, "Conversation avec Georges Braque," *XXe Siècle*, December 1973.

p. 319 Angèle Lamotte, "The Bouquet of Roses," *Verve* V, Nos. 17–18, 1947, pp. 3–8.

p. 320 Annette Vaillant, *Bonnard*, Thames and Hudson, London 1966, p. 146.

p. 320 Charles Terrasse, "L'Amandier en Fleur de Bonnard," *Revue du Louvre et des Musées de France* 14, no. 3, 1964.

p. 321 Georges Besson, Letter to Pierre Betz, *Le Point*, Revue Artistique et Littéraire, Lanzac, pp. 40–6.

p. 322 John Berger, *The Moment of Cubism and Other Essays*, Weidenfeld and Nicolson, London 1969, pp. 117–23.

p. 327 Rainer Maria Rilke, *Letters on Cézanne*, ed. Clara Rilke, Cape, London 1988 (letters of October 1907).

p. 330 Hélène Parmelin, *Picasso Says . . .*, George Allen and Unwin, London 1969, p. 72.

p. 330 Alfred H. Barr, trans. Myfanwy Evans, *Picasso: 50 Years of His Art*, Museum of Modern Art, N.Y. 1946, repr. in Wechsler, op. cit., p. 77.

p. 330 Maurice Merleau-Ponty, *Sense and Non-Sense*, trans. with preface by Hubert L. Dreyfus and Patricia Allen Dreyfus, Northwestern University Press, Illinois 1964, pp. 12–19.

p. 343 Clement Greenberg, *Art and Culture*, Boston 1961, pp. 50–8.

p. 348 Adrian Stokes, "The Image in Form – A Lecture," *British Journal of Aesthetics* 4, July 1966, repr. in *Reflections on the Nude*, Tavistock, London and N.Y. 1967, pp. 47, 48–50, 53–6.

p. 351 Bridget Riley, "The Artist's Eye: Seurat," *Modern Painters* 4, No. 2, Summer 1991, pp. 10–14.

p. 354 *The Diaries of Paul Klee*, ed. Felix Klee, Peter Owen, London 1965, pp. 223–4, 259–60.

p. 355 Georges Bataille, "Van Gogh as Prometheus," *Verve*, December 1937, repr. *October* 36, Spring 1986, pp. 58–60.

p. 365 René Magritte, "Van Gogh and Freedom," *Cahier de Nevelvlek–Van Gogh*, Antwerp, May–June 1955.

p. 366 W. H. Auden, *Forewords and Afterwords*, ed. Edward Mendelson, Faber, London, and Random House, N.Y. (1943) 1973, pp. 294–301.

p. 371 Meyer Schapiro, "The Still Life as a Personal Object," *The Reach of Mind: Essays in Memory of Kurt Goldstein*, ed. Marianne L. Simmel, Springer, N.Y. 1968, pp. 203–8.

CHRONOLOGY

1839
JANUARY 19. Birth of Paul Cézanne in Aix-en-Provence.

1840
APRIL 20. Birth of Odilon Redon in Bordeaux. His childhood is spent on his family's estate, Peyrelebade, in the Médoc.

1848
JUNE 7. Birth of Eugène-Henri-Paul Gauguin in Paris.

1849
Gauguin's family leaves France for Peru.

c. 1852–8
Cézanne at the Collège Bourbon where he makes friends with Émile Zola.

1853
MARCH 30. Birth of Vincent Willem van Gogh in Groot-Zundert, the Netherlands.

1855
Gauguin's father having died, his mother returns to France with the children to live in Orléans.

1858
NOVEMBER (until August 1859). Cézanne works at the Free Municipal School for Drawing, Aix.

1859
Cézanne studies law at the University of Aix, but dreams of becoming a painter.
DECEMBER 2. Birth of Georges Pierre Seurat in Paris.

1861
Cézanne abandons law studies. From April to autumn in Paris. He visits the Salon and studies painting at the Académie Suisse where he meets Pissarro. In September he returns discouraged to Aix and enters his father's bank.

1862
NOVEMBER. Cézanne returns to Paris, tries for entrance to the École des Beaux-Arts and fails.
Redon fails entrance to the École des Beaux-Arts.

1863
Cézanne exhibits at the Salon des Refusés, works at the Académie Suisse.
DECEMBER 12. Birth of Edvard Munch in Loeten, Norway.

1864
Cézanne rejected at the Salon; returns to Aix for the summer, visits L'Estaque in August.
Redon meets Rodolphe Bresdin in Bordeaux. Briefly a pupil of Jean-Léon Gérôme in Paris.
Munch's family moves to Oslo.

1865
Cézanne in Paris; returns to Aix for the summer.

Gauguin joins the merchant marine as an apprentice on a ship *en route* for Rio de Janeiro.

1866
Cézanne rejected at the Salon, writes letter of protest to the Director of Fine Arts. At Bennecourt on the Seine in July, develops interest in painting out of doors. August to December in Aix, begins palette-knife paintings.
Gauguin sails for South America as a second lieutenant in the merchant marine.

1867
Cézanne in Paris where he is rejected at the Salon, but defended by Zola in the press. In Aix for the summer.
Redon has an etching accepted at the Salon.
OCTOBER 13. Birth of Pierre Bonnard in Fontenay-aux-Roses.

1868
Cézanne rejected at the Salon. May to December in Aix, working at the Jas de Bouffan.
Redon publishes his "Salon de 1868" in *La Gironde*.
Gauguin joins the navy and completes his military service in 1871.
Munch's mother dies of tuberculosis.

1869
Cézanne in Paris, rejected at the Salon. He meets Hortense Fiquet, his future wife.
Van Gogh leaves his parents' home in Zundert after secondary school and starts work as a junior clerk for the art dealers Goupil & Co. in The Hague.
DECEMBER 31. Birth of Henri-Émile-Benoît Matisse in Le Cateau-Cambrésis, Picardy.

1870
Escaping from the draft (Franco-Prussian War), Cézanne lives with Hortense, working in Aix, and later in L'Estaque.

1871
Cézanne returns to Paris in the autumn.
Gauguin returns to Paris and secures a position at the brokerage firm of Paul Bertin. At around this time he begins painting and becomes familiar with Impressionism.

1872
Cézanne's son Paul is born in January. He moves with his family to Saint-Ouen near Pontoise where he works out of doors with Pissarro. At the end of the year he moves to Auvers-sur-Oise where Dr. Gachet has bought a house.
Gauguin meets Émile Schuffenecker at Bertin's firm. They study painting together at the Colarossi Academy.

1873
Cézanne spends the year at Auvers-sur-Oise.
Gauguin marries a Danish woman, Mette Sophie Gad.
Van Gogh is transferred to the London branch of Goupil's and until March 1876, when he is discharged from the firm, he works in London and Paris.

1874

JUNE. Cézanne returns to Aix, and then to Paris in the autumn. He participates in the first Impressionist group exhibition at the boulevard des Capucines where he exhibits *A Modern Olympia* and two landscapes.

Gauguin's first son, Emil, is born. At around this time Gauguin makes the acquaintance of Pissarro who introduces him to his Impressionist colleagues.

1875

Cézanne is introduced by Renoir to the collector Victor Chocquet whose portrait he paints. Lives in Paris, Quai d'Anjou.

1876

The Impressionists hold their second group exhibition at 11 rue le Peletier. Cézanne does not participate, but submits to the Salon instead and is rejected. He works in L'Estaque in the spring and returns to Paris in the autumn.

Gauguin submits to the Salon and is accepted.

After his discharge from Goupil's, Van Gogh returns to England where he becomes a teacher in Ramsgate and Isleworth.

After secondary school Seurat pursues his studies in drawing at the École Municipale de Sculpture et de Dessin. He meets Amand-Edmond Jean (Aman-Jean).

1877

Cézanne exhibits 16 works in the third Impressionist group show at 6 rue Le Peletier. He works with Pissarro at Pontoise, also Auvers and Issy.

Gauguin's daughter Aline is born.

Van Gogh returns to the Netherlands to prepare for entrance to the faculty of theology at the University of Amsterdam.

Munch's older sister dies of tuberculosis aged 15.

1878

Cézanne is rejected at the Salon. He works in Aix with Monticelli, a fellow Provençal painter, and in L'Estaque.

Redon exhibits a charcoal drawing at the Salon. He makes a first visit to the Netherlands.

Van Gogh abandons theological studies and enrolls in a course for evangelists. He fails to qualify and returns to parents' home in Etten. At the end of December he leaves for the Borinage, the coalmining district of Belgium, to begin missionary work.

Seurat is accepted at the École des Beaux-Arts and enters the studio of Henri Lehmann.

1879

Despite the intervention of Guillemet, a member of the jury, Cézanne is again rejected at the Salon. He returns to Paris in the spring, and then from April to December he lives in Melun, visiting Zola at Médan. The Impressionists hold their fourth group exhibition at 28 avenue de l'Opéra.

Redon publishes his first album of lithographs, "Dans le rêve."

Gauguin begins to collect the paintings of the Impressionists. Exhibits with them at the fourth group show, and in the summer paints with Pissarro in Pontoise.

Van Gogh is dismissed as preacher in July, but continues mission work in Cuesmes on his own.

Seurat begins military service in Brest.

Munch enters Technical College to study engineering.

1880

Cézanne divides his time between Melun, Paris, and Médan where he visits Zola and is introduced to J.-K. Huysmans. The Impressionists hold their fifth group exhibition at 10 rue des Pyramides. Gauguin exhibits eight works.

MAY 1. Redon marries Camille Falte.

With serious ambitions of becoming an artist, Van Gogh abandons evangelical work, and leaves the Borinage for Brussels to prepare for entrance to the Académie des Beaux-Arts.

Seurat completes military service and returns to Paris.

Munch drops engineering studies because of poor health. He begins to paint and to study history of art.

1881

Cézanne in Paris until April, spends May to October in Pontoise with Pissarro and meets Gauguin. Visits Zola in Médan and returns to Aix in November. The Impressionists hold their sixth group exhibition at 35 boulevard des Capucines. Gauguin exhibits six works.

Redon's first one-man show is held at the offices of *La Vie Moderne*.

Van Gogh visits The Hague where he meets his cousin, the artist Anton Mauve.

Seurat shares studio with Aman-Jean, reads scientific works of Sutter and Rood and takes an interest in Delacroix. Spends summer with Aman-Jean in Pontaubert.

Munch enters School of Design.

1882

Cézanne exhibits a portrait of a man (possibly a self-portrait?) at the Salon as a "pupil of Guillemet." Spends most of the year in Paris, but visits Zola at Médan, and returns to Aix in October where he works at the Jas de Bouffan.

Redon's second exhibition is held at the offices of *Le Gaulois*.

Gauguin exhibits in the seventh Impressionist show and in the summer paints in Pontoise.

Van Gogh moves into a small studio in The Hague where he lives with the prostitute "Sien" and her daughter.

Munch rents a studio with six friends. Their work is supervised by the naturalist painter Christian Krohg.

Matisse attends Lycée de Saint-Quentin.

MAY 13. Birth of Georges Braque in Argenteuil-sur-Seine.

1883

Cézanne spends most of the year around Aix; apparently attends Manet's funeral in Paris, May 4. From May to November in L'Estaque. In December meets up with Monet and Renoir working on the Riviera. Gauguin purchases two of Cézanne's paintings from Père Tanguy.

Redon publishes "Les Origines," an album of lithographs. For three months each year until 1885 he works in Morgat, Crozon, Douarnenez (Finistère).

At around this time Gauguin leaves the brokerage firm to devote himself entirely to painting.

Van Gogh breaks with Sien, leaves The Hague for Drenthe and in December moves back to his parents' in Neunen for the next two years.

Seurat exhibits a drawing at the Salon. Begins work on *Une Baignade* ("Bathing at Asnières").

1884

Cézanne submits to the Salon, but is rejected in spite of

intervention by Guillemet. Working mostly in and around Aix, Signac buys a Cézanne landscape from Père Tanguy.

Redon is a co-founder of the Salon des Indépendants. The first exhibition, held in May–July, includes Angrand, Cross, Dubois-Pillet, Redon, Schuffenecker, Signac, and Seurat who shows *Une Baignade*.

À Rebours ("Against Nature") by J.-K. Huysmans published. The mention of Redon creates interest in his work.

Gauguin's family moves to Denmark where he works for a French canvas manufacturer.

Van Gogh rents a studio in Neunen and begins giving painting lessons.

Munch establishes contact with Christian-Bohême, the avant-garde artists' and writers' group in Oslo.

1885

Cézanne spends most of the year in Aix. During June and July takes his family to stay with the Renoirs at La Roche-Guyon.

Redon meets Mallarmé. The lithographic album "Hommage à Goya" is published.

Disliking Denmark, Gauguin returns to Paris with his son Clovis and lives temporarily with Émile Schuffenecker. Works as a billposter.

Van Gogh moves into his studio following the death of his father. Visits Rijksmuseum in Amsterdam; especially admires Rembrandt and Hals.

Seurat works at Grandcamp during the summer and in October completes *Un dimanche à la Grande Jatte* ("Sunday Afternoon on the Island of La Grande Jatte"). Signac introduces him to Pissarro at Durand-Ruel's. At around this time Seurat begins a clandestine relationship with Madeleine Knobloch.

Munch makes a significant trip to Paris for three weeks. Studies at Louvre; particularly impressed by Manet's work.

After his *baccalauréat* Bonnard enrolls to study law.

1886

Cézanne marries Hortense Fiquet. Receives sizeable inheritance following the death of his father in October. Zola's *L'Oeuvre* ("The Masterpiece") is published in April and, deeply hurt, Cézanne breaks off their friendship.

Redon's son is born and dies in infancy. The lithographic album "La Nuit" is published. He exhibits in Brussels with *Les XX*, and in Paris at the eighth and final Impressionist exhibition and at the Salon des Indépendants.

Van Gogh enrolls at the Academy in Antwerp in January, but moves to Paris (*c.* February 28). He studies at Cormon's studio and lives with his brother Theo, through whom he is introduced to Pissarro, Bernard and Gauguin. He frequents the color shop of Père Tanguy and experiments with Impressionist techniques.

Gauguin participates in the final Impressionist exhibition at 1 rue Laffitte. He meets the ceramicist Ernest Chaplet with whom he makes his first ceramics. He moves to the artists' colony of Pont-Aven in Brittany where he boards at the Hôtel Gloanec and rents a small studio. He meets Émile Bernard. Returning to Paris in the autumn he meets Vincent van Gogh through the latter's brother Theo at the Galerie Boussod & Valadon.

Invited by Pissarro, Seurat participates in the eighth Impressionist exhibition with *Un dimanche à la Grande Jatte* together with works from Grandcamp and Honfleur. He also shows at the second Salon des Indépendants, where the Neo-Impressionists have a separate room.

Munch exhibits four paintings in the annual autumn salon. *The Sick Child* causes controversy.

Moréas publishes the "Symbolist Manifesto," Gustave Kahn: "Réponse des symbolistes." Mallarmé's Tuesday evening gatherings become an important venue for artists and writers.

1887

Cézanne spends most of the year working in and around Aix.

Redon's lithographs for Picard's *Le Juré* published in Brussels in book form, and in Paris as an album.

Gauguin leaves Paris with Charles Laval for Panama where he works as a navvy on the canal. They travel together to Martinique. Returning to Paris he lives with Schuffenecker who introduces him to Daniel de Monfreid. They become lifelong friends.

Van Gogh meets Signac with whom he works on the banks of the Seine at St-Ouen and at Asnières, where he also paints in the company of Bernard. Towards the end of the year he meets Seurat.

Seurat exhibits *Un dimanche à la Grande Jatte* with *Les XX* in Brussels. He works on *Les Poseuses* and begins *La Parade*.

Bonnard paints landscapes reminiscent of Corot at Grandcamp. While pursuing his law studies in Paris he also enrolls at the Académie Julian where he meets Sérusier, Denis, Ibels and Ranson.

Matisse goes to Paris to study law.

1888

Cézanne works with Renoir in L'Estaque, then in Paris and Chantilly. An article by Huysmans appears in *La Cravache* and Cézanne begins to be mentioned in Symbolist magazines.

Redon publishes "La Tentation de St. Antoine" (first series), an album of lithographs. He spends the summer in Samois near Valvins, seeing Mallarmé frequently. He begins the journal "À Soi-Même."

Van Gogh moves to Arles in February, renting rooms in the "Yellow House" in May.

Gauguin returns to Pont-Aven in February where he works with Laval, Sérusier, and Émile Bernard. Sérusier's *Talisman*, painted under tutelage of Gauguin, leads to the foundation in the winter of 1888–89 of the Nabi group by Sérusier, Denis, Bonnard, Ranson. They are joined in 1889 by Roussel and Vuillard. In October Gauguin is persuaded by Van Gogh to join him at Theo van Gogh's expense in Arles. They work together until Van Gogh's breakdown on December 23, after which he returns immediately to Paris.

Seurat exhibits ten works at the Salon des Indépendants. He returns to the Grande Jatte to paint with Angrand in the spring and spends the summer at Port-en-Bessin. Pissarro invites him to Eragny with Signac.

Munch travels in Norway.

Bonnard, having failed his oral law examination, begins work in a government office. Continues at Académie Julian.

Matisse passes his law examinations with distinction and returns to Picardy to practice as a solicitor.

1889

La Maison du Pendu ("The House of the Hanged Man") by Cézanne is shown at Paris World's Fair. He visits Chocquet in Normandy, spends most of year in Aix.

Redon publishes "À Gustave Flaubert," an album of lithographs. His second son Ari is born. Redon exhibits with the Society of Painter-Engravers at Durand-Ruel and will do so annually until 1893. He meets André Mellerio, his future biographer. Spends second summer in Samois.

Gauguin helps with the organization of the group exhibition of Impressionists and Synthetists at the Café Volpini which opens in May. Gauguin shows twelve works with *Les XX* in Brussels. The rest of the year is spent between Pont-Aven and Le Pouldu with Sérusier and Meyer de Haan.

Van Gogh is hospitalized for ten days following his attack and in May is voluntarily committed to the asylum of Saint-Paul-de-Mausole in Saint-Rémy, where he is diagnosed as suffering from an epileptic disorder. Two paintings are included in the Salon des Indépendants.

Seurat shows *Les Poseuses* and other works with *Les XX* in Brussels. Spends summer painting in Le Crotoy.

Munch has his first one-man show, with 110 paintings. He moves to Paris in October and studies with Léon Bonnat.

The Café Volpini exhibition and particularly the paintings by Gauguin make an impression on Bonnard and he resolves to become an artist. He is accepted at the École des Beaux-Arts where he meets Roussel and Vuillard.

1890

Cézanne exhibits three works with *Les XX* in Brussels. Spends summer in Switzerland; returns to Aix in the autumn where he works on *Card Players* series. Begins to suffer from diabetes.

Redon publishes illustrations to Baudelaire's *Les Fleurs du Mal* ("Flowers of Evil") in Brussels where he again exhibits with *Les XX*. He exchanges works with Gauguin, whom he sees frequently, and through whom he meets Sérusier. Begins to be friendly with the Nabis.

Gauguin divides his time between Paris, Pont-Aven and Le Pouldu. At around this time he conceives of the idea of founding a "studio of the tropics" in Madagascar or Tahiti. His request for a foreign appointment is rejected by the Colonial Department.

Article by Aurier on Van Gogh, "Les Isolés," published in the *Mercure de France*. He shows six paintings with *Les XX* in Brussels, and ten paintings with the Indépendants in Paris. In May Van Gogh moves to Auvers to be in the care of Dr. Gachet. He shoots himself while working in the Auvers countryside and dies on July 29. Theo after organizing a show of paintings in his Montmartre apartment suffers a serious breakdown and dies in January 1891.

Seurat's son Pierre Georges is born to Madeleine Knobloch. He exhibits *Le Chahut* at the Salon des Indépendants. Summer at Gravelines.

Munch lives in St-Cloud with the Danish poet Emanuel Goldstein. He returns to Norway in May. During course of visit to Le Havre in November he becomes ill with rheumatic fever.

Bonnard begins a period of military service in Bourgoin.

Recovering from an attack of appendicitis, Matisse does his first paintings with a set of watercolors given him by his mother.

1891

Cézanne divides his time between Aix and Paris. He becomes a devout Catholic at around this period.

Redon publishes "Songes," an album of lithographs.

A successful sale of Gauguin's paintings is held at the Hôtel Drouot, and he exhibits ceramics and sculpture with *Les XX* in Brussels. Charles Morice helps to arrange Gauguin's travel to Tahiti and before his departure a banquet is held in his honor at the Café Voltaire, presided over by Mallarmé. He arrives in Papeete, Tahiti, on June 9.

DECEMBER: Le Barc de Boutteville holds first "Exhibition of Impressionist and Symbolist Painters," including Gauguin and Bonnard.

Seurat exhibits *Le Cirque* and paintings from Gravelines at the seventh Salon des Indépendants. He dies suddenly after two days of illness on March 29.

After convalescing from illness in Nice, Munch returns to Norway via Paris. He participates in the autumn Salon in Oslo.

First Nabis group exhibition in Saint-Germain-en-Laye includes a painting by Bonnard. He also shows five paintings and four decorative panels at the Salon des Indépendants. He acquires a new studio which he shares with Vuillard and Denis in the rue Pigalle; a frequent visitor is Lugné-Poë, the actor and co-founder of the Théâtre d'Art, for which Bonnard works painting set designs. His successful poster "France-Champagne" inspires Lautrec.

Matisse returns to Paris to study art. He studies at the Académie Julian and with Adolphe Bouguereau.

1892

Cézanne works in Aix, Paris and in the forest of Fontainebleau. Aurier describes him as an important forerunner of Symbolism.

Requiring hospitalization and in need of funds, Gauguin applies to the French Government for repatriation. The first examples of his Tahitian paintings are sent back to France.

An exhibition of paintings by Van Gogh is organized by Bernard at Le Barc de Boutteville in April. The gallery holds the second Exhibition of Impressionist and Symbolist Painters in May and a third show in November to which Gauguin and Bonnard contribute.

A memorial retrospective exhibition for Seurat is held at the Salon des Indépendants.

Munch's exhibition of 55 paintings at the Verein Berliner Künstler closes after a week of scandal. The show travels to Düsseldorf and Cologne.

Bonnard shows seven paintings at the Salon des Indépendants and participates in the Nabi exhibition in Saint-Germain-en-Laye.

Matisse fails entrance to École des Beaux-Arts. He begins courses at the École des Arts Décoratifs where he meets Marquet. He is accepted as a student by Gustave Moreau. Meets Rouault.

1893

Cézanne continues working in Aix, Paris and the forest of Fontainebleau.

Gauguin exhibits 50 works in the Free Exhibition of Modern Art in Copenhagen; works are also included in an exhibition in the offices of *La Plume* organized by Le Barc de Boutteville. Gauguin succeeds in application for repatriation and returns to Paris in August, bringing 66 paintings with him. In November a major exhibition of Tahitian works is held by Durand-Ruel. At around this time Gauguin begins draft of *Noa Noa* in collaboration with Charles Morice.

Munch works in Berlin on *Frieze of Life*. He establishes connections with avant-garde writers and poets.

Bonnard exhibits four paintings at the Salon des Indépendants and in a group show at Le Barc de Boutteville. He meets Maria Boursin, "Marthe," his future wife.

1894
Cézanne visits Monet at Giverny and is introduced to Clemenceau, Rodin and Geffroy. Ambroise Vollard opens gallery in rue Laffitte, and buys works by Cézanne at the auction of Père Tanguy's stock following his death (1893).

Redon shows paintings and pastels in a major exhibition at Durand-Ruel in March–April. Exhibits at La Libre Esthétique in Brussels where Gauguin is also showing five paintings.

Gauguin participates in group exhibition at Le Barc de Boutteville. MAY: breaks his leg in brawl in Concarneau near Le Pouldu when assaulted by a group of local sailors.

Munch begins to make his first prints. A monograph including a piece by Julius Meier-Graefe is published.

Bonnard exhibits two paintings at Le Barc de Boutteville. He designs a poster for *La Revue Blanche* and becomes friendly with Thadée and Misia Natanson. Close friendship with Toulouse-Lautrec.

Birth of Matisse's daughter Marguerite to Caroline Joblaud.

1895
NOVEMBER. Cézanne's first one-man show is held at Vollard's gallery for which Cézanne has sent 150 works. In Paris from January to June, then in Aix with excursions to Bibémus quarry and Mont Sainte-Victoire.

Following an auction of 47 works at the Hôtel Drouot of which nine are sold, Gauguin leaves again for Tahiti, arriving in September in Papeete.

Munch's etchings are sold by the Paris office of the magazine *Pan*. *La Revue Blanche* reproduces *The Scream*. Meier-Graefe publishes portfolio of etchings.

Bonnard produces several lithographs for *La Revue Blanche*.

Matisse gains entrance to École des Beaux-Arts. Impressed by Corot exhibition at the Palais Galliéra.

Durand-Ruel shows Monet including the Rouen Cathedral series.

1896
Cézanne in Vichy, and Talloires on the Lac d'Annecy. Meets the poet Joachim Gasquet.

Redon publishes the lithographic albums "La Maison hantée," "La Tentation de St.-Antoine" (third series).

Gauguin without funds and suffering from severe leg pain for which he takes morphine, speaks of suicide and is hospitalized in July. Vollard holds a Gauguin exhibition at his gallery in late November.

Munch leaves Berlin for Paris where he makes his first color lithographs and woodcuts. Contributes *Anxiety* to Vollard's *album des peintres-graveurs*.

Durand-Ruel holds a first one-man show of Bonnard. In December Bonnard works with Sérusier, Lautrec, Vuillard, Ranson and Jarry on sets and masks for the Théâtre de L'Oeuvre production of Jarry's *Ubu Roi*.

Matisse exhibits first works at the Salon des Cent of the Symbolist magazine *La Plume*. Visits Brittany and Belle-Île in the summer.

1897
Cézanne works in Paris, in the forest of Fontainebleau, at Marlotte and Mennecy. Vollard purchases the entire contents of his studio. Returns to Aix in June.

Redon's family estate at Peyrelebade is sold. He begins a project to illustrate Mallarmé's "Un Coup de Dés . . ." which is never completed.

Gauguin learns of the death of his daughter Aline. Suffers from severe deterioration of health with symptoms of syphilis followed by series of heart attacks in October. He begins work on the "testament" painting *D'où venons-nous?* ("Where Do We Come From?"). Attempts suicide, but survives. *Noa Noa* completed by Morice is published in *La Revue Blanche*.

Publication of Mallarmé's poem "Un Coup de Dés . . ."

Munch remains in Paris. Designs program for Ibsen production at Théâtre de L'Oeuvre. Exhibits 150 paintings at the autumn Salon in Oslo.

A group exhibition including Bonnard is held at the gallery of Ambroise Vollard.

Matisse exhibits *The Dinner Table* at the Salon de la Société Nationale. He meets Pissarro.

At around this time Braque begins attending evening classes at the École des Beaux-Arts in Le Havre.

1898
Cézanne works in and around Aix, at the Château Noir. Returns to Paris in autumn, works near Pontoise.

Vollard holds a major Redon exhibition.

Gauguin enters hospital for three weeks in September. Vollard shows *D'où venons-nous* and eight other works, all of which he purchases for what Gauguin considers to be a derisory price.

Munch spends time between Norway, Copenhagen, Berlin and Paris where he exhibits at the Salon des Indépendants.

Bonnard participates in exhibition of French painting with Van Gogh, Gauguin and Vuillard in Oslo, Stockholm and Goteborg. Vollard commissions a series of prints from Bonnard, "Quelques aspects de la vie de Paris."

Matisse marries Amélie Parayre and honeymoons in London. Visits Ajaccio in Corsica. Reads Signac's "From Delacroix to Neo-Impressionism" serialized in *La Revue Blanche*.

Deaths of Stéphane Mallarmé and Gustave Moreau.

1899
Cézanne spends most of the year in and around Paris; returns to Aix in autumn. Forced to sell the Jas de Bouffan following his mother's death. Durand-Ruel buys works by Cézanne at the sale of Chocquet's collection.

Redon's "Apocalypse de Saint-Jean," an album of lithographs, is published.

Gauguin starts contributing to satirical magazine *Les Guêpes* ("The Wasps") and begins own broadsheet *Le Sourire*.

Munch visits Berlin, Paris, Nice, Florence and Rome. He convalesces in a Norwegian sanatorium.

Vollard publishes albums of color lithographs by Denis, Bonnard, Vuillard, which he shows in his gallery in March. Bonnard participates in a group show at Durand-Ruel.

Matisse's son Jean is born. He purchases Cézanne's *Three Bathers*. Meets Derain in Paris.

Having left school Braque becomes apprenticed to a painter-decorator in Le Havre.

1900
Cézanne in increasing retirement in Aix. Through the intervention of Roger Marx three paintings are exhibited at the Centennial Exhibition in Paris. Cassirer holds first exhibition of Cézanne in Berlin. All twelve paintings return to Durand-Ruel unsold.

APRIL. Durand-Ruel holds a Redon exhibition which includes paintings and pastels. A Seurat exhibition is held in the offices of *La Revue Blanche* which reunites some of the major paintings.

After many years of bitter negotiations with Vollard, Gauguin signs a contract agreeing a shipment of 20–24 paintings per year in return for a monthly stipend and shipment of painting materials.

Munch visits Berlin, Florence and Rome. He participates in the Oslo autumn Salon with 85 paintings and 95 prints and drawings. Stays in sanatorium in Switzerland.

Bonnard exhibits with the Nabis at Bernheim Jeune. Verlaine's *Parallèlement* with illustrations by Bonnard is published by Vollard. Bonnard begins to spend (until 1910) the spring working in Montval, L'Étang-la-Ville, Vernouillet, and the summer in Grand-Lemps.

Braque goes to Paris to continue his apprenticeship as a painter-decorator with Laberthe. Attends the Municipal Art Course at Les Batignolles.

1901

Cézanne in Aix. Buys land on the Chemin des Lauves to build a studio. Exhibits at the Salon des Indépendants, and at La Libre Esthétique in Brussels. Maurice Denis exhibits *Hommage à Cézanne* at the Salon.

Redon exhibits at Vollard's gallery.

Gauguin in and out of hospital in winter of 1900–01. Plans move to the Marquesas and arrives in Atuona on the island of Hivaoa. Begins construction of his "House of Pleasure."

An exhibition of 71 works by Van Gogh is shown at the Bernheim Jeune gallery. It is at this exhibition that Derain introduces Matisse to Vlaminck.

Vollard publishes, in collaboration with Jarry, Bonnard, Fagus, and Claude Terrasse *Almanach illustré du Père Ubu*. Bonnard shows nine paintings at the Salon des Indépendants.

Matisse exhibits for the first time at the Salon des Indépendants, showing ten works. His father discontinues his allowance, possibly as a result of seeing these paintings.

Braque begins one year of military service near Le Havre.

1902

Vollard visits Cézanne in Aix. He exhibits three paintings at the Salon des Indépendants.

Gauguin, finding it difficult to walk, considers leaving the islands to settle in Spain. Works almost exclusively on "journal" of recollections and observations, *Avant et Après*.

Munch exhibits 22 paintings from *The Frieze of Life* in the vestibule of the Berlin Sezession. He loses part of a finger from a gunshot wound in a struggle with woman friend Tulla Larsen.

Bonnard shows seven paintings at the Salon des Indépendants and participates in a group show with the Nabis at Bernheim Jeune. *Daphnis et Chloé* with lithographs by Bonnard is published by Vollard.

In Paris Braque studies painting at the Académie Humbert where he meets Marie Laurencin and Francis Picabia.

1903

Cézanne exhibits seven paintings at the Sezession in Vienna and three in Berlin. Attacked in the press.

Redon exhibits at Durand-Ruel in March.

Gauguin dies on May 8 in Atuona on the island of Hivaoa. The first exhibition of the Salon d'Automne in October–December includes Bonnard, Matisse, Rouault and a memorial exhibition of Gauguin organized by Morice. There is an exhibition at the Vollard gallery of 50 paintings and 27 transfer drawings in November.

Matisse exhibits at the Salon des Indépendants along with Camoin, Manguin, Marquet, and Puy.

Braque studies briefly in the studio of Léon Bonnat, joining two friends from Le Havre, Othon Friesz and Raoul Dufy.

1904

Cézanne receives visit in Aix from Émile Bernard who is preparing an article. Exhibits nine paintings at La Libre Esthétique in Brussels and at the Salon d'Automne in Paris. Has second one-man show at Paul Cassirer in Berlin.

Redon retrospective at the Salon d'Automne.

Munch signs contract with Bruno Cassirer in Berlin for exclusive rights to sale of prints in Germany. Becomes a member of Berliner Sezession.

Bonnard exhibits at the Salon des Indépendants and with Vuillard and Vallotton at Bernheim Jeune.

MAY–JUNE. Monet exhibits the *Thames* series at Durand-Ruel.

Matisse has a one-man show at Vollard's gallery. In the summer he visits St-Tropez with Signac and Cross. Exhibits at the Salon d'Automne.

Braque rents studio in Montmartre.

1905

Cézanne receives visit from R. P. Rivière and Jacques Schnerb in Aix, also from Maurice Denis. Exhibition of watercolors held at Vollard's in spring and summer. Ten works are shown at the Salon d'Automne. Durand-Ruel includes ten paintings in Impressionist exhibition at the Grafton Galleries, London.

Retrospectives for Van Gogh and Seurat are held at the Salon des Indépendants in March–April.

Matisse paints his first "fauve" works in Collioure with Derain. These paintings, along with those of Camoin, Derain, Manguin, and Marquet are shown in a room dubbed "cage of beasts" (*fauves*) at the Salon d'Automne. Matisse meets Gertrude and Leo Stein.

Braque, impressed with paintings at Salon d'Automne, is drawn into the Fauve orbit through his friendship with Dufy and Friesz.

1906

Cézanne shows ten works at Salon d'Automne. Vollard exhibits twelve paintings. Cézanne dies in Aix on October 22.

Redon is shown at Durand-Ruel in February–March.

Gauguin retrospective is held at the Salon d'Automne.

Bonnard has a one-man show at Vollard's gallery in April and at Bernheim Jeune in November. Visits Belgium and Holland in summer.

Matisse and Braque exhibit at the Salon des Indépendants. Matisse meets Picasso.

Braque paints first Fauve paintings working with Friesz in Antwerp during the summer. In October he goes to paint in L'Estaque on paintings very influenced by Cézanne.

1907

MARCH. A sale of works by Redon takes place at the Hôtel Drouot.

JUNE. Bernheim Jeune shows Cézanne watercolors.

Bonnard moves to Vernouillet in the spring. Participates in group show at Bernheim Jeune.

Braque exhibits six paintings at the Salon des Indépendants. He meets Matisse, Vlaminck, and Derain. In May he goes with Friesz to La Ciotat where they are joined

COLORPLATE 1. Paul Cézanne. *Trees and Houses. c.*1885–88. 21¼ × 28¾″ (54 × 81 cm).
Musée de l'Orangerie, Paris (Collection Walter-Guillaume).

COLORPLATE 2. Paul Gauguin. *Landscape in Arles*. 1888. 28⅜ × 36¼″ (72 × 92 cm).
Nationalmuseum, Stockholm.

COLORPLATE 3. Vincent van Gogh. *Flowering Garden*. July 1888. 36¼ × 28¾″ (92 × 73 cm).
Private Collection (on loan to the Metropolitan Museum of Art, New York).

COLORPLATE 4. Georges Seurat. *Port-en-Bessin, Entrance to the Harbor.* 1888.
Oil on canvas. 21⅝ × 25⅝″ (54.8 × 65.1 cm).
Museum of Modern Art, New York (Lillie P. Bliss Collection).

COLORPLATE 5. Edvard Munch. *From the Shore in Nice*. 1892. 18$^{1}/_{3}$ × 27$^{1}/_{2}$″ (46.5 × 69 cm). © Munch Museum, Oslo (1992).

COLORPLATE 6. Pierre Bonnard. *Normandy Landscape*. 1926–30. 24⅝ × 32″ (62.6 × 81.3 cm).
Smith College Museum of Art, Northampton, Mass. (Purchased Hillyer Fund, 1937).

COLORPLATE 7. Henri Matisse. *The Coast, Collioure: La Moulade.* 1905–06.
Oil on panel, 9½ × 12⅜″ (24.2 × 32.3 cm).
Private Collection (Courtesy of Barbara Divver Fine Art, New York).

COLORPLATE 8. Georges Braque. *The Canal, St-Martin.* Autumn 1906. 19¾ × 24″ (50.2 × 61 cm).
John A. and Audrey Jones Beck Collection,
on extended loan to the Museum of Fine Arts, Houston, Texas.

by Matisse and then on to L'Estaque. Braque exhibits at the Salon d'Automne. He meets Kahnweiler at around this time. Through Apollinaire he is introduced to Picasso and sees *Les Demoiselles d'Avignon* in his studio.

1908
JANUARY. 100 works by Van Gogh are shown at Bernheim Jeune.

Munch suffers nervous breakdown in Copenhagen and enters a clinic there.

Bonnard travels to Algeria and Tunisia. Exhibits at Salon d'Automne.

Matisse opens his own art school. His first American exhibition is held at the 291 Gallery in New York. He publishes "Notes of a Painter" in *La Grande Revue*.

Braque spends the summer working in L'Estaque on first Cubist paintings. These are rejected by the jury of the Salon d'Automne which includes Matisse. Kahnweiler's exhibition of Braque in November which includes his landscapes from L'Estaque leads to the christening of the "Cubist" movement.

1909
A major Redon exhibition is held at the Larensche Kunsthandel, Amsterdam.

Munch spends winter and spring in clinic in Copenhagen. Exhibition of 100 paintings and 200 prints in Bergen in June.

Bonnard shows 36 paintings at Bernheim Jeune. Exhibits at the Salon des Indépendants and La Libre Esthétique in Brussels.

Monet exhibits 48 *Waterlilies* at Durand-Ruel.

The Russian collector Schukin commissions large paintings *Dance* and *Music* from Matisse, who moves to Issy-les-Molineaux.

Braque exhibits in Salon des Indépendants for the last time until 1920. Period of close friendship with Picasso begins. Summer at La Roche-Guyon.

1910
Redon carries out a commission for decorative works at Fontfroide Abbey.

Bonnard exhibits 34 paintings at Bernheim Jeune.

Matisse has a large retrospective (65 paintings, 25 drawings) at Bernheim Jeune. He visits Munich to see exhibition of Islamic art.

"Analytical" phase of Braque's Cubism. Summer in L'Estaque.

NOVEMBER–JANUARY 1911. Roger Fry organizes "Manet and the Post-Impressionists" exhibition at the Grafton Galleries, London.

1911
Munch wins competition for the Aula decorations. He exhibits 111 paintings, 25 drawings and 111 prints in Oslo.

Bonnard spends large part of the year in St-Tropez. Shows 28 paintings at Bernheim Jeune.

Matisse visits Moscow at Schukin's invitation.

Braque spends summer with Picasso at Céret.

1912
Munch continues work on Aula decorations.

Bonnard shows 31 paintings at Bernheim Jeune. Purchases the villa "Ma Roulotte" in Vernonnet. From now

until around 1938 he divides his time between Paris and the south of France.

Matisse makes two visits to Morocco.

Braque joins Picasso in Sorgues for the summer. Makes first *papier collé* in September.

1913
André Mellerio's catalogue of Redon's prints is published.

Matisse exhibits Moroccan paintings at Bernheim Jeune. Matisse's *Blue Nude* is burned in effigy at the Armory Show in Chicago.

1914
Following the declaration of war Braque is mobilized and is assigned to 224th infantry regiment with rank of sergeant.

1915
Braque's serious head wound leads to an operation and long convalescence.

1916
JULY 6. Redon dies in Paris.

Munch buys the estate Ekely at Skoeyen where he is to spend most of the rest of his life. The Aula murals are officially unveiled.

1917
Matisse spends winter in Marseilles and Nice. Visits Renoir in Cagnes. He increasingly divides the year between Paris and Nice.

A banquet is held in Paris to celebrate Braque's recovery. He begins to paint again at Sorgues.

1921
Bonnard visits St-Tropez, St-Honoré-les-Bains, Luxeuil, St-Gervaise-les-Bains accompanying his wife who is seeking treatment for her poor health in the spas of the south. Many of Bonnard's paintings until his wife's death are completed in hotel bedrooms.

1922
Monet's mural-sized Waterlily Decorations are officially presented to the state for installation at the Orangerie des Tuileries.

Munch works on murals for workers' dining rooms in Freia chocolate factory in Oslo.

Braque exhibits at Salon d'Automne.

1924
A Bonnard retrospective (1891–1922) showing 69 works is held at the Galerie Drouet in Paris.

Matisse's largest exhibition to date (87 paintings) is held at the Ny Carlsberg Glyptotek in Copenhagen.

Braque has first exhibition at Paul Rosenberg.

1925
Bonnard purchases a villa in Le Cannet, "Le Bosquet," which becomes his permanent residence in the Midi.

1926
DECEMBER 5. Monet dies at Giverny.

1930
Munch suffers from problems with eyes.

Bonnard participates in "Painting in Paris" exhibition at Museum of Modern Art, New York.

Matisse visits Tahiti via New York and San Francisco. Returns to the United States and visits Etta Cone in Baltimore and the Barnes Foundation in Merion, PA. Dr. Barnes commissions a mural *Dance*.

1932
The Nazis confiscate 82 "degenerate" paintings by Munch in German public collections.

Georges Besson organizes an exhibition "Van Gogh, Gauguin, Toulouse-Lautrec, Bonnard and their era" at the Galerie Braun in Paris.

Matisse's illustrations commissioned by Skira for Mallarmé's *Poésies* are published.

1937
Bonnard is represented by 33 paintings at "Masters of Independent Art, 1895–1937" at the Petit Palais in Paris, Matisse by 61 paintings.

1939
Bonnard remains in Le Cannet during the war, returning to Paris only in 1945.

Matisse makes decision to remain in France during the war, staying most of the year in Nice.

1940
After German invasion Braque moves to Limousin, then to Pyrenees.

1941
Matisse undergoes surgery for duodenal cancer.

1942
The death of Bonnard's wife, Marthe.

1943
Matisse begins work on cut-outs eventually to become the book *Jazz*. Evacuated to Vence from Nice.

1944
JANUARY 23. Munch dies at Ekely leaving a bequest of over 1,000 paintings and 15,000 graphic works to the City of Oslo.

Matisse's wife and daughter are arrested for resistance activities.

1945
Bonnard returns for short visit to Paris after the liberation. Exhibits at J. Rodrigues-Henriques.

Large Matisse retrospective largely of paintings made during the war is held at the Salon d'Automne. Exhibition simultaneously with Picasso at the Victoria and Albert Museum, London.

1946
Bonnard retrospective at Bernheim Jeune.

1947
JANUARY 23. Bonnard dies in Le Cannet. A "Homage to Pierre Bonnard" is held at the Salon des Indépendants. The Orangerie in Paris holds a large Bonnard retrospective showing 100 paintings.

Matisse works increasingly with cut and pasted paper. Tériade publishes *Jazz*.

Aimé Maeght becomes Braque's dealer.

1948
Matisse begins work on the designs for the Dominican Chapelle du Rosaire in Vence.

1949
Braque has retrospective at the Museum of Modern Art, New York, showing 114 works.

1950
Braque exhibits at Galerie Maeght.

1951
Matisse retrospective is held at the Museum of Modern Art, New York.

1954
NOVEMBER 3. Matisse dies in Nice.

1963
AUGUST 31. Braque dies in Paris.

INTRODUCTION

The terminology of art history is often coined from the vocabulary of abuse. "Impressionist" was a term first used in derision by contemporary critics to describe the paintings of Monet and his friends, but the word stuck and quickly became how these artists were happy to describe themselves. "Post-Impressionism," on the other hand, began its career outside the historical context of the artists concerned, and a generation later than the art it describes. Although we now know Post-Impressionism as one of the familiar and established "isms" of modern art, when it was originally invented it was a label, improvised on the spur of the moment by an English critic to name a group of "modern foreign artists" whose work, he admitted, "could not be defined by any single term." Roger Fry settled on this "somewhat negative label" (as he later described it) for the paintings he selected for exhibition at the Grafton Galleries in London in 1910 to represent "avant-garde" French art. Cézanne, Van Gogh, Seurat, Gauguin and Matisse, who did not belong to any single movement defined or recognized at the time, were then entirely new to British audiences and the exhibition created a sensation. In a broadcast talk given in 1945 on "The Artquake of 1910" Desmond MacCarthy, who had worked with Fry as the exhibition's secretary, described how the name was invented.

> What was the exhibition to be called? . . . Roger and I and a young journalist who was to help with publicity met to consider this . . . Roger first suggested various terms like "expressionism" which aimed at distinguishing these artists from the impressionists; but the journalist wouldn't have that or any other of his alternatives. At last Roger, losing patience, said: "Oh, let's just call them the post-impressionists; at any rate they came after the impressionists."

Successive movements in art history are often seen as critical polarities. Roger Fry's invention of Post-Impressionism has had the lasting effect of pushing it apart from Impressionism and defining the two movements in terms of contrast and opposition. In the catalogue introduction that he and Desmond MacCarthy wrote for the exhibition, the Impressionists were seen to be painting strictly from objective perceptions of nature, promoting a "receptive, passive attitude toward the appearance of things," whereas the Post-Impressionists, rejecting the literal and naturalistic, sought "completer self-expression . . . exploring the emotional significance . . . in things and using abstract design as their principal means of expression."

Until recently these dichotomies between objective and subjective, naturalistic representation and abstract structure, have dominated the discussion of Impressionism and Post-Impressionism. John Rewald began his influential *Post-Impressionism: From Van Gogh to Gauguin* with the arrival of Van Gogh in Paris in 1886, the year of the last Impressionist exhibition, and treated the divergence between nature-based Impressionism and the inner-directed tendencies of Symbolism as an unbridgeable gap of generations. Venturi wrote in his history of the movement that "Impressionism, which was beginning to fragment in 1880, five years later no longer existed."

Yet the fact that in 1905 the critic and poet Charles Morice was asking "Is Impressionism over?" suggests that well into the twentieth century Impressionism was still regarded as a live issue. The results of his questionnaire on "Tendencies in Art Now," circulated to over 50 artists, were published in the *Mercure de France*. In a representative reply, Camoin, a close friend of both Cézanne and Matisse, stated that Impressionism was "still to be completed." In 1908 Matisse pointed to Impressionism with its pure color construction as providing his generation with "the starting point of Fauvism" – "the courage to return to the purity of means."

See page 296.
Roger Fry, Introduction to the catalogue of "The Second Post-Impressionist Exhibition," Grafton Galleries, London, October 5–December 31, 1912, pp. 7–8.

See page 302.

For the catalogue introduction see page 296. In making this distinction Fry had been influenced by Julius Meier-Graefe's emphasis on "expression." The German critic's Modern Art *had been translated into English in 1908.*

The exhibition "Post-Impressionism: Cross-Currents in European Painting," Royal Academy, London, November 1979– March 1980; National Gallery, Washington, May–September 1980, proposed an extension of Post-Impressionism by enlarging its catchment beyond the avant-garde protagonists within French art singled out by John Rewald in his Post-Impressionism: from Van Gogh to Gauguin, *New York 1956, but the principal revision of the predominantly socio-historical and stylistic approaches to the study of Impressionism and the art of the later nineteenth century has come from Richard Shiff. His "The End of Impressionism: A Study in Theories of Artistic Expression,"* The Art Quarterly, *I, no. 4 (Autumn 1978), and* Cézanne and the End of Impressionism, *Chicago 1984, have revised assumptions about the "objectivity" of Impressionism, and its relation to later nineteenth-century art and to Symbolism.*

Lionello Venturi, Les Archives de l'Impressionnisme, *I, Paris 1939, p. 75.*
See page 109.
See page 304.

Although painting from nature tied the Impressionists to a form of realism, the directness and clarity of their use of color, to which Matisse refers, also involved them in a radical and unprecedented abstractness. It was one of the contradictory effects of the immediate and improvisatory approach to their subjects that the Impressionists gave the pictorial realities of painting, the raw physical facts of the medium, a degree of exposure that had never been allowed in painting before. Monet, for example, had advised an American pupil to give a heightened attention to these aspects of painting: "Try to forget what objects you have before you, a tree, a house, a field or whatever. Merely think here is a little square of blue, here an oblong of pink, here a streak of yellow, and paint it just as it looks to you, the exact color and shape . . ."

See page 38.

In their later paintings, the first generation of Impressionists, Monet, Renoir, and Pissarro, respond to this abstractness of color and touch in ways which alter their approach to representation from the 1880s onward. But the artists of the "second generation," the Post-Impressionists, were learning painting from the Impressionists in a spirit of apprenticeship. Gauguin and Cézanne worked with Pissarro; Van Gogh discovered Impressionism for the first time in 1886, and worked with Pissarro and Signac; Seurat, trained at the École des Beaux-Arts, combined Impressionism with more formalized compositions. These artists took the abstractness of Impressionism on board as a *fait accompli*. Although still painting from nature they recognized the patch of color as raw material, not as the literal transcription of trees, houses or fields or any aspect of reality in itself, but as "fiction": raw material to be constructed inventively and imaginatively into anything. "You have to be a painter through the very qualities of painting," as Cézanne said, "you have to use crude materials." This opening up of understanding of how wide the symbolic function of very simple forms could be looks forward to the art of the twentieth century.

The paintings and documents in this book have been assembled with the intention of showing the cross-currents between Impressionism and the art which came to prominence in the 1880s, 90s and 1900s. Rather than interpreting Post-Impressionism as a reaction against Impressionism, I hope to redraw somewhat the lines of the debate, to indicate how aspects of representation and image-making were affected by and responded to the abstractness within Impressionism, to show that Post-Impressionism, which I interpret to include Bonnard, early Matisse,

Quoted by Émile Bernard, "Souvenirs sur Paul Cézanne," Mercure de France *I, October 16, 1907, reprinted in Michael Doran,* Conversations avec Cézanne, *Paris, 1978, p. 63.*

(*Below left*) Claude Monet. *Road in the Hollow, Pourville.* 1882. 23¾ × 32⅛" (60.4 × 81.5 cm). Museum of Fine Arts, Boston (Bequest of Mrs Susan Mason Loring).

(*Below*) Paul Gauguin. *Above the Abyss.* 1888. 28½ × 24" (72.5 × 61 cm). Musée des Arts Décoratifs, Paris.

Braque and Munch, was a counterpart to Impressionism, a second flood of the same tide, which has had a profound effect on twentieth-century art.

The first text is an excerpt from the private notes of Louis Le Bail, a young artist who consulted Pissarro about painting in the late 1890s. He records that Pissarro warned him that "precise drawing . . . destroys all sensations. Do not define too closely the outlines of things . . . work on everything simultaneously . . . placing tones everywhere . . . it is the brush-stroke of the right value and color which should produce the drawing." The emphasis here on the single mark, the individual touch of color, as opposed to the drawing of continuous outline is of more than technical importance. It has an immediate effect on representation, on our ability to see what a painting is "of." Rather than "producing drawing," these single patches of color in Impressionism tended to remain as discontinuous, visible strokes of paint, fragments which clung to the surface of the picture and refused to behave like objects in space. Placed across the boundaries of solid and air, foreground and background, and detached from all the focusing, organizing, and separating functions essential to drawing and describing form, these strokes of paint obstructed "likeness." They resisted being used as a representational means altogether. The Symbolist poet Jules Laforgue, writing about Impressionism in 1883, and comparing it to the music of Wagner, spoke of a form that was "symphonic" as opposed to "melodic," a form created not on a linear basis, but on the basis of a continuous interrelation and transition of color. "Where everything is obtained by a thousand little strokes dancing in every direction like straws . . . subject and object are then irretrievably in motion, inapprehensible and unapprehending." This abstractness seemed to be leading to a kind of painting only very tenuously connected with established symbols for representation.

We can guess at the assault mounted by Impressionism on conventions of painting from the violent reception it first received at the hands of contemporary critics. Later critics of the 1880s and 90s began to recognize the abstract qualities of Impressionism in a positive sense. In 1892 Georges Lecomte observed that the Impressionists "are gradually withdrawing from reality . . . they assemble lines, regulate gestures . . . they compose well away from nature . . . the draftsmanship becomes bolder, more summary and individual, the color tends to be simplified." Maurice Denis' much-repeated maxim "A painting before being a war horse, a nude woman or some anecdote is essentially a flat surface covered with colors arranged in a certain order" pointed to the shift he perceived in the art of Gauguin, Bernard and the school of Pont-Aven toward painterly qualities and the decorative and away from an image of nature. In his letters to Theo, Van Gogh conveys some of the excitement created by this new thinking. September 1889: "They [Gauguin and Bernard] are right, exasperated as they are by certain people's photographic and empty perfection. They will not ask the correct tone of the mountains, but they will say: By God, the mountains were blue, weren't they? Then chuck on some blue and don't go telling me that it was a blue rather like this or that, it was blue wasn't it? Good, make them blue and it's enough."

The little picture of the Bois d'Amour painted by Paul Sérusier under Gauguin's guidance during the summer of 1888, which he carried back with him to Paris in October to show to his fellow students at the Académie Julian, came to be known as *The Talisman*. Its abstractness of flat shape and bright color conveyed the quality of a magical initiation into a new awareness. Denis wrote that he was now searching for "a *painter*'s definition of that simple word 'nature'." In his obituary on Gauguin he described how extreme a definition Gauguin had provided to this group of young painters who had formed a secret society of initiates, the "Nabis." "Gauguin gave us a claim to lyricism . . . Why not translate impressions (of nature) plastically by exaggeration, which is justifiable in the metaphors of the poets? Why not stress even to the point of distortion?"

Georges Braque. *Landscape with Houses.* Winter 1908–09. 25⅝ × 21¼″ (65.5 × 54 cm). Art Gallery of New South Wales, Sydney, Australia (purchased 1980).

See page 39.

See page 50.

See page 99.

See page 85.

COLORPLATE 29

See page 99.

See page 86.

The plunge that Gauguin was taking into the painterly and abstract qualities of painting now raised serious questions about the new relation that painting seemed to propose to subject matter and meaning. "What worried me above all," Sérusier wrote to Denis on his return to Pont-Aven from Paris in the spring of 1889, "was this: what part should nature play in art? Where should the line be drawn? Too much freedom frightens me." Looking back on the changes that had recently taken place in his work, Signac wrote in his journal in August 1894, "A few years ago, I too was trying to prove to the world, through scientific experiment, that those blues, those yellows, those greens were to be found in nature. Now . . . I paint the way I do because this is the technique which [gives] the most harmonious, the most luminous, the most colorful result . . . and because that is how I like it." If "those blues, those yellows, those greens" were to be used in painting to radiate their own power, as Signac suggests, and were not to be found in nature, what were they to represent and how was their relation to meaning to be discovered? This question about how representation would respond to the inherent energies within the formal means of art was the legacy of Impressionism to this generation of artists. It was also a question that painters had in common with poets.

See page 97.

See page 101.

Téodor de Wyzewa, in an important article in the *Revue Wagnérienne*, one of the many new little magazines that had burst onto the scene in the 1880s, wrote very perceptively on the question of meaning as a shared ground between painting and writing. "Men of letters saw that words had taken on special resonances beyond their precise 'notional' meaning . . . syllables had taken on musical resonance . . . a whole new kind of painting . . . colors and lines, like words, had taken on an 'emotional' value independent of the actual objects they represented . . . They used colors and lines for purely *symphonic* groupings . . . each of the elements of painting has the value of a symphonic chord." Rimbaud's sonnet *Voyelles* begins with the lines: "Black A, White E, Red I, Green U, Blue O: vowels / Someday I will open your silent pregnancies." The poem proposes the breaking up of the whole word with its dictionary definition in favor of another kind of "dictionary," based on sensation and association, a set of symbols derived from a fragment of the whole, the individual "mark" of the word, the sound of a single syllable.

See page 153.

Arthur Rimbaud, Complete Works, *trans. Paul Schmidt, New York 1976, p. 123.*

This was a period of very close association between painters and poets. *Voyelles* appeared in Verlaine's essay on Corbière, Rimbaud, and Mallarmé, "Les Poètes Maudits," published in 1883 in the new Symbolist periodical *Lutèce*. The offices of the new magazines were frequently used as venues for exhibitions of art. The coteries that gathered around publications such as the *Revue Wagnérienne, Lutèce* and *La Vogue* overlapped with the groups of poets and painters who met at Mallarmé's "Tuesdays" in his apartment in the rue de Rome. These also included many of the original Impressionist generation. Mallarmé had been a close friend of Manet and later of Monet, Renoir and Berthe Morisot. Mallarmé's theory of poetry shared with Rimbaud the emphasis on the fragment, the individual sound or syllable or single word, detached from the organizing logic of the sentence as a whole as a source of meaning. In the painting of Impressionism and its legacy to the Post-Impressionists, the individual patch of color, like the word in Mallarmé, also achieves its meaning through suggestion rather than direct naming. "To name an object is to suppress three quarters of the enjoyment of the poem which lies in the delight of gradually guessing . . . to evoke an object little by little to show a state of mind."

Stéphane Mallarmé, quoted in Jules Huret, see page 48.

The word, like the luminous stroke of color in painting, which resists being narrowed and restricted to a single "likeness," is allowed to radiate a wide spectrum of meanings through evocation and association. This common ground between painting and poetry has, however, tended to become obscured. The decades of the 1880s and 90s were widely regarded as periods in which "confusion reigned." In the absence of "any single school" and "scarcely any groups," the poet and critic Émile Verhaeren

See section on "The Fragmentation of Artistic Movements," pages 103–122.

reported in 1891 that the splitting and fusing of tendencies within the circle of the new art made him think of the bewildering revolving fragments of a kaleidoscope. Two critics who came on the scene in the 1880s intent on marking out territory and erecting signposts, have been particularly influential in creating the dichotomy between Impressionism and Post-Impressionism on which later art historians have relied. Both Félix Fénéon and Albert Aurier emphasized Impressionism as an art of realism, Fénéon in order to demonstrate the even more precise "scientific" realism of Seurat and the Neo-Impressionists as an "improvement" on Impressionism, and Aurier in order to create a definition for Symbolism in painting against which Impressionism was used as a foil. Aurier's important article on Gauguin in *Mercure de France*, "Symbolism in Painting," made a distinction between the painting of objects in nature and the painting of the "Idea" – an essential and universal truth which could be known through the contemplation of its sign or symbol.

There is some evidence in Gauguin's and Van Gogh's writings and statements about painting that they thought in terms, similar to Aurier's, of the expression of ideas. In the manuscript *Cahier pour Aline* in which Gauguin describes *The Spirit of the Dead Watching* he speculates about the meaning of the pose of the "young native girl completely nude on the bed," and rejecting an erotic interpretation of the painting, proposes the idea of a symbolic contrast as its subject matter. "I see here only fear. What kind of fear? The *tupapau* (Spirit of the Dead) is clearly indicated . . . the spirit of a living person linked to the spirit of the dead. Night and Day." But it is significant that Gauguin distinguishes this aspect of painting – "the literary part" – from what he calls on many occasions "the musical part." In 1899 when the critic André Fontainas complained that Gauguin's large painting *Where Do We Come From?* was incomprehensible because "abstractions are not communicated through concrete images unless they have already taken shape in some natural allegory . . ." Gauguin replied, quoting Mallarmé, "It is a musical poem, it needs no libretto . . . I have tried to interpret my vision without recourse to literary means and *with all the simplicity the medium permits* . . ." (my italics).

In his letters Van Gogh frequently expresses the wish that his paintings should convey a specific idea or feeling. This is often with reference to the stock images of Romanticism: the empty chair, the sower or the reaper, which take on the allegorical meaning of "absence," "life," or "death." He also frequently elaborates a specific symbolism attached to colors: "I have tried to express the terrible passions of humanity by means of red and green." But as Rilke commented (1907), the fact "that Van Gogh's letters are so readable, that they are so rich, basically argues against him." The letters tend to be "literary" about the expression of specific ideas or feelings in a way that the paintings are not. In fact it is often in the more technical discussion in the letters that we find the most convincing accounts of Van Gogh's process of expression. With reference to the important series of paintings on the subject of the harvest in 1888, he compares the mental work of balancing the three pairs of complementary colors to the task of "an actor on a stage in a difficult part with a hundred things to think of at once." Gauguin also spoke of "a thought floating without direct, definitive expression" and frequently referred to painting as "dreaming." "Art is an abstraction: draw it out of nature while dreaming before it." The indeterminacy implied in Van Gogh's "hundred things to think of at once" and in Gauguin's references to the floating dream-thought may give a better account of the legacy of Impressionism, the indeterminacy of the means of painting, than the criticism of Symbolist writers who refer to "the externalization of the Idea," a more conceptual process. When Degas asserted that he was full of "ideas" for poetry, Mallarmé replied, "you can't make a poem with ideas . . . you make it with words."

In this respect Mallarmé's theory and practice of poetry are of crucial significance to this period. The individual word was seen to possess its

Émile Verhaeren, "Le Salon des Indépendants," La Nation, reprinted in L'Art Moderne, *April 5, 1891, cited by John Rewald,* Post-Impressionism: from Van Gogh to Gauguin, *New York 1956, p. 7.*

See page 73.

See page 175.

See page 199.

See page 200.

See page 203.

V. W. van Gogh (ed.), The Complete Letters of Vincent van Gogh, *London and Boston 1958, III, no. 533, pp. 28–29. See page 328.*

V. W. van Gogh (ed.), op. cit., II, no. 507, p. 606. See page 174.

Paul Gauguin, letter to Émile Schuffenecker, August 14, 1888, Correspondance de Paul Gauguin, I, *Victor Merlhès (ed.), Paris 1984, p. 210. For a discussion of the emphasis on conceptualization within Symbolism, see Norma Broude,* Impressionism: A Feminist Reading, *New York 1991, pp. 159–69. Paul Valéry,* Degas, Manet, Morisot, *trans. David Paul, London 1960, p. 62.*

own sensuous attributes of sound, texture, and rhythm and to contain a wealth of variable experience, imagery and association apart from its strictly denotative meaning or definition. In Mallarmé's poetry a wide range of functions can be assigned even to a single word. In Post-Impressionism the fragment within the language of painting, the single patch of color, plays a similarly expanded role. Like the individual word in Mallarmé which floats free from the representational structure of the poem and exhibits all of its sides and all of its associations, there is within Post-Impressionism, particularly in the later paintings of Van Gogh, Seurat and Cézanne, a consistent development of the fragment, the life of the small form. In Seurat's late study for *The Circus* (1891) and in Van Gogh's pen drawing *Hayricks* (1888), for example, individual marks and colors develop a vocabulary of their own, their own specific character and behavior. The simple way that the painter touches the canvas or paper has become something very beautiful in itself.

In the Cézanne *Portrait of the Artist's Son* (1875) the brushstrokes, flat rectangular touches of color, often seem to occupy two positions at once. They follow planes into depth, stipulating, through their juxtapositions of warm and cool color, each shift of direction taken by the form of the face. But they also hover together on the picture surface. It is there on the flat plane of the picture that the patches of color become detached from the outlines, facets of planes and all the depicted imagery. They also detach themselves from all the consciously conceived, intended or deliberate meanings they have been given by the artist, his own ideas and feelings, including his own notions of himself. It is there that they become subjected to that particular kind of contemplation Valéry described as "the speculative life of vision . . . an Impressionist is a contemplative whose meditation is retinal: he is aware of his eye as it creates, and he heightens this awareness of sensation into a revelation."

Richard Shiff has made the important point that within nineteenth-century criticism there was a term for this creative, meditative aspect of vision. Cézanne often spoke of "the sensations" he received from nature, from looking at landscape. "I paint as I see, as I feel, and I have very strong sensations." But he also said that sensations "reside in us." "I continue to seek," he wrote in June 1899, "the expression of the confused sensations which we bring with us when we are born." The way that late-nineteenth-century artists and critics used the word "sensation" shows that it had a much wider meaning than it carries now. Rather than the narrow sense of the objective perception *of* nature "out there," it represented a fusion of perception with thought and feeling. But it also referred to, and included, the means of painting. When Cézanne ("a forerunner in paranoia," as Greenberg described him) accused Gauguin of having stolen his "little sensations" and having "paraded them all over the South Seas," it was Cézanne's "reading of nature" that Gauguin had pinched "in terms of an interpretation in patches of color." Within the notion of "sensation" the divisions between objective and subjective, the painter's thought and the means of painting were broken down. Matisse puts his finger on it in 1908 in "Notes of a Painter" when he says that the separation of form and content is impossible to make. He refers to "the purely visual satisfaction that can be obtained from looking at a picture," but then writes, "But a painter's thought must not be considered as separate from his pictorial means, for the thought is worth no more than its expression by the means, which must be more complete . . . the deeper is his thought."

In fact the phrases of Symbolist criticism, "objectification of the subjective" or "externalization of the idea," fall wide of the mark as a means of describing the quality of the embodiment of thought in the painting of Van Gogh, Gauguin, Cézanne and Seurat. Their paintings seem less to do with ideas one may hold or feelings one may have. As Matisse explained, the painter's thought does not pre-exist, is not felt beforehand and then

Georges Seurat. *The Circus* (study). 1890. 21²/₃ × 18¹/₈″ (55 × 46 cm). Musée d'Orsay, Paris.

Vincent van Gogh. *Hayricks*. Arles, June 1888. 9¹/₂ × 12¹/₂″ (24 × 31.5 cm). Szépmüvészeti Museum, Budapest.

Paul Valéry, "Au sujet de Berthe Morisot," Écrits sur l'Art, *Paris 1960, p. 146.*
Richard Shiff, "The End of Impressionism: A Study in Theories of Artistic Expression," The Art Quarterly, I, *no. 4 (Autumn 1978),* Cézanne and the End of Impressionism, *Chicago 1984.*
John Rewald, "Un Article inédit sur Paul Cézanne," Arts (Paris), *no. 473, July 21–27, 1954, p. 8; cited in Rewald,* History of Impressionism, *New York 1961, p. 246.*
Paul Cézanne, letter to Henri Gasquet, June 3, 1899.
Maurice Denis, Journal, *II (1905–20), Paris 1957, p. 46.*

Henri Matisse, "Notes of a Painter," 1908, in Jack Flam (ed.), Matisse on Art, *New York and London 1973, pp. 35–36.*

"expressed." What Matisse refers to is a kind of thinking through painting where the painting itself is making the thinking.

In his review of the first Impressionist exhibition of 1874, Jules Castagnary wrote that the new painters should be called "Impressionists" because they render "not the landscape, but the sensation produced by the landscape." This distinction is anticipated, almost word for word, by Mallarmé in a letter to Henri Cazalis (October 1864). Poetry should *paint not the object but the effect it produces.* "All words," he wrote, "must retreat and be replaced by sensation." Their narrow definitions must be expanded to encompass the wider range of meanings that sensation implies. Cézanne's thinking about sensation suggests the same radical revision as Mallarmé's. In speaking about the importance of "realizing" his sensations, the project of "making real" seems to refer to a sense of completion and fulfillment – that is: each patch of color should express all the resources of seeing and feeling both objective and subjective contained within his "very strong" sensations. Not surprisingly his last letters, written in the month before his death, still complain of his "inability to realize." Yet when he referred to himself as "a primitive in the way that I have discovered" he indicated something of the unfolding from his work that is to take place within the twentieth century.

This discussion of the fragment and the wide range of meanings that could be felt to arise from the smallest unit of sensation, even a single brushstroke, shows how far painting had departed from any stable reference point. After his discussions with Gauguin in the spring of 1889 Sérusier had written, "too much freedom frightens me." The representation of nature had provided painting with a shared program of meanings, a universal content of experience that could be felt to belong equally to the artist and to the spectator. Insofar as Impressionism still seemed to be poised between an abstractness of means and the literal depiction of the recognizable look of the world, it still belonged to a familiar, understandable common language. Within Post-Impressionism, this poise between abstractness and literal representation alters. Whereas a painting by Monet of the rue Montorgeuil decked out for the Fourteenth of July shows fluttering brushstrokes doubling as flags flapping in the wind, Van Gogh's painting of the same subject shows abstract slashes of color that do not lock into any literal representational scheme for depicting a street. Adapting Impressionism, "using color more arbitrarily," as he writes in August 1888, he finds in it a sort of "savagery" which breaks down the order and continuity on which literal representation depends. His use of color is so simplified and generalized that it cuts across drawing, modeling, and perspective, the established means by which paintmarks are interpreted. But more radically, the patches of color that replace drawing also replace the conceptualization that goes with drawing; they replace the established meanings that these conventions for depiction might have had. This radical simplification results in the use of color as a pool of objective and subjective sensation, a fusion out of which something new of feeling and thought can be drawn.

Van Gogh often expresses an awareness of the extremism of his position: "a godsend to those people who have fixed preconceived ideas about technique." His struggle with the idea of "correctness" of drawing goes back to the period of his earliest attempts to become an artist while he was still in Holland. At one point, in exasperation at the dryness and weakness of feeling he found in academic art, he wrote to Theo: "Tell Serret *I should be desperate if my figures were correct* . . . Tell him that my great longing is to learn to make those very incorrectnesses, those deviations, remodellings, changes in reality, so that they may become, yes, untrue if you like – but truer than the literal truth." When he arrives in Paris in 1886, discovers Impressionism, and begins to develop the new brushmark as a strange new form of representation, almost as strange and beguiling a form as the abstraction within Japanese prints, he finds within it the means for an

Paul Cézanne. *Portrait of the Artist's Son.* 1881–82. Private Collection (Photo Sydney W. Newbery).

Jules Castagnary, "L'Exposition du boulevard des Capucines: Les impressionnistes," Le Siècle, *April 29, 1874, trans. in Martha Kapos (ed.),* The Impressionists: A Retrospective, *New York 1991, pp. 83–86.*

Stéphane Mallarmé, letter to Henri Cazalis, October 1864, *Correspondance 1862–1871,* Henri Mondor (ed.), *Paris 1959, p. 137.*

Paul Cézanne, letter to his son Paul, September 8, 1906, John Rewald (ed.), *Paul Cézanne,* Letters, *Oxford 1976, p. 327.*

Quoted by Émile Bernard, "Souvenirs sur Paul Cézanne," Mercure de France, *I, October 16, 1907, reprinted in Michael Doran (ed.),* Conversations avec Cézanne, *Paris 1978, p. 73.*

For Sérusier see page 97.

Vincent van Gogh, letter to Theo, August 1888, V. W. van Gogh (ed.), op. cit., *III, pp. 6–7.*

See page 216.

enormously widened and deepened range of "incorrectnesses, deviations . . . changes of reality." But he is often ambivalent about the expressive power of these new paintings: "Exaggerated studies like *The Sower* and like this *Night Café* usually seem to me atrociously ugly and bad, but when I am moved by something, as by this little article on Dostoevsky, then these are the only ones that appear to have any deep meaning." The reason for this ambivalence, it seems to me, is that Van Gogh is also aware of the enormous risks being taken through a kind of art based on the premises of Impressionism; that is, an art that had departed so far from established meanings and symbols for representation.

See page 220.

The isolation of the avant-garde artist and the apparent severing of art and poetry from society and from intelligible sources of meaning were issues of which the "Decadent" late nineteenth century was well aware. In the 1870s, marginalization and financial hardship had been the consequence of the Impressionists' decision to buck the system and to exhibit outside the mainstream outlets and institutions of art. But by the 1890s the obscurity and inaccessibility of both the art and the artists ("the thin wolf without a collar" as Degas described Gauguin) were both accepted and cultivated. "Be Mysterious," Gauguin advised. Huysmans' *Against Nature*, whose hero, Des Esseintes, read Mallarmé in an atmosphere of meticulously contrived isolation from the world, became the basic text of Symbolist aestheticism.

Paul Gauguin, letter to André Fontainas, Tahiti, March 1899. Quoting the La Fontaine fable to a "young man who didn't understand [Gauguin's] pictures," Degas commented, "he prefers liberty with starvation to servitude with abundance." Gauguin, Be Mysterious, illustrated on page 147.
For Huysmans see page 132.

Van Gogh, horrified to discover that his friend Émile Bernard's paintings had begun to reflect the rarefied and private ethos of literary Symbolism, wrote him an outraged letter condemning his recent painting of a mystical nativity, and contrasting it to a study by Millet "powerful enough to make one tremble – of peasants carrying . . . a calf which has been born in the fields. Now this my friend, all people have felt from France to America." The painting of "what all people have felt" is the way that we best know Van Gogh's paintings now and how he would have wanted them to be received. His initial idea for *La Berceuse*, one of the important "ugly" pictures, was that it would be a centerpiece for the *Sunflowers*, which, flanking it on either side, would shine out "like torches or candelabra." He thought of *La Berceuse* (which means both "the woman rocking the cradle" and "the lullaby") in terms of great closeness and intimacy, fantasizing about it being hung in the cabin of an Icelandic fishing boat, so that the sailors "being both children and martyrs would feel the old sense of being rocked come over them and remember their own lullabies."

See page 222.

See page 221.

By the 1890s critics had also begun to react against the esoteric and the obscure in painting and poetry. Jean Moréas, the poet-author of the original "Symbolist Manifesto" of 1886, five years later proposed what was in effect an anti-symbolist manifesto: a return to the lucid classical meters of Racine. The difficulty of understanding the increasing abstractness of Cézanne's paintings, which began to be exhibited regularly only in the decade after 1895, led critics to describe them as "brutal" or "clumsy." The terms "primitive" and "classical," both widely used in reference to Cézanne, imply a return to simple elemental construction and to the power of basic form. But Émile Bernard, one of his earliest supporters, concluded that his abandonment of drawing and tonal modeling in favor of construction with pure color had resulted in his "impotence" and "failure" as an artist. The critics Alphonse Germain, Charles Merki and Maurice Denis, trying to come to terms with the relationship between abstractness and representation in Cézanne, Van Gogh and Gauguin, wrestled with the problem of "distortion."

See page 148.

Jean Moréas, "Une Nouvelle École," Le Figaro, September 13 and 14, 1891. See also page 274.

See pages 124 and 280.

See page 284.

But it took the artists Matisse, Braque and Bonnard to recognize that "distortion" is measured by criteria that belong to pre-Impressionism. For them representation is understood to respond to the abstract qualities of the medium of painting. Drawing is a process of "drawing out," a forming of an image out of the rich resources of thinking, feeling and perception combined within the medium, particularly within color and touch.

See pages 181, 274, and 193.

THE
POST-
IMPRESSIONISTS

IMPRESSIONISM AND SYMBOLISM: SYMPHONIC FORM

CAMILLE PISSARRO

"Advice to a Young Painter"

1896

Look for the kind of nature that suits your temperament. The motif should be observed more for shape and colour than for drawing. There is no need to tighten the form which can be obtained without that. Precise drawing is dry and hampers the impression of the whole; it destroys all sensations. Do not define too closely the outline of things; it is the brush-stroke of the right value and colour which should produce the drawing. In a mass, the greatest difficulty is not to give the contour in detail, but to paint what is within. Paint the essential character of things, try to convey it by any

This passage, cited in John Rewald's History of Impressionism *(1946), is from the unpublished notes of Louis Le Bail, a young artist who sought Pissarro's advice in 1896–97. It summarizes many of the procedures of the Impressionist approach to painting.*

Camille Pissarro. *Study of Clouds.* 1887/88. Black chalk, $4 \times 6^2/_7''$ (10.1 × 15 cm). Ashmolean Museum, Oxford.

C. P.

L. P. 358 (17)

means whatsoever, without bothering about technique. When painting, make a choice of subject, see what is lying at the right and at the left, then work on everything simultaneously. Don't work bit by bit, but paint everything at once by placing tones everywhere, with brush-strokes of the right colour and value, while noticing what is alongside. Use small brush-strokes and try to put down your perceptions immediately. The eye should not be fixed on one point, but should take in everything, while observing the reflections which the colours produce on their surroundings. Work at the same time upon sky, water, branches, ground, keeping everything going on an equal basis and unceasingly rework until you have got it. Cover the canvas at the first go, then work at it until you can see nothing more to add. Observe the aerial perspective well, from the foreground to the horizon, the reflections of sky, of foliage. Don't be afraid of putting on colour, refine the work little by little. Don't proceed according to rules and principles, but paint what you observe and feel. Paint generously and unhesitatingly, for it is best not to lose the first impression. Don't be timid in front of nature: one must be bold, at the risk of being deceived and making mistakes. One must have only one master – nature; she is the one always to be consulted.

Monet's first studio in Giverny. *c.*1905–06. Lilla Cabot Perry Papers, 1889–1909 (Archives of American Art, Smithsonian Institution, Washington, D.C.).

LILLA CABOT PERRY
THE AMERICAN MAGAZINE OF ART
"Reminiscences of Claude Monet 1889–1909"
March 1927

In spite of his intense nature and at times rather severe aspect, he was inexpressibly kind to many a struggling young painter. He never took any pupils, but he would have made a most inspiring master if he had been willing to teach. I remember his saying to me:

"When you go out to paint, try to forget what objects you have before you, a tree, a house, a field or whatever. Merely think here is a little square of blue, here an oblong of pink, here a streak of yellow, and paint it just as it looks to you, the exact colour and shape, until it gives your own naïve impression of the scene before you."

He said he wished he had been born blind and then had suddenly gained his sight so that he could have begun to paint in this way without knowing what the objects were that he saw before him. He held that the first real look at the motif was likely to be the truest and most unprejudiced one, and said that the first painting should cover as much of the canvas as possible, no matter how roughly, so as to determine at the outset the tonality of the whole. As an illustration of this, he brought out a canvas on which he had painted only once; it was covered with strokes about an inch apart and a quarter of an inch thick, out to the very edge of the canvas. Then he took out another on which he had painted twice, the strokes were nearer together and the subject began to emerge more clearly.

Monet's philosophy of painting was to paint what you really see, not what you think you ought to see: not the object isolated as in a test tube, but the object enveloped in sunlight and atmosphere, with the blue dome of Heaven reflected in the shadows.

Lilla Cabot Perry (1848–1933), an American painter who met Monet in 1889 at Giverny.

In these recorded remarks, Monet emphasizes the purely visual aspect of Impressionism as fragments of color sensation. As with Pissarro's advice, "do not emphasize the outlines of things," this resulted in a loosely organized, freely painted surface consisting of patches of color which often appeared independent of the objects or scene represented.

Claude Monet in 1899 (photograph, Collection Durand-Ruel, Paris).

Camille Pissarro in his studio at Éragny-sur-Epte. Photograph, *c.*1890. Pissarro Museum Archive, Pontoise.

JULES LAFORGUE

IMPRESSIONISM

"The Eye and the Poet"

October 1883

Jules Laforgue (1860–87), Symbolist poet and critical writer. His interests were wide-ranging and brought together ideas from science, philosophy and psychology which he applied to art. His poetry, in its combination of irony and fantasy with untraditional vocabulary and meters, influenced the early T. S. Eliot.

The article of which this is an extract was written on the occasion of an exhibition which included Monet, Pissarro, Renoir and Degas at the Gurlitt Gallery in Berlin in October 1883. It is unclear whether the magazine in which it was to have appeared ever came out, but it was published in Laforgue's Mélanges Posthumes *in 1902. Laforgue's description of the fluidity of touch and image, and the merging of the objective and the subjective, make this article one of the most perceptive pieces of contemporary writing about Impressionism.*

THE ACADEMIC EYE AND THE IMPRESSIONIST EYE: POLYPHONY OF COLOUR. In a landscape flooded with light, in which beings are outlined as if in coloured grisaille, where the academic painter sees nothing but a broad expanse of whiteness, the Impressionist sees light as bathing everything not with a dead whiteness but rather with a thousand vibrant struggling colours of rich prismatic decomposition. Where the one sees only the external outline of objects, the other sees the real living lines built not in geometric forms but in a thousand irregular strokes, which, at a distance, establish life. Where one sees things placed in their regular respective planes according to a skeleton reducible to pure theoretic design, the other sees perspective established by a thousand trivial touches of tone and brush, by the varieties of atmospheric states induced by moving planes.

The Impressionist eye is, in short, the most advanced eye in human evolution, the one which until now has grasped and rendered the most complicated combinations of nuances known.

The Impressionist sees and renders nature as it is – that is, wholly in the vibration of colour. No line, light, relief, perspective or chiaroscuro, none of those childish classifications: all these are in reality converted into the vibration of colour and must be obtained on canvas solely by the vibration of colour.

In the little exhibition at the Gurlitt Gallery, the formula is visible especially in the work of Monet and Pissarro ... where everything is obtained by a thousand little dancing strokes in every direction like straws of colour – all in vital competition for the whole impression. No longer an isolated melody, the whole thing is a symphony which is living and changing like the "forest voices" of Wagner, all struggling to become the great voice of the forest – like the Unconscious, the law of the world, which is the great melodic voice resulting from the symphony of the consciousness of races and individuals. Such is the principle of the *plein-air* Impressionist school. And the eye of the master will be the one capable of distinguishing and recording the most sensitive gradations and decompositions on a simple flat canvas. This principle has been applied not systematically but with genius by certain of our poets and novelists.

This refers to Act II of Siegfried *in which the hero tries to understand the song of the birds.*

FALSE TRAINING OF THE EYES. Now everyone knows that we do not see the colours of the palette in themselves but rather according to the illusions which the paintings of the past have developed in us, and above all we see them in the light which the palette itself gives off. (Compare the intensity of Turner's most dazzling sun with the flame of the weakest candle.) What one might call an innate harmonic agreement operates automatically between the visual effect of the landscape and the paint on the palette. This is the proportional language of painting, which grows richer in proportion to the development of the painter's optical sensibility. The same goes for size and perspective. In this sense, one might even go so far as to say that the painter's palette is to real light and to the tricks of colour it plays on reflecting and refracting realities what perspective on a flat canvas is to the real planes of spatial reality. On these two things, the painter builds.

MOBILITY OF LANDSCAPE AND MOBILITY OF THE PAINTER'S IMPRESSIONS. You critics who codify the beautiful and guide the development of art, I would have you look at this painter who sets down his easel before a rather evenly lighted landscape – an afternoon scene, for example. Let us suppose that instead of painting his landscape in several sittings, he has the good sense to record its tonal values in *fifteen minutes* – that is, let us suppose that he is an Impressionist. He arrives on the scene with his own individual optic sensibility. Depending on the state of fatigue or preparation the painter has just been through, his sensibility is at the same time either bedazzled or receptive; and it is not the sensibility of a single organ, but rather the three competitive sensibilities of Young's fibrils. In the course of these fifteen minutes, the lighting of the landscape – the vibrant sky, the fields, the trees, everything within the insubstantial network of the rich atmosphere with the constantly undulating life of its invisible reflecting or refracting corpuscles – has undergone infinite changes, has, in a word, lived.

In the course of these fifteen minutes, the optical sensibility of the painter has changed time and time again, has been upset in its appreciation of the constancy and relative values of the landscape tones. Imponderable fusions of tone, opposing perceptions, imperceptible distractions, subordinations and dominations, variations in the force of reaction of the three optical fibrils one upon the other and on the external world, infinite and infinitesimal struggles.

One of a myriad examples: I see a certain shade of violet; I lower my eyes towards my palette to mix it and my eye is involuntarily drawn by the white of my shirt sleeve; my eye has changed, my violet suffers.

So, in short, even if one remains only fifteen minutes before a landscape, one's work will never be the real equivalent of the fugitive reality, but rather the record of the response of a certain unique sensibility to a

COLORPLATE 9. Claude Monet. *Morning on the Seine*. 1896–97. 35²⁄₅ × 36¹⁄₂ (89.9 × 92.7 cm).
© 1992 The Art Institute of Chicago (Martin A. Ryerson Collection, 1933.1156).
All Rights Reserved.

COLORPLATE 10. Claude Monet. *Waterlilies – Reflection of Willow*. 1916–19. 78³/₄ × 78³/₄″ (200 × 200 cm). Musée Marmottan, Paris.

COLORPLATE 13. Claude Monet. *Waterlilies at Twilight*. 1916–22.
6′ 6¾″ × 19′ 8¼″ (200 × 600 cm). Kunsthaus, Zurich.

COLORPLATE 11. Claude Monet. *Wisteria*. 1919–20. 39⅓ × 118″ (100 × 300 cm).
Musée Marmottan, Paris.

COLORPLATE 12. Claude Monet. *The Japanese Bridge.* 1918. 39⅓ × 78¾″ (100 × 200 cm).
Musée Marmottan, Paris.

Claude Monet. *Rue St-Denis, Festivities of June 30, 1878 (Rue Montorgueil with Flags)*. 1878. 30 × 20½″ (76 × 52 cm). Musée des Beaux-Arts, Rouen.

moment which can never be reproduced exactly for the individual, under the excitement of a landscape at a certain moment of its luminous life which can never be duplicated.

There are roughly three states of mind in the presence of a landscape: first, the growing keenness of the optical sensibility under the excitement of this new scene; second, the peak of keenness; third, a period of gradual nervous exhaustion.

To these should be added the constantly changing atmosphere of the best galleries where the canvas will be shown, the minute daily life of the landscape tones absorbed in perpetual struggle. And, moreover, with the spectators the same variation of sensibility, and with each an infinite number of unique moments of sensibility.

Subject and object are then irretrievably in motion, inapprehensible and unapprehending. In the flashes of identity between subject and object lies the nature of genius. And any attempt to codify such flashes is but an academic pastime.

JULES HURET

ECHO DE PARIS

"Inquiry into Literary Evolution"

March 3–July 5, 1891

In making the distinction between the direct naming of an object and its gradual apprehension by means of nuance and suggestion, Mallarmé is indicating qualities that were seen, in the 1890s, to belong to both Symbolism and Impressionism.

M. STÉPHANE MALLARMÉ

One of the most widely loved *littérateurs* in the world of letters . . . Average height, pointed greying beard, long straight nose; large pointed satyr's ears, extraordinarily bright wide eyes, an expression of unusual shrewdness tempered by an air of great kindliness. He gestures perpetually as he speaks – variously, gracefully, precisely, eloquently; he lingers slightly over the ends of words, his voice softening a little; he exerts a powerful charm, and one also senses in him, soaring above all, a perennial pride, as of a god or visionary before whom – once one has understood this – one must immediately make an inward gesture of obeisance.

We are now witnessing a truly extraordinary phenomenon, he said to me, one unique in the history of poetry: each poet is withdrawing to his own corner, to play whatever tunes he likes on his own special flute; for the first time ever, poets are no longer singing in unison. Hitherto, do you not think, the poet's accompaniment was necessarily the great organs of official metre. But now these have been overplayed, and people have become tired of them.

*   *   *

Stéphane Mallarmé photographed next to his portrait by Manet.

This new kind of verse has arisen above all because people are weary of official verse; even its supporters share this weariness. Is it not an aberration to open up any book of poetry whatsoever and to be sure to find uniform and conventional rhythms throughout, just where, in fact, we are allegedly being drawn by the essential variety of human feelings! Where is the inspiration, where is the unexpected? and what lassitude! Official verse should serve only in moments of spiritual crisis; today's poets quite understand this; they have skirted around it with a very delicate feeling of caution, or approached it with singular timidity, one might even say alarm, and instead of making it their principle and starting-point, they have suddenly caused it to rise up as the climax of the poem or sentence!

Furthermore, the same transformation has occurred in music: the firmly drawn melodies of former times have been succeeded by an infinity of broken melodies which enrich the fabric without one feeling the cadence so strongly marked.

Is this indeed the root of the split? I asked.

Oh yes. The Parnassians, lovers of very strict verse, of verse which is intrinsically beautiful, did not see that this new kind was just an effort that was completing their own; an effort which at the same time had the advantage of creating a sort of interregnum for "great" verse, which was exhausted and begging for mercy. Furthermore people should know that the latest arrivals are not attempting to do away with "great" verse; they aim to make the poem more airy, to create a sort of fluidity, of mobility between the endless flow of verses – something which hitherto had been somewhat lacking. In an orchestra you may suddenly hear a very lovely outburst from the brass; but you know quite well that if that were the whole piece, you would soon weary of it. The young are sparing with these high points, producing them only when they may have the greatest effect: it is thus that the Alexandrine, which no one actually invented but which sprang up spontaneously from the instrument of language, instead of remaining obsessional and fixed as at present, will be freer, more unexpected from now on; it will acquire a grandeur through association only with the solemn impulses of the soul. And in the volume of poetry of the future, the greatest classical verse will be punctuated by an infinitude of motifs borrowed from the individual ear.

* * *

You have talked of form, I said to M. Stéphane Mallarmé. What of content?

I think, he replied, that, as to content, the young are nearer the poetic ideal than the Parnassians, who still treat their subjects in the fashion of the old philosophers and orators, presenting objects directly. Whereas I think that poetry is purely a matter of allusion. It is contemplation of the object, the image released by the reveries it arouses; the Parnassians take hold of the thing in its entirety and proclaim it; thus they lack mystery; they deny the imagination the delicious joy of believing that it is creating. To *name* an object is to suppress three-quarters of the enjoyment of the poem, which lies in the delight of gradually guessing; to *suggest* it, that is the dream. It is the perfect use of that mystery that constitutes the symbol: to evoke an object little by little to show a state of mind or, inversely, to choose an object and abstract a state of mind from it, through a series of decipherings.

Here, I said to the master, we are approaching a serious objection I have to put to you . . . that of obscurity!

Indeed, he replied, it is equally dangerous, whether the obscurity comes from the reader's incapacity, or from that of the poet . . . but it would be cheating to shrink from this demanding process. For if a person of average intelligence, and with inadequate literary grounding, should happen by chance to open a book written in this fashion and claim enjoyment from it, misunderstanding ensues, and things must be sorted out. There must always be mystery in poetry, and it is the aim of literature – its sole aim, indeed – to *evoke* things.

* * *

The Parnassians were a group of poets, including Théophile Gautier (1811–72), Théodore de Banville (1823–91) and Leconte de Lisle (1818–94), successors to the Romantics, who appeared regularly in an anthology of contemporary poetry published between 1866 and 1876, Le Parnasse Contemporain.

Paul Gauguin. *Portrait of Stéphane Mallarmé.* 1891. Etching, $7^{1}/_{4} \times 5^{3}/_{4}''$ (18.5 × 14.6 cm). Bibliothèque Nationale, Paris (Cabinet des Estampes).

What do you think of the aims of naturalism?

Hitherto, literature had been sufficiently childish to believe, for example, that to select a certain number of precious stones and put their names down on paper – even very vividly – is to *make* precious stones. Since poetry consists in *creating*, you must take states, glimmers in the human soul, of a purity so absolute that, well sung and well-set, the result will indeed constitute the jewels of man: here there will be a symbol, here there will be true creation, here the word poetry will come into its own. It is, in short, the only human creation possible.

Basically, you see, said the master, shaking my hand, the world was made to end up in a Book.

GEORGES LECOMTE
LA REVUE INDÉPENDANTE
"L'Art Contemporain"
April 1892

Georges Lecomte (1867–1958), writer and friend of Pissarro and Fénéon, who shared their anarchist sympathies. He edited the Symbolist weekly La Cravache in 1888–89. In this article Lecomte's discussion of "the decorative" reflected current thinking within the Symbolist movement about the equivalence of poetry, music and painting and about the expression of qualities of feeling and states of mind through the abstract organization of painting apart from nature.

Masters of all ages have probably composed their pictures in accordance with systems of lines that were interesting in themselves irrespective of any precise meaning: colours were brought together in captivating harmonies to complete the linear ornamentation. And we have no memory of a truly great work which is not simultaneously characteristic and decorative. It would thus not be in the least novel to observe this concern for ornamentation in the specific efforts of such and such a contemporary painter, since this concern is common to the great talents of all centuries. But what is peculiar to our own is the systematic and general nature of this tendency. With the decorative in view, all innovatory artists (however diverse and sometimes indecisive their means of execution may be) try to disengage the permanent characters of natural Beauty from all that is secondary and superfluous.

The unanimity of this concern also bears witness to a very elevated understanding of art, raising the contemporary schools above the discredit in which too many people unjustly hold them. It proves the abandoning of the immediate copying of nature, a greater intellectuality and a more complex plastic ideal, since a preconceived and considered system is here aiming to achieve what the masters offered, whether intentionally or unconsciously.

Furthermore, do not all great works appear clothed in special, as it were decorative beauty? The alliteration of syllables in a line of verse, the development and echoes of certain lines in a stanza which complete its thought and rhythm, the repetition of stanzas within a poem, these are the astragals and dentils which trace their arabesques over the coloured web of the words, whose graceful flow creates an overall harmony and brings together the various aspects of the basic idea. Poems in prose, if their writing is artistic, may also be mentioned here by virtue of the recurrence of ideas and phrases whose supple and highly decorative over-archings embroider both thought and text. But above all, decorative arrangement is evident in music. Motifs are developed, abandoned for a moment and taken up again: they alternate, they interconnect; not only do they explicitly describe states of mind, they are also united to create an overall harmony. These successions of motifs in a symphony have a movement which ornaments the lyrical development of the theme.

* * *

Édouard Manet. *Raven Sitting on Bust.*
Illustration for Mallarmé's translation
of Poe's *The Raven*, 1875. Lithograph,
17½ × 12¾″ (44.5 × 31.8 cm).
Bibliothèque Nationale, Paris.

The *plein-air* painters known by common accord as the "Impressionists" at first sought decorative beauty solely on the basis of colours rigorously revealed by light. And this exclusive concern appeared very rational, bearing in mind that these painters were interested above all in covering their canvases with the most radiant colours and with rendering the splendour of the natural scene in all its harmonic intensity. What particularly seduced them in the work of Delacroix was his knowledge of colour, the unexpectedness of certain distributions of colour to achieve a more vivid effect and more meaningful overall harmonies. In truth, their concern for decoration through colour was, at first, quite instinctive. They sought above all to render place, mood and enveloping brightness in all their truth and individuality. And it is because they were drawing nearer to authentic natural colouring that their studies acquired a decorative beauty. Only later, when they observed the results achieved through faithfulness in the rendering of outer appearance, did they think to arrange the distribution of their colours not only with a view to the exact description of the effect, with adequate brightness, but also with a view to overall harmony.

Still, they did not modify the outer aspect of things as deliberately as they do today; they did not prune away the superfluous and the momentary through a process of synthetic elimination. The natural setting was far from being the essential leitmotif, a pretext for a decorative interpretation. Quite simply, to translate the appearance of nature, they would choose one among twenty possible aspects which their painter's eye saw as both significant and harmonious. But they have not ceased working directly from nature and are still too much under her immediate influence to distort her suggestions in order to intensify the meaning and ornamental beauty of the work.

They are gradually withdrawing from reality. They continue to be scrupulously inspired by it, but they use exact data which they take from it as a starting point to build up compositions which are beautiful both for their basic character and for their decoration: they assemble lines, regulate gestures, orchestrate the lie of the land in accordance with that of the attitude of the human being who moves upon it; they compose, well away from nature. At the same time as the draughtsmanship becomes bolder, more summary and individual, the colour tends to be simplified. The sense of proportion between line and colour disappears. The painter who, along with M. Cézanne, first freed himself from too strict a communion with nature, our venerable friend M. Camille Pissarro, set gracefully outlined clouds sailing through his limpid skies, completed the curve described by the trunk of a tree by the rounded rump of an animal or the bent back of a peasant woman, linked the rise and fall of the ground to the pretty scrolls of the fronds and branches. M. Renoir, ravished by the linear beauty and relief of the human anatomy, organizes the attitudes and gestures of the body and the mobility of its physiognomy in accordance with a very ingenious decorative ensemble. Lastly, the vigorous talent of M. Claude Monet, who long restricted himself (but with what evocative power) to rendering rapid natural effects in their fleeting intensity, seems increasingly to be isolating the lasting character of things from their complex appearances, to accentuate their decorative meaning and beauty by a more synthetic and more reflective rendering.

MARCEL PROUST

BY WAY OF SAINTE-BEUVE

"Portraits of Painters – Monet"

1908–10

A lover of pictures, of Claude Monet's landscapes, let us say, or Sisley's, will inevitably come to know and feel a liking for rivers where a sailing-boat streaks its wake between grassy banks, for the blue sea at Antibes, for various times of day, for certain aspects of Rouen where the cathedral appears among the houses, with its spire and ribbed Gothic walls standing out among flattened roofs and smooth house-fronts – just as a man who loves a singer inevitably loves the character of Juliet or of Ophelia, in which, as in the bread of the altar, the being he adores is made manifest to him. Picture lovers who will make a journey to look at a Monet painting of a poppy-field will not, perhaps, take a walk to look at a field of poppies; but meanwhile, like astrologers who had a speculum that showed them everything in the world, but which had to be consulted in some place of solitude since astrologers did not mingle in the world's affairs, they have hanging on their walls mirrors of a no less magic kind called pictures, in which if one knows how to look at them steadily, slightly withdrawing oneself the while, important constituents of reality are unveiled. There we stand, bent on the magic mirror, standing a little back from it, trying to drive out every other thought, seeking to understand the purport of each stroke of colour, each of them calling to mind past impressions which gather into a construction as atmospheric and multicoloured as the strokes

Proust, a great admirer of Monet, had made him the chief model for the painter Elstir in Remembrance of Things Past, *and saw in Monet's aesthetic a reflection of his own interest in the fusion of memory and new experience.* Contre Saint Beuve *is a collection of writings that engaged Proust during the years immediately after he embarked on* Remembrance of Things Past *in 1908, but was not unearthed and published until 1954. Scholars have debated whether this fragment on Monet, which was entitled "Le Peintre. Ombres – Monet" in the Pléiade edition, 1971, should properly be included in the collection.*

of colour on the canvas and build up a landscape in the imagination; mirrors consulted by old men with long beards who do not know that the wind parches and the sun scorches, but who are entranced to discover all these truths, which are, besides, based on the real wind and the real sun. Just as the singer's lovers know the author whom she admires and whose characters they see her playing, a picture by Monet makes us love the landscape which pleases us in it. He often painted the banks of the Seine at Vernon. No doubt we can be of the opinion that he would have seen things as lovely elsewhere, and that perhaps it was his personal circumstances that took him there. Never mind. To draw out the truth and beauty of a place we must know that they are there to be drawn out, that gods are everywhere latent in its soil. Apart from those places where on some high and holy day we ourselves have been granted a revelation, we can pray only on consecrated ground. Certainly it is not a vain idolatry for Monet or Corot that will do our loving for us. We shall love for ourselves. But on the threshold of love we are bashful. There has to be someone who will say to us: Here is what you may love; love it. And then we love. Monet's pictures show us the magic vein in Argenteuil, in Vetheuil, in Epte, in Giverny. So we set off for these holy lands. They show us, too, the heavenly pasturage our imaginations can find in things less localised, islet-dotted rivers during those motionless hours of afternoon when the river is blue and white with sky and clouds, and green with trees and lawns, and pink with sunbeams already sloping on tree-trunks, and splashed with scarlet in the shadow of the garden hedges where the tall dahlias push through. The pictures make us adore a field, a sky, a beach, a river, as though these were shrines which we long to visit, shrines we lost faith in when we see, strolling through the field, walking briskly along the shore, a lady drawing her shawl closer, a man and woman holding hands. We rank the divinities of our worship so high that whatever brings them down to the level of the already known breaks the spell for us. It is the ideal we give our hearts to. Believing that the painter is going to tell us about the place itself, a mysterious personage with a vast countenance of cliff and a sunset glance reddening through the rain into the very depths of the sea, we see a couple thrust themselves between it and us. And we who believed this personality of places to be such a mystery that we believed the painter entirely given over to calling it up amid the silence and the furrowing boom of waves on that beach, we are astounded to see that he was in the upshot no more concerned with it than with this couple, who strike us as in no way mysterious and whom he has put into his picture too. We thirsted for parts of the world that are themselves and nothing but themselves, beaches that never see more than a particular corner of the cliff and hear the sea's lament all day and all night, towns built on the slope of a hill that see only a river and in summer lilac groves; the sight of mankind embedded in these things irks us, since it was them only, them unbelittled, that we wanted to see. Such is the unreasonableness of our ideals. When we are children, and we try to find the moon and the stars in books, we are enraptured by the moon in *Picciola* because it is a glistening luminary, and are disappointed by it in *Columba* because it is compared to a cheese and a cheese seems vulgar to us and the moon appears divine. And in de Musset's *Histoire d'un Merle blanc*, so long as it is a matter of white wings and a rosy beak and little drops of water, we are charmed, but after the white blackbird has addressed the dove as *Madame la Marquise* these men and women who at that time represent the real world, which we think to be ugly, to be unpoetical, irk us and take away all our pleasure. It is the period of our life when the only things we enjoy in a picture gallery are works by Gleyre or Ingres, when we require faultless symmetry, moons like silver crescents in a star-strewn heaven, and when all the colouring of the *Marriage at Cana* seems as far removed from the world of poetry, and as vulgar, as the coat-tails over the chair or the wine-stains on the table-cloth.

Marcel Proust, photograph
(© Collection Harlingue-Viollet, Paris).

Alfred de Musset (1810–57), Romantic poet, novelist and playwright.

Charles Gleyre (1806–74), academic painter.
Veronese (1528–88): The Marriage at Cana, *1562–3, Louvre.*

Claude Monet at Giverny, 1926. Photograph by Nickolas Muray. 9⁹/₁₆ × 7⁵/₈″ (24.3 × 19.3 cm). Museum of Modern Art, New York (Gift of Mrs Nickolas Muray).

PIERRE FRANCASTEL

L'IMPRESSIONNISME

"Impressionism and Poetry"

1937

There are two aspects to Monet's painting: one that we might call technical, and one that we might call poetic and ideological. Drawing closer to the classic definition of Impressionism: it is an art of light, a synthesis of the world in colour. However, it is certain that the effect produced by a form of art must be taken into account quite as much as its means; Monet, in fact, worked more for the achievement of an aesthetic ideal than for the refinement of a method; more precisely put, the technical developments evident in his work were inspired not by a concern for artistic means, but by the desire to convey new effects.

For example, when he told a friend about his first idea for the *Water-lilies*, he told him not that he was intending to create a virtuosic work where classical composition would tend to melt away, where the artist would capture the reflections of things and not the things themselves, where "divided" tones would express the make-up of light, but that he wished to paint "the impossible – water with water-weeds, rippling in the depths under the sun's rays." The starting-point for his research, the standpoint he referred to in order to assess the value of his efforts, was undoubtedly emotional.

* * *

Pierre Francastel (1900–70) was one of the first art historians to question the received definition of Impressionism as an art concerned with the recording of objective perceptions of light in nature. Here he notes the subjectivity and emotional content of Impressionism and the close relationship between Impressionism and Symbolism. In this excerpt he discusses the common ground between Monet and Mallarmé.

Letter to Gustave Geffroy on June 22, 1890. When Monet started painting his water garden, in the 1890s, it was also the period of his closest association with the Symbolist movement and particularly with Mallarmé.

The critic must make one vital distinction: it is tempting to say that Monet banishes man from the domain of painting. Clearly he banishes the representation of man, but does this mean that his art is necessarily anti-human? The anti-realism of Monet's art, characteristic of its development from 1889 onwards, self-evidently and *a priori*, is ill-adapted to the denial of spiritual values. But in ceasing to represent human actions, Monet tends to make art into a direct act of witnessing which embraces and vividly evokes the rhythms of an inner life. His painting, stripped of all anecdotal representation, takes on the value and meaning of a symbol. And it is almost superfluous to stress *en passant* that Monet's art is thus comparable to contemporary poetry.

*   *   *

Like literary symbolism, in its definitive form Monet's Impressionism emerges as essentially distinct from allegory. Monet's endeavour is no more a rejuvenation of the old subject than Mallarmé's poetry is an attempt to develop a traditional system of images under another name. The problem of expression and the meaning of a work of art was a topic dear to all "independent" circles. Puvis de Chavannes and Gustave Moreau are concerned with it, the former in love with brightness and naivety, the latter with erudition and violent colours, but both, the designer of cartoons as much as the mystical intellectual, remain faithful to the classic conception which seeks the intelligible through the subject, through the paths of memory and the association of ideas.

Monet's dream, like Mallarmé's, is to link meaning to emotion and not to knowledge. Furthermore, the role of technique is crucial for both, since they feel a need to forge new relationships, to create a novel mechanism; but each senses that the secret of a new art must be sought elsewhere than in its formal means. . . .

Just as Monet rejects lines and local colour, so Mallarmé rejects the descriptions of the Parnassians and the rhetoric of the Romantics. The Symbolists' definitions of their poetic art are curiously similar to those of Monet. Like Symbolism – and above all like the Symbolism of Mallarmé, isolated among his rivals and disciples (as is Monet) and being the sole representative, not of a movement, but of a tendency – Impressionism is a return to the personal poetry proscribed equally by the Parnassians and the realists. It is an impassioned appeal to life and liberty, but at the same time it is quite the reverse of anarchic. It seeks relationships of an intuitive kind, but it accepts the need for method, and the value of rules.

*   *   *

The parallel between Symbolism and Impressionism does not end with this general comparison. Its thirst for novelty and pure emotion means that Symbolism uses certain formal means which have a strange similarity to those of Impressionism. It draws its effects essentially from rhythm; and the suppression of outlines and subject matter, likewise of classic images and descriptiveness, gives the new art a fluidity hitherto unknown, which enables it to evoke the volatile and the ephemeral. Both these arts, enamored as they are of visual evocation, preclude any firm definition of their images; they aim to engender them not through representation, but through analogy, through emotion. Rhythm, a free form as different as may be from traditional symmetry, from which it borrows only selectively and occasionally, plays a vital if hidden role. It is rhythm which enables the *Water Lilies* to give us the illusion of witnessing the emergence of a whole world of forms, a marvelous refuge dreamt by the poet, who avoids imposing his own vision upon the spectator, but who seeks only to put him in a state of mind where he himself can become a poet, through a simultaneous train of emotions of an optical and emotional kind. Mallarmé's aim in his famous *Coup de Dés*, for example, is to transmute our

Pierre Puvis de Chavannes (1824–98), Gustave Moreau (1826–98): Symbolist painters whose "symbolism" was more a question of the illustrated subject matter than the handling of form. This is the distinction from Monet.

Mallarmé's radical and typographically innovative poem was first published in the magazine Cosmopolis *in May 1897.*

reminiscences into a wave of images, though here, with evident awkwardness, he has recourse to effects of a typographical and visual kind.

The comparison should be pursued further to extend to the neighboring realm of music. For it is not true, as has already been said, that a parallel between the effects sought by artists expressing themselves through different forms of art is necessarily superficial and misleading. To claim as much is to forget that technique is only the servant of inspiration and, more precisely, that there are, so to speak, intermediaries at work between the phase of pure inspiration and that of technique: the laws of harmony, of composition, of proportion, are common to all the arts; indeed, to some degree, music evokes images and painting evokes rhythms. One may therefore quite legitimately accept that different artists of a single period, expressing themselves through different means, might represent very similar states of mind and that they might have recourse to closely related methods.

What is much more delicate, in the case which concerns us, is sensing with what music Impressionism, and Mallarmé's Symbolism, should truly be associated. One immediately thinks of Wagner and Wagnerism. All the more so since the same men, open as they were to generous ideas, undertook the defence of both Wagner and Claude Monet to the public. But one may wonder how much the critics of *La Revue Wagnérienne* really understood of this fairly complex adventure. This is not the place to embark upon a history of Wagnerism in France; we would simply like to point out how Wagnerism, on the one hand, and Impressionism and Symbolism on the other, are inspired by indomitable forms of the ideal.

La Revue Wagnérienne, *a Symbolist magazine, was founded in 1885 by Téodor de Wyzewa and Édouard Dujardin, members of Mallarmé's circle.*

THE SUBJECTIVITY OF SENSATIONS

PAUL GAUGUIN
Letter to Émile Schuffenecker
January 14, 1885

Charles-Émile Schuffenecker (1851–1906), minor Impressionist painter and an assiduous supporter of Gauguin. He was selfless in his efforts on Gauguin's behalf, advancing him money, frequently supplying him with lodgings, studio space and every kind of hospitality. Gauguin was unstinting in his advice.

Armand Guillaumin (1841–1927), painter who belonged to the Impressionist group.

COPENHAGEN

My dear Schuffenecker,

I have received a letter from Guillaumin, apparently you wanted one of his exhibited paintings and it was already reserved. Why do you not go and see him to choose another one, I think it would be good for you to have an example of his work at your place, as well as wanting a sale for this poor but talented artist.

For myself, sometimes I feel that I am mad, and yet the more I ponder at night in bed, the more I think I am right. Philosophers have long discussed phenomena which seem to us supernatural but of which we have the *sensation*. Everything is there, in this word. Raphael and others, artists in whom sensations were formulated well in advance of thoughts, were allowed to work on them, without crushing them, and to remain artists. And for me the great artist is the hallmark of the greatest intelligence, one open to feelings, to the most delicate translations (and hence the least visible) achieved by the brain.

Look into the immense creation of nature and you will see that there are laws which generate all human feelings, unalike in their aspects yet similar in their effects. Look at a big spider, or a tree-trunk in a forest, both produce powerful sensations in you without your knowing why. Why do you feel revulsion at touching a rat and suchlike: no logic holds before these feelings. All our five senses *reach the brain directly*, affected by an infinity of things which no schooling can destroy. I conclude from this that there are noble lines, others that are deceptive, etc. The straight line creates infinity, the curve limits creation, not to mention the fatality of numbers. The figures 3 and 7 have been endlessly discussed. Colours, though there are fewer of them, speak even more loudly than lines, because of their power over the eye. There are noble tones, others which are common, peaceful and soothing harmonies, and others which arouse you by their boldness. Graphology may show you the features of an honest man, or of a liar; why should an ordinary man not be able to discern the more or less imposing character of the artist through his lines and colours? Take Cézanne, the misunderstood, the quintessential mystical man of the East (he even looks like an elder from the Levant): his forms tend to have the mystery and weighty serenity of the dreamer, his colour is as grave as the character of an oriental; a man of the South, he spends whole days on mountain tops reading Virgil and looking at the sky. Thus his horizons are lofty, his blues very intense and his reds astonishingly vibrant.

Furthermore, this Virgil of his can be interpreted at will; and his paintings too have a parabolic meaning with two aims; his backgrounds are as much imagined as real. To sum up: when you see a painting by him, the word "strange" comes to your lips. But he is a mystic and he draws like one.

The further I go along this path – the translation of thought into a medium other than literature – the more convinced I am of my theory; we shall see who is right. If I am wrong, why does your whole Académie, which is acquainted with all the means employed by the old masters, not

A new awareness of the dimensions of the term "sensation" is indicated in Gauguin's exclamation: "Everything is there, in this word." Inherited from Impressionism it had become a loaded term understood, as the documents in this section indicate, to mean not only the objective impressions received from the external world, from nature, but also the subjective feelings and thoughts that were inseparable from them.

Paul Gauguin photographed in 1888 at Pont-Aven. Musée départemental du Prieuré, St-Germain-en-Laye.

produce masterpieces? Because one does not create a nature, an intelligence and a heart for oneself. The young Raphael knew these things intuitively and his paintings create harmonies of line which cannot be accounted for, for they are the veiled reflection of the inmost part of man. Look at the lesser details, the landscape background, of a picture by Raphael: you will find the same feeling as in the head. It is all of a piece. A landscape by Carolus Durand [sic] is as much of a shambles as one of his portraits. (I can't explain it but that is what I feel.)

Here I am more exercised by art than ever, undistracted by either money worries or business inquiries. You say that I would do well to join your Société d'Indépendants, but do you know what will happen? There are a hundred of you now, tomorrow there will be two hundred. Artist-dealers are two-thirds schemers; soon you will see Gervex and others commanding attention, and then what shall we do, we, the dreamers, the misunderstood? This year you had a *favorable press*, next year the painters of seascapes (there are Raffaëllis everywhere) will be throwing mud at you in order to appear clean themselves.

The equilateral triangle is the most solid and perfect form of triangle. The isosceles triangle is more elegant. Truth cannot be viewed obliquely. In our view, right-hand lines come towards you and left-hand lines retreat. The right hand strikes, the left is on the defensive. A long neck is graceful but a sunken head is more pensive. A duck with its head cocked is on the alert, I don't know, I'm rambling. Your friend Courtois makes better sense, but his painting is so dull. Why are weeping willows so called? Is it because downward lines are mournful? And is the sycamore mournful because it is planted in cemeteries – no, it is the colour that is mournful.

As far as business is concerned, I won't be seeing any results, if there ever are any, for six months. Meanwhile I haven't a penny, I'm in it up to here, so I console myself by dreaming.

Bit by bit my wife and I will extricate ourselves, giving French lessons. You'll laugh, me giving French lessons?

I wish you better luck than mine.

My greetings to your wife.

P. GAUGUIN.

Photograph of Camille Pissarro with palette. Detail. Ashmolean Museum, Oxford.

Émile-Auguste Carolus-Duran (1838–1917), popular academic painter. Jean-François Raffaëlli (1850–1924), realist and anecdotal painter associated with the Impressionists.

LUCIEN PISSARRO
Letter to his Father Camille
May 1891

LONDON

My dear Father,

... I had the nerve to begin a painting at the studio with very little information, and I'm quite amazed to discover that I'm going to be able to do it. It's really a revelation! I had imagined it would be so difficult, that by comparison, it seems rather easy! I'm obliged to do things this way because it is very difficult to paint from nature when you live in the city. There are distances and changes of effects in a country where there aren't two days in a row that are alike. Besides, since my idea is to paint emphasizing the decorative aspect, I have no other choice.

I'm not surprised that Anquetin made his way in that manner. It was inevitable. And what a faker Gauguin is! Come now, seriously, do you think he has all that many ideas? We've talked with him and know, there's not a chance that we'd be taken in! In Aurier's article there's a point you didn't notice and that shows how empty it is: at one point, after a long procession of words (words, nothing but words!), he admits that everything he has just said means nothing if the artist isn't endowed with the gift of *emotivity*. But that's what we call *sensation*. So what did he prove??

Lucien Pissarro (1863–1944), Pissarro's eldest son, a painter and printmaker, had been living in London since 1883. His letter shows that "sensation" was understood by the Impressionist generation to signify qualities of feeling ("emotivity") as well as qualities of perception.

On May 9 Pissarro had written to his son from Paris: "Anquetin is getting somewhere. ... he sent [to the Indépendants*] ... a rather good nude figure imitated from the primitives, but carefully done ... but also some horrible landscapes and a huge prostitute whose enormous breasts hang outside her bodice. Naturally there was a storm. ... [he sent] eight objects to the* Champs de Mars, *seven were rejected. Tumult in the newspapers, meetings of discontented artists, then a third organization was formed, Anquetin, president. . ."*

Albert Aurier's article "Le Symbolisme en peinture: Paul Gauguin" had just appeared in Mercure de France *in March 1891.*

CAMILLE PISSARRO

Letter to his Son Lucien

November 22, 1895

PARIS

My dear Lucien,
I am always haggling with Durand who hesitates. I hope he doesn't abandon me. Yesterday he talked to me at length, saying that he would like nothing better than to buy everything I did, but that he wasn't selling my work, that he had four million francs' worth of paintings that cost him tremendous interest.

Mauclair has published an article [on Cézanne] which I am sending you. You will see that he is ill informed like most of those critics who understand nothing. He simply doesn't know that Cézanne was influenced like all the rest of us, which detracts nothing from his qualities. People forget that Cézanne was first influenced by Delacroix, Courbet, Manet and even Legros, like all of us; he was influenced by me at Pontoise, and I by him. You may remember the sallies of Zola and Béliard in this regard. They imagined that artists are the sole inventors of their styles and that to resemble someone else is to be unoriginal. Curiously enough, in Cézanne's show at Vollard's there are certain landscapes of Auvers and Pontoise [painted in 1871–74] that are similar to mine. Naturally, we were always together! But what cannot be denied is that each of us kept the only thing that counts, the unique "sensation"! – This could easily be shown.

Paul Durand-Ruel (1831–1922), the Impressionists' first dealer who had regularly purchased the work of Pissarro since 1871.

"Choses d'Art", Mercure de France, November 1895. Camille Mauclair (1872–1945), art critic for Mercure de France.

Cézanne exhibited a group of 150 paintings at Vollard's gallery in November 1895.

PAUL CÉZANNE

Letters

1899, 1903, 1904

TO HENRI GASQUET   PARIS, JUNE 3, 1899

My dear Henri,
Last month I received a number of the *"Memorial d'Aix"* which published at the head of its columns a splendid article of Joachim's about the age-old titles to fame of our country. I was touched by his thoughtfulness and I ask you to interpret to him the sentiments which he has re-awakened in me, your old school-fellow at the Pensionat St. Joseph; for within us they have not gone to sleep for ever, the vibrating sensations reflected by this good soil of Provence, the old memories of our youth, of these horizons, of these landscapes, of these unbelievable lines which leave in us so many deep impressions.

As soon as I get down to Aix, I shall come and embrace you. For the time being I continue to seek the expression of the confused sensations which we bring with us when we are born. When I die everything will be finished, but never mind.

Whether I shall be the first to come down to the South, or whether you will come to Paris before me, I commend myself to your good thoughts; let me know and we shall meet again.

Please give my respects and best wishes to Mme. Gasquet, your mother and convey the expression of my sincerest wishes to your son, your wife; and for you, my warmest greetings, in the hope of meeting you again soon, from your old comrade

Paul Cézanne

Henri Gasquet, a schoolmate whose son Joachim (1873–1921) Cézanne met in 1896 and with whom he remained a close friend until 1904. Joachim wrote the account of his conversations with Cézanne in 1912–13. It was published in 1921.

Mémorial d'Aix: *a widely read Aix weekly had recently published an article asserting that the cultural traditions of Aix were dead. Joachim had written a passionate defence of his home town.*

TO CHARLES CAMOIN   AIX, SEPTEMBER 13, 1903

Dear Monsieur Camoin,

I was delighted to get your news and congratulate you on being free to devote yourself entirely to your studies.

I thought I had mentioned to you that Monet lived at Giverny; I wish that the artistic influence which this master cannot fail to have on his more or less immediate circle, may make itself felt to the strictly necessary degree, which it can and ought to have on a young artist willing to work. Couture used to say to his pupils: "Keep good company, that is: go to the Louvre. But after having seen the great masters who repose there, we must hasten out and by contact with nature revive within ourselves the instincts, the artistic sensations which live in us." I am sorry not to be able to be with you. Age would be no obstacle were it not for the other considerations which prevent me from leaving Aix. Nevertheless I hope that I shall have the pleasure of seeing you again. Larguier is in Paris. My son is at Fontainebleau with his mother.

What shall I wish you: good studies made after nature, that is the best thing.

If you meet the master whom we both admire, remember me to him. He does not, I believe, much like being bothered, but in view of the sincerity he may relax a little.

Believe me very sincerely yours,

Paul Cézanne

Charles Camoin (1879–1965), painter, and a fellow student with Matisse of Gustave Moreau, was introduced to Cézanne by Vollard in 1901. He later became a Fauve, influenced by Cézanne and by Signac.

Thomas Couture (1815–79), academic painter respected as a teacher. Manet spent six years as his pupil.

Léo Larguier (1878–1950), poet, friend of Joachim Gasquet, who introduced him to Cézanne. He wrote Le Dimanche avec Paul Cézanne *(1925).*

Claude Monet.

AIX, JANUARY 25, 1904

My dear Monsieur Aurenche,

Thank you very much for the good wishes you and your family sent me for the New Year.

Please accept mine in turn for you and all at home.

In your letter you speak of my realization in art. I believe that I attain it more every day, although a bit laboriously. Because, if the strong feeling for nature – and certainly I have that vividly – is the necessary basis for all artistic conception on which rests the grandeur and beauty of all future work, the knowledge of the means of expressing our emotion is no less essential, and is only to be acquired through very long experience.

The approbation of others is a stimulus of which one must sometimes be wary. The feeling of one's own strength makes one modest.

I am happy at the success of our friend Larguier. Gasquet, who lives completely in the country, I have not seen for a long time.

I send you, dear Monsieur Aurenche, my very warmest greetings.

Paul Cézanne

Louis Aurenche, a writer, who had been introduced to Cézanne in Aix by Gasquet, and became part of the small circle of young friends, including Gasquet and Camoin, surrounding Cézanne during his last years.

LAWRENCE GOWING

CÉZANNE: THE LATE WORK
"The Logic of Organized Sensations"

1977

Sir Lawrence Gowing (1918–91), British painter and art historian.

Our understanding of Cézanne's purpose is evidently incomplete if we do not follow the determination, of which he spoke so often, to read nature. It was one of his favorite phrases. It recurs in the letters; it was his constant objective. "Reading the model (*la lecture du modèle*) and realizing it are sometimes very slow in coming for the artist." The word echoes through the "opinions" transcribed by Bernard. He begins with a couple of remarks differentiating the " 'pernicious classicists' who deny nature or copy it with their minds made up" from Gothic art, which "belongs to the same family as we do." Then he begins his exhortation: "Let us read nature, let us realize our sensations in an aesthetic that is at once personal and traditional." So Bernard made him say, at all events, without provoking any complaint. Indeed, the record was approved "on the whole." The observation ends: "The strongest will be the one who sees most deeply and realizes fully, like the great Venetians." Two observations later, he gives the definition that I have quoted: "To read nature is to see it . . . in terms of an interpretation in patches of color," and the fifteenth observation (which forms a conclusion, though Bernard added conversational remarks and paragraphs out of recent letters) notes that the doctrine "is all summed up in this: to possess sensations and to read nature."

To follow Cézanne's thought we have to feel the force of his terminology. Here too he seems to have been well aware of the situation. Over and over again the crux of his art theory was a definition of the terms that he was using or a meditation on the validity of definitions. Theory was indispensable to him, though from another standpoint it was obviously superfluous – totally useless. He told Bernard, who was the recipient not only of the largest part of his theoretical teaching but of his warnings against art talk, that he did not want to be right in theory but in nature. In a jocular mood at a café, he announced to Aurenche that it was not his business to have ideas and to develop them. But it was his business,

Letter to Charles Camoin, December 9, 1904.

Letter to Émile Bernard, May 26, 1904. Bernard recorded Cézanne's "opinions" in an article in L'Occident, *"Paul Cézanne," July 1904.*

Letter to Émile Bernard, May 26, 1904.

and he remained haunted by the two parallel necessities. For painting one had to have both a way of seeing and a system of thought – both *une optique* and *une logique*. Devoting oneself entirely to a study of nature, one tried "to produce pictures that are an instruction." Fifteen years earlier, he had already explained his isolation: 'I must tell you . . . that I had resolved to work in silence until the day when I should feel myself able to defend in theory the results of my attempts." His regret in the last months of his life was that he could not "make plenty of specimens of my ideas and sensations." The two aspects of painting were inseparably coupled. They occupied him equally. "There are two things in the painter," he announced in the fifth of the "opinions" that Bernard recorded, "the eye and the mind; each of them should aid the other. It is necessary to work at their mutual development, in the eye by looking at nature, in the mind by the logic of organized sensations, which provides the means of expression."

Has any painter explained his artistic constitution more intelligently and exactly? Cézanne's terminology was precise; yet it is enigmatic in just the same way as the visual propositions in the late pictures. What did he mean by "sensations"? What did "realization" in fact involve? The late works are his own meditations on just these questions. Sensations were the root of everything for Cézanne. From the beginning to the end of his career, they were his pride and justification. In 1870, when he was interviewed for the *Album Stock* on submitting his entries for the Salon, the sensations of which he boasted seem to have comprised not only the data of sight but feelings also. "I paint as I see, as I feel – and I have very strong sensations. The others, too, feel and see as I do, but they don't dare . . . they produce Salon pictures . . ." In his last years, they were sometimes still described in the same terms, as "the strong sensation of nature – and certainly I have that vividly." The pride and the assurance that sensations gave him remained unaltered; they served him as a defense. "As sensations form the foundation of my business, I believe myself invulnerable." Yet at the same time they were also being defined rather differently. The fifth "opinion" in 1904 established them as something organized by logic in the mind. So far from regarding them simply as sense data (as is often thought), he more than once implicitly distinguished them from perceptions. The sensations for which he continued to seek an expression to the end of his life, as he explained to Henri Gasquet, the friend of his youth, were "the confused sensations which we bring with us when we are born." The word had, in fact, a double meaning – contact with nature "revived within us the instincts, the artistic sensations (*sensations d'art*) that reside within us." The double meaning of the word corresponds to the dual significance attaching to the paint marks themselves in the late work. It is in the last two years of Cézanne's life that the sensations are identified precisely as color sensations, the sensations of color that give light. It was in view of these that he most regretted his age, as he told his son two months before he died.

At this final stage sensations were thus senses of color which were as much innate as experienced. They were the chief object of the painter's efforts; they influenced all the "opinions" published by Bernard. Painting was first and foremost a matter of "realizing" them.

Photograph of Paul Cézanne carrying his painting materials in Auvers, *c.*1874.

The quotations on this page are from, respectively: Léo Larguier, Le Dimanche avec Paul Cézanne *(Paris: L'Édition, 1925), p. 136. Émile Bernard, "Souvenirs sur Paul Cézanne et ses lettres" (Paris:* La Rénovation Esthétique, *1921), p. 27. Letter to Émile Bernard, May 26, 1904. Letter to Octave Maus, November 27, 1889. John Rewald, "Un Article inédit sur Paul Cézanne en 1870,"* Arts *(Paris), July 21– 27, 1954; cited in Rewald,* The History of Impressionism, *4th ed. (New York: Museum of Modern Art, 1973), p. 246. Letters to Louis Aurenche, January 25, 1904; to his son Paul, October 15, 1906; to Émile Bernard, May 26, 1904; to Henri Gasquet, June 3, 1899; to Émile Bernard, July 25, December 23, 1904, October 23, 1905; to his son Paul, August 3, 1906.*

COLORPLATE 14. Georges Seurat. *Suburb*. *c*.1881–82. 12¾ × 16″ (32.3 × 41 cm).
Musée d'Art Moderne, Troyes, France.

COLORPLATE 15. Georges Seurat. *The Rainbow*. 1882–83. Oil on wood, 6 × 10″ (15.5 × 24.5 cm).
Berggruen Collection, on loan to the National Gallery, London.

COLORPLATE 16. Georges Seurat. *The Strand at Bas-Butin, Honfleur.* 1886. 26⅓ × 30¾″ (67 × 78 cm). Musée des Beaux-Arts, Tournai.

COLORPLATE 17. Georges Seurat. *Study for La Grande Jatte: Woman with a Monkey.* 1884.
Oil on wood, 9¾ × 6¼″ (24.8 × 15.9 cm).
Smith College Museum of Art, Northampton, Mass. (Purchased 1934).

COLORPLATE 18. Georges Seurat. *Study for La Grande Jatte: Seated Women and a Baby Carriage.* 1884. Oil on wood, 6¼ × 10″ (15.9 × 25 cm). Musée d'Orsay, Paris.

COLORPLATE 19. Georges Seurat. *Study for La Grande Jatte: View of Background with Several Figures.*
1883–84. Panel, 6⅛ × 9½″ (15.6 × 24.1 cm).
Metropolitan Museum of Art, New York (Robert Lehman Collection, 1975.1.207).

COLORPLATE 20. Georges Seurat. *La Poseuse* (study for *Les Poseuses*). 1886.
Oil on panel, 9¾ × 6″ (25 × 15.7 cm).
Vente Renand, Paris, Hôtel Drouot, November 20, 1987/Compagnie des Commissaires-Priseurs de
Paris (All Rights Reserved).

COLORPLATE 21. Georges Seurat. *Sunday Afternoon on the Island of La Grande Jatte, 1884.* 1884–86.
81¾ × 121¼″ (207.6 × 308 cm).
© 1992 The Art Institute of Chicago (Helen Birch Bartlett Memorial Collection, 1926.224).
All Rights Reserved.

"SCIENTIFIC" IMPRESSIONISM: THE NEO-IMPRESSIONIST REACTION

ROBERT REY

LA RENAISSANCE DU SENTIMENT CLASSIQUE

"The Return to Classical Order"

1931

Cézanne refused to philosophize and wanted only to be a painter. Seurat too guarded against all other ambition. Several of his friends have left us statements similar to that found in a letter, written after Seurat's death, by the painter Charles Angrand to the painter H.-E. Cross, and which M. Félix Fénéon has kindly communicated to us:

"... Last week, being at Dieppe where I was spending a couple of weeks, I was thinking of him [Seurat], as indeed I always do when I am by the sea. He was the first to render the feeling the sea inspires on calm days. He said to me, when we were coming back from la Grande-Jatte, through the streets of Courbevoie: 'Some critics do me the honour of seeing poetry in my work. I merely paint according to my method [he always referred to 'my method'], without any other concern.' He refused to put anything on the canvas apart from the paint itself. The truth is that the tone of his palette, which was unique, conjured up the essence of the sea – its unbounded, iridescent fluidity. The seascapes he has done are wonderful . . ."

Now is it not very unsettling to see not only that Seurat quickly and unconsciously rose above the realism of the Impressionists, but also that he sought a scientific method of recreating the art of painting from its very beginnings? And was that not a completely new concern in his time? In fact, this need to reconceive everything – technique as well as expression – bedevilled all the great artists of the end of the century: not only Seurat but also Cézanne, Gauguin, and Renoir. Now with a personality such as that of Gauguin, one might take the opposite view and think that this return to the source was dictated by vague literary needs. But with Seurat, no such interpretation is possible. All these artists do indeed wish to return to the very roots of plastic art. For with the deaths of Ingres and Delacroix (and this cannot be said too often), the torch of inspiration was laid low – it was not extinguished, but there was no hand to pass it on. Thus those who hoped to take it up again, and pass it on, had to look to the roots of art.

Increasingly, in looking closely at the production of the artists who concern us here, we become convinced that, however alive it was, however close to the shifting reality of the moment, the art of Édouard Manet held no fruitful promise of development for the future. It cast light upon one path alone, that of quick and intelligent realism, but without any sense of creative activity. And Impressionism had set off down that same blind alley. In Western culture, the need for intellectualized and ordered creativity is so deeply ingrained in the genius of the race that even those artists, who believe that their concerns are purely those of realistic Impressionists, search, in spite of themselves, for an order that is both more arbitrary and more rational. In this context, the example of Seurat admirably complements that of Cézanne.

Robert Rey, French art historian whose influential study of Degas, Renoir, Gauguin, Cézanne and Seurat interpreted Post-Impressionism as a reaction against the informality, looseness and lack of structure in Impressionism in favor of classical order and rationality.

Charles Angrand (1854–1926), Henri-Edmond Cross (1856–1910): Neo-Impressionist painters.

Photograph of Georges Seurat (place and photographer unknown). © Archives Signac.

CAMILLE PISSARRO
Letter to Lucien
March 1886

My dear Lucien,

Because of Degas I missed the post last night. We went in a body to meet him to determine the number of paintings each would be allowed to exhibit. As usual, he arrived at an impossible hour. We had to stand in the street discussing the matter. Things are going well.

I went to dinner with the impressionists. This time a great many came: Duret brought Burty, an influential critic, Moore, the English novelist, the poet Mallarmé, Huysmans, M. Deudon, and M. Bérard; it was a real gathering. Monet had been in Holland, – he arrived from The Hague at eight o'clock, just in time for dinner. – I had a long discussion with Huysmans, he is very conversant with the new art and is anxious to break a lance for us. We spoke of the novel *His Masterpiece*. He is decidedly of my opinion. It seems that he had a quarrel with Zola, who is very worried. Guillemet, who is furious about the book, also wrote to Zola, but only to complain that *Fagerolles* is too easily identifiable. They are telling a charming anecdote in connection with the book: Guillemet, who worships Zola, and with good reason, wanted his name to appear on this work, which he was certain would add to Zola's renown. He wrote Zola, requesting that the book be dedicated to him. Zola, very embarrassed, as you can imagine, by this expression of admiration, replied that he was reserving all dedications until the whole *Rougon-Macquart* series appeared. But since *His Masterpiece* was published, Guillemet's ardor has melted like butter in the sun; he wrote Zola a long letter of complaint. Zola assured him that it was Gervex he had described. Guillemet calmed down, completely content with this explanation. – As for Gervex, he takes a different attitude. He has his friends call him "Fagerolles." At X's marriage he paraded this name.

What I have written you should not be repeated.

Yesterday I had a violent run-in with M. Eugène Manet on the subject of Seurat and Signac. The latter was present, as was Guillaumin. You may be sure I rated Manet roundly. – Which will not please Renoir. – But anyhow, this is the point, I explained to M. Manet, who probably didn't understand anything I said, that Seurat has something new to contribute which these gentlemen, despite their talent, are unable to appreciate, that I am personally convinced of the progressive character of his art and certain that in time it will yield extraordinary results. Besides I am not concerned with the appreciation of artists, no matter whom. I do not accept the snobbish judgments of "romantic impressionists" to whose interest it is to combat new tendencies. I accept the challenge, that's all.

But before anything is done they want to stack the cards and ruin the exhibition – Monsieur Manet was beside himself! I didn't calm down. – They are all underhanded, but I won't give in.

Degas is a hundred times more loyal. – I told Degas that Seurat's painting was very interesting. "I would have noted that myself, Pissarro, except that the painting is so big!" Very well – if Degas sees nothing in it so much the worse for him. This simply means there is something precious that escapes him. We shall see. Monsieur Manet would also have liked to prevent Seurat from showing his figure painting. I protested against this, telling Manet that in such a case we would make no concessions, that we were willing, if space were lacking, to *limit our paintings* ourselves, but that we would fight anyone who tried to impose his choice on us.

But things will arrange themselves somehow!

Schuffenecker has been to see Monsieur and Madame Manet. The latter went to see his work and *accepted it*. What do you think of that? After his letter which was so dignified! – I have just seen a still life of his, and it's truly terrible.

Pissarro had met Seurat in October 1885 and had become a convert to the rationality of concept and method of Neo-Impressionism. This letter to his son reveals the difficulties he was having in persuading the "romantic" Impressionists to include Seurat and Signac in the Eighth and last Impressionist Exhibition which was to be held May 15–June 15, 1886 at the Maison Dorée.

The Impressionist "dinners" had become an institution in the 1870s when they had been held on a weekly basis at the restaurant of the pastrycook and collector Eugène Murer.

Théodore Duret, critic and collector (1838–1927); Philippe Burty (1830–90); Charles Deudon (1832–1914); Paul Bérard (1833–1905): friends and patrons of Renoir.

Zola's controversial novel L'Oeuvre *(published in serial form by* Gil Blas *in 1886), in which several artists recognized themselves, terminated his lifelong friendship with Cézanne.*

Fagerolles was a painter of cynical character in Zola's novel, who adapts the theories of the Impressionists to suit the corrupt tastes of the public.

Antoine Guillemet (1842–1918), painter who belonged to the Impressionist group.

Rougon-Macquart: *title given to the cycle of 20 novels written (1871–93) by Zola.*

Henri Gervex (1852–1929), academic painter linked with the Impressionist group.

Eugène Manet (1833–92), Édouard Manet's brother, who married Berthe Morisot. They were both involved in organizing the Eighth Impressionist Exhibition.

Émile Schuffenecker (1851–1934), painter of the Impressionist group and close friend of Gauguin.

FÉLIX FÉNÉON
LA VOGUE
"Eighth Impressionist Exhibition"
June 7 and 15, 1886

From the beginning, the Impressionist painters, with that concern for the truth which made them limit themselves to the interpretation of modern life directly observed and landscape directly painted, have seen objects conjointly related to one another, without chromatic autonomy, participating in the luminous qualities of their neighbors; traditional painting considered them [these objects] as ideally isolated and lighted them with a poor and artificial daylight.

These color reactions, these sudden perceptions of complementaries, this Japanese vision, could not be expressed by means of shadowy sauces concocted on the palette: these painters thus made separate notations, letting the colors arise, vibrate in abrupt contacts, and recompose themselves at a distance; they enveloped their subjects with light and air, modeling them in the luminous tones, sometimes even daring to sacrifice all modeling; sunlight was at last captured on their canvases.

They thus proceeded by the decomposition of colors; but this decomposition was carried out in an arbitrary manner: such and such a streak of impasto

Félix Fénéon (1861–1944), Symbolist writer and art critic, a founder editor of the Revue Indépendante *in 1884, and, more covertly, an anarchist propagandist for workers' rights. He first introduced the term "Neo-Impressionist" to describe the paintings of Seurat and his followers. His review of the Eighth Impressionist Exhibition, of which this is an excerpt, was the first serious explanation of the theory and practice of their work; its authority was endorsed by Seurat himself in a letter (published by Rewald – see "Artists' Wrangles", page 78) to Signac, August 1888, as "the exposition of my ideas on painting." His collected reviews from June 7, 15, 28 and September 20 were reprinted by* La Vogue *in December 1886 as a pamphlet under the title* Les Impressionnistes en 1886.

happened to throw the sensation of red across a landscape; such and such brilliant reds were hatched with greens. Messieurs Georges Seurat, Camille and Lucien Pissarro, Dubois-Pillet, and Paul Signac divide the tone in a conscious and scientific manner. This evolution dates from 1884, 1885, 1886.

If you consider a few square inches of uniform tone in Monsieur Seurat's *Grande Jatte*, you will find on each inch of its surface, in a whirling host of tiny spots, all the elements which make up the tone. Take this grass plot in the shadow: most of the strokes render the local value of the grass; others, orange tinted and thinly scattered, express the scarcely felt action of the sun; bits of purple introduce the complement to green; a cyanic blue, provoked by the proximity of a plot of grass in the sunlight, accumulates its siftings towards the line of demarcation, and beyond that point progressively rarefies them. Only two elements come together to produce the grass in the sun: green and orange tinted light, any interaction being impossible under the furious beating of the sun's rays. Black being a nonlight, the black dog is colored by the reactions of the grass; its dominant color is therefore deep purple; but it is also attacked by the dark blue arising from neighboring spaces of light. The monkey on a leash is dotted with yellow, its personal characteristic, and flecked with purple and ultramarine. The whole thing: obviously merely a crude description, in words; but, within the frame, complexly and delicately measured out.

These colors, isolated on the canvas, recombine on the retina: we have, therefore, not a mixture of material colors (pigments), but a mixture of differently colored rays of light. Need we recall that even when the colors are the same, mixed pigments and mixed rays of light do not necessarily produce the same results? It is also generally understood that the luminosity of optical mixtures is always superior to that of material mixture, as the many equations worked out by M. Rood show. For a violet-carmine and a Prussian blue, from which a gray-blue results:

$$\underbrace{50 \text{ carmine} + 50 \text{ blue}}_{\text{mixture of pigments}} = \underbrace{47 \text{ carmine} + 49 \text{ blue} + 4 \text{ black}}_{\text{mixture of rays of light}}$$

for a carmine and green:

$$50 \text{ carmine} + 50 \text{ green} = 50 \text{ carmine} + 24 \text{ green} + 26 \text{ black}$$

We can understand why the Impressionists, in striving to express extreme luminosities – as did Delacroix before them – wish to substitute optical mixture for mixing on the palette. Monsieur Seurat is the first to present a complete and systematic paradigm of this new technique. His immense canvas, *La Grande Jatte*, whatever part of it you examine, unrolls, a monotonous and patient tapestry; here in truth the accidents of the brush are futile, trickery is impossible; there is no place for bravura – let the hand be numb, but let the eye be agile, perspicacious, cunning. Whether it be on an ostrich plume, a bunch of straw, a wave, or a rock, the handling of the brush remains the same. And if it is possible to uphold the advantages of "virtuoso painting," scumbled and rubbed, for rough grasses, moving branches, fluffy fur, in any case "la peinture au point" imposes itself for the execution of smooth surfaces, and, above all, of the nude, to which it has still not been applied.

The subject [of the *Grande Jatte*]: beneath a canicular sky, at four o'clock, the island, boats flowing by at its side, stirring with a dominical and fortuitous population enjoying the fresh air among the trees; and these forty-odd people are caught in a hieratic and summarizing drawing style, rigorously handled, either from the back or full-face or in profile, some seated at right angles, others stretched out horizontally, others standing rigidly; as though by a modernizing Puvis.

The atmosphere is transparent and singularly vibrant; the surface seems to flicker. Perhaps this sensation, which is also experienced in front of other such paintings in the room, can be explained by the theory of Dove: the retina, expecting distinct groups of light rays to act upon it, perceives in very rapid alternation both the disassociated colored elements and their resultant color.

Photograph of Félix Fénéon in 1886. Paulhan Archives, Paris.

Ogden N. Rood (1831–1902), an American physicist and professor at Columbia University whose Modern Chromatics (Student's Text-Book of Color), *1879, had explained the superior luminosity of mixing light (additive mixture) as opposed to mixing pigment (subtractive mixture). These ideas had a profound influence on Seurat's painting practice.*

Seurat: Sunday Afternoon on the Island of la Grande Jatte, *1884–86, The Art Institute of Chicago,* COLORPLATE 21.

"La peinture au point": pun on pointillism (literally "done to perfection" – as in cooking).

Heinrich-Wilhelm Dove (1803–79), German physicist whose "theory of luster" influenced Seurat.

JORIS-KARL HUYSMANS

LA REVUE INDÉPENDANTE
"Chronicle of Art: The Independents"
April 1887

Joris-Karl Huysmans (1848–1907), novelist and art critic. In the 1870s the writer of proletarian novels under the influence of Zola, he became, in the 1880s, the arch-spokesman for the Symbolist movement with his novel À Rebours *("Against Nature"), 1884.*

COLORPLATE 21

Seurat: The Hospice and Lighthouse at Honfleur, *1886, National Gallery of Art, Washington.*

. . . Last year, Monsieur Seurat exhibited, in addition to the *Grande Jatte*, several truly beautiful seascapes, quiet seas beneath calm skies; these canvases, light and blond, enveloped in a grey dust of light, reveal a very personal yet very accurate conception of nature. . . .

The seascapes he exhibits this year, his views of Honfleur, especially his *Lighthouse*, affirm the very real talent of which he has already furnished indisputable proof. These pictures still depend upon the sensation they express of a nature more dormant than melancholy, a nature calmly at ease beneath wrathless skies, sheltered from the wind . . . I find in them a repose for the quiet soul, a distinction of pallid indolence, a caressing sea that lulls all weariness and disperses it.

Strange thing! This landscape painter whose seascapes can induce monotonous dreams becomes all unsuggestive façade when he places painted personages upon his stage; and it is here that his technique – that

Georges Seurat. Study for *La Grande Jatte: Man Standing by a Tree. c.*1884–85. Conté crayon, 24 × 18″ (61 × 46 cm). Von der Heydt Museum, Wuppertal.

arpeggio of little strokes, that mesh of tiny stitches, those mosaics of colored points – trips him up.

. . . Monsieur Seurat succeeds – but no better than did his predecessors the Impressionists – in rendering the vision of the human figure in light; and as a result of concentrating all of his efforts on this goal, he neglects to penetrate further and deeper. Strip his figures of the colored fleas with which they are covered, and underneath there is nothing; no soul, no thought, nothing. Nothingness in a body of which only the contours exist. Thus in his picture of the *Grande Jatte*, the human armature becomes rigid and hard; everything is immobilized and congealed.

I fear that there are too many methods here, too many systems, and not enough of the flame that ignites, not enough of life. . . .

J. U. HALPERIN
FÉLIX FÉNÉON, AESTHETE AND ANARCHIST
Letters: Georges Seurat and Félix Fénéon
1988

Seurat "hardly ever wrote," Fénéon once explained, and then "always laconically, with difficulty, as can be seen by his schoolboy's hand-writing." But in his anxiety Seurat scribbled off a letter to Fénéon which is one of the rare documents that have survived showing the relationship between the two men. In fact, several rough drafts of it exist; it is hard to say which was the final version, since all contain crossed-out words, unfinished sentences and little punctuation. Scholars have appreciated this letter for the information it contains on the painter's development. But it also reveals much of the man.

PARIS, JUNE 20, 1890

My dear Fénéon
Allow me to point out a mistake in the biography of Signac – or rather to remove any doubt allow me to specify – "It [optical painting] appealed – around 1885," p. 2, par. 4 Begun ~~in~~ the evolution of Pissarro and Signac was slower I protest and I re-establish to within a fortnight the following dates:
The purity of the spectral element being the keystone of ~~my~~ the technique – ~~and being~~ which was first consecrated by You
Seeking as long as I have held a brush an optical formula on this basis 1876–1884
[*Seurat here names the authors and painters who had influenced his thinking*]
I must insist on establishing the following dates indicating my earlier paternity
1884 Grande Jatte study   exhibition of indépendants
~~and the discussions that I had~~
1884–1885 Grande Jatte composition
1885 studies at the grand Jatte and at Grand-camp
resumption of la Grande Jatte composition 1886 October
October ~~85 I meet Pissarro~~ at Durand-Ruel's
1886 January or February little canvas of Pissarro at Clozet dealer on rue Châteaudun divided and pure Signac finally convinced and who had just modified [his painting] the milliners – while I was finishing la Jatte – painted in ~~my~~ accordance with my technique
1. passage du puits Bertin-Clichy, March–April 1886

Joan Ungersma Halperin (b. 1932), American scholar and professor of modern languages, was the editor of Fénéon's Oeuvres plus que complètes, *Geneva, 1970.*

Letter to John Rewald, October 9, 1937. Fénéon's monograph on Signac, published in Les Hommes d'Aujourd'hui *no. 373, 1890, illustrated by Seurat's conté portrait of Signac, did not mention Seurat by name as the instigator of Neo-Impressionism. The article was also illustrated by a strange dotted circle, "a seductive work" as Fénéon explained in a note to Seurat (April 1890) "due to the collaboration of Henry and the bottom of a saucepan."*
Fénéon had written: "It matters not that the old Impressionists did not embrace optical painting . . . It appealed to several young painters of a more philosophical bent of mind. This happened around 1885."

Charles Henry. *Une Tache (A Spot).* La Vogue, May 2, 1886, page 110. Bibliothèque Nationale, Paris.

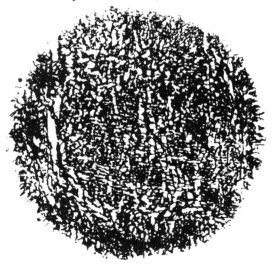

2. les gazomètres Clichy, March–April 1886
(catalogue of the indépendants   For these reasons
coolness with Guillaumin who had introduced me to Pissarro and whom
I saw because of Signac's long-standing friendship. You have to admit
that there is a difference and that if I was unknown in 85 I was none the
less alive, I and my vision which you have just described so superbly
under an impersonal form apart from one or two insignificant details.

Seurat was referring to the "synopsis" of technique that Fénéon had
published in his biography of Signac. Finally, after citing yet more names
and dates to justify his claim that in 1885 he was virtually alone on the
path to optical painting, Seurat concluded his letter:

Then You brought me out of eclipse, with Signac who benefited from
my research. I am counting on your loyalty to communicate these notes
to M. Jules Christophe and Lecomte.
I shake your hand cordially and loyally – Seurat

Two days later Fénéon sent his reply:

Your little chronological account, so heavily documented, my dear
Seurat, did not teach me anything essential: I know very well that the
technique of optical painting was established by you, and, as you gra-
ciously remember, I printed it long ago.

If I had been given the honor of writing your biography I, like Jules
Christophe, would have printed it again.

I do not need to re-read my article to ~~know~~ be sure that ~~neither
directly nor by way of the sort of insinuation of which I would be
incapable~~ it contains nothing ~~that might~~ likely to mislead the public on
the origin of this technique that the old impressionists did not greet at
all kindly and which appealed to more recent painters, in 1885.

I simply, and deliberately, dispensed with informing the reader about
this, judging that it was not the place ~~to do it~~ for such a disclosure.

As you requested, your letter of the 20th was communicated to Messieurs Christophe and Lecomte: to the former on the 21st; to the latter
on the 22nd. On the same 22nd, at 5:29 I presented myself at your
studio with M. Lecomte, marking with a card the futility of my visit.
Not knowing when I can go to see you nor if you will soon be leaving
Paris, I am writing you – which permits me, ~~my dear Seurat~~ to ~~send~~
offer you my most cordial ~~respects~~ regards and to dispel, my dear
Seurat, your anxiety.

félix fénéon

Both men strove in vain to hide their feelings behind "statements of fact."
Fénéon's emotion is betrayed by the controlled irony of his reply and the
numerous blacked-out words, which did not often mar his correspondence. His pride and sense of justice were obviously offended. He
had been writing reviews stressing the priority of Seurat for the past four
years, and the painter had responded only with increasing distrust. Control overrode emotion, though, sending him in search of expressions that
would soothe Seurat's feelings without falsifying his own position. Always
the attentive critic, he preserved Seurat's letter and, two years later (a year
after the painter's untimely death), published the information Seurat had
furnished on his development.

Seurat's anxiety is evident in the broken phrases of his writing, which
cannot be attributed solely to a lack of aptitude. He clearly thought of
Fénéon as his primary interpreter: "You brought me out of eclipse . . ."
He felt not only betrayed but abandoned by the critic. Jules Christophe, in
his biography of Seurat, had named all his friends – including Fénéon. It
seemed to Seurat that Fénéon had obviously meant to slight him by
omitting his name entirely from the biography of Signac. Others had also
noticed the insult; Angrand had expressed an offensive sympathy for him
on the subject.

Jules Christophe's biography of Seurat appeared in Les Hommes d'Aujourd'hui *no. 368, 1890. It was in response to the inaccuracies in this article that Seurat wrote the well-known letter to Maurice Beaubourg (August 28, 1890).*

Félix Fénéon in 1894. Photograph by Alfred Natanson. Courtesy Archives Annette Vaillant, Paris.

Félix Fénéon, "Au Pavillon de la Ville de Paris," Chat Noir, *April 2, 1892.*

In late afternoon, the proper time to call, Fénéon and Lecomte had presented themselves at Seurat's door to make amends. Seurat refused, however, to see them. Fénéon makes this clear in his letter by noting both the hour and the minute of their call (as if to say, "You know and I know you were home") and the likely futility of future visits. He did not know that the artist had a personal reason for not admitting visitors to his studio. Madeleine Knobloch had given birth in February and Seurat had legally recognized his son. But he avoided any conflict with his devout, bourgeois family by continuing to keep his mistress and child a secret. None of his friends knew about the baby, either. By moving to the new studio and not receiving anyone there, he had meant to convey the idea that, like Delacroix, he considered his atelier private. Therefore it was doubly offensive that the two critics had sought him out in his refuge and tried to violate that privacy. His behavior was incomprehensible to Fénéon, who could attribute this wariness and hostility only to an unreasonable fear that he or another comrade would spy out the "secret" of the painter's art. The day after he received Fénéon's reply, Seurat wrote again. Rather than an answer, this letter is a continuation of his first, with no acknowledgment of Fénéon's response or his visit.

TUESDAY JUNE 24, 1890

My dear Fénéon out of 30 articles referring to me as innovator I count you 6 times so that is not what made me write.

If you had done my biography and if you had asked for my opinion I would have asked you not to lay any stress on technique. That's what I did with respect to Mr. Christophe ....

Signac must be suffering as much as I from technical popularization He was of my opinion two months ago.

People who have read you feel sorry for me they no doubt do not understand very well if   very offensive condolences for me there. They believe I have been wronged. That is the reason why I am taking a very open stand and why I am telling you what I think without any kind of bitterness.

In 1885 since you want to move things up several months it appealed to an old master Pissarro and a young man Signac. I therefore do not find it in its place, and I am saying so because I am hurt.

Your friend Seurat

I am going to the département du Nord around Calais.

Georges Seurat. *Paul Signac*. 1890. Conté crayon, 13½ × 11" (34.5 × 28 cm). Private Collection, Paris.

JOHN REWALD
GEORGES SEURAT
"Artists' Wrangles"
1948

Reserved and mistrustful, Seurat fiercely avoided confidences, even to his friends. His letters to Signac, for example, were written in an almost telegraphic style. They related facts, imparted the occasional piece of news, and mentioned painting as little as possible. "Mild weather," he informed his friend, "no one in the streets (provinces). Slight depression. From 22 August to 18 September, 28 days. Dubois-Pillet very bothered, could be ousted. Serious. That's life."

He wrote from Honfleur, on June 25, 1886: "The weather has been good here for two days. I'm hoping to get down to serious work on my canvases. So far I've only done sketches to get my hand in. If you find les Andelys colourful, I'm looking at the Seine – an expanse of grey water that is almost indefinable, even in the strongest sunlight and with a blue sky, at

It was at Gravelines, near Calais, that Seurat painted his last series of seascapes.

John Rewald (b. 1912), art historian, whose History of Impressionism *(1946) and* Post-Impressionism from Van Gogh to Gauguin *(1956) are the pioneering works on which all subsequent studies of these subjects depend. The documents quoted in this chapter of the French edition of his book on Seurat (Editions Albin Michel, Paris, 1948) were not available for the earlier American editions (1943, 1946). They were unpublished, provided to Rewald by Mme Charles Cachin-Signac and M. Rodo Pissarro.*
Albert Dubois-Pillet (1846–90), member of the Neo-Impressionist group.

least during the last few days." A little later, he continues: "Nothing much of interest. Have just got to keep going . . . Have received only two letters, one of which is a writ of summons. Wind and hence clouds hampering me these last few days. The finer weather of the first few days should return . . . Are your studies going well? Have you done many? I'm sure you have. No need to answer. So, what else? Well, that's all for today. Let's go and get drunk on light once again, it is consoling."

At the end of his summer campaign, he announced laconically: "Only six canvases; four of size 25, one of 15, one of 10. One considered finished, the motif having long disappeared (boat in a corner of a port). Two others worked on but still not satisfactory (beach scenes). One canvas of size 10, in cloudy weather, still needs to be taken further (end of jetty). Then there is one canvas size 25 and another of 15, started. That's all I've been able to do." On another occasion, talking of his work, he writes: "Gesso-coated canvas deplorable, makes me despair. Completely confused. Everything makes a stain – uphill work."

Seurat said little about his friends in his letters. "Lucien [Pissarro] is doing chromo-lithography in rue du Cherche-midi (difficult)." He mentioned that Dubois-Pillet "often meets Guillaumin on the quayside (exchange of courtesies)." His relations with Guillaumin, a friend of Pissarro and Signac, were somewhat strained. "Guillaumin nurses a slight grudge against me . . . The other day at Vetzel's Guillaumin lost his temper with Fénéon (the article) because Fénéon happened to mention Dubois-Pillet and placed him in the vanguard of Impressionism. Misinter-

July 5, 1886.

(*Above*) Georges Seurat. *Place de la Concorde in Winter.* 1882–83. Conté crayon and charcoal, $9^{1}/_{8} \times 12^{11}/_{16}''$ (23.2 × 30.7 cm). Solomon R. Guggenheim Museum, New York.

COLORPLATE 4

Seurat in a letter to Signac, August 1887. While he was working on Les Poseuses, *1887–88, he had closed the door of his studio to everyone for several weeks.*

Armand Guillaumin (1841–1927), Impressionist painter who, in spite of his close friendship with Pissarro and Signac in the mid-1880s, remained uninfluenced by Neo-Impressionist theories.

preting this, Guillaumin said to me: 'Dubois-Pillet is no more in the vanguard *than you and Signac.*' I instantly clammed up and stuck my nose in a newspaper. Apparently these things are measured by age. Guillaumin had clearly just been wound up by Gauguin, who has a special key."

Seurat was very bitter towards the original Impressionists. He resented Degas' "devil-may-care impertinence", as Signac put it, and Monet's coldness. He was particularly vexed that Gauguin and Guillaumin treated him somewhat patronizingly, as he could see them merely as more or less skilful imitators of the real Impressionists. Pissarro was the only one among the "old guard" to join the scientific Impressionists and his efforts at rallying his pupils Gauguin and Guillaumin to the new cause proved vain.

"I am not surprised that Gauguin and Guillaumin no longer follow you to the Indépendants," wrote Pissarro to Signac in August 1886. "Gauguin, it seems, is much better off now.... I hope that success will make him a little less sectarian. Nothing soothes an overheated temperament better than a good deal! As for my old friend Guillaumin, I'm sorry about it for his sake. He sees intrigue in our struggle. That's absurd. We don't need that. We only have to appear with our optical mixture for the whole pack to respond with fellow feeling or to howl for blood."

Seurat himself was beginning to tire of seeing each of his works become the centre of discussions which rapidly deteriorated into flurries of disapproval and suspicion, all argument failing in the face of prejudice or the simple desire not to change course. On the other hand it worried him to see new adepts joining his artistic circle and it was not without regret that he observed the efforts of these new recruits to appropriate his theories and technique for themselves. He even said that he would stop exhibiting, so that no one would be able to copy him, and on that occasion Pissarro wrote in February 1887 to his son Lucien: "He carries caution to extremes. But we, or rather I, can see no harm in exhibiting, since I do not believe that painting holds any *secret* except that of one's own artistic feeling, which is not so easy to pinch!!!"

The question of caution naturally became even more delicate when the new theory had to be explained to his critic friends, who sometimes came up against a wall of silence on the part of Seurat.

"I was a bit embarrassed," wrote Pissarro to Signac in April 1887, "by M. Félix Fénéon's request for information about our working methods and our observations on the analysis of colour. This was not easy, since I did not want to rend the veil of mystery completely on the one hand, and yet on the other I was unable to refuse to comply with M. Fénéon who, all in all, has been very good to us. I wanted to say only what the public would understand. What I did say was most inadequate. Indeed, I do not believe that my observations arrived in time for correction at the printer's. What I regret the most (I was late) is my advice that one should generalize as far as possible where the personality of an artist is concerned, though there was one thing I thought I should stress, which was not to fail to give first place to Seurat as the initiator of the whole scientific movement."

However, Pissarro was not too disappointed in Fénéon's article: with his usual modesty, he objected only that it contained "too much praise for the doyen who, all in all, is merely a follower." All his letters, and indeed his actions, reveal Pissarro's almost touching concern not to offend Seurat. Thus he wrote to Signac on June 16, 1887:

> Yesterday I visited Seurat's studio. His large painting [*Les Poseuses*] is making progress. It is already charming in its harmony. It will clearly be very beautiful, but the real surprise will be the execution of the frame. I've seen how he has begun it. It's indispensable, really, my dear Signac. We shall all be obliged to do the same. The picture is not the same with white or anything else around it. Clearly, one can give no idea of sunshine or overcast weather except by this vital complement. I too shall try it; I shall not exhibit, of course, until after our friend Seurat has established his precedence in the matter, as is only fair!

Dubois-Pillet was thirteen years older than Seurat.

Degas' comment on Dubois-Pillet: "du bois pillet [sawdust]: good for pointillism" was recorded by Coquiot in Les Indépendants *(Paris, 1920).*

Édouard Vuillard. *At the Revue Blanche (Portrait of Félix Fénéon)* (detail). 1901. 18¼ × 22⅝" (46.3 × 57.5 cm). Solomon R. Guggenheim Museum, New York (Hilla Rebay Collection, 1971).

Les Poseuses, 1888, Merion, PA., Barnes Foundation.

But despite all these precautions, Seurat's sensitivity was never completely assuaged. He knew how to "clam up" when he found it politic, but he forgot nothing. He may have been acrimonious despite himself, for he was above all meticulous to the point where nothing that interested him ever escaped him or faded from his memory. More than once his friends were struck by how incapable he was of forgetting the least slight. Knowing him to be so touchy, they came to be almost afraid of him; yet even with the best will in the world awkward moments could not always be avoided. Thus when in 1887 a journalist called Seurat "a newcomer, a pupil of Pissarro," the young painter had been quite incapable of excusing this phrase, though he knew perfectly well that it was nothing to do with Pissarro himself. From then onwards he tried to prove to the art critics of his circle that it was he who had been followed by Pissarro, a fact which the older master had always been quick to maintain. But the outcome of this campaign was soon to be self-defeating.

On 13 August 1888, Arsène Alexandre published an article on the movement in the journal *Paris*, whose conclusion was that a little science does no harm, while too much leads away from art. Having thus formulated several reservations, Alexandre had observed: "The artists who use the small brushstroke are blazing with conviction, and several are very talented. One need only mention, for instance, Pissarro *père*, who has rallied to the new school and is still managing to produce beautiful work; or Seurat, the true apostle of the lentil, who planted it and saw it grow: Seurat, the dogged toiler who was in danger of seeing himself deprived of the paternity of his theory by ill-informed critics and unscrupulous friends."

Signac was naturally highly indignant at this last phrase which, as he wrote to Pissarro, "impugns our honesty, and which I cannot allow to pass. I am writing to Seurat to ask him if it is he who fed it to Alexandre. I expect a *frank* answer. At all events, you will agree that if Seurat had not slunk off to wail on Alexandre's shoulder, the man would be quite unaware of the petty jealousies of our excellent fellow artist." Seurat's answer was not long in coming. It is dated Sunday, August 26, 1888.

My dear Signac,
I know nothing of this article save the phrase quoted in your letter. If M. Alexandre had told me what he was going to write, I would have replied: but you will offend either Signac, or Pissarro, or Angrand or Dubois. I don't want to offend anyone. Now I have never told him anything but what I have always thought: the more numerous we are, the less original we shall be, and the day when everyone practises this technique, it will be valueless and people will look for something new, which is happening already.

It is my right to think that and to say it, since I painted in this manner only in order to break new ground, to find a style of my own.

That is all I may have told him. As to the beginning of the phrase, it must be referring to an article in *Le Matin* where I am described as Pissarro's pupil . . . Now this I will not allow because it is not true. And I could prove as much.

This is a regrettable business, for which I am not responsible. M. Alexandre came to see me over a year ago. I exhibited with you in a special room, which I would not do if I had the ideas you attribute to me about my fellow-painters.

I take account not of personalities, but of facts.
Cordially yours,

Seurat.

This letter has the following words in the margin: "Anyway, I do not talk much," and a little note attached: "Firstly, I have never described anyone as an 'unscrupulous friend'. Secondly, I still regard Fénéon's pamphlet as the statement of my ideas on painting."

Seurat's explanations did not immediately succeed in mollifying Signac, but Pissarro regarded the incident more philosophically:

Maximilien Luce. *Portrait of Paul Signac.* 1892. Lithograph.

Seurat, Signac, Pissarro and his son Lucien showed in a separate room which featured La Grande Jatte *at the eighth Impressionist exhibition in 1886.*

Les Impressionnistes en 1886 *appeared initially in* La Vogue, *June 13–20, 1886.*

Really, if Seurat is the instigator of the article you have brought to my attention, it is enough to make one believe he is taking leave of his senses. From the start we have taken the greatest care (we said as much to Fénéon, Durand-Ruel and all those who have been involved with the new painting), to leave Seurat the distinction of being the first in France to have the idea of applying science to painting. And still it was not enough. Now he wants to own it absolutely! . . . It's absurd! . . . My dear Signac, we shall have to give Seurat a patent, if that gratifies his pride . . . In a word, the whole of art does not lie in scientific theory. If Seurat had only that, I confess he would interest me only moderately. Can one not create masterpieces with black and white? My dear Signac, do you yourself believe that this is the basis of your talent? No, fortunately. So do not let yourself be influenced by this tittle-tattle; remain calm, carry on with your work and let the jealous cry aloud. You have what it takes to make art . . .

But it is worrying from another point of view. For the future of our "impressionist" art we absolutely must keep clear of Seurat's sphere of influence. You yourself sensed as much. Seurat is steeped in the tradition of the École des Beaux-Arts, he is riddled with it. So let us take care, that is where the danger lies. Here it is neither technique nor science that is at stake, it is our tradition, which we must safeguard.

So apply the science, which belongs to everybody, but keep for yourself the gift you have, to feel as a free spirit, and leave Seurat to resolve problems which clearly have their use. That is his lot. But creating is something higher! A word to the wise . . .

Yet his friends soon forgot these differences of opinion and hostilities when Seurat showed them his new works. If they were sometimes hurt by his manner, they remained faithful in their admiration of the artist. Looking at Seurat's canvases, Pissarro and Signac above all were able once again to feel respect for the man whose intransigence may have concealed singular shyness, revealing itself as pride. They forgave him or, rather, they understood him; they could not long deny Seurat their affection. But other members of the small Neo-Impressionist group were not always able to rise above matters of amour-propre. Floundering amidst the rigours of Seurat's method, they were hurt by the scorn which he expressed for those who followed it without making any original contribution. Thus, far from being bolstered by his advice, they ended by feeling themselves the butt of a veiled cloud of hostility. It was thus that Hayet, the young friend of Lucien Pissarro, wrote to Signac at the beginning of 1890:

> When I found myself drawn into the Impressionist movement, I thought of its members as a group of like-minded intelligent people offering each other mutual help in their researches with no ambition other than that of creating pure art, and I believed that for five years. Then a succession of minor clashes occurred and gave me food for thought: looking at things more closely, I saw the past more clearly, and I saw this group, which I had taken for a select band of seekers, as divided into two camps, one seeking, the other wrangling (though perhaps not intentionally) and having but one aim: a fight to the death . . . And this series of occurrences made me lose all confidence. Not being able to live in doubt and not wanting to suffer permanent anguish, I decided to withdraw . . .

Seurat seems to have remained unmoved amidst all these quarrels and controversies and misunderstandings. But if he did not modify his attitude, he nonetheless finally understood that it was his duty to formulate his ideas clearly. Pissarro was right: there can be no secrets in art; it was preferable that he himself should provide the necessary information and affirm his incontestable priority yet again. It was thus that, after long reflection and several rough drafts, in the summer of 1890 Seurat finally came to commit the principles of his aesthetic to paper.

The Exhibition of the Indépendants. Caricature by F. Lunel, 1890. Bibliothèque Nationale, Paris.

Pissarro to his dealer Durand-Ruel: November 6, 1886.

Louis Hayet (1864–1940).

He is referring to the Neo-Impressionists.

Seurat's letter to Maurice Beaubourg, August 28, 1890.

PAUL SIGNAC

FROM EUGÈNE DELACROIX TO NEO-IMPRESSIONISM

"The Neo-Impressionist Contribution"
1898

1. It was in 1886, at the latest of the exhibitions of the Impressionist group, that we saw the first appearance of works painted solely with pure, separate, balanced colours, mixed optically, in accordance with a systematic method. There Georges Seurat, who was the founder of this development, exhibited the first "divisionist" picture, *Un dimanche à la Grande-Jatte*, an epoch-making canvas which also bore witness to his rare qualities as a painter; grouped around it, Camille Pissarro, his son Lucien Pissarro and Paul Signac also exhibited canvases painted in accordance with a roughly similar technique.

The unaccustomed brightness and harmony of the paintings of these innovators were immediately remarked upon, if not well received. These qualities were the result of the application of the fundamental principles of *division*. Since then – thanks to the researches and contributions of MM. Henri-Edmond Cross, Albert Dubois-Pillet, Maximilien Luce, Hippolyte Petitjean, Théo van Rysselburghe, Henry van de Velde and some others, and despite cruel losses, attacks and desertions – this technique has continued to develop and has come to constitute the very precise method summed up at the beginning of this study and designated as that of the Neo-Impressionist painters.

If these painters, who would be better described by the epithet *chromo-luminarist*, have adopted the name Neo-Impressionist, it was not out of sycophancy (the Impressionists were still in mid-struggle), but to pay homage to the endeavours of their precursors and to underline their shared aims, namely, *light* and *colour*, despite the divergence of procedures that lay beneath. It is in this sense that this word *Neo-Impressionist* must be understood, for the technique used by these painters has nothing impressionistic about it: theirs is as much a painting of deliberation and constancy as that of their predecessors is one of instinct and spontaneity.

2. The Neo-Impressionists, like the Impressionists, have on their palette only pure colours. But they absolutely reject any mixture on the palette except, of course, the mixture of colours that are contiguous on the colour circle. These, shaded into each other and lightened with white, will tend to reinstate the variety of the colours of the solar spectrum and all their tones. An orange blending with a yellow and a red, a violet shading into red and blue, a green passing from blue to yellow, together with white, are the only elements they make use of. But through the optical mixture of these few pure colours, by varying their proportions, they obtain an infinite range of colours, from the most intense to the dullest.

Not only do they banish all mixture of muddy colours from their palette, they even avoid sullying the purity of their colours by any juxtaposition of contrary elements on the support. Each brushstroke, taken pure from the palette, remains pure upon the canvas. In this way, and as though they were using colours prepared with more brilliant pigments and richer materials, they can claim to outstrip the Impressionists in intensity of light and colour, since the latter sullied and dulled the pure colours of a reduced palette.

3. Not only does the technique of *division* ensure a maximum of luminosity and colour through the optical mixture of pure elements: the measuring

Signac's study was first published serially in the Revue Blanche *in 1898 and in the* Revue Populaire des Beaux-Arts *in 1898–99. Until its re-evaluation by W. I. Homer in* Seurat and the Science of Painting, *MIT, 1964, it was considered to be the definitive source of information about the theory and practice of Neo-Impressionism. It is now seen to be more in the nature of a manifesto. Seurat had been dead for seven years when it was first published and the role of leader and propagandist for the movement had fallen to Signac. He used the opportunity to expand on the progressive aspects of Neo-Impressionism compared with Impressionism's absence of method and haphazard results. 1886 was the year of the eighth and last Impressionist exhibition. The exhibitors included Bracquemond, Cassatt, Degas, Forain, Gauguin, Guillaumin, Morisot, Camille and Lucien Pissarro, Redon, Rouart, Schuffenecker, Seurat, Signac, Tillot, Vignon, Zandomeneghi. The Neo-Impressionist group included Henri-Edmond Cross; Albert Dubois-Pillet; Maximilien Luce (1858–1927); Hyppolyte Petitjean (1854–1941); Théo van Rysselberghe (1862–1926); Henri van de Velde (1863–1957). Seurat had died in 1891. The term "Neo-Impressionism" was first used by Félix Fénéon in his article* L'Impressionnisme aux Tuileries *for* L'Art moderne, *September 19, 1886, published in Brussels. It reappeared in Paris the next day in* La Vogue.

O.-N. Rood. Illustration from *Théorie Scientifique des couleurs et leur application à l'art et à l'industrie* (page 43). Bibliothèque Nationale, Paris.

Fig. 13. — La fumée parait bleue sur un fond sombre et brune sur un fond clair.

and balancing of these elements, in accordance with the rules of contrast, gradation and irradiation, further ensures the total harmony of the work.

These rules, which the Impressionists observed only sporadically and instinctively, are always and rigorously applied by the Neo-Impressionists. This is a precise and scientific method, which does not weaken their sensibility, but guides and protects it.

4. It seems logical that the first concern of a painter before his empty canvas should be: to decide what curves and arabesques should divide up its surface, what colours and tones should cover it. A very rare concern at a period when most pictures resemble snapshots or pointless illustrations.

To reproach the Impressionists for having neglected these concerns would be pointless, since their aim was obviously to capture the arrangements and harmonies of nature, as they present themselves, without any care for order or grouping. "The Impressionist sits down beside a river," as their critic Théodore Duret said, "and paints what is before him." And they have proved that they could do wonders in this manner.

Duret's Les Peintres Impressionnistes *was published in Paris in 1878.*

The Neo-Impressionist, here following the advice of Delacroix, will not begin a canvas without having decided on the way it is to be disposed. Guided by tradition and science, he will harmonize the composition to his way of thinking, that is, he will adapt the lines (directions and angles), the chiaroscuro (tones), the colours, in accordance with the character he wishes to see prevail. The lines will be predominantly horizontal for a sense of calm, upward for joy and downward for sorrow, with all the intermediary lines to indicate all other sensations in their infinite variety. A play of colours, no less expressive and diverse, combines with this linear play: warm colours and light tones correspond to the upward lines; predominantly cold colours and dark tones to the downward ones; a more or less perfect balance of warm and cold colours, and of pale and intense tones, will add to the calm imparted by the horizontal lines. Thus subjecting colour and line to the emotions he has felt and that he wishes to translate, the painter will play the part of the poet, the creator.

This relates to Seurat's theory, embodied in his later paintings, of the expressive values of particular linear directions and colors.

5. Generally speaking, one may allow that a Neo-Impressionist work is more harmonious than an Impressionist work since, first, thanks to the constant observation of contrast, its harmony of detail is more exact, and secondly, thanks to its systematic composition and to the aesthetic language of the colours, it implies a harmony of the work as a spiritual whole which the Impressionist work deliberately does not have.

But perish the thought of comparing the merits of these two generations of painters: the Impressionists are established masters whose glorious task is done; they have compelled recognition; the Neo-Impressionists are still pursuing their researches and they understand how much they still have to do. Here it is not a question of talent, but of technique, and it shows no lack of the respect we owe to these masters to say: more than that of the Impressionists, the technique of the Neo-Impressionists ensures the purity of the luminosity, colour and harmony of a work; similarly we can say that the paintings of Delacroix are less luminous and colourful than those of the Impressionists.

THE DISCOVERY OF
PAINTING AS ABSTRACTION

VINCENT VAN GOGH

Letter to Theo

September 10, 1889

My dear Theo,

. . . When you say in your letter that I have always only been working, no – I cannot agree – I am myself very, very dissatisfied with my work, and the only thing that comforts me is that people of experience say you must paint ten years for nothing. But what I have done is only those ten years of unfortunate studies that didn't come off. Now a better period may come, but I shall have to get the figure stronger and I must refresh my memory by a very close study of Delacroix and Millet. Then I shall try to get my drawing clearer. Yes, misfortune is good for something, you gain time for study. I am adding a study of flowers to the roll of canvases – nothing much, but after all I do not want to tear it up.

Altogether I think nothing in it *at all* good except the "Field of Wheat," the "Mountain," the "Orchard," the "Olives" with the blue hills and the portrait and the "Entrance to the Quarry," and the rest tells me *nothing*, because it lacks individual intention and feeling in the lines. Where these lines are close and deliberate it begins to be a picture, even if it is exaggerated. That is a little what Gauguin and Bernard feel, they do not ask the correct shape of a tree at all, but they do insist that one can say if the shape is round or square – and honestly, they are right, exasperated as they are by certain people's photographic and empty perfection. They will not ask the correct tone of the mountains, but they will say: By God, the mountains were blue, were they? Then chuck on some blue and don't go telling me that it was a blue rather like this or that, it was blue, wasn't it? Good – make them blue and it's enough!

Gauguin is sometimes like a genius when he is explaining that, but as for the *genius* Gauguin has, he is very fearful of showing it, and it is touching the way he likes to say something that will really be of some use to the young ones.

What a queer creature he is all the same.

I am very pleased to hear that Jo is well, and I think that you will feel much more in your element thinking of her condition, and of course having worries too, than alone without these family worries. For you will feel more in nature.

When you think of Millet and Delacroix, what a contrast. Delacroix without a wife, Millet surrounded by a big family, more than anybody.

And yet what similarities there are in their work.

* * *

Do you know what I think of pretty often, what I already said to you some time ago – that even if I did not succeed, all the same I thought that what I have worked at will be carried on. Not directly, but one isn't alone in believing in things that are true. And what does it matter personally then!

Paul Gauguin. Sketch of boys wrestling, in a letter to Van Gogh dated July 25, 1888. Rijksmuseum Vincent van Gogh Foundation/Van Gogh Museum, Amsterdam.

I feel so strongly that it is the same with people as it is with wheat, if you are not sown in the earth to germinate there, what does it matter? – in the end you are ground between the millstones to become bread.

The difference between happiness and unhappiness! Both are necessary and useful, as well as death or disappearance . . . it is so relative – and life is the same.

Even faced with an illness that breaks me up and frightens me, that belief is unshaken.

* * *

It is a great advantage that my stomach is behaving well, and then I do not think I am so sensitive to cold. And besides I know what to do when the weather is bad, having this project of copying several things that I like.

I should very much like to see Millet reproductions in the schools. I think there are children who would become painters if only they saw good things.

Regards to Jo and a handshake. Good-by for now.

Ever yours, Vincent

MAURICE DENIS

L'OCCIDENT

"The Influence of Paul Gauguin"

October 1903

Gauguin is dead, and now that Séguin's well-documented study has been published in *L'Occident*, it is more appropriate to examine his influence on the artists of his time than his own work, which we hope will soon be brought together in a complete exhibition.

The most daring young artists among us who around 1888 attended the *Académie Julian* were almost completely ignorant of the great movement in art which under the name of Impressionism had just revolutionized the art of painting. They had gotten to Roll, to Dagnan; they admired Bastien-Lepage; they spoke of Puvis with a respectful indifference, although secretly doubting that he knew how to draw. Thanks to Paul Sérusier, then *massier* [monitor] for the little studios of the Faubourg Saint-Denis and executing his duties with brilliant imaginativeness, the milieu was, without a doubt, much more cultivated than those of most of the academies. It was customary there to speak of Péladan and of Wagner, of the Lamoureux concerts, and of decadent literature, about which, by the way, we knew little enough.

It was at the beginning of 1888 that the name of Gauguin was revealed to us by Sérusier, back from Pont-Aven, who showed us, not without a certain mystery, a cigar box cover on which could be seen a landscape [later called the "Talisman."] It seemed crude because of its synthetic formulation in purple, vermilion, Veronese green and other pure colors – just as they came out of the tube – with almost no white mixed in. "How do you see this tree," Gauguin had said, standing in one of the corners of the *Bois d'Amour*. "Is it really green? Use green then, the most beautiful green on your palette. And that shadow, rather blue? Don't be afraid to paint it as blue as possible."

Thus was introduced to us for the first time, in a paradoxical and unforgettable form, the fertile concept of the "plane surface covered with colors assembled in a certain order." Thus we learned that every work of art was a transposition, a caricature, the passionate equivalent of a sensa-

In this obituary article Maurice Denis (1870–1943), a painter and critic within the Symbolist/Synthetist orbit of Gauguin, gives an account of Gauguin's ideas conveyed through the little painting The Talisman *painted under Gauguin's guidance by Sérusier. The simplification of color and line, the emphasis on the artist's "inner thought" and the symbolic properties of formal elements rather than on the representation of nature came as a revelation to Denis and his contemporaries who, according to Denis, had hardly heard of Impressionism.*

Armand Séguin (1869–1903), painter who met Gauguin in Le Pouldu in 1891 and wrote a series of three articles on him in L'Occident, *March, April, May 1903.*

Académie Julian: an informally run studio and refuge for young artists who wanted to work independently of the École des Beaux-Arts; they included Sérusier, Denis, Bonnard and Vuillard (1868–1940).

COLORPLATE 29

Alfred Philippe Roll (1846–1919), painter of genre and military subjects and a friend of Manet. Isidore Dagnan (1794–1873), landscape painter. Jules Bastien-Lepage (1848–84), academic painter who adopted some aspects of Impressionism. Joséphin ("Sar") Péladan (1859–1918), Symbolist writer who founded in 1892 the Salon de la Rose†Croix.

COLORPLATE 22. Maurice Denis. *Sunlight on the Terrace*. October 1890.
7³/₄ × 7³/₄″ (20 × 20 cm). Musée d'Orsay, Paris.

COLORPLATE 23. Vincent van Gogh. *The Fourteenth of July*. Late 1886.
17¼ × 15¼″ (44 × 39 cm). Private Collection.

COLORPLATE 24. Paul Gauguin. *The Vision after the Sermon: Jacob Wrestling with the Angel.* Summer 1888. 28³/₄ × 36¹/₄″ (73 × 92 cm). Scottish National Gallery of Art, Edinburgh.

COLORPLATE 25. Georges Seurat. *La Parade* (oil sketch). *c.*1888. Panel, 6¼ × 10¼″ (16 × 26 cm). E. G. Bührle Foundation, Zurich.

COLORPLATE 26. Georges Seurat. *Le Chahut* (study). 1889–90.
Border painted by Seurat on canvas. 22 × 18⅕″ (55.7 × 46.2 cm).
Albright-Knox Art Gallery, Buffalo, N.Y. (General Purchase Funds).

COLORPLATE 27. Paul Gauguin. *The Mermaid and the Ape.* 1895–1901.
Woodcut printed in black, green, brown, white, block size 8 × 16½″ (20.2 × 42.1 cm).
Öffentliche Kunstsammlung, Kupferstichkabinett, Basle.

COLORPLATE 28. Edvard Munch. *Women beside the Sea*. 1898.
Colored wood-engraving, 17¾ × 19¾″ (45 × 50 cm). © Munch Museum, Oslo (1992).

COLORPLATE 29. Paul Sérusier. *The Talisman*. 1888. Oil on panel, 10¾ × 8¾″ (27 × 22 cm).
Musée d'Orsay, Paris.

tion received. This was the origin of an evolution in which H. G. Ibels, P. Bonnard, Ranson, M. Denis participated without delay. We began to frequent some places completely unknown to our patron, Jules Lefebvre: the mezzanine of the Maison Goupil on the boulevard Montmartre, where Van Gogh, the painter's brother, showed us, along with the Gauguins from Martinique, the Vincents, the Monets and the Degas'; Père Tanguy's shop in the rue Clauzel where, with such emotion, we discovered Paul Cézanne.

The extremely philosophical intellect of Sérusier very quickly transformed the least words of Gauguin into a scientific doctrine, which made a decisive impression on us. . . .

It was perhaps not he who invented Synthetism, which became Symbolism through contact with the literary men. Emile Bernard is very positive on this controversial question. All the same Gauguin was the Master, and the undisputed one. His paradoxes were welcomed and quoted by everyone. He was admired not only for his talent and inexhaustible imagination, but for every trait in his romantic behavior – his gesticulation and fluency, his physical strength, his capacity for alcohol, and his pugnacity. The mystery of his ascendancy was to furnish us with one or two very simple and essential verities at a time when we were completely lacking in instruction. Thus, without ever having sought beauty in the classic sense, he soon had us engrossed in it. He wanted above all to convey character, to express the "inner thought," even in ugliness. He was still an Impressionist, but he claimed to read the book "wherein are

Henri Gabriel Ibels (1867–1936); Pierre Bonnard (1867–1947); Paul Ranson (1861–1909). Jules-Joseph Lefebvre (1836–1911), genre and portrait painter.

(Above) The Gloanec Inn, Pont-Aven, in *c.*1890. Photograph (© Collection Harlingue-Viollet, Paris).

Paul Sérusier's studio photographed in 1890, with Ranson, Sérusier and Madame Ranson. Private Collection.

From Gauguin's preface to Armand Séguin's catalogue reprinted in Mercure de France, February 1895. See page 191.

written the eternal laws of Beauty." He was fiercely individualistic and yet he clung to the most collective and most anonymous of the popular traditions. And we extracted a law, instructive principles, and a method from his contradictions. . . .

As it had always been explained by its proponents' works and by their paradoxes, Impressionism meant a return to the sun, to diffused light and freedom of composition. It meant the sense of values seen in Corot's work, an iridescent technique, a taste for fresh color, and finally the Japanese influence, that leaven which little by little permeated the whole mixture. It was all that, yes, but much else besides. Along with this bequest, Gauguin announced to us a second, presenting both at the same time.

Gauguin freed us from all the hindrances imposed upon our painters' instincts by the idea of copying. In our studio the grossest realism had followed the colorless academicism of the last students of Ingres. . . . We were, however, aspiring to the joy of "self-expression," an idea which was then dominating the young writers just as insistently as it is now. The theory of equivalents, which we had extracted from Gauguin's expressive imagery, furnished us with the means toward this goal. Gauguin gave us a claim to lyricism; for instance, if we could paint in vermilion that tree which appeared to us very reddish at a certain moment, why, then, not translate these impressions plastically by exaggeration, which is justifiable in the metaphors of poets? Why not stress even to the point of distortion the curve of a lovely shoulder, overdo the pearly whiteness of a flesh tint, stylize the symmetry of a branch not moved by any wind?

*   *   *

Thus at the perfect moment it had been Gauguin's role to project into the spirit of several young men the dazzling revelation that art is above all a means of expression. He had taught them, perhaps without wanting to, that all objects of art must be decorative. And finally, by the example of his work, he had proven that all grandeur, all beauty is worth nothing without simplification and clarity, or without a homogeneity of *matière*.

He was not the sort of "gentleman artist" that had become so distasteful to us for the past fifteen years – indeed, his sensuality was uncommon – but his works were rugged and sound. He fully justified Carlyle's etymological play on words with *genius* and *ingenuity*. Something of the essential, of the profoundly true, emanated from his savage art, from his rough common sense, and from his vigorous naïveté. The paradoxes which he brought out in conversation, undoubtedly in order to seem just as pretentious as the others, and because he was a Parisian, concealed basic teachings, deep truths, eternal ideas, which no art in any era has been able to do without. With them he invigorated painting again. He was for our corrupt time a kind of Poussin without classical culture, who, instead of serenely going to Rome to study the antiquities, became inflamed by a passion to discover a tradition beneath the coarse archaism of Breton calvaries and of Maori idols, or in the crude coloring of the *Images d'Epinal*. Yes, but like the great Poussin, he passionately loved simplicity and clarity, which he incited us to desire unreservedly. For him too, *synthesis* and *style* were almost synonymous.

Thomas Carlyle (1795–1881), Scottish historian and writer.

PAUL SÉRUSIER

Letter to Maurice Denis
March 1889

Paul Sérusier (1864–1927). Having spent the summer of 1888 working with Gauguin at Pont-Aven in Brittany, on his return to Paris in October he became the principal interpreter of "Symbolism/Synthetism" for the group of young painters at the Académie Julian, including Maurice Denis, Paul Ranson, Édouard Vuillard and Pierre Bonnard, who formed themselves into the secret society, the Nabis. Here Sérusier reveals the crisis created for him by Gauguin's ideas about the abstract qualities of painting. Confused and anxious, he felt he no longer understood what the artist's relationship to nature should be.

PONT-AVEN

Lucky, twice-lucky Denis, you seem pleased with your work, and I have only sad tidings to give you. I'm not doing anything worthwhile. I was so optimistic on leaving Paris, and when I arrived here, I found myself thoroughly at a loss. What worried me above all was this: what part should nature play in art? Where should the line be drawn? In a word, from the material point of view of the execution, should one work directly from nature, or merely look and remember? Too much freedom frightens me, I'm a poor copyist, and yet I find there is so much in my head, triggered off by any number of images, that nature seems to me petty and banal.

As soon as I arrived, I realized that Gauguin, who is here with me, is not the artist I had thought; I saw points in his line of reasoning where we are not in agreement, and, in his works, a lack of delicacy, an illogical, childish affectation in the draughtsmanship, a pursuit of originality taken to the point of mystification. I therefore refrained from showing him what I'd done. So I feel very alone. I could do with a word of encouragement, sometimes it's discouraging to find yourself in front of your canvases wondering whether they're good or ridiculous.

Painting aside, my life is most agreeable; I'm here with Taupin, Jourdan, Maurice Lefèvre, Bouffar and some others, all good fellows, but with nothing of the Nabi about them. So I envy you when you mention the new brother [Vuillard] sent to you by Jahvé. I welcome him wholeheartedly. For the future, I dream of a hand-picked brotherhood, consisting only of convinced artists, lovers of the beautiful and the good, filling their works and days with that indefinable quality I understand by Nabi. I'm sure you know what I mean.

I've had news of two Nabis, Séguin and Ibels; they ate the monthly meal together, all dressed up in oriental garments. They seem fairly pleased with their work, particularly Séguin, whose words imply excellent principles; we shall see the proof of it on our return.

In a few days I'm going to move nearer the sea; I love it so much, in all its vastness; it has always filled me with great emotion. So I am going to

Paul Sérusier. *Portrait of Paul Ranson in Nabi Dress.* 1890. 24 × 18" (46 × 61 cm). Private Collection.

take leave of the girls with the beautiful white coifs in order to gaze upon the ragged, sallow little girls, scrawny and strong, who tend their sheep on the great rocky cliffs amidst piles of wrack. So far I have worked in little flower-filled gardens; I yearn for the bare and simple solitude of the coast. I dream of such great things when I am there, that I'm afraid.

MARS DAY, POULDU

I am happy to be able to end this letter, begun so sadly three days ago, upon a gayer note. Yesterday I arrived at these magnificent beaches, where I am going to live for a fortnight, alone with Gauguin, without distracting worries or apéritifs. I'm seized with a fever for work, all is going well. Be with me in spirit, I feel that at last I am going to do something worthwhile.

Till I see you again, brother Nabi; I feel such happiness, I wish I could share it with you.

P. SÉRUSIER

Are these drawing lessons you're talking about? Don't do it. By all means do coaching in French, Latin or Greek etc.

Le Pouldu: a little seaside resort near Pont-Aven.

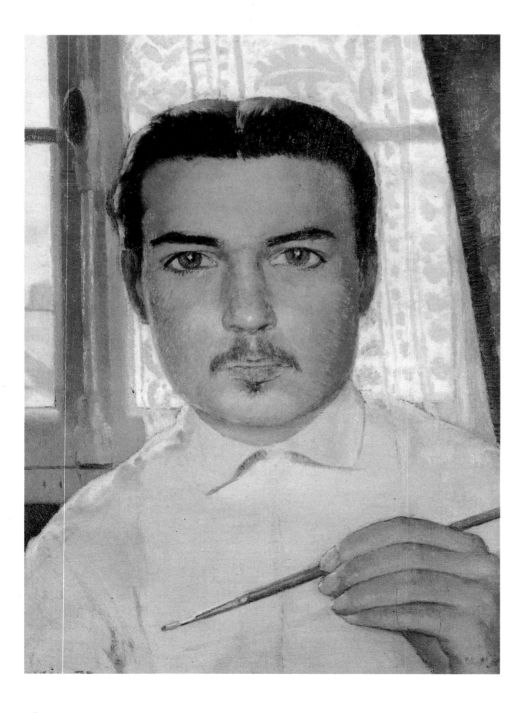

Maurice Denis. *Self-Portrait of the Artist.* 1896. Oil on canvas, 13 × 9½″ (33 × 24 cm). Collection Dominique Denis, St-Germain-en-Laye.

Before ending this letter, I'd like to write out for you something I read in a book and wrote out on the wall of our room. It's our personal *credo*.

"I believe in a last judgment when terrible punishment will be meted out to all those who in this world dared to traffic in chaste and sublime art, to all those who have defiled and degraded art through the baseness of their emotions, and by their vile greed for material gain.

"But I believe that the faithful disciples of great art will be crowned with glory; wrapped in celestial array woven of sunbeams, perfumes and melodious chords, they will return once more for all eternity to lose themselves in the bosom of the divine source of all harmony. R. Wagner."

MAURICE DENIS

ART ET CRITIQUE
"Definition of Neotraditionism"
August 23 and 30, 1890

I

It is well to remember that a picture – before being a battle horse, a nude woman, or some anecdote – is essentially a plane surface covered with colors assembled in a certain order.

II

I am seeking a *painter's* definition of that simple word "nature," the word which is both the label and the definition of the theory of art most generally accepted by our dying century.

Is it perhaps: the totality of our optical sensations? But, not to mention the disturbance natural to the modern eye, who is not aware of the power mental habits have over our vision? I have known young men who gave themselves over to fatiguing gymnastics of the optic nerves in order to see the *trompe l'oeil* in the *Poor Fisherman* [by Puvis de Chavannes]; and they found it, I am sure. With irreproachable scientific method, M. Signac can prove to you the absolute necessity of his chromatic perceptions. While M. Bouguereau, if his classroom corrections are sincere, is totally convinced that he is copying "nature."

This article, written when Maurice Denis was only nineteen years old, was first published under the pseudonym "Pierre Louys"; it was reprinted in Denis' Théories: 1890–1910 *(Paris, 1912). Denis was the first to formulate the ideas transmitted from Pont-Aven to the future "Nabis" via Sérusier's* The Talisman. *The opening paragraphs of Denis' article indicate the conflict with representation ("nature") that the new awareness of the abstract formal qualities of painting had introduced into late nineteenth-century art.*

Pierre Puvis de Chavannes, The Poor Fisherman, *1879, Musée d'Orsay.*

Adolphe-William Bouguereau (1825–1905), academic painter popular at the Salon.

III

Go to the museum and consider each canvas apart, isolated from the others: each one will give you even if not a complete illusion at least an aspect of nature that pretends to be true. You will see in each picture what you want to see.

However, if it should happen that by an effort of the will one should see "nature" in the pictures, the reverse is true. Painters have an ineluctable tendency to merge those aspects perceived in reality with aspects of painting already seen.

It is impossible to determine all that can modify the modern vision, but there is no doubt but that the torment of intellectuality, through which most of the young artists pass, results in the creation of very real optical deviations. One sees very readily grey violets when one has for a long time sought whether or not they are violet.

The irrational admiration of old pictures because they must be admired, in which one seeks conscious renditions of nature has certainly deformed the eye of the masters of the schools.

From the admiration of modern pictures, which one studies in the same spirit, comes an infatuation that leads to other difficulties. Has it been observed that this indefinable "nature" perpetually modifies itself, that it is not the same in the salon of 1890 as in the salons of thirty years ago, and that there is a fashion in "nature" – a changing fantasy as with clothing and hats?

IV

Thus the modern artist forms, by choice and synthesis, a certain eclectic and exclusive habit of interpreting optical sensations – which becomes the naturalist criterion, the idiosyncratic character of the painter, what *littérateurs* later called temperament. It is a kind of hallucination about which aesthetics has nothing to say, since reason itself depends upon it and exerts no control.

V

When one says that nature is beautiful, more beautiful than all of painting – assuming that we remain within the limitations of aesthetic judgment – he means to say that one person's impressions of nature in himself are better than those of others. That we must readily admit. But does one want to compare the hypothetical and imagined plenitude of the original effect with the mere notation of that effect by such and such a consciousness? Here the great question of temperament presents itself: "Art is nature seen through a temperament."

A very just definition because it is very vague, and which leaves uncertain the important point, the criterion of temperaments. The painting of M. Bougereau is nature seen through a temperament. M. Raffaëlli is an extraordinary observer, but do you think he is sensitive to beautiful forms and colors? Where does the "painter" temperament begin and end?

There is a science which is concerned with these things: aesthetics (is it not known?) which, thanks to the research of Charles Henry, defines and bases itself on the psychology of Spencer and Bain.

Before exteriorizing sensations such as those, it would be necessary to determine their value from the point of view of beauty.

VI

I do not know why painters have so misunderstood the word "naturalist" when applied in a uniquely philosophic sense to the Renaissance.

I maintain that the predellas of Angelico which are in the Louvre, *The Man in Red* of Ghirlandaio, and many other works of the Primitives, recall for me more precisely "nature" than Giorgione, Raphael, Da Vinci. They are another manner of seeing – they are different fantasies.

VII

And then in our sensations everything changes, both object and subject. One must be very well trained to perceive the same model on the table on two successive days. There is life, the intensity of coloration, light, mobility, air, a host of things which one does not render. I am now on familiar themes that are, however, very true and quite obvious.

VIII

Finally, I recognize that there is a strong possibility that general assent, in this as in other insoluble questions, has some value, namely, that the photograph conveys to a greater or less degree the reality of a form, and that a facsimile of nature is "as much nature as possible."

Therefore, I will say of these sorts of works and of those that tend toward them that they are "nature." I will call "nature" the *trompe l'oeil* of the crowds, like the grapes of the antique painter pecked by the birds, and the panoramas of M. Detaille, where one is uncertain (O, aesthetic emotion) if a certain caisson in the foreground is real or on the canvas.

Zola's famous aphorism is from "Proudhon et Courbet" in Le Salut Publique, *July 26, 1865.*
Raffaëlli exhibited with the Impressionists in 1881–82.

Charles Henry (1859–1926), scientist and art theorist whose ideas influenced Seurat and his followers. Herbert Spencer (1820–1903) and Alexander Bain (1818–1903), materialist and positivist philosophers.

The call for a return to classicism came later in Denis' development as a critic. "Neotraditionism" proposes the principles of an alternative which Denis and his Nabis friends were developing in opposition to academic as well as to Impressionist and Neo-Impressionist art.

PAUL SIGNAC
JOURNAL
1894-95

Material from Signac's diary, edited by John Rewald, was first published in the Gazette des Beaux-Arts, *July–September 1949.*
The last paragraph of the August entry in Signac's diary (1894) shows a significant change in his awareness: that color in painting no longer needed to be justified by its correspondence to "exact" or "scientific" color in nature, but could be determined by independent and abstract painterly concerns.

ST. TROPEZ, AUGUST 23, 1894

The size 25 canvas [81 × 60 cms] from nature seems to me increasingly a waste of time. The theory is: (1) to do some quick sketches from nature according to one's needs or sensations, (2) to create the work from these sketches. This size 25 canvas, done entirely from nature, is a waste of time. Let us leave that to the "Impressionists" – actually, they have created some wonderful work using this system ... And to think that these painters (because they have committed themselves to working entirely from nature) regard themselves as "naturalists" – No, M. Monet, you are no naturalist ... Bastien-Lepage is much closer to nature than you are! There are no blue trees in nature, nor violet people ... and your great virtue is precisely to have painted them like that, as you feel them to be, and not as they are ...

A few years ago, I too was trying to prove to the world, through scientific experiment, that those blues, those yellows, those greens, were to be found in nature. Now I simply say: I paint the way I do because this is the technique which seems to be the best suited to producing the most harmonious, the most luminous, the most colourful result ... and because that is how I like it ...

* * *

SEPTEMBER 15, 1894

How unfair people are to Seurat. To think that they refuse to recognize him as one of the geniuses of the century! The young are full of admiration for Laforgue and Van Gogh – who are also dead (that's crucial, apparently) – but for Seurat, oblivion, silence. Yet he's a greater painter than Van Gogh, who is interesting only as a phenomenon, by virtue of his mad side ... and whose only interesting paintings are those done at the time of his illness, in Arles. At the time of Seurat's death, the critics were recognizing his talent but claiming that he did not leave a complete body of work. It seems to me, on the contrary, that he has given all that he could give, and that admirably. He would certainly have produced many more paintings and progressed further, but his task was done. He surveyed the scene and has made these very important contributions: his black and white, his harmony of line, his composition, his contrast and harmony of colour, even his frames. What more can you ask of a painter?

Jules Laforgue (1860–87), Symbolist poet and critical writer. He also died young at the age of 27.

Our pictures' lack of success is easily explained: what pleasure could they offer people without a painterly eye, since we seek merely beautiful lines and colours, with no care for fashion, anecdote or literature! Moreover, this is the fate of all truly painterly painters. Does anyone look at the paintings of Delacroix nowadays? How many people visit St-Sulpice? They still have no time for him, alive or dead. They admire his work on principle, but they don't look at it. Why should the public look at it, anyway? They wouldn't understand it. Who, among public or critics alike, has an eye sufficiently trained to enjoy beautiful lines and beautiful colours? I am sure I could do a painting with all the rules of harmony reversed, where I would paint the contrary of what I believe to be beautiful ... and no one would notice anything! If there are dots, it will still be a Signac!

The two murals painted in the Chapel of the Holy Angels in St-Sulpice (1854–61) had been the occasion of widespread discussion in the 1860s about the radical aspects of Delacroix's use of color.

* * *

OCTOBER 3

I attach more and more importance to the purity of the brushstroke – I try to give it maximum purity and intensity. Any defiling sleight of hand or smearing disgusts me. When one can paint with jewels, why use shit? Each time that my brushstroke happens to come up against another, not yet dry, and this mixture produces a dirty tone, I feel great physical disgust! It is this passion for beautiful colours which makes us paint as we do ... and not the love of the "dot", as foolish people say.

Georges Seurat. *Nurse and Child.* 1881–82. Conté crayon, 12 × 9½″ (31 × 24 cm). Louvre, Paris, Department of Graphic Arts (Gift of Paul Jamot).

OCTOBER 9

What fumisterie, this business of "literature" in art! What "advanced critics" at the time of naturalism most admired in the *Grande-Jatte* was the woman on the right, who is walking with a young man and a monkey; and they admired her because she looked "like the tough sort of woman you wouldn't dare stand up!" Nowadays the young symbolists appreciate this painting for "the hieratic poses of the figures, who look like the descendants of an Egyptian bas-relief or a fresco by Benozzo Gozzoli . . ." None of the critics of 1885 or 1894 saw the superb and uniquely "painterly" qualities of poor Seurat. And how time disposes of these marginal concerns, which are merely a matter of fashion. How little we now care about the realism of Courbet or the Romanticism of Delacroix! Their draughtsmanship, their colour, their style alone are of any importance to us.

* * *

MAY 25, 1895

[Georges] Lecomte . . . is not enthusiastic about the *Cathedrals.* Not enough sky around them, not enough ground . . . a curtain backdrop. Magnificent masses. I completely understand what these *Cathedrals* are: marvellously executed walls.

Georges Lecomte (1867–1958), writer and critic who edited the Symbolist weekly La Cravache *in 1888–89: "Les Cathédrales de M. Claude Monet,"* La Nouvelle Revue, *June 1, 1895.*

THE FRAGMENTATION
OF ARTISTIC MOVEMENTS

CAMILLE PISSARRO

Letter to Lucien
December 28, 1883

OSNY

My dear Lucien,
I am sending you *Les Fleurs du Mal* and the book of Verlaine. I do not believe these works can be appreciated by anyone who comes to them with the prejudices of English, or what is more, bourgeois traditions. Not that I am completely in favor of the contents of these books; I am no more for them than for Zola, whom I find a bit too photographic, but I recognize their superiority as works of art, and from the standpoint of certain ideas of modern criticism, they have value to me. Besides it is clear that from now on the novel must be critical, sentiment, or rather sentimentality, cannot be tolerated without danger in a rotten society ready to fall apart.

The discussion you had about naturalism is going on everywhere. Both sides exaggerate. It is clear that it is necessary to generalize and not lean on trivial details. – But as I see it, the most corrupt art is the sentimental, the art of orange blossoms which makes pale women swoon.

Charles Baudelaire, Les Fleurs du Mal *(1857)*.

Lucien Pissarro. *Vincent van Gogh and Félix Fénéon.* Drawing, black crayon, 8⅝ × 6⅞″ (22 × 17.5 cm). Ashmolean Museum, Oxford.

Henri de Toulouse-Lautrec. *Portrait of Vincent van Gogh.* 1887. Pastel, 21¼ × 18½″ (54 × 47 cm). Rijksmuseum Vincent van Gogh Foundation/Van Gogh Museum, Amsterdam.

VINCENT VAN GOGH
Letter to Émile Bernard
Late July 1888

ARLES

My dear comrade Bernard,
I have just sent you – today – nine more sketches after painted studies. In this way you will see subjects taken from the sort of scenery that inspires "father" Cézanne, for the Crau near Aix is pretty similar to the country surrounding Tarascon or the Crau here. The Camargue is even simpler, for there is often nothing, nothing more than the poor soil with its tamarind bushes and the coarse grasses which are to these meager pastures what esparto grass is to the desert.

As I know how much you like Cézanne, I thought these sketches of Provence might please you; not that there is much resemblance between a drawing of mine and one by Cézanne. Oh, for that matter, no more than there is between Monticelli and me! But I too very much like the country they have loved so much, and for the same reasons: the color and the logical design.

My dear comrade Bernard, by the word *collaboration* I did not mean to say that I think two or more painters ought to work at the same pictures.

Adolphe Monticelli (1824–86), Provençal painter much admired by Van Gogh.

What I meant by it rather was divergent works which nonetheless belong together and complement each other.

Look here! Take the Italian primitives, take the German primitives, take the Dutch school, take what we call the Italians proper – in short, look here, take the whole art of painting! Unintentionally their works form "groups," "series."

Well, at the moment the Impressionists form a group too, notwithstanding all their disastrous civil wars in which they are all trying to cut each other's throats with a zeal worthy of a better cause and a better final aim.

Rembrandt is the head of our northern school, seeing that his influence makes itself felt by anyone approaching him. For instance, we see Paulus Potter paint animals rutting and passionate in equally passionate landscapes, in a thunderstorm, in the sun, in the melancholy of autumn; whereas, before he came to know Rembrandt, this same Paulus Potter was dry and meticulous enough!

Here are two people, Rembrandt and Potter, who belong together like brothers; and though Rembrandt probably never touched a picture by Potter with his brush, that does not alter the fact that Potter and Ruysdael owe him all that is best in them: that something which moves us so deeply, as soon as we know how to see a corner of old Holland through the medium of their temperament.

Paulus Potter (1625–54); Salomon van Ruysdael (1600/3?–1670), Dutch painters.

Furthermore, the material difficulties of a painter's life make collaboration, the uniting of painters, desirable (as much so as in the days of the Guilds of St. Luke). By safeguarding their material existence, by loving each other like comrades-in-arms instead of cutting each other's throats, painters would be happier, and in any case less ridiculous, less foolish and less culpable.

But for all that I won't labor the point. For I know that life drags us along so fast that we haven't time both to argue and to act. For which reason, as the said union exists only very incompletely, we are at present sailing the high seas in our wretched little boats, all alone on the great waves of our time.

Is it a renaissance? Is it a decadence? We are unable to judge, because we are too close to things not to be misled by distortions of perspective, as contemporary occurrences probably assume exaggerated proportions in our eyes, at least with regard to our misfortunes and our merits.

A hearty handshake, and I hope to have some news from you soon.

Sincerely yours, Vincent

The Atelier Cormon photographed in 1883. Musée Toulouse-Lautrec, Albi.

JACQUES DAURELLE
ECHO DE PARIS
"Young Painters at Home"
December 28, 1891

Recently we reviewed the exhibition of young Impressionist and Symbolist painters held at rue le Peletier. We thought it might be interesting to pay a visit to the ateliers of some of the most individualistic of them: MM. Anquetin, de Toulouse-Lautrec, Émile Bernard, Maurice Denis and Pierre Bonnard. We asked them all the same questions:

1. How do you define the artistic tendencies of the young school of painters, and what label do you group them under?
2. What do you think of the contemporary masters and particularly of Meissonier – whose name and works have recently given rise to an inheritance dispute between his widow and his children?
3. Which is the master whom you most admire?

We expected to hear established painters such as Cabanel, Henner, Carolus-Duran etc. described as "doddering, hidebound idiots."

But our young painters proved tolerant interviewees. They are politely reserved. They answered us without any outburst of offensive epithets. How little they resemble our young writers, all eager to speak ill of their forebears and to proclaim themselves geniuses and leaders. This is quite excusable, of course. Is it not typical of youth to be uncompromising in its ideas, implacable in its antipathies, excessive in its enthusiasms, extreme in its ambitions?

Our young painters are thoroughly moderate, well-disposed, praiseworthy! These rebels of the palette are very fair-minded fellows. Only

The exhibition opening in December 1891 at Le Barc de Boutteville's gallery in the rue Le Peletier showed a small group of artists including members of the Nabis under the title "Impressionists and Symbolists." Since Jules Huret had published his discussions with Mallarmé and others in the Echo de Paris, *interviews about the current scene in art and literature had become a popular journalistic form. Jacques Daurelle went along to interview the exhibitors, Anquetin, Toulouse-Lautrec, Bernard, Denis and Bonnard.*

Alexandre Cabanel (1824–89); Jean-Jacques Henner (1829–1905); Jean-Louis Meissonier (1815–91): academic history painters.

Pierre Bonnard. *Place Clichy* with, *left to right*, Bonnard, Roussel, Vuillard, Toulouse-Lautrec, Tapié de Céleyran and Maurice Denis. Pen and ink, wash drawing, page 12½ × 9½" (32 × 24 cm). Galerie Huguette Berès, Paris.

occasionally do they let slip the odd guarded word of contempt for those who are already established in the métier they are embarking on, paint-brush tucked behind ear and easel awry.

First we spoke to:

M. ANQUETIN. M. Anquetin is a little older than the rest of the crowd. Twenty-two or twenty-three. Erect, slim and vigorous. Brown hair, cut *en brosse*; a frizzy, fan-shaped beard; bright, alert eyes, a slightly sarcastic mouth.

M. Anquetin is a great lover of fencing. He never misses his daily bout, to limber up and calm his nerves. He works in a stylish atelier on the rue de Rome, behind Gare St-Lazare, where engines moo and whistle ceaselessly.

We found M. Anquetin smoking his faithful cherrywood pipe in the company of two of his friends. We chatted about generalities, even about painting. He showed us his sketches, and canvases in varying stages of completion. The most striking thing about his works is the wonderfully intense combination of imagination and reality. The forms are clear, the lines precise and the colours arranged with as much tact as ingenuity.

We asked M. Anquetin how he would describe himself. Pipe in hand, he replied gravely:

"I would describe myself quite simply as Anquetin. Unfortunately, I have indeed been subject to certain influences; but I am working hard towards disengaging myself from them. Talk of Symbolism or Impressionism is all nonsense. There are no theories, no schools, there are only temperaments."

As we must be very brief, we proceed to another question.

"Which contemporary painters do you admire the most?"

"Cézanne, and also Renoir. Two pure geniuses demanding recognition."

"What do you think of the others, Cabanel, Henner, Carolus-Duran, Meissonier?"

"I think nothing. All Meissonier achieved was a sort of photography of costume. All I can say of his work is that I wouldn't want to have painted a Meissonier."

M. DE TOULOUSE-LAUTREC. We meet M. de Toulouse-Lautrec at the exhibition. He is small, dark and heavily-bearded, wearing pince-nez. We talk.

Interspersing his sentences with little sniggers, M. de Toulouse-Lautrec tells us:

"I am not part of any school. I work on my own small patch. I admire Degas and Forain. I have no opinion on the contemporary masters. I'm trying to become one of them.

"As to Meissonier, I feel that he has taken infinite pains, and one must always feel a degree of respect for someone who has taken pains."

And M. de Toulouse-Lautrec gives a little snigger. He is very much the man of his pictures, with their bitter irony. And indeed his women, too, dreaming mournfully on the divans of public "cloisters," exhibit truly cruel powers of observation.

M. ÉMILE BERNARD. M. Émile Bernard has had an interesting life. Expelled from Cormon's atelier at sixteen for Impressionism, he went to Brittany on foot, penniless, sleeping in barns, with vagrants, eating when people felt disposed to give him a crust of bread.

He is a seeker, an extremist, who would die of hunger rather than make the least concession where art is concerned. He is also an ardent and practising Catholic, which explains the mysticism of his paintings.

M. Émile Bernard lives with his parents at Asnières, where he has a small weatherboard atelier; here we were able to see a number of interesting sketches, highly original canvases, stained glass of surprising beauty, panels sculpted with infinite care, and tapestries of extreme originality.

Jean-Louis Forain (1852–1931), painter, caricaturist and friend of Degas.

We notice a *Christ taken down from the Cross* in his small room; it is intensely moving.

The impression we gained from this visit to his atelier is that M. Émile Bernard – who has been accused of plagiarizing Paul Gauguin – resembles him not at all.

M. Émile Bernard is purely a religious painter, nothing else. His painting translates only religious feelings. As to his methods, they are very simple: few colors, and those dim and faint.

M. Émile Bernard is twenty-four. Tall, slender, long-haired, blue-eyed, with a fair, pointed beard and a mild expression, he brings to mind a figure from Velazquez. He is an interesting talker, clear and knowledgeable. "I am a committed Christian," he tells us, "and I try to express my Christian feelings. Ideally, I would like to create a religious style rising above modernity, above topicality. As to methods and inspiration, you have to go back to the Primitives, be technically very concise, use line only to determine form and colour only to determine its states. In a word, you have to create a style for our own time."

"How do you judge our contemporary masters?"

Without the slightest hint of malice in either tone or gesture, Émile Bernard replies:

"I think that Cabanel, Carolus-Duran, Cormon etc. are all fools who never understood anything about the masters they wanted to immortalize: Raphael, Leonardo etc. . . .

"As to Meissonier, his early paintings are well-made cakes and his later ones are gravy. The only contemporary masters I admire are Cézanne, and Odilon Redon."

M. MAURICE DENIS. M. Maurice Denis lives with his family at St-Germain. For four years he attended the École des Beaux-Arts and the atelier Julian. He too is a practising Catholic and paints religious works. His *Catholic Mystery*, exhibited at rue Le Peletier, attracts much attention.

Maurice Denis: Catholic Mystery, *1890, Private Collection, France.*

Currently M. Maurice Denis is apparently engaged in researches which he hopes will lead to a satisfactory outcome.

Although he is only twenty-one, he talked to us with the moderation of an old man:

"We are not pretentious people, living with the conviction that we have discovered the definitive Art. We are deeply humble seekers.

"Personally, I can admire people very different from myself. Contemporary masters hold some interest for me. Briefly put, Meissonier is an estimable man who knows his métier as painter, thanks to his imitation of the Dutch *petits maîtres*.

"I think that first and foremost a painting must be decorative. The choice of subjects and scenes counts for nothing. It is through the coloured surface, through the tonal values and harmony of its lines that I hope to reach the spirit of the viewer and arouse emotion."

Édouard Vuillard. *Portrait of Bonnard.* 1891. Oil on paper, 12¾ × 8½″ (32.5 × 21.5 cm). Galerie Huguette Berès, Paris.

M. PIERRE BONNARD. M. Pierre Bonnard is also very young. His friends regard him as a decorative painter and an admirably gifted illustrator. His decorative panels exhibited at rue Le Peletier do indeed give proof of great imagination in the combination of motifs and colors.

"Painting," as M. Pierre Bonnard tells us furthermore, "must be above all decorative. Talent will emerge in the way lines are arranged.

"I belong to no school. I seek only to create something personal, and at the moment I am unlearning what I had so much difficulty learning during four years at the École des Beaux-Arts.

"Some time ago I was very worked up against those painters who, to some degree or other, are members of the Institut. But now I do not believe that one should hold anything against these people for not being geniuses. They have their reasons for doing what they do."

As we have said, our young painters are extremely well-bred young people, amiable rebels, hardliners with palettes of velvet.

CHARLES MORICE
MERCURE DE FRANCE
"Inquiry into the Tendencies of Art Now"
August–September 1905

It is clear that at the present time the plastic arts are poised between memory and desire, the former weighing heavily upon the latter, and hampering their ascent. The result, particularly among the young, is deep disarray, long evident in the annual exhibitions. It is the morning after "something." Is it the eve of "something else?"

The primitive and decadent masters have met together in our time and are walking side by side with those of the century of Pericles, and those of the Renaissance, and those of the centuries of Louis XIV and XV. All centuries brush shoulders in our own. And here we have not only a singular mingling of simplicity and rottenness, we also see rottenness in simplicity, we see the same soul torn between these opposing directions, living, painfully, and creating, in a fragile fashion, in this unstable balance.

Optimists maintain that these were ever the conditions of Art, that there is nothing to worry about, that this apparent chaos is an inevitable part of our current disorder, that genius and talent were always able to pick their way through it. They do not take into account the great novelty which characterizes the present moment, against which it is not possible to invoke the authority of tradition, for it belies it; and this novelty is, precisely, that our contemporaries believe in the possibility of *novelty in art.*

This, for me, gives a strange timbre and colour to the present moment.

It was inevitable; given the characteristics of current thought – drunk on scientific conquests as it is and deeply stricken by a sick Faith in the indefinite progress of the species, ringing with incomprehensible scorn for the past – the crisis which art and artists are experiencing today might have been foreseen.

* * *

But we have recently discovered *peinture claire*, and the decomposition of the tone, and in the name of these inventions we condone the proposal that the doors of our museums be closed. This is our lamentable triumph: our conviction that we have created something new. We are left dazzled by this blaze of colours, this conflagration set off by the Impressionists, and while the fireworks are fizzling out, we are somehow struck by blindness. These late midsummer bonfires leave ageing humanity wandering distraught amidst the half-shadows of the last twilight.

I know of no more striking or poignant example of the break-up of the modern universe. Now all schools, in the arts, all religions, all philosophies, rub shoulders and contradict each other with the lamentable serenity of indifference: we have the Impressionists and the official party, the symbolists and the realists of Faith, of social science, of politics as well as those of the plastic arts. There is no accord; each one merely seeks out, and exclusively cultivates, his own differences instead of trying to reach out to his fellows – only there are no fellows any more!

* * *

But what is most evident, and often most comforting, is the passion put into these very disparate hopes. It is a turbulent "morning after," but maybe this agitation is that of life itself. All these artists, who will shortly be allowed to speak for themselves, are seeking the future, their own and that of their race; they are seeking it in all directions and rarely by the same paths. The brief conclusions they have been good enough to offer me

Charles Morice (1861–1919): Symbolist poet, critic and regular contributor to the Mercure de France, *mainly on the work of Gauguin who was a colleague and friend. He collaborated with him on the first editions of* Noa-Noa, *and included Gauguin's controversial account of his visit to Van Gogh in Arles in his article on him in* Mercure de France *in October 1903.*

Fifty-six painters replied to Morice's questionnaire on the state of modern art. In inquiring about the "death" of Impressionism and its possible revival, Morice emphasized its continuing significance for young artists even as late as 1905.

His final question (should the artist expect everything from nature, or only the plastic means of giving expression to the thought which is within him?) poses as alternatives "nature" and the "plastic means" of painting. It addresses one of the central dilemmas Impressionism left as a legacy to this generation. It also anticipates Matisse's statement in Notes of a Painter, *1908: "a painter's thought must not be considered as separate from his pictorial means."*

Peinture claire: *Painting expressing light by means of pale luminous color, as in Impressionism.*

on their meditations reflect their own works and comment upon them. Not all this movement is sterile; and I am convinced that by offering my correspondents the opportunity of meeting one another, of joining forces, if I might so put it, around certain key aims – those which are the subject of their perpetual dialogue with themselves – perhaps, who knows, I shall usefully have sparked off comparisons, the reconsideration of departures and returns – again, who knows, the happy acknowledgement of certain features common to minds hitherto dispersed and which may now find some comfort in this discovery of some mysterious spiritual correspondence.

At all events, this opportunity to have their say, here, now, on this "morning after" Impressionism and on the eve of the unknown, may at least be of some historical interest.

Without classifying them, and roughly in the order in which they were given, I shall note down the answers they have been good enough to provide me. The questions I put to them were the following:

1. Do you feel that art today is tending towards new directions?
2. Is Impressionism over? Can it take on new life?
3. Whistler, Gauguin, Fantin-Latour . . . What did these dead painters take away with them? What have they left us?
4. How do you evaluate Cézanne?
5. In your view, should the artist expect everything from nature, or only the plastic means of giving expression to the thought which is within him?

Maurice Denis. *Homage to Cézanne*. 1900. 71 × 95″ (180 × 240 cm). Musée d'Orsay, Paris (Gift of André Gide).

COLORPLATE 30. Georges Seurat. *La Parade (Invitation to the Side-Show). c.*1887–88.
39¼ × 59″ (99.7 × 149.9 cm).
Metropolitan Museum of Art, New York (Bequest of Stephen C. Clark, 61.101.17).

COLORPLATE 31. Henri Edmond Cross. *The Golden Isles.* 1891–92.
23¹/₂ × 21⁵/₈″ (60 × 55 cm). Musée d'Orsay, Paris.

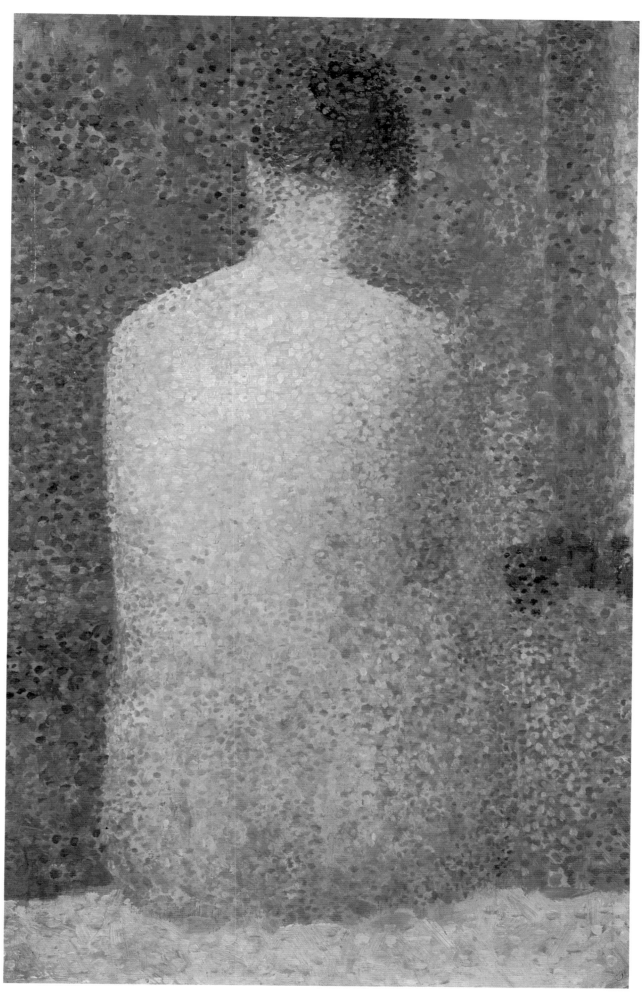

COLORPLATE 32. Georges Seurat. *Poseuse from the Back*. 1886.
Oil on wood, 9⅝ × 6″ (24.5 × 15.5 cm). Musée d'Orsay, Paris.

COLORPLATE 33. Henri Edmond Cross. *Hair. c.*1892. 24 × 18″ (61 × 46 cm).
Musée d'Orsay, Paris.

COLORPLATE 34. Édouard Vuillard. *Woman in Blue with a Child. c.*1899. Oil on card, 20 × 23″
(50.8 × 58.4 cm). © Glasgow Art Gallery and Museums, Scotland.

COLORPLATE 35. Édouard Vuillard. *Félix Vallotton*. 1900. Distemper on cardboard mounted on panel, 29⅝ × 19⅝″ (75 × 49.8 cm). Musée d'Orsay, Paris.

COLORPLATE 36. Édouard Vuillard. *Still Life with Artist's Paint Box and Moss Roses.*
14 × 16½″ (35.6 × 41.9 cm).
National Gallery of Art, Washington, D.C. (Ailsa Mellon Bruce Collection).

COLORPLATE 37. Georges Seurat. *The Circus* (sketch). 1891. 21½ × 18″ (55 × 46 cm).
Musée d'Orsay, Paris.

Several artists, as was their absolute right, grouped their replies into a sort of general profession of faith; others kept strictly to my questions; yet others rejected the possibility, for them, of any historically-based answer; all are significant.

* * *

M. KEES VAN DONGEN. Art will always take new directions, and something is about to begin, is beginning – but only beginning. The Impressionist movement is dead, though it may not be quite lying down.

The dead take nothing away with them.

Gauguin leaves a fine *oeuvre*; and I regard him as the precursor of a new religion of art which will draw upon the source of life itself to make life into a flower, and death into a flower, and eternity into a crown of multi-coloured flowers.

Fantin and Whistler leave us – pictures.

Cézanne is the finest painter of his time. But many singe their wings at his lamp!

I myself do not hark back to the masters of yesteryear, nor to those of yesterday. Today, I think of tomorrow – and what I ask of nature is how one should live.

* * *

M. CHARLES CAMOIN. I believe art is constantly developing, that it revitalizes and renews itself ceaselessly through the diversity of individual temperaments and, in a general way, it seems to me that the task of the current generation will be to complete what Impressionism has begun.

Impressionism was a rebirth. It cannot be completely over. The artists of the future will have to free themselves from it, or fall into pastiche, but they will not be able to ignore it.

The novelty and power of Cézanne's imagination make him a genius. He is one of those who move art forward. He is the Primitive of the *plein air*. He is deeply classical and he often says that he aimed simply to *redo Poussin from nature*. He does not see objectively and through the patch of colour like the Impressionists; he deciphers nature slowly, through light and shade, which he expresses in sensations of colour. Yet his aim is purely to "make an image."

I would like to quote some of his views and the advice I've had from him:

"Since you are here in Paris and since you are interested in the Masters in the Louvre, by all means do studies from the great decorative painters, Veronese, Rubens, as you would from nature; this is something I myself was able to do only in part. But you are right to work from nature above all ... Go to the Louvre but, after having seen the great masters who repose there, we must hasten out and by contact with nature revive within ourselves the instincts, the artistic sensations which live in us. We probably talk better about painting while on the motif, rather than devising purely speculative theories, where we often lose our way.

"A new artistic era is indeed on its way, as you foresaw. Continue to study, do not falter. God will do the rest.

"Everything, especially in art, is theory developed and applied in contact with nature. When I see you again I shall talk to you more honestly about painting than anyone else. I have nothing to hide in art. Nothing but primary force, that is, his temperament, which can carry a person toward the end he should attain.

"Whichever the master you prefer, he must be no more to you than a guide. Another's advice and methods must not cause you to change your own way of feeling.

"Drawing is only the configuration of what you see.

"Michelangelo is a 'constructor', and Raphael an artist who, however great, is always limited by the model. When he wants to become 'reflective', he falls below his great rival."

Kees van Dongen (1877–1968), Dutch painter who settled in Paris in 1899 and exhibited with the Fauves in the 1905 Salon d'Automne.

From Cézanne's letter to Camoin, February 3, 1902.

Quoted from Cézanne's letter to Camoin, September 13, 1903.

From Cézanne's letter to Camoin, January 28, 1902.

Cézanne's letter to Camoin, February 22, 1903.

119

Here I would like to say that Cézanne has the greatest admiration for Monet, and wants people to know as much. For me Fragonard and Renoir are the masters who come most naturally to mind.

Yes, I look to the study of nature to provide all I need.

* * *

M. E. SCHUFFENECKER. In my view, the nineteenth century has had no art; it has had only artists.

Currently, for me, only what is known as Art Nouveau is really interesting and may have a future, because it was created by a race that is strong and self-aware, the Anglo-Saxons.

Impressionism does not need to be revitalized, but completed. Its founding father, its god, was Delacroix. Pissarro, Monet, Manet initiated *plein air*, but they never made complete paintings, an *oeuvre*, in a word. Puvis did, but he is not an Impressionist in the strict sense of the word.

Impressionism is a beautiful, intelligent, logical way forward. It remains since the great Delacroix for a body of work to be produced.

Whistler has a very Anglo-Saxon temperament, dreamy, gentlemanly, deep but limited. Not a single complete picture – several fine portraits, some engaging notations.

Gauguin was a phenomenon, a hostile and disconcerting giant, mainly. He was not able to show what he was capable of, he was too widely hated. But one can conclude from what he did do that he had a quite extraordinary ability to dominate his material. He turned every substance into a work of art; canvas, clay, wood, sheet metal, cloth . . . That man was truly possessed by the daemon of art. But he loved ugliness. He never gave us a glimpse of heaven.

Fantin is the author of pretty poetic sentimentalities, charmingly picturesque pieces. His portraits and still lifes were very popular.

But of these three, only Gauguin seems to have left a following, to have blazed a trail.

Cézanne is the great, raw primitive. His powerful temperament left neither complete pictures nor an *oeuvre*.

The master to whom I myself always turn, the Father, the Initiator, the God, is: Delacroix.

The artist should be reliant only upon himself, upon what is lit within him by nature. But Nature is the necessary setting through which he moves, in which he delights, and finds peace, from which he draws certain elements, even inspiration. But the source of his whole art lies within himself.

* * *

M. GEORGES ROUAULT. . . . You ask me whether the artist must be entirely reliant on nature, or whether he should borrow from her only the means to give expression to a thought which is within him. To my way of thinking, the artist must dominate nature and not be enslaved by her. To let oneself be fully taken over by one's emotion before nature is not to be totally reliant on her, and I am bold enough to believe that the individuality of the artist plays some part in this emotion. . . .

The pioneers of Impressionism took a robust and very healthy stand amidst all manner of jeers, idiotic sniggers and betrayals. But the question of whether the movement can take on new life seems to me very secondary. If new artists emerge who are as moved by the same aspects of things as were the Impressionists, why should they not convey their emotions to us? It is crucial that the lovers of light should be sustained by this "luminous radiance;" but it is no less crucial that such as I, *a bird of night*, an *owl*, should be granted the right to disengage themselves from it. Everyone has to seek to mine the universal treasure from those nuggets which are the purest in his eyes, however modest these may be in the eyes of others. Essentially one must express what one has loved *very earnestly and very wholeheartedly*.

(*Opposite*) Félix Vallotton. *The Five Painters: Vallotton, Bonnard, Vuillard, Cottet, Roussel.* 1903. 56¼ × 73⅝″ (142.8 × 187 cm). Kunstmuseum, Winterthur.

Émile Schuffenecker (1851–1934).

Georges Rouault (1871–1958), a fellow student with Matisse of Gustave Moreau. He exhibited in the 1905 Salon d'Automne.

* * *

M. PAUL SÉRUSIER. Like everything in nature, I believe that art *non fecit saltus*. Like heavenly bodies and ideas, it follows a curve which I visualize in the form of an irregular spiral.

... Impressionism? First we must define it. It would seem, to take it as it were literally, that it was an art where the *moment* would emerge as the main factor, without activity of thought; it would be instantaneous painting. It is clear that neither Claude Monet nor Cézanne proceeded in this fashion. Both worked upon nature for weeks on end. And did Manet do his paintings in an instant? With all artists, the brain is active quite as much as the eyes and the hand.

I think that Impressionism should be understood as a group of very different artists who, each in his own fashion, escaped the tyrannies of the schools and yet did not constitute a school themselves. Their liberation led them back to the true tradition. In this sense, Impressionism had no beginning, so when you ask me if it is over, I would reply that what has no beginning, has no end.

Gauguin used to say: "Do what you want, as long as it isn't dull." And those who heeded him became Impressionists. Indeed, I believe that an Impressionist is someone who doesn't paint like everyone else.

Does not take leaps.

Whistler and Fantin are painters, true artists. But I do not think that they have great influence on living art.

Gauguin? You know, he rescued me, and many others. He broke the bonds which bound us to the École. I myself shall always be grateful to him. It was after meeting him in Brittany while I was still at the Académie Julian that I launched the cry of freedom which rallied Denis, Vuillard, Roussel, Bonnard, Ranson, Ibels and others.

Members of the Nabis.

However, I must acknowledge that Gauguin is not the initiator of the current movement. Led at first by Pissarro, this movement was then put on course again by Cézanne, to whom Gauguin introduced us.

Cézanne was able to free pictorial art of all the mustiness which time had deposited upon it. He proved clearly that imitation is only one means, that the artist's sole aim is to arrange lines and colours on a surface so as to delight the eye and speak to the spirit; in a word, to create a language through purely plastic means, or rather to rediscover the universal language. He is accused of roughness, of dryness; these apparent faults are the outward facets of his power! His thought is so clear in his mind! His desire for expression so imperious! If our time gives birth to any new tradition – as I dare hope it will – it is from Cézanne that it will spring. Then others will come after, clever cooks, and garnish the leftovers with more modern sauces; but Cézanne will provide the basic meat. This is not a new art, but a resurrecting of all art that is solid, pure and *classical.* . . .

Nature provides us only with inert matter. Only the human spirit can arrange it in such a way that it may express its thoughts and feelings by means of correspondences. This is how one arrives at Style, the final aim of all art.

* * *

M. PAUL SIGNAC. It is probably too late to reply to your questions and I deeply regret this, for I would greatly have liked to express all my admiration for Whistler, Fantin and Cézanne, and to have talked briefly to you about that fine painter, Gauguin.

I would also have told you that the master most often in my mind is Turner. It is he who gives me the most cogent lessons concerning that *freedom* towards which I strive.

In my answer to your last question I would have tried to show that the painter must make a choice from among all the elements of beauty and variety which nature offers him, and that a picture where all the lines and colours are carefully thought out will be of a higher order than one suggested by the random and direct copy of a "motif."

In short:

Art cannot take new directions: it is unchangeable and constant. As for *painting*, it is always distinguished by: (1) harmony of line (composition, design); (2) harmony of tone (chiaroscuro); (3) harmony of colour. The masterpiece combines all these qualities: in very fine works, one quality dominates at the expense of the others. As to subject and format, these are matters of literary fashion and social milieu, and are unimportant. A still life by Cézanne, a box lid by Seurat are as beautiful as the Mona Lisa or the two hundred square metres of Tintoretto's *Paradise*.

GEORGE MOORE

REMINISCENCES OF THE IMPRESSIONIST PAINTERS

Monet and Cézanne

1879

Of the originality of these two painters, and of the originality of the Impressionist school, one cannot think too often or too long; there arose suddenly an art in France unlike any other art that had ever been seen in the world before and no country, not even France, is prepared for such surprising innovations as Monet's and Sisley's pictures. Monet especially paid dearly for the gift of his genius, he very nearly starved; there were times when he could not get more than one hundred francs apiece for his pictures, very often no price could be obtained, and Monet went without his dinner. He began by imitating Manet, and Manet ended by imitating Monet. They were great friends. Manet painted Monet and Madame Monet in their garden, and Monet painted Manet and Madame Manet in the same garden; they exchanged pictures, but after a quarrel each returned the other his picture. Monet's picture of Manet and his wife I never saw, but Manet's picture of Monet and Madame Monet belongs to a very wealthy merchant, a Monsieur Pellerin, who has the finest collection of Manet's and Cézanne's in the world. I do not remember ever to have seen Cézanne at the Nouvelle Athènes; he was too rough, too savage a creature, and appeared in Paris only rarely. We used to hear about him –

George Moore (1852–1933), Irish writer and friend of Manet and Whistler. He came to Paris in 1873, initially to study under Cabanel. His Reminiscences *helped to spread the "wild-man" myth of Cézanne.*

(*Left*) The Café de la Nouvelle-Athènes, rue Pigalle (photograph), meeting place of artists and writers in the 1870s and 80s.

(*Below*) Draner. *Le Charivari*, April 23, 1879. *Ex-refusé ci-devant réaliste, antérieurement impressionniste, intentioniste, luministe, actuellement nihiliste* ("Former *refusé* previously realist, impressionist, intentionist, luminist, presently nihilist"). British Library, London.

he used to be met on the outskirts of Paris wandering about the hillsides in jack-boots. As no one took the least interest in his pictures he left them in the fields; when his pictures began to be asked for, his son and daughter used to inquire them out in the cottages, and they used to keep watch in the hedges and collect the sketches he had left behind him. It would be untrue to say that he had no talent, but whereas the intention of Manet and of Monet and of Degas was always to paint, the intention of Cézanne was, I am afraid, never very clear to himself. His work may be described as the anarchy of painting, as art in delirium. It is impossible to deny to this strange being a certain uncouth individuality; uncouth though it be there is life in his pictures, otherwise no one would remember them. I pause to ask myself which I would prefer – one of Millet's conventional, simpering peasants or one of Cézanne's crazy cornfields peopled with violent reapers, reapers from Bedlam. I think that I prefer Cézanne.

GUSTAVE GEFFROY
LA VIE ARTISTIQUE
"Paul Cézanne"
1894

Gustave Geffroy (1855–1926), novelist, art critic and the biographer and friend of Monet who introduced him to Cézanne on November 28, 1894.

For a long time Paul Cézanne has had a singular artistic destiny. He could be defined as a personage at once unknown and celebrated, having but rare contacts with the public and considered as an influence among the uneasy and experimental spirits of painting, known only by certain ones, living in an unsociable isolation, reappearing, disappearing brusquely to the eyes of his intimate friends. From all the ill-known facts of his biography, from his quasi-secret production, from the scarcity of his canvases which do not seem to be submitted to any of the accepted laws of advertising, a kind of peculiar renown has come to him; already remote, a mystery enveloped his being and his work. Those who are in search of the unexpected, who love to discover things not yet seen, used to talk about Cézanne's canvases with knowing airs, supplied information as though they were giving out passwords. Those who were just arriving, impassioned and earnest in the region – new to them – of modern art, the fields under cultivation where from day to day are to be seen shoots blossoming and growing, all the shoots, the wheat and the tares – these latter asked their elders about this phantom-like Cézanne, who lived in this way on the margin of life, without bothering any longer with a role or supporting players. What did his canvases look like? Where were they to be seen? It was replied that there was a portrait at Émile Zola's, two trees at Théodore Duret's, four apples at Paul Alexis', or else that the preceding week a canvas had been seen at Père Tanguy's, the artists' supply dealer on the Rue Clauzel, but that one had to hurry up to find it, for there were always, in the case of the Cézannes, art lovers swift to pounce upon this widely spaced prey. There was talk also of extensive collections, of various canvases in considerable numbers: it would have been necessary, in order to become acquainted with them, to penetrate into the household of M. Choquet [sic] in Paris, or M. Murer in Rouen, or Dr. Gachet at Auvers, near Pontoise.

Actually, the encounters with the paintings of Cézanne were rare in everyday life, since the artist quickly enough gave up putting himself forward and took part only in the first exhibition of the independent group in 1874. So one only caught a glimpse, here and there, of a landscape or a still life, a canvas often unfinished, with parts solid and beautiful, and one kept one's opinion in suspense.

Cézanne had virtually vanished from public view, since he had last shown with the Impressionists in 1874 and 1877, until Vollard's large retrospective in November 1895. From 1899, however, until his death in 1906 he featured in the major annual exhibitions such as the Salon des Indépendants and the Salon d'Automne. This excerpt from the chapter on Cézanne in Volume III of Geffroy's La Vie Artistique, 1892–1903, shows Cézanne in 1894 as "both unknown and famous," a shadowy, almost mythical figure.

Victor Chocquet (1821–91), a customs official with private means, a passionate collector first of Delacroix, and then of Impressionism, particularly the work of Renoir and Cézanne. Eugène Murer (Eugène-Hyacinthe Meunier) (1846–1906), an important collector of Impressionism. Dr. Paul-Ferdinand Gachet (1828–1909), physician and collector, in whose care in Auvers Van Gogh spent the last two months of his life.

(*Above*) Stock. Caricature of Paul Cézanne with two paintings rejected by the Salon Jury of 1870.

(*Left*) Camille Pissarro. *Portrait of Cézanne.* 1874. 29 × 23⅝″ (73 × 60 cm). Collection Robert von Hirsch, Basle.

MAURICE DENIS
L'OCCIDENT
"Cézanne"
September 1907

There is something paradoxical in Cézanne's fame; and it is no easier to explain his fame than to explain the man himself. The case of Cézanne creates two irreconcilable camps: those who love painting, and those who prefer its accessories, literary or otherwise. I know, alas, that it is fashionable to love painting. Discussions on this subject no longer have the passionate seriousness they used to have. Too much admiration is suspect. Snobbery and speculation have involved the general public in painters' disputes, and they take sides according to fashion or self-interest. It is thus that the apotheosis of a great artist has been engineered, with the complicity of a public that is by nature hostile, but which has been cunningly schooled by critics and dealers: a great artist who, for those who love him the most, nonetheless remains a difficult painter.

I have never heard an admirer of Cézanne giving any clear and precise reasons for his admiration; and it is rare even among artists, those who experience his art most directly. I have heard words – quality, essence, importance, interest, classicism, beauty, style.... With Delacroix or

Monet, for example, it is possible to express a reasoned, easily intelligible, concise opinion. But being precise about Cézanne is difficult.

The mystery surrounding the entire life of the master from Aix-en-Provence has contributed much to the obscurity of the commentaries which have further added to his renown. He was a shy man, an independent spirit, a loner. Exclusively concerned with his art, perpetually restless and most usually dissatisfied with himself, he eluded public curiosity until his final years. Even most of those who claimed kinship with his methods failed to understand him. The author of these pages admits that around 1890, at the time of his first visits to Tanguy's shop, he regarded Cézanne as a myth, possibly the pseudonym of an artist engaged in other activities, and that he doubted his existence. Since then he has had the honor of meeting him in Aix, and the remarks he has gathered together, along with those which M. Émile Bernard published in *L'Occident*, may help to throw some light on his aesthetic.

VINCENT VAN GOGH
Letters to Theo
September–October, 1888

My dear Theo,   ARLES
Many thanks for your letter and the 50-franc note which it contained. It isn't cheery news that the pains in your leg have come back – Good Lord – you ought to be able to live in the South too, because I always think that what *we* need is sun and fine weather and a blue sky as the most efficacious cure. The weather here remains fine, and if it was always like this, it would be better than the painters' paradise, it would be absolute Japan. I keep thinking of you and Gauguin and Bernard all the time wherever I go. It is so beautiful, and I so wish you were here.

Enclosed a little sketch of a square size 30 canvas, the starry sky actually painted at night under a gas jet. The sky is greenish-blue, the water royal blue, the ground mauve. The town is blue and violet, the gas is yellow and the reflections are russet-gold down to greenish-bronzes. On the blue-green expanse of sky the Great Bear sparkles green and pink, its discreet pallor contrasts with the harsh gold of the gas.

Two colorful little figures of lovers in the foreground.

Also a sketch of a size 30 canvas representing the house and its surroundings in sulphur-colored sunshine, under a sky of pure cobalt. The subject is frightfully difficult; but that is just why I want to conquer it. It's terrific, these houses, yellow in the sun, and the incomparable freshness of the blue. And everywhere the ground is yellow too. I shall send you a better drawing than this rough improvised sketch out of my head later on.

The house on the left is pink with green shutters, I mean the one in the shadow of the tree. That is the restaurant where I go for dinner every day. My friend the postman lives at the end of the street on the left, between the two railway bridges. The night café I painted is not in the picture, it is to the left of the restaurant.

Milliet thinks this horrible, but I need not tell you that when he says he cannot understand anyone amusing himself doing such a dull grocer's shop, and such stark, stiff houses with no grace whatever, remember that Zola did a certain boulevard at the beginning of *L'Assommoir*, and Flaubert a corner of the Quai de la Villette in the midst of the dog days at the beginning of *Bouvard et Pécuchet*, and neither of them is moldy yet.

And it does me good to do difficult things. That does not prevent me from having a terrible need of – shall I say the word? – of religion. Then I go out at night to paint the stars, and I am always dreaming of a picture like this with a group of living figures of our comrades.

* * *

Julien-François Tanguy (Père Tanguy) (1825–94), color merchant and smallscale art dealer in whose shop in 14 rue Clauzel Impressionist paintings, including Cézannes, could be seen.
Émile Bernard's article on Cézanne, which quoted at length from the artist's letters and his verbatim "opinions," was published in L'Occident *in July 1904. See page 252.*

COLORPLATE 42

The Yellow House, 1888, Rijksmuseum Vincent van Gogh, Amsterdam.

Paul-Eugène Milliet, a second lieutenant in the third regiment of the Zouaves, who met and befriended Van Gogh in June 1888.

Vincent van Gogh. *The Starry Night.*
Sketch in a letter, September 1888. Pen.
Rijksmuseum Vincent van Gogh
Foundation/Van Gogh Museum,
Amsterdam.

My dear Theo,
Enclosed a very, very remarkable letter from Gauguin. Do put it on one
side as a thing of extraordinary importance.

I mean his description of himself, which moves me to the depths of my
soul. I got it along with a letter from Bernard which Gauguin probably
read and perhaps approved of, in which Bernard says once more that he
wants to come here . . . I should not ask anything better, but when it is a
question of several painters living a community life, I stipulate at the
outset that there must be an abbot to keep order, and that would naturally
be Gauguin. That is why I would like Gauguin to be here first . . . As for
me, I want two things, I want to earn back the money which I have
already spent, so as to give it to you, and I want Gauguin to have peace
and quiet in which to produce, and to be able to breathe freely as an artist.
If I can get back the money already spent which you have been lending me
for several years, we shall enlarge our enterprise, and try to found a studio
for a renaissance and not for a decadence. I am pretty sure that we can
count on Gauguin staying with us always, and that neither side will lose.
Only by associating thus, each of us will be more himself, and union is
strength.

By the way, of course I shall not give anything to Gauguin in exchange
for his portrait, because I think that it is sure to be too good, but I shall ask
him to hand it over to us for his first month, or as payment for his fare. . . .

Do you realize that if we get Gauguin we are at the beginning of a very
great thing, which will open a new era for us.

When I left you at the station to go South, very miserable, almost an
invalid and almost a drunkard, I still felt vaguely that we had put our very
heart into our discussions with so many interesting people and artists that
winter, but I hadn't the courage to hope.

After continued efforts on your part and mine, now at last something is
beginning to show on the horizon: Hope.

It does not matter if you stay with the Goupils or not, you have committed yourself to Gauguin body and soul.

So you will be one of the first, or the first dealer-apostle. I can see my
own painting coming to life, and likewise a work among the artists. For if
you try to get money for us, I shall urge every man who comes within my
reach to produce, and I will set them an example myself.

And if we stick to it, all this will help to make something more lasting
than ourselves.

* * *

*The project of "getting Gauguin" to come
to Arles and be the head of a "studio of the
South" was one of deep significance to Van
Gogh. Because of Gauguin's reputation and
authority, it represented the legitimation of
certain qualities in his own painting over
which he suffered profound doubt. "The
studio of the South" would also have meant
the establishment of Impressionism as a
movement on which the value of his own
painting as expression and communication
depended.*

The "Vines" that I have just painted are green, purple and yellow, with violet bunches and branches in black and orange.

On the horizon are some gray willows, and the wine press a long, long way off, with a red roof, and the lilac silhouette of the distant town.

In the vineyard there are little figures of women with red parasols, and other little figures of men working at gathering grapes with their cart.

Over it is a blue sky, and the foreground is of gray gravel. This is a pendant to the garden with the clipped bush and the oleanders.

I think you will prefer these ten canvases to the batch I last sent, and I venture to hope to double the number in the autumn.

Day after day it grows richer and richer. And when the leaves start to fall – I do not know if this happens in the beginning of November here the way it does with us – when all the foliage is yellow, it will be amazing against the blue. Ziem has given us that splendor many a time already. Then a short winter, and after that we shall have got to the orchards in bloom again.

What Gauguin says about "Persian" painting is true. I don't believe that it would shock anybody in the Dieulafoi Museum, one might put it there without any difficulties. But, but, but . . . I myself do not belong to the world of the great, not even to any world at all . . . and . . . I prefer the Greeks and Japanese to the Persians and Egyptians. All the same, I do not mean to say that Gauguin is wrong in working in the Persian style.

But I should have to get used to it.

Paul Gauguin and Camille Pissarro. *Portrait of Gauguin* by Pissarro juxtaposed with *Portrait of Pissarro* by Gauguin. *c.*1879–83. Black chalk and pastel on blue laid paper, 14 × 19¼″ (35.8 × 49.5 cm). Musée du Louvre, Paris (Cabinet des Dessins).

PAUL GAUGUIN
Letter to Émile Bernard
November 1889

My dear Bernard,

What can I say to you now that everything is crumbling around me. Debt is keeping me tied to Le Pouldu, and I have little hope of seeing it sorted out. No news from Van Gogh because he can't be of any help, and from what I suspect, from what Schuff tells me, our affairs are not going very well, because Van Gogh has married, and is at the mercy of the whims of the ménage, which bodes no good for us. So the only person so far who has bothered with me has had to let me drop, and I am not at the point where I am ready to opt out. I've made enquiries about going to Tonkin, but the response is more or less negative for the moment. The people who are sent to the colonies are usually those who've done something silly, dipped into the till, etc. . . . But I'm an Impressionist, i.e. an insurgent . . . it's out of the question. Then I'm building up so much bile, and gall, as a result of this run of bad luck, and it's making me ill, I hardly have the strength to work at present. And work used to make me forget. In the end this isolation, this concentration upon myself, particularly when the main joys of life are elsewhere and inner satisfaction is lacking, cries out in hunger like an empty stomach. In the end this isolation is a delusion in terms of offering happiness, unless one is made of ice and absolutely unfeeling. Despite all my efforts to become so, I am not unfeeling, the old Adam will always out. Like Gauguin the cook, burning his hand in the oven, unable to suppress a cry. But I would pass over all that, what is man in this vast creation, and who am I to complain more than anyone else? But all the same, in this I can unfortunately see the results in other people, and what could help an evil man to put up with the company of others has the opposite effect on me. I am touched by your words "You know how much we love you," strengthened as they are, intentionally or not, by that plural "we." Did you send me that issue on art and criticism? What an idiotic article. But at least idiocy offends no one. Fénéon actually wrote that I was

The exhibition of work Gauguin had organized at the Café Volpini of the "Groupe Impressionniste et Synthétiste" during the summer of 1889 had opened to disappointing reviews and closed without any sales. The following autumn, during which this letter to Bernard was written, his prospects seemed to be at their lowest ebb.

Émile Bernard. *Nightmare.* The portraits are of Schuffenecker, Bernard and Gauguin. *c.*1888. Pencil, $7^{1}/_{8} \times 10^{5}/_{8}$" (18 × 26 cm). Musée du Louvre, Paris (Cabinet des Dessins).

imitating Anquetin, whom I didn't know. It seems that Eve didn't speak pidgin but my God what Language did she speak, she and the Serpent. Thanks for the photograph.

Though it is well arranged in terms of line and effect, your fine group of the Magdalen supported by two women puts too much emphasis on the intimate aspect of the scene for other figures to be able to share equally in the pain. These figures may be necessary to the arrangement of lines, but I would have them rather dazed than suffering. This beautiful image of Mary Magdalen, who by her love did so much for belief in the resurrection, is enough. And, I repeat, you have captured her admirably; I look at her now as at a different Magdalen from the one I knew. Do not be offended by my criticism, for at this moment I feel so bitter that I see nothing clearly.

I embrace you both from the depths of my pain-racked heart.

P. Gauguin.

Félix Fénéon, "L'Autre Groupe Impressionniste," La Cravache, July 6, 1889: see page 173.

Madeleine Bernard, Émile Bernard's sister.

PAUL GAUGUIN

Letter to Odilon Redon
September 1890

LE POULDU

My dear Redon,
Your silence did indeed surprise me, I had judged the man by his Art, then later by himself, and the only explanation I could see was some hiccup in the post. In these circumstances I was doubly pleased to get your letter, and I am happy to learn that you are enjoying the *inner* conditions which make for relative happiness.

The reasons you give for my remaining in Europe flatter me rather than convince me. My mind is made up, and since I have been in Brittany I have made a new decision. Madagascar is still too near the civilized world; I am going to go to Tahiti, where I hope to end my days. I regard my art (for which you express admiration) as the merest seedling, and I hope to cultivate it there for myself alone in its primitive and savage state.

For that I need peace and quiet. I don't care about others' success!

Gauguin is finished here, you will see no more of him. As you see, I am an egoist. In photographs and drawings I shall take with me a small world of comrades who will speak to me every day; of you I have, in my head, the memory of about everything you have done, and also a canvas; seeing it, in my hut on Tahiti, I shall no longer think of death, I promise you, but of eternal life, not death in life, but life in death. In Europe, this death with its serpent's tail may seem quite likely, but in Tahiti it should be seen with roots that sprout again with flowers. I haven't said goodbye to the artists who are in sympathy with me. I remember a passage by Wagner which explains my thoughts:

I believe that the faithful disciples of great art will be crowned with glory; wrapped in celestial array woven of sunbeams, perfumes and melodious chords, they will return once more for all eternity to lose themselves in the bosom of the divine source of all harmony.

So, my dear Redon, we shall meet again.

I don't yet know when I'll be leaving, since the matter I mentioned to you is not yet concluded and I'm in Brittany, waiting, which is making me thoroughly nervous.

My regards to your wife:
Cordially yours,

Paul Gauguin.

This letter was written when Gauguin had abandoned his plan to move to Madagascar and had decided on Tahiti.
Gauguin had proposed the founding of a "studio of the tropics," a plan which Redon had advised him against. Gauguin wrote at around the same time to the Danish painter J. F. Willumsen, "I want to forget all the evils of the past and to die down there [Tahiti] unknown by those here, free to paint without any glory at all for the others . . . A terrible ordeal is in store in Europe for the coming generation: the kingdom of gold. Everything is rotten, men as well as the arts."

(Opposite) Odilon Redon. Self-Portrait. c.1895(?) Crayon, 13⅜ × 8⅞" (34 × 22.5 cm). Netherlands Institute for Art-Historical Documentation, The Hague.

The passage from Wagner is also quoted by Sérusier: see page 99.

Gauguin was waiting on the outcome of an offer made by a Dr. Charlopin, an inventor, to purchase a group of paintings for the total sum of 5,000 francs. This fell through in October.

JORIS-KARL HUYSMANS

AGAINST NATURE

1884

"Lord, how few books there are that are worth reading again!" sighed Des Esseintes . . . There were now only two thin booklets left on the table. . . . He began looking through one of these, comprised of a few pages bound in onager-skin that had been glazed under a hydraulic press, dappled in water-colour with silver clouds, and provided with end-papers of old lampas, the floral pattern of which, now rather dim with age, had that faded charm which Mallarmé extolled in a truly delightful poem.

These pages, nine in all, had been taken out of unique copies of the first two *Parnasses*, printed on parchment, and preceded by a title-page bearing the words: *Quelques vers de Mallarmé*, executed by a remarkable calligrapher in uncial letters, coloured and picked out, like those in ancient manuscripts, with specks of gold.

Among the eleven pieces brought together between these covers, a few, *Les Fenêtres*, *L'Épilogue*, and *Azur*, he found extremely attractive, but there was one in particular, a fragment of *Hérodiade*, that seemed to lay a magic spell on him at certain times.

Often of an evening, sitting in the dim light his lamp shed over the silent room, he had imagined he felt her brush past him – that same Herodias who in Gustave Moreau's picture had withdrawn into the advancing shadows, so that nothing could be seen but the vague shape of a white statue in the midst of a feebly glowing brazier of jewels.

The darkness hid the blood, dimmed the bright colours and gleaming gold, enveloped the far corners of the temple in gloom, concealed the minor actors in the criminal drama where they stood wrapped in their dark garments, and, sparing only the white patches in the water-colour, drew the woman from the scabbard of her jewels and emphasized her nakedness.

His eyes were irresistibly drawn towards her, following the familiar outlines of her body until she came to life again before him, bringing to his lips those sweet, strange words that Mallarmé puts into her mouth:

> . . . . *O miroir!*
> *Eau froide par l'ennui dans ton cadre gelée*
> *Que de fois et pendant les heures, désolée*
> *Des songes et cherchant mes souvenirs qui sont*
> *Comme des feuilles sous ta glace au trou profond,*
> *Je m'apparus en toi comme une ombre lointaine,*
> *Mais, horreur! des soirs, dans ta sévère fontaine,*
> *J'ai de mon rêve épars connu la nudité!*

He loved these verses as he loved all the works of this poet who, in an age of universal suffrage and a time of commercial greed, lived outside the world of letters, sheltered from the raging folly all around him by his lofty scorn; taking pleasure, far from society, in the caprices of the mind and the visions of his brain; refining upon thoughts that were already subtle enough, grafting Byzantine niceties on them, perpetuating them in deductions that were barely hinted at and loosely linked by an imperceptible thread.

Huysmans' novel established Des Esseintes, its hero, as the prototype of the "decadent" aesthete attempting to create an artificial paradise full of strange thrills as a bulwark againt modern materialism. Mallarmé's poem "Prose pour Des Esseintes", published in La Revue Indépendante *in January 1885, was a subtle and ironical reply to Huysmans. This poem, in its turn, furnished the material for the hilarious satires on Mallarmé by "Adoré Floupette,"* Les Déliquescences, *published in May 1885 (see page 134).*

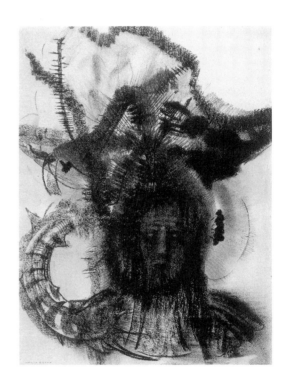

Odilon Redon. *Chimera.* 1902. Charcoal, $21^5/_8 \times 15^1/_4''$ (54.5 × 39 cm). Musée du Louvre, Paris (Cabinet des Dessins).

"Oh mirror! cold water frozen by boredom within your frame, how many times, for hours on end, saddened by dreams and searching for my memories, which are like dead leaves in the deep hole beneath your glassy surface, have I seen myself in you as a distant ghost! But, oh horror! on certain evenings, in your cruel pool, I have recognized the bareness of my disordered dream!"

These precious, interwoven ideas he knotted together with an adhesive style, a unique, hermetic language, full of contracted phrases, elliptical constructions, audacious tropes.

Sensitive to the remotest affinities, he would often use a term that by analogy suggested at once form, scent, colour, quality, and brilliance, to indicate a creature or thing to which he would have had to attach a host of different epithets in order to bring out all its various aspects and qualities, if it had merely been referred to by its technical name. By this means he managed to do away with the formal statement of a comparison that the reader's mind made by itself as soon as it had understood the symbol, and he avoided dispersing the reader's attention over all the several qualities that a row of adjectives would have presented one by one, concentrating it instead on a single word, a single entity, producing, as in the case of a picture, a unique and comprehensive impression, an overall view.

* * *

Of all forms of literature, the prose poem was Des Esseintes' favourite. Handled by an alchemist of genius it should, he maintained, contain within its small compass and in concentrated form the substance of a novel, while dispensing with the latter's long-winded analyses and super-fluous descriptions. Many were the times that Des Esseintes had pondered over the fascinating problem of writing a novel concentrated in a few sentences and yet comprising the cohobated juice of the hundreds of pages always taken up in describing the setting, drawing the characters, and piling up useful observations and incidental details. The words chosen for a work of this sort would be so unalterable that they would take the place of all the others; every adjective would be sited with such ingenuity and

Gustave Moreau. Study for *Chimera.* *c.*1880. Pencil. Musée Gustave Moreau, Paris.

Photograph of Joris-Karl Huysmans in his study. Bibliothèque Nationale, Paris (Cabinet des Estampes).

133

finality that it could never be legally evicted, and would open up such wide vistas that the reader could muse on its meaning, at once precise and multiple, for weeks on end, and also ascertain the present, reconstruct the past, and divine the future of the characters in the light of this one epithet.

The novel, thus conceived, thus condensed in a page or two, would become an intellectual communion between a hieratic writer and an ideal reader, a spiritual collaboration between a dozen persons of superior intelligence scattered across the world, an aesthetic treat available to none but the most discerning.

In short, the prose poem represented in Des Esseintes' eyes the dry juice, the osmazome of literature, the essential oil of art.

This succulent extract concentrated in a single drop could already be found in Baudelaire, and also in those poems of Mallarmé's that he savoured with such rare delight.

When he had closed his anthology, the last book in his library, Des Esseintes told himself that in all probability he would never add another to his collection.

The truth of the matter was that the decadence of French literature, a literature attacked by organic diseases, weakened by intellectual senility, exhausted by syntactical excesses, sensitive only to the curious whims that excite the sick, and yet eager to express itself completely in its last hours, determined to make up for all the pleasures it had missed, afflicted on its death-bed with a desire to leave behind the subtlest memories of suffering, had been embodied in Mallarmé in the most consummate and exquisite fashion.

HENRI BEAUCLAIR AND GABRIEL VICAIRE
LES DÉLIQUESCENCES
"The Life of Adoré Floupette"
1885

My old friend and classmate, Adoré Floupette, a decadent poet, came round the other day to make me an unusual proposal. Namely, to write a preface to his astounding collection of verses, *Les Déliquescences*. At first I objected strenuously. "Oh, Adoré, what an idea. Me, a mere pharmacist's assistant from rue des Canettes, a *potard*, as they say, write an introduction for a man like you! They will have a good laugh over this in the *Panier Fleuri*." Unfortunately, Adoré stood his ground. Quite rightly, he despises the public profoundly. A pack of fools, as he says gleefully when we're alone. Yet this contempt is not without a touch of pity. He is a good fellow at heart; he feels that we should do something for those who, unlike ourselves, have not had the good fortune to be introduced to the great Arcana. Ninnies, maybe, but it is not their fault. They do not *know*; that is all. Adoré would not dream of stooping to spreading enlightenment himself; one cannot really expect him to. He floats on high, that is his function, we should not ask for more.

* * *

After our initial effusions, we sat down side by side, on a faded old sofa that graced my humble lodgings, and the questions came thick and fast. What a good-hearted chap Adoré is! As a poet, an artist, he might so easily despise ordinary folk like us, yet he forgets no one. He wanted to know what had happened to M. Tourniret the notary and how little Marguerite Clapot, the daughter of the sacristan at Orgelet, was getting on, and

In May 1885 the radical publisher Léon Vanier issued a small collection of poems, Les Déliquescences: Poèmes Décadents d'Adoré Floupette avec sa Vie par Marius Tapora, *purporting to be by a previously little-known Symbolist poet, Adoré Floupette, introduced by a "friend of the poet's," a pharmacist, Marius Tapora, with a short biography of the poet. The introduction gradually reveals that Floupette's outlook on life is as bizarre as that of Huysmans' personification of decadence in* À Rebours: Des Esseintes *and his poems display the same strangeness of vocabulary and convoluted syntax as those of Mallarmé. In fact, Floupette declares his masters to be poets whose names, "Bleucoton" (blue cotton) and "Arsenal," bear a punning resemblance to Verlaine (green wool) and Mallarmé. The actual authors of the satire were the poets Henri Beauclair and Gabriel Vicaire. The book was a sell-out; reviews fanned the flames of dispute surrounding the ethos of "decadence" which was subsequently defined (for example by Paul Bourde in his article "Les Décadents" in* Le Temps, August 6, 1885) *as a literature displaying the same perverted mysticism and obscurantism as Adoré Floupette (adored weathervane) himself. This in turn provoked the poets Jean Moréas and Gustave Kahn to rush to the defence, with more precise definitions – see Moréas: "Un Manifeste Littéraire, Le Symbolisme,"* Le Figaro Littéraire, September 18, 1886 (page 148), *and Gustave Kahn: "Réponse des Symbolistes,"* L'Événement, September 28, 1886 (page 151).

COLORPLATE 38. Paul Gauguin. *Nirvana (Portrait of Meyer de Haan). c.*1890.
Gouache on silk, 8½ × 11¼″ (22 × 28.5 cm).
Wadsworth Atheneum, Hartford, Conn. (Ella Gallup Sumner and Mary Catlin Sumner Collection).

COLORPLATE 39. Edvard Munch. *Melancholia (The Yellow Boat: Jealousy)*. 1895.
25 × 37¾″ (64 × 96 cm). Nasjonalgalleriet, Oslo.

COLORPLATE 40. Pierre Bonnard. *Interior with Woman in Wicker Chair.* 1920.
28³⁄₈ × 20¹⁄₈″ (72.1 × 51.1 cm). Statens Konstmuseer, Stockholm.

COLORPLATE 41. Vincent van Gogh. *Still Life: Vase with Fourteen Sunflowers*. Arles, January 1889.
39½ × 30″ (100 × 76 cm). Seiji Togo Memorial Yasuda Kasai Museum of Art, Tokyo.

COLORPLATE 42. Vincent van Gogh. *Starry Night over the Rhône*. 1888. 28¾ × 36¼″ (72.5 × 92 cm). Collection Mr and Mrs R. Kahn-Sriber (on loan to the Musée d'Orsay, Paris).

COLORPLATE 43. Paul Gauguin. *The Little Dreamer*. 1881. 23¼ × 28⅝″ (59.5 × 73.5 cm). Ordrupgaard Collection, Copenhagen.

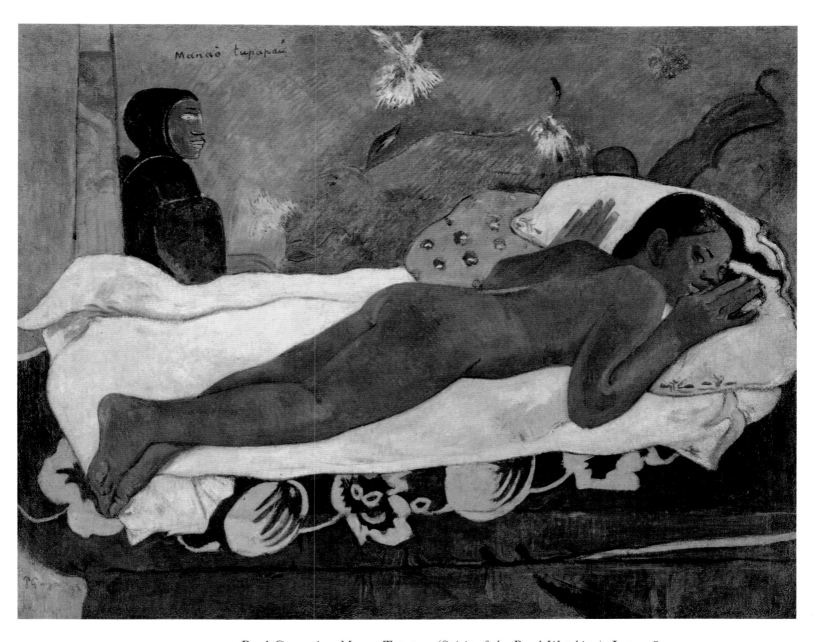

COLORPLATE 44. Paul Gauguin. *Manao Tupapau (Spirit of the Dead Watching)*. Late 1892.
28½ × 36⅜" (72.5 × 92.5 cm).
Albright-Knox Art Gallery, Buffalo, N.Y. (A. Conger Goodyear Collection, 1965).

COLORPLATE 45. Edvard Munch. *Self-Portrait with Cigarette*. 1895. 43½ × 33½″ (110.5 × 85.5 cm).
Nasjonalgalleriet, Oslo.

whether the Trouillet family from Lons was still flourishing, etc., etc. At last I asked: "What about your poetry?" "It's going from strength to strength," he replied. "I mustn't grumble." "How is Zola?" – "Pooh," he replied with a striking pout, "very vieux jeu." "And Hugo?" "In the grave, like his own burgraves." "Coppée?" "Thoroughly bourgeois." I do not know why, but these words dismayed me. I was surprised, and I showed as much. This was a mistake, for Adoré noticed; but he continued with his usual goodness: "My dear fellow, you have just arrived from the provinces; you do not know the score. Don't worry, we'll educate you." "Well, what about the Parnassians?" "*So* old hat." – "Rustic poetry?" – "Just about fit for the Félibres." – "And naturalism?" – "Ho hum. No dreams, no hereafter; mere mechanical warbling." By now I was worried; unthinkingly, I exclaimed: "So what is left?" He fixed me with his gaze and, in a grave voice that trembled a little, he proclaimed: "What is left is the *Symbol*."

Victor Hugo (1802–85), Romantic poet. "Burgrave": an "old fossil." François Coppée (1842–1908), poet known for his popular treatment of the life of the poor.

Les Félibres: a group of poets formed in 1854 to revive Provençal language and culture.

Edvard Munch. *Portrait of Stéphane Mallarmé.* 1896. Lithograph. Munch Museum, Oslo.

I now understand these words, or at least I think I do, for I may as well admit that I am not entirely certain; but at that time they were Greek to me. Adoré probably read the bewilderment in my eyes, and giving the hearty laugh of a son of Lons-le-Saulnier: "Fiddlesticks," said he, "it is not as abstruse as you imagine. All will soon be made plain, you'll see. But this evening I'm taking you to the *Panier Fleuri*! You shall hear the *Poets*." Thereupon he left me, having, apparently, to finish a sonnet which was to have three meanings: one for society people, one for journalists and a third, hideously obscene, for the initiate. The *ne plus ultra*, as you know.

Hear the Poets! What an adventure! All day the thought obsessed me and when, around half-past seven, after a modest meal chez Petiot, Floupette came to pick me up to introduce me to his coterie, my heart was beating hard. Yet the café we entered, the *Panier Fleuri*, was utterly unassuming, as though unaware of the glorious reputations of those it was accommodating, and I confess that for my part I had imagined them as more imposing. But I soon reflected that true talent is modest and, like the violet, reveals itself only by its scent. Moreover, "We're in luck," said Adoré as we entered; "they're all here." And indeed, nonchalantly lounging on the seats at the end of the room, several young persons of the most agreeable appearance were engaged in lively discussion. They were the flower of the new Parnassus, MM. d'Estoc, Bornibus, Flambergeot, Carapatidès and Caraboul; amongst them, adding to the charm of the gathering, were two or three persons of the opposite sex, still very alluring, though a little timeworn. However, as their role in the general conversation was limited to repeating: "You'd like me to have a chartreuse, wouldn't you, old chap?" or "Aristide, a glass of beer," from time to time, I shall be forgiven, I hope, if I say little about them.

Meanwhile, the introductions concluded, the one who struck me as the oldest of these gentlemen, though perhaps not yet thirty – a bald little man, fashionably attired, a monocle set firmly in his eye and a slight pointed beard in the manner of Henri III – rose and, acknowledging me with an infinitely gracious inclination of the head, said: "Sir, you can scarcely imagine my pleasure upon making your acquaintance. My friend and brother in Jesus Christ, Adoré Floupette, has spoken to me of you in the most flattering terms."

While I was thanking him as best I could, touched to the bottom of my heart, he added: "Are you a poet?" I blushed and replied that I was but a hapless pharmacist's assistant, quite unworthy of the honor of such company. "A pharmacist!" he exclaimed with an air of joyful surprise, as though this revelation had plunged him into ravishment, "a pharmacist! Then you *are* a poet. Since Haussmann's asinine demolitions, it is only the pharmacies, and the omnibuses, which continue to bring a little charm and poetry into our Paris streets. Your multicolored bottles are the true stars of the modernist firmament. I myself am but a dilettante, a society man who writes verse; I claim all your indulgence."

Beside us, discussion was of the liveliest. Floupette was treating the company to some *ternaires* he had composed over dinner, since the famous symbolic sonnet had clearly not come up to scratch. Moreover he recited admirably, his voice carrying throughout the estaminet. I recall the following tercet:

Georges Eugène Haussmann: city planner under Napoleon III whose new "grands boulevards" changed the face of Paris from the late 1850s through the 60s.

Je voudrais être un gaga	["Would that I were an old fogey
Et que mon coeur naviguât	And that my heart might float
Sur la fleur du seringa	Upon the flower of the mock-orange"]

"Old fogey!" exclaimed one of the ladies who had hitherto kept her own counsel, "my poor friend, you already are." The downright impropriety of this remark shocked me. Hush hush, they murmured on all sides, and the offender, with no further care for what was going on around her, fell back into deep contemplation of a Sherry-Gobler.

"I think 'old fogey' is fine," said Caraboul, "though I'm a little perturbed by the 't' of 'naviguât'."

"Oh, but why?" asked Floupette. "Bleucoton had no qualms about using it in similar circumstances." He quoted examples.

Bleucoton was an undisputed authority. All bowed before him.

Floupette continued:

Je voudrais que mon coeur fût	["Would that my heart were
Aussi roide qu'un affût,	As unyielding as a gun carriage,
Aussi rempli qu'un vieux fût.	As full as an old cask"]

"Oh come now, Floupette," exclaimed my first interlocutor, "*fût, affût,* what horrible words! No sensitive soul could fail to be shocked by them. Your words lack all subtlety, all fantasy, all gleam of paradise. If we are Poets at all, it is because we deliver the impossible, express the ineffable." Then gradually becoming more heated, for he is naturally eloquent and fond of the sound of his own voice: "The dream, the dream! My friends, let us take ship for dreamland! The Church, our mother, teaches that to dream is to pray. Lost in ecstasy, the female saints were poetesses, the poet was a seer. Today, brutal denial is everywhere; the man of action is a savage. But we, refined by life and thought – if reason keeps us from belief, let us at least grant ourselves the illusion of faith through dreams!"

He fell silent and sighed deeply. Now Bornibus, who had been showing increasing signs of agitation throughout this speech, burst out: "Floupette, I'm sorry to say this, but you stole your 'mock-orange' from me. You should reread my *Foul Purity*."

"Well," said Floupette good-humouredly, "accept my *Cyclamen* and my *Oegypans* in fair exchange. You know I have a considerable stock of them and, between ourselves, I suspect you of having dipped into my reserve." Everyone began to laugh, but Bornibus took no part in the general hilarity, and as he was leaving the café we heard him still murmuring "Mock-orange indeed," in a plaintive voice.

* * *

"Nonetheless," exclaimed Carapatidès, a burly fellow built like Hercules, with powerful shoulders, "we must acknowledge that Roman decadence did know a thing or two about love. By larding it with perverse inventions and satanic conceits, it managed to make love positively piquant. Oh decadence, long live decadence! Love is the flower of an evil spell that grows on tombs, a heady flower, with troubling scents . . ."

"Streaked with green," slipped in the young Flambergeot.

"Yes, streaked and marbled with the whole subtly delicious range of organic decomposition; its chalice is swollen with poisonous juices, exquisitely desirable, for he who inhales it, dies. Find me a flower like that in the countryside; not even all the artifice of all our deeply corrupt civilization could produce one like it; the plants of nature are dull and callow. Oh – health!

"What could be more sickening! If there are any among you who might be gladdened by the buxom charms of a dairy maid, I pity you with all my heart. Speak to me of a lovely bloodless face, fringed with long hair, spangled with gold, and eyes brightened by black pencil, lips of purple or of vermilion, cut in two by a broad sabre slash; show me the languid charms of a soft body, bound by triple wrappings like a mummified Cleopatra twelve times steeped in aromatic herbs. Such is the eternal sorceress, the true daughter of the devil."

"The devil, who is talking of the devil?" enquired a new arrival whose mysterious serpentine gait had something vaguely ecclesiastical about it. "I do not believe in God but I do believe in the devil; the devil is my master; let us not speak ill of him!"

"Oh, we wouldn't dream of doing so," said Carapatidès. "We know too much about his charming manners. He is a real gentleman, and damned to all eternity to boot, which makes him interesting."

Thereupon, as the beermats, piled high upon each other, were beginning to form a tall leaning tower, the conversation became increasingly heated and each one had his say. Eyes rolling fearfully, one of them, of ghoulish inclination, claimed that a cemetery, at twilight, would make an admirable setting for a love idyll and that nothing rivalled a death's head for sheer good company. Another praised the *Imitation of Christ* and admitted that he preferred it even to the *Justine* of the divine Marquis. A third became roundly hysterical. Altogether they made a fine racket, which would doubtless have continued and redoubled, had closing-time not arrived, so that we had to take leave of my new friends. While the waiters put up a scaffold of rush chairs on the marble tables, cordial handshakes were exchanged. Each one went off, some with their women, others alone; I found myself accompanied by Floupette, who was clinging to me desperately. He was very worked up: he has never had a strong head, and I must admit that I myself was somewhat befuddled. The fine things I had just heard were spiralling around in my brain as if on some demonic whirligig. I was finding it difficult to regain my composure, so necessary to a herbalist. Meanwhile Adoré was trotting at my side, zigzagging a little and sometimes pulling me to a halt to shout thunderously in my ear: "Well, what do you say? First-rate, wasn't it? Never fear, I'll complete your education for you. Perversity, my dear Tapora, let us be perverse." I promised him I would, to calm him down, and, as we arrived at his lodgings, he begged me in a low voice not to make a noise on the stairs, as this was a respectable establishment. Such an injunction, coming at such a moment from such a man, struck me as unworthy; however, I complied with it.

Adoré's room, which was on the fifth floor, was not distinguished by any particular luxury, but everything seemed arranged in a most orderly fashion. Here and there Japanese prints were pinned to the wall. The mirror reflected a magnificent drawing by the great artist Pancrace Buret: a gigantic spider with a bouquet of eucalyptus flowers at the end of each long leg, its body consisting of one enormous, fearfully meditative eye, the very sight of which made one shudder; another symbol, no doubt. I put Adoré to bed for he was incapable of undressing himself; seeing him calmer now, I made as if to tiptoe out, but he seized me by the arm: "No, don't go yet; I need to talk to you. What you heard just now is nothing! Your thanks, o happy pharmacist – for you I shall lift the veils of Isis." Then, half-sober now, with a volubility which I had never suspected, he began to unfold what he called the *Great Mystery*. It was not enough to find a new source of inspiration, at a time when imagination seemed to have run dry, when faith was dying, when all was base and vulgar. This fleeting inspiration, these dream blossoms, these elusive nuances, more varied than those of an infinite rainbow, had to be given lasting form. And the French language was decidedly too poor for that. Our ancestors had made do with it, but they were blinkered spirits, whose visions were modest and uninteresting – good folk, blameless but unsophisticated, who loved jam and never thought to put a pinch of cayenne pepper into the patriarchal soup. Whereas our delicious modern corruption, our exquisite disordering of the soul, must be couched in language that is sweetly neurotic. The forms used by Corneille, by the good La Fontaine, Lamartine and Victor Hugo were unsuitably innocent. Hysterics on paper, that was what modern writing was! Sometimes the sentence would flame and crackle in a great blaze, you could hear its joints creak; at others, with the unconscious charm of a *grande dame* who has returned to her childhood, deliquescent, a trifle gamey, it would let itself go, crumple, begin to fall apart, and nothing was sweeter than these dangling flakes of style. Sometimes, as though alarmed by some wind of fear blowing through the forest of things, she would start, or bristle.

"Words are as jumpy as hens," as Bleucoton put it.

Here Floupette sat bolt upright on his bed and began speaking urgently:

The Imitation of Christ, *devotional treatise by Thomas à Kempis (c. 1380–1471).*
Justine, ou les malheurs de la vertu *(1791) by the Marquis Donatien-Alphonse-François de Sade (1740–1814).*
Pierre Corneille *(1606–84); Jean de La Fontaine (1621–95); Alphonse de Lamartine (1790–1869).*

"Les mots ont peur comme les poules": compare "il pleure dans mon coeur" ["weeping in my heart"] (Verlaine).

"Do you know, *potard*, what words are? You think they are mere combinations of letters. Wrong! Words are as alive as you are, more so indeed; they walk, they have legs like little boats; there are as many words as there are colours; there are green ones, yellow and red ones like the jars in your shop; some are the colour dreamed of by the seraphim, and which pharmacists know nothing of. When you utter the word RANUNCULUS, is your soul not filled with all the tender softness of an autumn evening? People talk about dark cigars. What an absurdity! As though cigars were not the very embodiment of blondness. Campanula is pink, an innocent pink; triumph, blood-red; adolescence, pale blue; mercy, deep blue. Nor is that all: words sing, murmur, whisper, lap, coo, grate, twinkle; they may express the sigh of water on moss, the glaucous song of the sea, the basso profondo of the storm, the eerie howling of wolves in the wood . . . ."

Here there was a sharp rap on the dividing wall behind which I had thought I heard a faint drumming for some time now. "Monsieur," said a hoarse voice, "will you be good enough to let me get some sleep? It's four in the morning, and I must get up at six. Tomorrow, you may depend upon it, I shall inform the landlord."

Paul Gauguin. *Soyez Mystérieuses* ("Be Mysterious"). 1890. Painted wood relief, 29 × 37½″ (73 × 95 cm). Musée d'Orsay, Paris.

Compare Rimbaud: "A noir, E blanc, I rouge, U vert, O bleu: voyelles" [A black, E white, I red, U green, O blue: vowels"].

Paul Gauguin. *Soyez Symboliste* ("Be Symbolist"). Caricature portrait of himself with Jean Moréas, from *La Plume*. 1891. Pen, brush, ink, 13¼ × 15¾" (34 × 40 cm). Bibliothèque Nationale, Paris.

JEAN MORÉAS

LE FIGARO LITTÉRAIRE

"A Literary Manifesto: Symbolism"

September 18, 1886

For two years now, the Parisian press has been much concerned with a school of poets and prose-writers known as the 'decadents'. M. Jean Moréas, the narrator of *Thé chez Miranda* (in collaboration with M. Paul Adam, the author of *Soi*), the poet of *Les Syrtes* and *Les Cantilènes* and one of the most talked of among these revolutionaries, . . . has formulated the basic principles of the new artistic phenomenon for the readers of the Supplement, at our request.

SYMBOLISM

Like all the arts, literature moves forward: it develops in a cyclical fashion, with strictly determined phases further complicated by modifications brought about by the march of time and upheavals in various milieus. It would be superfluous to add that each new phase of development in art corresponds closely to the senile decrepitude, the ineluctable end of the school immediately preceding it. Two examples will suffice: Ronsard triumphed over the inadequacies of the last imitators of Marot, and Romanticism unfurled its oriflamme over the classical debris ill-defended by Baour Lormian and Étienne de Jouy. For every artistic phenomenon is fated to become enfeebled and exhausted; endlessly copied and imitated, what was originally full of sap and freshness dries up and shrivels; what was once spontaneous becomes conventional and commonplace.

Thus Romanticism, after having sounded the tumultuous tocsins of revolt, having had its days of glory and of battle, lost some of its power and charm, renounced its heroic stance, became orderly, sceptical and full of good sense; it sought in vain for rebirth through the honorable and insignificant endeavors of the Parnassians, then finally, like a monarch in his

Jean Moréas (1856–1910), poet who, in his article "Les Décadents" in XIX Siècle, *August 11, 1885, introduced the term "Symbolist" to describe the new literary movement, and designated the first "Symbolists" as Mallarmé, Verlaine and himself. This 1886 "manifesto" had the polemical purpose of presenting, to a wider audience, the aims and principles of the movement which had been gradually taking shape in a series of little magazines. Much public debate in the national newspapers ensued, including a refutation by Anatole France (1844–1924), a leading member of the literary establishment (* Le Temps, *September 26, 1886).*

Paul Adam (1862–1920), a disciple of Zola turned Symbolist and the author of Soi *(1886) and* Le Thé Chez Miranda *(1886). Moréas:* Les Syrtes *(1884),* Les Cantilènes *(1886).*

Pierre de Ronsard (1524/5–85), Renaissance poet who established the dominance of the twelve-syllable line, the Alexandrine. Clément Marot (1496–1544), early Renaissance poet using ballade *and* rondeau *forms. Pierre-François Marie Baour-Lormian (1770–1854).*

second childhood, it allowed itself to be deposed by naturalism, whose only true value was one of a legitimate but ill-conceived protest against the vapidity of several novelists who were fashionable at the time.

Some new artistic manifestation was thus to be expected; it was necessary, inevitable. Long in the making, this manifestation has just emerged into the public view. And all the bland witticisms of our journalistic jesters, all the puzzlement of the critics, all the ill-humor of the public, rudely awakened from its sheeplike indolence, are so many tributes to the vitality of the current development in French literature, a development which harassed judges, through some inexplicable paradox, have dubbed decadence. But it should be noted that decadent literatures are by nature essentially thick-skinned, long-winded, timorous and servile: all the tragedies of Voltaire, for example, are tarred with the brush of decadence. And what objections could be made, what objections are made, to the new school? Its abuse of ostentation, the strangeness of its metaphors, a new vocabulary where harmonies are combined with colors and lines: a characteristic of every renaissance.

Voltaire (François-Marie Arouet) (1694–1778).

We have already suggested the term *Symbolism* as the only one capable of aptly designating the current tendency of the creative spirit in art. This term may stand.

As we said at the beginning of this article, developments in art have a highly complex cyclical nature; thus, accurately to chart the exact ancestry of the new school, we would have to go back to certain poems by Alfred de Vigny, to Shakespeare, to the mystics, and further still. A whole volume of commentary would be required; let us therefore say that Charles Baudelaire is to be considered as the true precursor of the current movement; M. Stéphane Mallarmé gave it its sense of mystery, and of the ineffable; in its honor M. Paul Verlaine broke the cruel shackles of the verse which M. Théodore de Banville had previously weakened. However, the *Supreme Enchantment* has not yet been accomplished: our newcomers will have to labor doggedly and jealously.

Alfred de Vigny (1797–1863), Romantic poet.

Théodore de Banville (1823–91), Parnassian poet.

The enemy of instruction, declamation, false sensibility and objective description, symbolist poetry aims: to clothe the Idea in a sensible form which, nonetheless, is not an end in itself, but which, while serving to express the Idea, remains subject to it. The Idea, in its turn, must not allow itself to be stripped of the sumptuous rayment of external analogies; for the essential character of symbolist art lies in stopping short of the conception of the Idea itself. Thus Symbolism will never depict the sights of nature, human actions or any concrete phenomenon as such: they are palpable appearances intended to suggest their esoteric affinities with primordial Ideas.

It is no surprise that such an aesthetic has been made the target for accusations of obscurity by certain readers who are wide of the mark. What can one expect? Were not Pindar's *Pythian Odes*, Shakespeare's *Hamlet*, Dante's *La Vita Nuova*, Goethe's *Faust Part II*, Flaubert's *Temptation of St Antony*, also taxed with ambiguity?

For the exact translation of the desired synthesis, symbolism requires an archetypal and complex style: a virgin terminology, firmly-planted phrases alternating with softly flowing ones, meaningful pleonasms, mysterious ellipses, suspended anacoluthia, all manner of daring and manifold tropes; in a word, the good language – rooted and modernized – the good and luxuriant and lively French language as it was before Vaugelas and Boileau-Despréaux and their like, the language of François Rabelais and Philippe de Commines, Villon, Rutebeuf and so many other unfettered writers, who wielded it with all the accuracy of the Thracian archers with their sinuous arrows.

Vaugelas, critic and grammarian: Remarques sur la langue française (1647). Nicolas Boileau ("Despréaux") (1636–1711), writer whose L'Art Poétique (1674) defined classical rules of poetry. François Rabelais (1490–1553). Philippe de Commynes (c. 1445–1511), French medieval historian; François Villon (1431–63?), French medieval lyric poet; Rutebeuf (fl. 1250–85), French medieval poet; Stendhal (Henri Beyle) (1783–1842); Honoré de Balzac (1799–1850); Gustave Flaubert (1821–80).

Rhythm: the old metrics refurbished; expertly ordered disorder; rhymes as sparkling and emphatic as a golden breastplate, together with rhymes that are abstrusely fluid; the Alexandrine with varied and movable caesuras; the use of certain uneven numbers of syllables.

* * *

Odilon Redon. *The Eye like a Strange Balloon mounts toward Infinity*. Plate I from *À Edgar Poë*. 1882. Lithograph, printed in black, 10¼ × 7¹¹/₁₆″ (26 × 19.5 cm). Museum of Modern Art, New York (Gift of Peter H. Deitsch).

Prose – novels, novellas, short stories, fantasies – develops in a similar way to poetry. Here apparently heterogeneous elements are brought together: Stendhal contributes a pellucid grasp of psychology, Balzac an intemperate vision, Flaubert sentences full of sinuous, rhythmical cadence, M. Edmond de Goncourt an evocative sense of impressionistic modernity.

The conception of the symbolist novel is polymorphous: sometimes a single character will move through settings distorted by his own hallucinations, or his temperament; in this distortion lies the only *reality*. Mechanically propelled beings, with cloudy outlines, weave to and fro around this single character: they are mere pretexts for his sensations and conjectures. He himself is a tragic or comic mask, at the same time perfectly human as well as rational. Sometimes, superficially affected by the sum of the images that surround them, crowds are borne, now jostling, now motionless, towards actions which remain for ever incomplete. Sometimes, individual *desires* become apparent; they attract each other, bond together, become generalized for an aim which, achieved or otherwise, disperses them once more into their original elements. Sometimes mythical phantasma are conjured up, from the ancient Demagorgon to Belial, from the Kabyres to the Nigromans, and appear lavishly decked out on Caliban's rock or in Titania's grove, to the mixolydian modes of barbitons and octochords.

In this way, disdainful of the puerile Method of Naturalism – though Zola was saved by his wonderful writer's instinct – the symbolist novel will be built upon *subjective distortion*, armed with this axiom: that art may use the *objective* merely as an extremely meagre starting-point.

GUSTAVE KAHN
L'ÉVÉNEMENT
"Reply of the Symbolists"
September 28, 1886

One of the leaders of the Symbolist school has sent us the following article, which we are publishing here in all impartiality.

THE SYMBOLISTS' REPLY

An article by M. Jean Moréas, which recently appeared in *Le Figaro*, has aroused a trail of irrelevant words and idle comments concerning the writers disqualified by the soubriquet of decadents. Although all labels are empty, we feel compelled, for the exact information of those interested, to remind them that *decadent* is pronounced *symbolist*. We would also like to say that some, lacking any connection with ourselves, any link, however remote, with our aims, are picking up this word *decadent*, beating the drum and attempting a surreptitious tag-along, marvellously assisted by the little tactic unveiled here:

The silence that had descended upon *La Vogue* was broken by discussion of the décor for *Le Thé chez Miranda* and by aggressive but documentary notes appearing in *L'Événement* under the heading *Notes parisiennes*.

The article by Jean Moréas put forward the general aims of the school quite clearly. Nonetheless, *Le Temps*, *Le Gaulois* and *La Justice* etc. put on a show of knowing nothing of the published novels and poems, then proceeded to concern themselves with very young writers, as yet unformed, and maliciously described as clustering around the name of Paul Verlaine.

Quoting a line from Rimbaud, wrenching it unhappily from its context and, in complete ignorance of the proven scientific facts which legitimized the special vision experienced by the poet of *Les Illuminations*, they sniggered unrestrainedly. They collected together everything in hack journalism which was unclear, or superfluous, an aggravation of silence. Which obliges us to stand up and be counted.

The poets: MM. Verlaine and Mallarmé, Jean Moréas, Jules Laforgue, Gustave Kahn, Charles Vignier, whose books are: *Les Romances sans paroles*, *Sagesse*, *Jadis et naguère*, *L'Après-midi d'un faune*, *Les Syrtes*, *Les Cantilènes*, *Les Complaintes*, *L'Imitation de Notre-Dame la Lune*, *Les Palais Nomades*;

M. Paul Adam, exclusively a writer of prose, wrote *Soi* and *Le Thé chez Miranda*;

Félix Fénéon inaugurated a new theory of art criticism in his work on the Impressionists;

M. Barrès has already written articles and will be writing books. This winter the struggle over the *Demoiselles Goubert*, the *Moralités Légendaires*, *Être*, *La Reine de Saba* etc. will continue.

The general characteristic of these books, and their unifying tendency, is the repudiation of the old, monochordic technique of the line, the desire to break up the rhythm, to use the shape of the stanza as the outline for a particular sensation. As minds develop, sensations become more complex; they need more apposite terms, not ones exhausted by an identical use over twenty years. We are also mindful of the normal expansions of language, through its inevitable neologisms, and the founding of an older vocabulary made necessary by a return of the imagination to the epic and the marvelous.

The main point which separates ours from all other similar attempts is that we take as our main principle the perpetual inflection of the line or rather of the stanza, which thus becomes the sole unit.

Banal prose is the instrument of conversation. For the novel we claim the right to give the sentence rhythm, to accentuate its declamation; the

Gustave Kahn (1859–1936), Symbolist poet, critic and writer on art who became editor of the Symbolist journal La Vogue *in 1886. This article, which was his contribution to the feuds that followed the publication of* Les Déliquescences d'Adoré Floupette *and Moréas' manifesto in* Le Figaro Littéraire, *explained the principles underlying the theory and practice of Symbolism, listed its principal practitioners, stressing the importance of Mallarmé's role, and attempted to describe the common ground held between music, literature and art.*

Arthur Rimbaud (1854–91), with Baudelaire and Mallarmé, among the most radically innovative nineteenth-century French poets. La Vogue was the first to publish his collection, Les Illuminations. *Gustave Kahn also reprinted the very rare* Saison en Enfer.

Maurice Barrès (1862–1923).

Paul Gauguin. *Self-Portrait.* 1889. Oil on wood, 31 × 20″ (79.2 × 51.3 cm). National Gallery of Art, Washington, D.C. (Chester Dale Collection).

tendency is towards a poem in prose, very mobile and with a variety of rhythms, following the pace, the oscillation, the digressions or the simplicity of the Idea.

In his article, M. Deschaumes seems to believe that we are borrowing the methods of Ronsard. This opinion is mistaken. Ronsard was the first to hamper the line by uniformity of prescription. The present attempt consists in broadening and freeing it from precisely those gothic procedures.

As far as the subject of these works is concerned, weary of the intrusion of the everyday, the obligatory contemporary setting, we have set the unfolding of the symbol in any epoch whatsoever, or even in the dream (*the dream being indistinguishable from life*). We want to substitute for the struggle of individuals the struggle of sensations and ideas and, for the milieu of the action, to replace the oft-repeated decor of crossroads and streets with the whole or part of the brain. The essential aim of our art is to objectify the

Edmond Deschaumes (1856–1916), novelist and critic for L'Événement *and* L'Echo de Paris.

subjective (the externalization of the Idea) instead of subjectifying the objective (nature seen through a temperament).

Similar reflections have led to the multi-tonality of Wagner and the latest techniques of the Impressionists. With us, literature adheres to the scientific theories, inductively built up and experimentally checked, of M. Charles Henry, expounded in an introduction to the principles of mathematics and experimental aesthetics. These theories are based on the purely idealist philosophical principle that causes us to reject the utter reality of matter and only admit the existence of the world as representation.

So we wish to take the analysis of the *self* to the extreme, to make the multiplication and interlacing of rhythms accord with the measure of the Idea, to create literary enchantment by doing away with a modish, constrained and spiritual modernism, to build up a personal vocabulary on all levels of the work, and to seek to break out of the banality of all received molds.

"The latest techniques of the Impressionists," i.e. Neo-Impressionism.

Charles Henry (1859–1926), chemist and mathematician, whose lectures at the Sorbonne beginning in 1884 on the emotional value of colors and lines brought him into contact with avant-garde painters and poets. His publications included Introduction à une esthétique scientifique *(1885);* Le Rapporteur Esthétique *(1888).*

TÉODOR DE WYZEWA
LA REVUE WAGNÉRIENNE
"Outline of an Idealist Aesthetic"
May and June 1886

WAGNERIAN ART: PAINTING

I am firmly convinced that true Wagnerism does not lie solely in admiring the works of Richard Wagner: that his works should affect us above all as examples of an artistic theory, and that this theory – repeatedly clarified by the Master in his books – calls for the fusion of all forms of art for one common end. Wagner inspired his admirers to work for the renewal of art; and he showed them the means by which art, in all its forms, was to be renewed, and for what ends.

Thus true Wagnerians do not limit themselves to music – music, alas, which has been dead since Wagner died; they are also concerned for the progress of the Wagnerian spirit in the works of men of letters, poets and painters. . . .

Painting, being one form of art, must be joined with the total purpose of art.

Art, as Wagner tells us, must create life. Why? Because it must deliberately pursue the natural function of all the activities of the spirit. For the world we live in, and which we call real, is a pure creation of the soul. . . . But a fateful over-familiarity with this same creation has caused us to lose the joyous awareness of our creative power; we believed those dreams to which we had given birth were real, along with this personal *self*, conceived by us, and which is limited by things, and subject to them.

From that moment we have been slaves to the world; and the contemplation of this world, which had engaged our interest, has now ceased to be a pleasure to us. The Life we had created – created in order to give us a sense of creative joy – has thus lost its foremost quality. Therefore it needs to be recreated; beyond this world of profaned familiar appearances, we must build the holy world of a better life: better, because we can create it deliberately, and know that we are so doing. This indeed is the task of Art.

Téodor de Wyzewa (1862–1917), Polish-born critic and writer on art. He belonged to the Symbolist circle which included Fénéon, Kahn, and Moréas and which met at the famous gatherings, the mardis *(Tuesdays), held by Mallarmé at his apartment in the rue de Rome. De Wyzewa co-founded with Édouard du Jardin* La Revue Wagnérienne *in 1885, and gradually those who gathered at Mallarmé's apartment became collaborators on the magazine. Wagner had had a widespread influence among writers at least since Baudelaire's piece on* Tannhäuser *(1861). De Wyzewa uses Wagner to propose the thesis of a total art in which the qualities of poetry and music could be combined in painting. In its understanding of the integration of form and meaning, and the central role of sensation, this article is an important statement of the Symbolist basis of modernism.*

* * *

Art must quite consciously, by means of *signs*, recreate the total life of the Universe, that is, of the soul, where the motley drama that we call the Universe is played out. But the life of the soul is made up of complex elements; and their differing complexities produce the specific modes of life which can, through arbitrary classification, be reduced to the three distinct and successive modes of Sensation, Concept and Emotion.

In reality, all three are made up of one simple, common element: sensation.

At first, the soul feels *sensations*, phenomena of pain and pleasure; namely, the various colors, textures, smells and sounds, all of which we believe to be external qualities, but which are uniquely inner states of the spirit.

* * *

Sensation is the initial mode; the first arts had sensation as their aim. But sensations are various – smells, sounds, flavors and textures. Was a special art needed for each of these groups? One alone, plastic art, sufficed for all. For, long before the birth of art, the various sensations had become associated; our senses had acquired the ability to call to one another, and one of them in particular, sight, had obtained this power of suggestion to a marvelous degree.

Slowly schooled by habit, our visual sensations became capable of evoking the whole range of other sensations within us by their mere presence. Now man needed only to see colors in order to perceive relief and texture, and even the temperature and smell and sound of objects without further assistance.

The first artists thus had no need to recreate the different sensations by means of special devices. Their purpose was served by recreating *visual sensations*.

Thus, from the first, the art of sensations was the plastic art of *sight*.

Here I cannot even begin to sketch in the history of this plastic art, to show how it was always realistic, and the different forms it took, under the influence of the various ways of feeling and seeing.

First came the polychrome sculpture of the Egyptians, then the monochrome sculpture of the Greeks, whose divine masterpieces were no less concerned with fidelity and life.

Then came the sculpture of the Middle Ages, that incomparable statuary of the Romanesque and Gothic buildings, translating the vision of naive and pious souls with loyal exactitude. But then – despite the delightful works produced by the Florentine and French masters, and the entire Renaissance where, briefly, the intellectual achievements of the ancients were almost emulated – great sculpture came to an end. Why? Because *sight* was becoming the sense increasingly favored by plastic art, with light as its instrument; but above all because, as spirits become increasingly refined, art increasingly requires processes different from those used by reality to suggest this same life. Thus, because of its material, a polychrome statue too closely resembles the models it has reproduced. From then on we cannot see it as fully alive: we cannot help thinking that, similar in appearance as it is to a real man, this statue is inferior in one essential way: it cannot move.

In the same way a play, when read, will seem more alive to sensitive souls than the same play acted, on the stage, by living actors. In order to preserve the feeling of art as art, we have an ever keener need for the impressions of life to be given to us, in artistic form, by means other than those of real life itself.

Painting answers this need. The means it employs to suggest sensations to us artistically, differ entirely from the means employed in reality. For colors and lines, in a picture, do not reproduce the quite different colors and lines of reality; they are merely conventional signs which have become suitable for what they signify as a result of an association between images;

Louis Anquetin. Caricature of Téodor de Wyzewa. *c.*1890. Pastel, 20⅞ × 13¾″ (53 × 34.9 cm). Collection Madame C. du Ferron-Anquetin, Paris.

but as different from real colors and lines as a word is from a concept, or a musical sound from the emotion it suggests.

And painting, since its glorious appearance in the Middle Ages, remained a fully realistic art as sculpture had once been.

*   *   *

Later, the vision of reality was further refined. Outstanding masters, gifted with an almost unhealthy sensitivity, accustomed artists to see things as steeped in the air around them. Then the vocabulary of painting was modified: new signs were introduced which created new sensations in their turn.

Meanwhile the art of *concepts* had emerged: namely, literature. Then, finally, the art of *emotions*, music. Wagner, after Beethoven, practised it with all the mastery of his supreme genius.

But he understood that now music, like the other arts, could no longer exist in isolation; and he brought the three separate forms of art together for the production of total life.

Painting, literature and music suggested only one mode of life. But life lies in the intimate union of its three modes. Soon painters, like men of letters, felt that their art was inadequate for the expression of the whole of life as they conceived it. They had long wanted to broaden the functions of their art, to use it to reconstruct life's different forms. Men of letters, for instance, saw that words had taken on special resonances beyond their precise "notional" meaning, and that syllables had taken on musical resonances, as well as giving rhythm to the sentence. Then they attempted a new art, *poetry*. They used words no longer for their "notional" value, but as symbols in sound, evoking emotion by means of harmonic groupings.

This same need, to translate the life of the emotions through the procedures of their art, soon led painters to venture beyond the limits of the completely realistic reproduction of their sensations.

Now they embarked upon a whole new kind of painting, made possible by a happy combination of natural circumstances: namely, the fact that, as a result of habit, colors and lines too, like words, had taken on an "emotional" value independent of the actual objects that they represented. We had always seen such and such a facial expression, such and such a color or such outlines accompanying certain objects which, for quite other reasons, inspired us with such and such an emotion: and now these colors, these outlines and expressions, were linked in our soul to these emotions: through this chance linking they had become not merely visual sensations, but *emotional signs*, like the syllables of poetry, like the notes in music. Thus certain painters were able to go beyond painting's original purpose, namely, to suggest the precise sensations offered by sight. They used colors and lines for purely symphonic groupings, heedless of any visual object to be painted directly. And today these colors and these lines, the formal means of painting, are used in painting of two very different types: one "sensational" and descriptive, recreating the exact appearance of things; the other "emotional" and musical, heedless of the objects which these colors and lines represent, taking them only as the signs of emotions, marrying them up in such a way as to produce in us, through their free play, a total impression comparable to that of a symphony.

But what is the purpose of this new music? Would the music of sounds not be sufficient to translate all emotion? By no means. These "symphonist" poets and painters do indeed create emotions, as do the composers; but they create quite different emotions, though these differences cannot be defined, since emotion is indefinable by its very nature. But consider a painting by the "symphonist" Rembrandt, or the masters we call Colorists. Usually we are unconcerned by the actual objects in these paintings: they show us nothing, or what they show us is devoid of reality or life, powerless to suggest any visual reality. This is because these paintings move us above all by the play of the light and the lines steeped in this light. Here each of the elements of the painting has the value of a symphonic chord; and these painters, though they are not representing something truly seen, are no less powerfully realistic in that they recreate a total emotion, living and real.

* * *

WAGNERIAN ART: LITERATURE

Art must create life, as Wagner said; not the life of the senses nor of the spirit, nor of the heart, but the whole of human life, which is all these. Art must still be realistic: the life which it has to create must be made up of the elements which make up so-called *real* life, because the higher, joyous life of art cannot but recreate the modes already experienced in this lower reality.

The first aspect of life is sensation: the first form of art was the plastic form, recreating sensations. But soon these latter, often repeated, left an imprint upon the soul; they became linked, within it, until at last one of them evoked the others. They became further limited: groups formed, separate and abstract; the frequent perception of red objects led the soul to imagine a new object where *redness* would be the dominant quality. Thus *concepts* were born, groups of general, abstract sensations fixed in the mind by *names*; along with what we call the inner life, thought, calculated judgment, reasoning: this was a new mode of life, the logical outcome of sensation.

Art recreates life by means of *signs*, linked in the soul to other ideas and evoking them inwardly. The signs of plastic art had been the visual sensation of certain lines or colors; the signs in literature, the art of concepts, had been *words*, sensations which were auditory at first, but which then became visual in their turn, in the form of the written word.

Through words, literature recreated concepts. Its development submitted to the consistent laws of all artistic development, the same ones which ruled the progress of plastic art from the first sculptures of the Egyptians down to modern drawing. Here are the most important of these laws:

1. First, the constant progress from a simple, relatively homogeneous state to a more complex state of heterogeneity. Concepts, very numerous and vague at first, break up further, become refined, multiply. Life appears to be made up of ever subtler elements. The resemblances between sensations decrease; differences are more clearly perceived as sensations are repeated. Soon the general terms "a marriage, a struggle" no longer suffice to recreate life; the soul requires more precise concepts. Thus art gradually charts a more detailed life of concepts: it takes an increasingly narrow total subject, so as to draw more numerous elements from it. And the analysis of ideas and facts becomes more complicated, while the number of ideas and facts in the mind does likewise.

2. At the same time, the reproduction of certain natural phenomena, following a set order, causes men to perceive this order as necessary, and further modifies their perception of things. Thus a sense of the possible and of the real is born, in terms of which, from now on, all life will have to be created. By virtue of an illusion, to which he submits – and which he has imposed upon himself – man now sees the universe as ruled by constant laws; and facts become inconceivable if they do not obey these laws. And art, which recomposes the elements of ordinary reality on a higher plane, thus loses the power to make facts which are supernatural come alive for us (legends and myths may reappear in a more perfect art, in order to achieve the value of symbols, and recreate certain very subtle modes of mental life in the absence of more direct means).

Then, as the sense of the real and the possible becomes further refined, art soon finds itself abandoning the creation of events that seem merely unusual; after miraculous actions, even adventures too become impossible to recreate artistically. *In its essential effort to make life more lifelike, literature marches ceaselessly toward the complete and minute analysis of the most ordinary facts.*

3. Yet another law of artistic development is the gradual disappearance of any intermediary between the soul of the artist creating life and the souls of those who recreate it. In order to conceive of life in art as real, we cannot tolerate anything belonging to a different reality coming between it and ourselves. Hence signs gradually tend to become simplified, at the same time as concepts become complicated. Thus the first literature was narrative: a man told a story. Then, one day, people no longer wanted to be separated from the story by this narrator: history was presented before them, acted out by living people, on a stage. Then the theater became powerless to produce the illusion of life. For actors, men of one reality, to play the roles of those in a different reality – even this was too intrusive an intermediary, preventing a fully ideal life from coming into being. But men still needed some intermediary, a *sign*, less akin to the things signified, and more capable of being taken solely as a sign, outside its own reality. Then literature began to be written; letters – few in number and soon overlooked as linear values – were called upon to evoke a world of concepts that were not their own.

4. Finally, this development resulted in the multiplication and refining of the various minds. While most still retained an identical number of identical concepts, some, privileged by age-old circumstances, experienced the law of gradual heterogeneity faster and more intensely. The result was that they demanded – for themselves alone – more subtle artistic forms than those which sufficed for the majority of their contemporaries.

* * *

The real champion of modern literature, the intellectual father of our times, was the philosopher René Descartes. Never did a man exert so telling an influence upon his time as this retiring writer over the thoughts and *mores* of the seventeenth century. For those spirits ready to receive it, his doctrine was decisive: and France and the world at large have been more or less *Cartesian* ever since.

The fundamental principle of this revolution was the distinction between two substances, one the mind – pure reason, capable of what is true, beautiful, and divine; while the senses were dependent on the other substance; they were the fount of all that was erroneous, false and deceiving, and palpable, base, and despicable. Hence the cult of reason and contempt for the senses. And these scorned, palpable perceptions faded from the spirit: the world became a harmonious arrangement of concepts. Now the arrangement of facts was perceived in preference to facts themselves, which were seen no more.

* * *

The first effect of the growth of democracy was, at around this time, the revelation of the palpable world and the dethroning of reason. The concept of material objects took on color and refinement. And Romanticism took it upon itself to translate this sudden advent of new thought into the form of art: by Hugo, enamored of warm, precise images; by Honoré de Balzac, the creator of a somewhat chaotic world, but one alive with the deep desire for financial gain and worldly luxuries. These first Romantics, dazzled by new sensations, had not yet managed to forge themselves a sense of the real: to them, all sensations seemed possible.

* * *

From primitive legends down to contemporary novels, literature, the art of concepts, always had one single purpose, that assigned by Wagner himself to all forms of art: beyond everyday reality, to create the higher and truer reality of an artistic life, using its free and joyous power to inform it with elements provided by everyday life. There is no antagonism between the epic tale, the play and the novel: they are three successive forms of a single art, each having fulfilled, and still able to fulfill, the artistic needs of certain spirits. There is no antagonism between the so-called realistic novel, which is purely descriptive, and the so-called idealist novel, which is purely psychological. They are two different aspects of the same life; and they must be reconciled within a total art, recreating the life of both reason and the senses as one complete whole.

But with the development and bonding of ideas, literature, the art of concepts, and painting, the art of sensations, have produced new arts, particularly "emotional." Painting produced the work of Da Vinci and Rubens, which evokes emotion through the groupings of colors and lines; literature produced a symphonic art, Poetry, arousing emotion through the musical arrangement of rhythm and syllables.

*   *   *

True poetry, while alone remaining irreducible to mere literature, is an emotional music of syllables and rhythms. Thus we see poets, still hampered from making pure poetry by a range of conventions, and by the inadequacy of their theoretical vision, becoming increasingly indifferent to the "notional" subjects of their works. . . .

M. Mallarmé was the first to attempt to write poetry skillfully composed in terms of total emotion. As his subject, he deliberately took the emotion produced by the creation and contemplation of philosophical dreams. And he sought the ideal form for purely emotional poetry, but registering the reason for this emotion at the same time as translating it. . . .

M. Mallarmé believed he should retain the set form of the poem; other artists found this a hindrance, which they tried to shatter. They thought that rhyme and regular rhythm were precise musical procedures, with special "emotional" significance; they believed that, henceforth, such shackles should no longer be imposed upon poets, like frames, but should be used as required by the emotional complexities they suggested. They dreamed of a renewal of verbal music comparable to that made in instrumental music by Wagner, which did not do away with tunes and cadences and reprises, but gave them a particular meaning, and used them only to produce very specific emotions. . . .

Gustave Kahn, for example, was credited with being one of the first practitioners of vers libre.

Thus the laws of artistic forms themselves have led to the creation of a new literature, using the formal means of "notional" literature; and as a color, today, can variously suggest a sensation and an emotion, similarly the syllables of our words are signs of both concepts and emotions. These are two arts, sharing the same means: two quite different literatures, but equally valuable for the common purpose of all the arts. For both the literature of concepts, and musical literature alike, recreate different modes of life, but of the same life.

Such – too briefly stated – was the development of literary art. What would Wagnerian literature be in such conditions?

When will a writer emerge who will bring together the different forms of his art, to produce a complete literary "life"?

COLORPLATE 46. Paul Gauguin. *The Harvest at Arles (Human Miseries)*. 1888.
28³/₄ × 36¹/₄″ (73 × 92 cm). Ordrupgaard Collection, Copenhagen.

COLORPLATE 47. Paul Gauguin. *Still Life: Fête Gloanec.* 1888. Oil on wood, 15 × 20⅞″ (38 × 53 cm).
Musée des Beaux-Arts, Orléans, France.

COLORPLATE 48. Paul Gauguin. *Still Life with Ham*. 1889. $19\frac{5}{8} \times 22\frac{3}{4}''$ (50 × 58 cm).
Phillips Collection, Washington, D.C.

COLORPLATE 49. Gustave Moreau. *Abstract Study. c.* 1890. Oil on wood, 8¼ × 10⅝″ (21 × 27 cm).
Musée Gustave Moreau, Paris.

COLORPLATE 50. Odilon Redon. *Landscape, Peyrelebade. c.*1880.
Oil on paper stuck on card, 18⅛ × 17⅜″ (46.8 × 45.4 cm). Musée du Louvre, Paris.

COLORPLATE 51. Edgar Degas. *Landscape.* 1890–93.
Monotype in oil colors with pastel, 10 × 13⅜″ (25.6 × 34.2 cm).
Metropolitan Museum of Art, New York (Purchase, Mr and Mrs Richard J. Bernhard Gift, 1972).

COLORPLATE 52. Odilon Redon. *Orpheus*. After 1913. Pastel, 27½ × 22¼″ (70 × 56.5 cm).
Cleveland Museum of Art (Gift of J. H. Wade, 26.25).

COLORPLATE 53. Odilon Redon. *Cyclops*. *c.*1898. Oil on wood, 25¼ × 20″ (64.1 × 50.8 cm).
Rijksmuseum Kröller-Müller, Otterlo.

REDON: "SUGGESTIVE ART"

JORIS-KARL HUYSMANS
CERTAINS
"The Monster"
1889

Here we have a new starting-point, almost a new topic; it seems to have been discovered by the only painter currently fascinated at the fantastical, M. Odilon Redon. For the creation of his pullulating, prodigiously disquieting monsters, he has plumbed the depths of all that is fluid, mercurial, shifting, he has trawled the realms of the imperceptible, enlarged by projection, and hence more terrifying than the extraordinary beasts of the old masters, but essentially inspired by them.

Thus in one of his albums, he aimed to translate the phrase from Flaubert in The Temptation of St. Antony: "All sorts of terrifying beasts loom forth."

Liquid and phosphorous beings, bladders and bacilli, hair-fringed corpuscles, aqueous, villous blebs fly wingless through a sky of deep and steadfast black, entangled in the ribbons of threadworm and tapeworm; it is as though all manner of worms, whole legions of parasites, were swarming in the darkness of this engraving where the human face suddenly looms, incomplete, borne aloft at the end of these living whorls or thrust like a nucleus into the life-giving protoplasm.

Thus in order to recreate the monstrous, M. Redon has been obliged to have recourse to ancient concepts and to marry the horror of the face of man to the undulating hideosity of the caterpillar.

Marshaling imagined *Infusoria* and larvae of all kinds, he was also to interpret more clear-cut phrases concerning the dance of Lust and Death, also in The Temptation; the following, for example:

"We see before us a death's head with a crown of roses, set upon a woman's torso of pearly whiteness; below, a stained shroud shaped like a tail. The whole body billows like some gigantic upright worm."

The lithograph inspired by this description is one of the most formidable he ever made.

The monster stands out against an expanse of impenetrable, muffled black, velvety as that of the bat, haloed in white, and goffers the darkness with the bucking form of a great C.

The death's head, with its exaggerated rictus, its eyes brimming with shadow, leans against the bust of a swaddled mummy, hands crossed upon a breast of solid resin. Coiffed with a long embroidered hennin, this head emanates a certain chilling grace, while the monster braces its diaphanous rump, ringed with the oscillating annuli standing out under its cold skin.

Here and there, scattered across the shadow, faint apparitions, white cocoons, tremble around this fearful image of lust, which, as the poet intended, merges with the effigy of Death itself.

In a second album, also dedicated to the glory of Flaubert, as well as in another collection entitled "Origins," the painter again projects his monsters using similar combinations.

The former is strewn with a world of embryonic flying monads, sprouting tadpoles, amorphous beings, minuscule discs with vague, incipient eyelids and emergent mouths.

Gustave Flaubert (1821–80), The Temptation of St Antony *(1874)*. *Odilon Redon's albums of lithographs:* The Temptation of St Antony *(1888)*; To Gustave Flaubert *(1889)*; Origins *(1883)*.

Odilon Redon. *I, myself, have sometimes seen in the sky what seemed like forms of spirits*. Plate XXI from *The Temptation of St Antony*. 1896. Lithograph, printed in black, $10\frac{1}{2} \times 7\frac{1}{4}''$ (26.5 × 18.2 cm). Museum of Modern Art, New York (Gift of Abby Aldrich Rockefeller).

The latter, entitled "a long red chrysalis," depicts the parvis of an improbable temple, before which the body of a slender specter is rolled around a low column, its woman's head placed where the capital should stand.

Gaunt, pale, heart-rending with its closed eyes and pained and pensive mouth, this face seems vainly to await the liberating fall of an invisible ax, like a victim on the block.

Despite its thoroughly modern structure, the profound and singular expression of the features takes us back over the centuries to the mournful works of the Middle Ages; it links M. Redon to the chain, unbroken since the Renaissance, of fantastic Bestiaries, of seers fascinated by the monstrous.

But the great science of Religious Symbolism is no more. In the realm of the Dream, art remains alone, in these times when the soul's hunger is sufficiently assuaged by the ingestion of the theories of the likes of Moritz, Wagner and Darwin.

ODILON REDON

Letter to André Mellerio
August 16, 1898

My dear Mellerio,   PEYRELEBADE

I have your letter here in front of me, but I find your questions somewhat awkward. I cannot answer them completely. Why should you want to know whether I put myself in front of my easel, or lithographic stone, with a definite preconceived idea? I've been wondering the same thing myself for thirty years.

You can't imagine how it shocks my sense of reserve – I've never answered it. What is the point of divulging anything other than the actual result? Those who see me working in the intimacy of my private life may perhaps be more enlightened on these matters, and Ari or his mother could tell you more – laughingly – than I, in all probability.

I could however tell you, should it be of interest, about certain peculiarities of my nature. For instance, I have a horror of a blank sheet of paper. It fills me with such awe that it renders me unproductive, so that I lose all taste for work (unless, of course, I am intending to portray something real, a study or a portrait for example); I find a sheet of paper so daunting that as soon as it is on the easel, I have to scribble on it with charcoal, or some other material, so as to bring it to life. I think that suggestive art owes much to the effect that the material itself has on the artist. A truly sensitive artist does not find the same invention from different materials, because each impresses him differently.

I say this to explain the extremely relative and indirect nature of this preconception of which you speak. It is often more like the sort of forward plan which is abandoned in mid-enterprise, in order to follow those charming and unexpected by-ways of the imagination – that sovereign queen who lies in wait for us with swift seductions – magnificent, enthralling. Imagination has been my guardian angel, less today than in the past, alas. She loves a puzzled, furrowed brow. Above all she loves youth and childhood, and it is wise always to remain something of a child where the creative act is involved.

She is also the harbinger of the "unconscious," that lofty and mysterious figure whose arrival is so longed for in over-circumspect old age. She comes unbidden, according to her hour, her place, even her season. That should enlighten you and tell you how hard it is to give an answer to these whys and wherefores; for the fatal crucible where the work of art is forged is utterly dependent upon the precious whim of this unknown.

Odilon Redon.

André Mellerio, critic, friend and biographer of Redon, was in the course of preparing an article on the artist, and had put to him a series of questions about his working methods.

Ari Redon (1889–1972), the son of Odilon Redon.

Odilon Redon. *The Light of Day*. Plate VI from *Dreams*. 1891. Lithograph, printed in black, 8¼ × 6⅛″ (20.9 × 15.6 cm). Museum of Modern Art, New York (Lillie P. Bliss Collection).

ODILON REDON

LA VIE

"Confidences of the Artist"

November–December 1912

What was it that at the beginning made my work difficult and at the same time slowed it down so? Was it a way of seeing that was not in accord with my particular talents? A kind of struggle between the heart and the mind? – I do not know.

The fact remains that at the very beginning I always aimed at perfection and (could you believe it) at the perfection of form. But let me tell you now that no plastic form – and I mean form observed objectively, exactly for what it is, according to the laws of light and shadow and by the rather conventional means of modeling – could be found in any of my works. At the very most, I often tried in the beginning to reproduce (for one must insofar as possible know everything) objects of the exterior world accord-

"Confidences d'Artiste" was the title first used by Redon for the publication of a letter to his friend, the publisher Edmond Picard. It appeared in Dutch in Nieuwe Rotterdamsche Courant *on July 4, 1894, and was then republished in French in* L'Art Moderne *on August 25, 1894. Redon used the title "Confidences d'Artiste," again, for this different and longer autobiographical text of May 1909 dedicated to Andries Bonger. It was reprinted in the issue of* La Vie, *"Hommage à Odilon Redon" in 1912 and in* À Soi-Même *(1867–1915), Paris, 1922.*

ing to the rules of an art which was based on the old way of seeing. I simply did it as an exercise. But now in my maturity, I declare, indeed I insist, that all my work is limited exclusively to the resources of chiaroscuro. It also owes a great deal to the effects produced by the abstract character of line – that agent from a profound source acting directly upon the spirit. Suggestive art can fulfill nothing without going back uniquely to the mysterious play of shadows and the rhythm of imaginatively conceived lines. Ah, they were never more successfully realized than in the work of da Vinci. The mystery of his art and the boundless fascination which it exerts on our spirits would be impossible without them. They are the very roots of the words which constitute his language. And it is through a sense of perfection, excellence and reason, and through a quiet submission to the laws of nature that this admirable and supreme genius has mastered the entire art of form; he dominates it in its very essence. "Nature is overflowing with an infinite number of principles which are not a part of experience," he writes. Nature was for him, as it must be for all masters, both an absolute necessity and a basic axiom. What painter would ever think otherwise?

It is nature then that decrees that we obey the needs of the gifts which she has bestowed upon us. My own talents have directed me into the realm of dreams. I gave myself over to the torments of the imagination and to the various surprises that nature provided for me by means of my pencil, but I channeled and trained these surprises according to the basic laws of the organism of art that I know and feel. My sole aim: to instill in the spectator, by means of quite unexpected allurements, all the evocations and fascinations of the unknown on the boundaries of thought.

I said nothing, moreover, that was not already nobly stated by Albrecht Dürer in his print *Melancholia*. It was thought to be incoherent. No, it is clearly defined, it is defined solely in terms of line and according to its great powers. His is a grave and profound spirit that lulls us like the dense and complicated accents of a rigorous fugue. Compared to him, we can only chant abbreviated motifs of a few measures.

Suggestive art is like an illumination of things for dreams, toward which thought also is directed. Decadence or not, it is so. Let us say rather that it is growth, the evolution of art for the supreme elevation and expansion of our personal life through a necessary exaltation – our highest point of strength or moral support.

This suggestive art lies completely within the exciting realm of the art of music, and more freely and radiantly. It is also my own art through a combination of various elements brought together, of forms that are transposed and transformed without any relation to the contingencies at hand, but which nevertheless possess a logic all their own. All the errors made by critics concerning my first works were the result of their inability to see that it was not at all necessary to define, to understand, to limit, to be precise, because everything that is sincerely and humbly new – such as the beautiful from elsewhere – carries its meaning within itself.

The designation of my drawings by titles is often redundant, so to speak. A title is justified only when it is vague, indeterminate and when it aims even confusedly at the equivocal. My drawings *inspire* and do not offer explanations. They resolve nothing. They place us, just as music does, in the ambiguous world of the indeterminate.

They are a sort of *metaphor*, explained Remy de Gourmont in setting them apart, far from any sort of geometric art. He sees in them an imaginative logic. I believe that this writer has said more in a few lines than anything else formerly written about my first works.

Imagine arabesques or various types of linear involutions unwinding themselves not on a flat surface but in space, with all that which the deep and indeterminate limits of the sky can offer the spirit; imagine the play of

Albrecht Dürer (1471–1528), "Melancholia" (1514).

Remy de Gourmont (1858–1915), critic, novelist and apologist for Symbolism.

their lines projecting upon and combining with the most diverse elements imaginable, including that of the human face. If this face possesses the particularities of him whom we encounter daily in the street, along with its very real, immediate but unexpected truth, you will have then the usual combinations that appear in many of my drawings.

Further explanation could hardly make the fact any clearer that they are the reverberations of a human expression, that, by means of the license of fantasy, they have been embodied in a play of arabesques. I believe that this action will originate in the mind of the beholder and will arouse in his imagination any number of fantasies whose meaning will be broad or limited according to his sensitivity and imaginative aptitude to enlarge or diminish.

Moreover, everything derives from universal life; a painter who neglects to draw a wall vertically draws poorly because he diverts the spirit from the idea of stability. The same is true of the painter who fails to render his water with consideration for the horizontal (to cite only the very simplest of phenomena). But in the vegetal world, for example, there are certain secret and inherent life tendencies that a sensitive landscape painter could not possibly misinterpret: the trunk of a tree forcefully thrusts out its branches according to the laws of growth and the flow of sap. A true artist must feel this and must represent it accordingly.

The same is true with animal or human life. We cannot move a hand without our entire body being displaced in obedience to the laws of gravity. A draftsman knows that. In creating certain fantastic creatures I believe that I have complied with these intuitive suggestions of the instincts. Contrary to the insinuations of Huysmans, they do not owe their conception to that terrifying world of the infinitely minute as revealed by the microscope. Not at all. While creating them I took the greatest care to organize their structure.

Huysmans: see "Le Monstre", Certains, *1889 (page 167).*

There is a method of drawing which the imagination has liberated from those bothersome worries presented by the details of the exterior world in order to represent only imaginary objects. I have created various fantasies based on the stem of a flower, the human face, or even on certain skeletal elements, which, I believe, were drawn, constructed and formed as they had to be. They are thus formed because they possess an organism. Any time a human figure cannot give the illusion that it is about to leave the picture frame, so to speak, to walk, act or think, the drawing is not truly modern. They cannot take away from me the merit of giving the illusion of life to my most fantastic creations. All my originality consists, therefore, in endowing completely improbable beings with human life, according to the laws of the probable and in placing, as much as possible, the logic of the visible at the service of the invisible.

This method proceeds naturally and easily from the vision of the mysterious world of shadows for which Rembrandt, in revealing it to us, supplied the key.

But, on the other hand, as I have often said, the method that has been the most fruitful and the most necessary to my development is the copying of real things, carefully reproducing the objects of the exterior world in their most minute, individual and accidental details. After attempting to copy minutely a pebble, a sprout of a plant, a hand, a human profile or any other example of living or inorganic life, I experience the onset of a mental excitement; at that point I need to create, to give myself over to representations of the imaginary. Thus blended and infused, nature becomes my source, my yeast and my leaven. I believe that this is the origin of my true inventions. I believe that this is true of my drawings; and it is likely that, even with the weakness, unevenness, and imperfection inherent in all that man recreates, one could not for an instant stand the sight of them (because they are humanly expressive), if they were not, as I have just said, created, formed, and built according to the law of life and the moral transmission necessary to all existence.

Odilon Redon. *I was plunged into solitude. I dwelt in the tree behind me.* Plate IX from *The Temptation of St Antony.* 1896. Lithograph, printed in black, 11¾ × 8⅞″ (30 × 22.5 cm). Museum of Modern Art, New York (Gift of Abby Aldrich Rockefeller).

GAUGUIN: SYMBOLISM IN PAINTING

PAUL GAUGUIN

Letters to Émile Schuffenecker

1888

OCTOBER 8

I made a painting for a church; naturally, it was refused, so I'm sending it back to Van Gogh. Useless to describe it to you – you'll see it. This year I sacrificed everything – execution, color – for style, wanting to force myself to do something other than what I know how to do. I think it's a transformation which hasn't borne fruit but which will. I made a portrait of myself for Vincent, who asked me for it. I think it's one of my best things; so abstract that it's absolutely incomprehensible (I suppose). A bandit's head at first sight, a Jean Valjean (*Les Misérables*) also personifying an Impressionist painter, run down and bearing the chains of the world. Its drawing is very special (complete abstraction). Eyes, mouth, and nose are like flowers of Persian carpets which also embody the symbolic aspect. The color is rather far from nature; it reminds you vaguely of my pottery gone lopsided because of a hot kiln. All the reds, the violets slashed through with fiery sparks, like a furnace shining in the eyes, the seat of the painter's struggling thoughts – everything on a pure chromium background sprinkled with childish bouquets – pure little girl's room....

* * *

Gauguin had offered Vision after the Sermon, Jacob Wrestling with the Angel, *1888 (National Gallery of Scotland) to the small Breton church of Nizon near Pont-Aven.*

Self-Portrait: "Les Misérables", *1888 (Rijksmuseum Vincent van Gogh, Amsterdam). Victor Hugo (1802–85),* Les Misérables *(1862).*
The term "abstraction" referred to representation away from the model, or the motif, from imagination.

Paul Gauguin. *Self-Portrait, "Les Misérables à l'ami Vincent."* 1888. 16⁷/₈ × 21¹/₄" (43 × 54 cm). Rijksmuseum Vincent van Gogh Foundation/Van Gogh Museum, Amsterdam.

You speak to me of my *formidable* mysticism. Be an Impressionist to the end and do not be frightened of anything. Obviously, this Symbolist road is full of pitfalls and I have only just taken the first step, but it is in the depths of my nature and one must always follow his temperament. I well know that people will understand me *less and less*. What does it matter if I distance myself from others? For most I will be a puzzle, for a few I will be a poet, and sooner or later what's good will earn its place – no matter what, I tell you, I will end up doing things of *the first order*; I feel it and we will see. You well know that in art I am always right in the end. Be aware that right now there is a current among *the artists* that is highly favorable *to me*; I know of it because of certain indiscretions; don't worry, as much as Van Gogh loves me, he would not undertake to feed me in the Midi for my beautiful eyes. He studied the lay of the land like a cool Dutchman and intends to push things as much as possible, exclusively. I asked him to lower the prices to attract buyers. He replied that he intended, on the contrary, to raise them. Always the optimist, this time I am certainly walking on solid ground. . . .

Theo van Gogh was handling Gauguin's paintings at Boussod & Valadon. The project of sending him to Arles at Theo's expense was still under discussion.

FÉLIX FÉNÉON

LA CRAVACHE
"The Other Impressionist Group"
July 6, 1889

Their mysterious, hostile, and rough aspect isolated the ambiance of the works of M. Paul Gauguin, a painter and sculptor of the Impressionist exhibitions of 1880, 1881, 1882, and 1886; many details of execution, and the fact that he carved bas-reliefs in wood and coloured them was a sign of a tendency towards archaicism; the form of his earthenware vases bore witness to an exotic taste: all characteristics which attain their degree of saturation in his recent canvases.

This article, acutely perceptive of the common ground between Seurat and Gauguin, was written on the occasion of the exhibition of "Impressionists and Synthetists" at the café Volpini in May 1889.

The means of the *tachistes*, so appropriate to the representation of brief visions, were abandoned about 1886 by several painters concerned about an art of synthesis and premeditation. While M. Seurat, M. Signac, M. Pissarro, M. Dubois-Pillet realized their conception of this art in paintings in which the episodes were abolished in a general docile orchestration conforming to the code of optical physics, and in which the personality of the author remains latent, like that of a Flaubert in his books, *M. Paul Gauguin was working towards an analogous goal, but by other means*. Reality for him was only the pretext for a far distant creation: he rearranges the materials reality furnishes; disdains trompe-l'œil, be it the trompe-l'œil of the very atmosphere; uses prominent lines, limits their number, hieraticizes them; and within each of the spacious cantons formed by their interlacings, an opulent and heavy color sits in bleak glory without attempting to meet its neighboring colors, unclouded. . . .

M. Louis Anquetin speculates on the hypothesis posed by Humboldt about the gentleman brusquely transferred from Senegal to Siberia. . . . It is probable that M. Anquetin's style, with its intractable contours, flat and intense colors, had some slight influence on M. Paul Gauguin: but only a formal influence, for it does not seem that the least feeling flows through these knowing and decorative works.

M. Emile Bernard is showing Breton landscapes and scenes; M. Charles Laval, scenes and landscapes of Brittany and Martinique – M. Gauguin's favorite territories. Both of them will free themselves from the stamp of this painter, whose work is arbitrary, or at least is the result of a too special state of mind for newcomers to be able to use it as their point of departure.

Poster for the Impressionist/Synthetist Group Exhibition at the Café Volpini, Paris, 1889.

GROUPE IMPRESSIONNISTE ET SYNTHÉTISTE

CAFÉ DES ARTS

VOLPINI, DIRECTEUR

EXPOSITION UNIVERSELLE

Champ-de-Mars, en face le Pavillon de la Presse

EXPOSITION DE PEINTURES

DE

Paul Gauguin	Émile Schuffenecker	Émile Bernard
Charles Laval	Louis Anquetin	Louis Roy
Léon Fauché	Daniel	Nemo

Affiche pour l'Intérieur

PAUL GAUGUIN

Letter to Émile Bernard

June 1890

Paul Gauguin photographed in 1891. Musée Gauguin, Papeari, Tahiti (lent by Madame Hue de Monfreid).

My dear Bernard,
Thank you for your good, kind letter. Yes, I am depressed and that is why I have not yet answered it. All matters of the heart touch me more than I can say, despite all the efforts I make to harden my own against them. The coteries who howl before my paintings mean little to me, all the more so since I myself know that these works are incomplete, more an approach to comparable things. One has to sacrifice things in art, at times, to make approximate efforts, a thought floating without direct, definitive expression. Anyway, one minute you feel you've achieved your aim, the next it recedes before you; yet this *half-seen* dream is more powerful than any material thing. Yes, we are destined (we artists, seekers and thinkers) to perish beneath the blows of the world, but to perish as mere matter perishes. The stone will perish, the word will remain. We're in deep trouble but we are not yet dead. They won't have *my* skin yet. To think I might get what I'm asking for right now, a good position in Tonkin where I'll work on my painting and put aside some savings. The whole of the East, all that great thought written in letters of gold throughout its art, is well worth studying; I feel I shall be rejuvenated out there. The West is rotten right now. Like Antaeus, we gain new strength when touching land out there. And we'll come back after a year or two, solvent again.

At the moment I am gathering my strength, tired but not exhausted. There is very little good daylight and I'm resting, sculpting and doing still life. A storm has been blowing for ten days, the sea is breaking on our beach and it's all very gloomy at the moment, with no news from Paris.

I find this purchase of *Olympia* very odd now that the author is dead. Will the Louvre take it? I don't think so and this is to be hoped for.

Still, pressure is mounting, and ultimately they'll probably have to buy *Olympia* at a higher price, like the Millet. Right now the more madness there is around, the more certainly better times will appear on the horizon; you who are young will profit from them. As to writing an article on the subject, I'm not encouraged by the response to the one I wrote this year. Aurier *has failed to answer* two letters, just like dogshit along a wall. The *Moderniste* has not arrived and I haven't been able to read "Le Maudit."

I liked the thought of your sister in front of my pot. Between ourselves I made it like that partly on purpose to test the limits of her admiration for such objects, then I wanted to give her one of my best, though not very successful as far as the firing is concerned.

As you have known for some time, and as I have written in the *Moderniste*, I am scanning each material for its essential nature. Now the nature of stoneware embodies a sense of intense heat, and I think this figure, baked in this inferno, expresses its character fairly strongly. Like an artist glimpsed by Dante during his visit to Hell.

A poor devil thrown in upon himself to endure his suffering. At all events, the most beautiful girl in the world can give only what she has.

Vincent wrote me more or less what he wrote to you: that the tendency is toward affectation. I answered him accordingly.

Oh, I'd like to ask you a favor. Could you take a photograph of the pot, well-lit, with reflections giving color to the surface, standing out against a light background.

A warm handshake. P. Go.

All my excuses to Madeleine for the crudeness of her pot.

Monet had raised a subscription fund to purchase Manet's Olympia. *It was offered to the nation and hung in the Musée du Luxembourg.*

In 1889 at the Sacrêtan sale Millet's Angelus *had achieved the price of 553,000 francs.*

Gauguin, deeply offended by Fénéon's article in La Cravache *of July 6, 1889 (above), had been lobbying Aurier for a major article to support his position. Instead the critic chose to write about Van Gogh ("Les Isolés: Vincent van Gogh,"* Mercure de France, *January 1890). A collection of poems by Aurier was published in 1889 under the title* L'Oeuvre Maudite. *Gauguin had two articles published in* Le Moderniste, *"Notes sur l'art à l'Exposition Universelle" 4, June 13, 1889, and "Qui trompe-t-on ici?" September 21, 1889.*

G.-ALBERT AURIER
MERCURE DE FRANCE
"Symbolism in Painting: Paul Gauguin"
March 1891

G.-Albert Aurier (1865–92) was introduced by Bernard to Gauguin, whom he came to regard as the leading representative of Symbolism in painting. In this article, Aurier makes the important distinction between Impressionism as an art of realism and Symbolism as the expression of the universal "Idea" by means of its sign or symbol.

How do you think he would answer if he were told that until then he has seen only ghosts, that now, before his eyes, are objects more real and closer to the truth? Would he not think that what he saw before was more real than what he is being shown?

Plato

Far, very far away, on a fabulous hill, where the earth seems to glow bright red, Jacob's Biblical struggle with the Angel is taking place.

While the two legendary giants – transformed by the distance into pygmies – fight their fearsome battle, a group of women are watching, interested and naive, uncertain, doubtless, about what is happening over there, on the fabulous crimsoned hill. They are peasant women. And by the breadth of their white headdresses, which spread like seagull wings, and by the typical array of colors in their scarves, and by the shapes of their gowns and jackets, they reveal their Breton origins. Their respectful manners and their wide-eyed faces are those of simple creatures listening to extraordinary and somewhat fantastic tales affirmed by some incontestable and revered mouth. They might be in church, so silently do they pay attention, so collected, so worshipful, so pious is their bearing; they might be in church, with a vague scent of incense and prayer fluttering amidst the white wings of their headdresses, and with the respected voice of an old priest soaring above their heads. . . . Yes, certainly, in a church, in some poor church in some poor Breton market-town. . . . But, if so, where are the moldy and green pillars? Where are the milk-white walls with their infinite multichromatic stations of the Cross? The pine pulpit? The old priest preaching, whose mumbling voice we hear, yes, to be sure, we hear? Where is it all? And why, over there, far, very far away, the swell of that fabulous hill, whose earth seems to glow bright red?

Ah! The moldy and green pillars, and the milk-white walls, and the little multichromatic stations of the Cross, and the pine pulpit, and the old preaching priest vanished some minutes ago, no longer exist for the eyes and the souls of the good Breton peasant women! . . . What marvelously stirring intonation, what luminously vivid description, strangely appropriate to the rough ears of his lumpish congregation, has he found, this droning village hunchback? All the surrounding objects have dispersed into vapors, have disappeared; he himself, the evocator, has faded away, and it is his Voice, his poor old pitiful stammering Voice that has now become visible, imperiously visible, and it is his Voice that the white-coiffed peasant women contemplate, with naive and pious attention, and it is his Voice, this rustically fantastic vision that has risen over there, far, very far away, his Voice, that fabulous hill with its earth the color of vermilion, land of a child's dream, where the two Biblical giants – transformed by the distance into pygmies – fight their arduous and imposing battle!

Now, before this marvelous canvas by Paul Gauguin, which truly illuminates the riddle of the Poem, during primitive humanity's paradisiacal hours; which reveals the ineffable charms of dream, mystery, and the symbolic veils only half-lifted by the hands of the simple-hearted; which resolves, for the wise reader, the eternal psychological problem of the possibility of religions, politics, and sociologies; which, finally, shows the fierce primordial beast tamed by Chimera's magical philters; before this miraculous canvas, not just a certain fat and Prudhommesque banker, priding himself on a gallery full of Detailles (a sure thing) and Loustauneaus (an investment), but even a certain art enthusiast, known to

Gauguin: The Vision after the Sermon, COLORPLATE 24.

Monsieur Prudhomme, a fictional character created by Henry Monnier and depicted by Daumier.
Édouard Detaille (1848–1912), popular academic painter of military scenes; Louis Auguste Loustauneau (1864–98), landscape and genre painter.

be intelligent and sympathetic to youthful audacities to the point of accepting the Pointillists' harlequinesque vision, exclaimed:

"Oh, no! Absolutely not! . . . It's too much! . . . Ploërmel's headdresses and scarves, Breton women, at the end of this century, in a painting entitled *Jacob Wrestling with the Angel*!! I am certainly no reactionary, I accept Impressionism, in fact, I only accept Impressionism, but. . . ."

"And who says, my dear sir, that this is Impressionism?"

In fact, it is perhaps time to clear up a troublesome misunderstanding, undoubtedly created by the word "Impressionism," which has been all too misused. The public – I mean that tiny, more or less intelligent public that still cares about art, that useless anachronism – acknowledges only two categories of painters: academic painters, that is, those who, adequately educated, qualified, and licensed by the Art Faculty in the rue Bonaparte, deal, at Israelite prices, in official beauty, in the classical, modern, or other manner, certifiably backed by a government guarantee: and, on the other hand, the Impressionist painters, that is, all those who rebelled against the idiotic tastes of the boulevard critics and against the ignorant academic formulators, and who now allow themselves the presumptuous freedom of not copying someone else.

That would be fine, and the latter term would be as good as another. Unfortunately, however broadly the term is used, it implies a meaning, a precise meaning, in fact, that can confuse the public. The word "Impressionism," indeed, whether one wishes or not, suggests an entire aesthetic program based upon sensation. Impressionism is and can only be a variety of Realism, a sharpened, spiritualized, amateurized Realism, but Realism nonetheless. The desired goal is still the imitation of materiality – no longer, perhaps, in its own form or its own color, rather in its perceived form and its perceived color – and the translation of sensation, with all the unexpected qualities that arise from instantaneous notation, all the deformations that arise from rapid, subjective synthesis. Although Messieurs Pissarro and Claude Monet without a doubt translate forms and colors differently than Courbet, nevertheless, in essence, like Courbet, even more than Courbet, they translate only form and color. The substratum and the ultimate goal of their art is the material subject, the real thing. Thus the public, in speaking the word "Impressionism," inevitably has the vague notion of a program of a special kind of Realism; they expect works that are but the faithful translation – *and nothing more* – of an *exclusively sensory impression*, of a sensation. So that, if there were, by chance, among the heterogeneous group of independent painters labeled with the title in question, a few artists pursuing different, even opposite paths, the good public, that eternal and blissful adorer of catalogues, would clearly be unable to make heads or tails of it, as they say, and – I can see it now – would shrug its omnipotent shoulders and sneer:

"This is absurd! . . . This Impressionist is painting impressions that no one can ever have felt! . . ."

Might this not, possibly, explain the similar tirade before Gauguin's painting by the aforementioned "art enthusiast, known to be intelligent and sympathetic to youthful audacities to the point of accepting the Pointillists' harlequinesque vision?"

In any event, now that it is becoming evident that we are witnessing, in literature, the death-throes of Naturalism, even as we are seeing an idealist, even mystical reaction taking shape, it would be surprising if the plastic arts showed no tendency toward a similar evolution. *Jacob Wrestling with the Angel*, which I attempted to describe in the beginning of this piece, is evidence enough, I believe, of this tendency, and one must understand that it is entirely in the interest of the painters committed to this new path to be free of the absurd label of "Impressionists," which implies – and this bears repeating – a program diametrically opposed to their own. This quibbling over words may appear ridiculous, but it is, in my opinion, necessary; the public, the supreme judge where art is concerned, has the incurable habit,

Ploërmel: a Breton village known for its production of cloth.

as we all know, of only judging things by their names. Therefore, let there be a new -ist word invented (there are already so many that it won't be noticed!) for the newcomers whom Gauguin leads: Synthetists, Idéistes, Symbolists, as you please, as long as this foolish general term "Impressionist" is abandoned, except as a specific title for those painters for whom art is only a translation of the artist's sensations and impressions.

Oh, how truly rare, among those who pride themselves on their "artistic aptitudes," how rare are those happy beings whose soul's eyelids are half-open and who can exclaim, with Swedenborg, that inspired hallucinator: "That very night, the eyes of the inner man were opened: they were made fit to look into the heavens, into the world of ideas and into the nether regions! . . ." And yet, is that not the necessary, prerequisite initiation that the true artist, the absolute artist must undergo? . . .

Paul Gauguin seems to me to be one of these sublime voyeurs. To me, he appears to be the pioneer of a new art, not in history, but at least in our time. Let us, therefore, analyze this art from the standpoint of a general aesthetic. This would amount, it seems to me, to studying the artist himself, and perhaps improving upon the superficial monograph consisting of the descriptions of some twenty canvases and ten flattering clichés that usually satisfies today's body of critics.

It is evident – and it is almost a platitude to say it – that there exist in the history of art two great and opposite tendencies that incontestably depend, the one, on blindness, the other on the acumen of "man's inner eye," as Swedenborg says; the Realist tendency and the Idéiste tendency (I do not say Idealist, we shall see why).

Undoubtedly, Realist art, that art whose sole aim is the representation of the material exteriorities, of the perceptible appearances of things, constitutes an interesting aesthetic manifestation. It reveals to us, in some way, by indirection, the worker's soul, since it shows us the deformations that the object underwent in passing through it. Furthermore, no one disputes that Realism, though it was the pretext for many hideous works, as impersonal and banal as photographs, has also produced, at times, some undeniable masterpieces that shine in the museums of all our memories. And yet it is no less indisputable that to whomever wishes to reflect honestly, it is Idéiste art that seems purer and nobler – purer and nobler by all the purity and nobility that divides matter from idea. One could even state that the highest art could only be Idéiste, since art is, by definition (as we intuit), only the representative materialization of what is noblest and most truly divine in the world, of what is, in the final analysis, the only living being, the Idea. Are not those who can neither see the Idea nor believe in it, worthy therefore of our compassion, as were, for free men, the poor, stupid prisoners of Plato's allegorical Cave?

And yet, with the exception of most of the Primitives and a few of the great Renaissance masters, the general tendency in painting, as we know, has, until now, been almost exclusively Realist. Indeed, many confess that they cannot understand how painting – the representational art par excellence, which can copy, to the point of illusionism, all the visible attributes of matter – can be anything but a faithful and exact reproduction of objectivity, an ingenious facsimile of the allegedly real world. The Idealists themselves (whom, I repeat, one must avoid confusing with the artists whom I choose to call "Idéistes") were more often than not, whatever they claim, only Realists; the aim of their art was only the direct representation of material forms. They were content to order objectivity according to certain conventional and preconceived notions of quality; they prided themselves on presenting us with objects that were beautiful, but that were beautiful considered as objects, the focus of their works residing always and still in the qualities of the form, that is, the qualities of reality. What they called ideal was never other than the artful cosmeticizing of ugly, tangible things. In short, they have painted a conventional objectivity, but an objectivity nonetheless and, to paraphrase the famous dictum of one of

Emanuel Swedenborg (1688–1772), Swedish scientist, philosopher and theologian whose theory of "correspondences" between material reality and the spiritual world created great interest among Symbolist writers.

Paul Gauguin. Detail of photograph, 1891. Courtesy Musée Gauguin, Papeari, Tahiti.

The term "primitive" was understood to refer, not to tribal art, but to the art of the late Middle Ages and early Renaissance before Raphael.

them, Gustave Boulanger, basically, the only difference between today's Idealists and Realists is the choice "between a hat and a cap"!

They, too, are poor, stupid prisoners of the allegorical Cave. Let us, therefore, leave them to grow more stupid as they contemplate the shadows that they take to be reality, and let us return to the men who, their chains broken, are entranced by the contemplation, far from their cruel native dungeon, of the radiant heaven of ideas.

The usual and ultimate goal of painting, as I have said, moreover that of all the arts, cannot be the direct representation of objects. Its finality is to express ideas by translating them into a special language.

Indeed, in the artist's eyes – that is, in the eyes of whomever must be the *evocator of the absolute beings* – objects – the relative beings that are but a translation, adjusted in proportion to our intellects, of the absolute and essential beings, of Ideas – can have no value only insofar as objects. They can only appear to him as *signs*. They are the letters of an immense alphabet that the man of genius alone can spell out.

To write his thought, his poem, with these signs, keeping in mind that the sign, as indispensable as it may be, is nothing in itself and that the idea alone is everything, appears therefore to be the task of the artist whose eye has known how to discern the essence of tangible objects. The first consequence of this principle, too obvious to belabor, is, one divines, a necessary simplification in the writing of the sign. If it were not so, in fact, would the painter not resemble the naive writer who believes that he is adding something to his work by polishing his penmanship and ornamenting it with useless flourishes?

But, if it is true that, in the world, ideas are the only real beings, if it is true that objects are but the outward forms that reveal those ideas, and thus are important insofar as they signify ideas, it is no less true that in our human eyes, that is, in the eyes of the arrogant *shadows of pure beings* that we are, shadows living in ignorance of their illusory condition and in the beloved falsity of the spectacle of a deceptive reality, it is no less true that in our myopic eyes objects appear most often to be objects, nothing but objects, independent of their symbolic significance – to the point that, at times, we cannot imagine them as signs despite our sincere efforts.

This vile propensity to consider, in our practical lives, an object to be only an object is obvious and, one might say, virtually universal. Only the superior man, enlightened by that supreme virtue that the Alexandrians so rightly called ecstasy, can persuade himself that he is but a sign, cast by some mysterious preordination amidst a numberless crowd of signs; he alone, tamer of the illusion-monster, can walk as master within this fantastic temple

> Where living pillars
> Let out, at times, confused words. . . .

whereas the idiot human herd, duped by appearances that lead it to deny the essential ideas, will ever blindly pass

> Through the forest of symbols
> That observe him with intimate gazes.

The work of art must not, even to the eye of the common cattle, lend itself to such an error. Indeed, the dilettante (who is not an artist and who therefore has no sense of symbolic correspondences) would find himself before it in a position similar to that of the crowd faced with natural objects. He would perceive its represented objects only as objects – and it is important to avoid this. Thus, the Idéiste work must not allow this confusion; thus, we must be allowed to know for certain that the objects in the painting have no value as objects, that they are but signs, words of no other importance in themselves.

Consequently, certain appropriate laws must govern pictorial imitation. The task of the artist will necessarily be to avoid carefully the paradox of all art: concrete truth, illusionism, *trompe l'oeil*, so as not to give, through one's painting, a deceptive impression of nature that would act upon the

Gustave Rodolphe Boulanger (1844–88), painter of everyday life in classical antiquity.

From Baudelaire's sonnet "Correspondances," Les Fleurs du Mal (1857).

viewer as nature herself does, that is, without any possible suggestion, that is (if I may be forgiven the barbarous neologism), in an Idéiste manner.

It is logical to imagine him fleeing, so as to guard himself against the perils of concrete truth, the analysis of the object. Indeed, each detail is, in reality, only a partial symbol, more often than not useless with regard to the total significance of the object. The Idéiste painter's strict duty is, therefore, to make a reasoned selection among the multiple elements combined in objectivity, to use in the work only the general and distinguishing lines, forms, and colors that will help to write clearly the Idéiste significance of the object, plus those partial symbols that corroborate the overall symbol.

Indeed, as one may easily deduce, the artist will always have the right to exaggerate, attenuate, deform the directly signifying characters (forms, lines, colors, etc.) not only according to his individual vision, not only molding it by his personal subjectivity (as happens even in Realist art), but, further, to exaggerate, attenuate, deform them according to the requirements of the idea to be expressed.

Therefore, to sum up and conclude, a work of art, as I have chosen to evoke it logically will be:

1. *Idéiste*, since its unique ideal will be to express the idea;

2. *Symbolist*, since it will express the idea through forms;

3. *Synthetic*, since it will present these forms and signs in a commonly intelligible fashion;

4. *Subjective*, since the object will never, in the work of art, be considered as an object, but as the sign of an idea perceived by the subject;

5. (This is a consequence) *decorative* – for decorative painting, properly speaking, as the Egyptians and quite probably the Greeks and the Primitives understood it, is nothing other than a manifestation of art that is at once subjective, synthetic, symbolist, and idéiste.

Now, if one pauses to consider, decorative painting is, strictly speaking, the true art of painting. Painting could only have been invented to *decorate* with thoughts, dreams, and ideas the banal walls of human edifices. The easel painting is but an illogical refinement, invented to satisfy the whim or the commercial spirit of decadent civilizations. In primitive societies, the first pictorial attempts could not have been other than decorative.

The art that we have attempted to legitimize and to characterize with all the preceding deductions, the art that may have seemed complicated and that certain chroniclers will gladly call decadent art, thus becomes, in the final analysis, a return to the formula of simple, spontaneous, and primordial art. Therein lies the criterion for the soundness of the aesthetic arguments applied. Idéiste art – which had to be justified with abstract and complicated reasoning, so paradoxical does it seem to our decadent civilizations that have forgotten all the initial revelations – is thus, indisputably, the genuine and absolute art, since, it is not only legitimate from a theoretical standpoint, but it also happens to be fundamentally identical with Primitive art, with art as it was divined by the instinctive geniuses of humanity's first ages. But is this all? Is there not a further element missing that would make art as we have understood it truly Art?

The man who, because of his native genius, because of his acquired qualities, can, in the face of nature, read the abstract significance, the primordial and underlying idea of every object, the man who, by his intelligence and his skill, knows how to use objects as a sublime alphabet to express the ideas that are revealed to him, would he truly be, by virtue of these qualities, a complete artist? Would he be the Artist?

Is he not, rather, an inspired scholar, a supreme formulator, who is able to write ideas as does a mathematician? Is he not in some sense an algebraist of ideas, and is his work not a marvelous equation, or, better, a page of ideographic writing that recalls the hieroglyphic texts of the obelisks of ancient Egypt?

Yes, to be sure, the artist who has not some further psychic gift will be nothing more, for he will be nothing more than an understanding evocator, and while understanding complemented by the power to express may be enough to make a scholar, it is not enough to make an artist.

To be really worthy of this fine title of nobility – so polluted in our industrialist present – he must join to the capacity to understand a still more sublime gift: I mean the gift of *emotivity*. Not, to be sure, the emotivity every man knows in the face of the illusory, passionate combinations of beings and objects, not the emotivity known to nightclub singers and chromo-print manufacturers – but that transcendental emotivity, so great and so precious, that causes the soul to shiver in the face of the undulating drama of abstractions. Oh, how rare are those whose bodies and hearts are stirred by the sublime sight of pure being and ideas! But that as well is the gift *sine qua non*, it is the spark that Pygmalion wanted for his Galatea, it is the illumination, the golden key, the Daimon, the Muse. . . .

With this gift, symbols, that is, ideas, rise from the darkness, animate, begin to live with a life that is no longer our contingent and relative life, a dazzling life that is the essential life, the life of art, the being of being.

With this gift, complete, perfect, absolute art exists at last.

Such is the art it is consoling to dream of, such is the art that I like to imagine, in my compulsory strolls amidst the miserable or base art trash that clutters our industrialist exhibitions. Such, too, I think – unless I have misinterpreted the thought in his work – is the art that Paul Gauguin, that great artist of genius with the soul of a primitive and, somewhat, of a savage, wanted to establish in our deplorable and rotten nation.

I can neither describe nor analyze his already marvelous work here. It is enough for me to have tried to characterize and legitimize the highly laudable aesthetic conception that seems to guide this great artist. Indeed, how can one suggest in words all that is inexpressible, the whole ocean of ideas that the clear-sighted eye can glimpse in those masterful works: *The Calvary*; *Jacob Wrestling with the Angel*; *The Yellow Christ*; in those marvelous landscapes of Martinique and Brittany, where each line, each form, each color is the word for an idea; in that sublime *Garden of Olives*, where an incarnadine-haired Christ, seated in a desolate place, seems to mourn the ineffable sorrows of dreams, the death-throes of Chimeras, the treason of chance, the vanity of the real, of life, and, perhaps, of the hereafter. . . . How can one relate the philosophy sculpted in the bas-relief that reads, ironically, *Be in love and you will be happy*, in which all lust, all the struggle of flesh and thought, all the sorrow of the sexual pleasures writhe and, so to speak, gnash their teeth? How to evoke that other wood sculpture: *Be mysterious*, which celebrates the pure joys of esotericism, the disturbing caresses of the riddle, the fantastic shadows of problem's forests? How to describe, finally, those strange, barbarous, and savage ceramics, into which he kneaded, sublime potter, more soul than clay?

And yet, if one thinks about it, as disturbing, as masterly, and as marvelous as this work may be, it is little enough, compared with what Gauguin could have produced, had he been placed in another civilization. Gauguin, it must be repeated, like all the Idéiste painters, is, above all, a decorator. His compositions find themselves confined by the limited field of the canvases. One would be tempted, at times, to take them for fragments of immense frescoes, and they nearly always seem ready to explode the frames that unduly limit them!

So! We have in our dying century only one great decorator, two perhaps, counting Puvis de Chavannes, and our idiotic society of bankers and polytechnicians refuses to give this rare artist the least palace, the meanest national hovel wherein the sumptuous mantles of his dreams may hang! The walls of our Pantheons of Stupidity are soiled by the ejaculations of the Tom, Dick, and Harrys of the Institute!

Ah, gentlemen, how posterity will curse you, mock you, and spit on you, if one day the meaning of art awakens in humanity's spirit! . . . Come now, a little common sense, you have among you a decorator of genius: walls! walls! give him some walls! . . .

Gauguin: Christ in the Garden of Olives, *1889, Norton Gallery and School of Art, West Palm Beach, Florida;* The Vision after the Sermon, *1888, National Gallery of Scotland, Edinburgh;* The Yellow Christ, *1889, Albright-Knox Art Gallery, Buffalo, New York;* The Calvary – Green Christ, *1889, Musées Royaux des Beaux-Arts, Brussels;* Be in Love and You Will be Happy, *1889, Museum of Fine Arts, Boston;* Be Mysterious, *1890, Musée d'Orsay, Paris.*

ALPHONSE GERMAIN

LA PLUME

"The Distorters' Theory"

September 1, 1891

EXPOSÉ AND REFUTATION

Certain young people are dissociating themselves from the desire to create art from scratch, to capture sensations purely instinctively. They preach a return to tradition, indeed to the sources of tradition – to the artlessness of exotic art. Their aim is piously to retain the original sensation and to render it through truly rare and harmonious line and color, but using *primitive* means and a freedom of interpretation verging upon the strange, upon distortion; summary outlines, little or no modeling, tones laid on without gradations, even without value relationships. "Neo-traditionism", as Pierre Louis [*sic*] has put it, "can have no dalliance with highly-wrought and learned psychological matters, with subtleties of feeling, none of which are within its emotional domain. It goes straight to the final synthesis. Everything is contained within the beauty of the work."

If they were applying such principles to react *artistically* against the technical complexities and the excessive importance given to the formal means of painting, these newcomers would deserve an enthusiastic welcome; unfortunately, they confine themselves to embryonic impressions; their espousal of distortion, ill-justified by their desire to render an aesthetic state of mind when faced with some natural effect, leads them back to the silhouettes of Saurias. This is the equivalent, in literature, of suppressing all syntax, with the pretext of giving images a more natural flavor.

Nothing can justify the exclusion of perspective and the suppression of relief, nothing, not even the pursuit of this sort of fine tapestry-making which is dear to the "traditionists;" an aim far better expressed by the telling images exhibited by Anquetin at the Champ-de-Mars than by the equations of Bernard and the *kakemonos* of Bonnard. A truly healthy western eye will always feel the need for gradation, which Ruskin rightly saw as the source of the value and beauty of a color: "Gradation," he states, "is to color what the curve is to the line; both appear beautiful to the human spirit guided by instinct alone, and both, considered as types, express the law of the change and gradual progress of the human soul itself."

Furthermore, to cease to take account of relief in order to avoid the paltriness of *trompe-l'oeil* is to leap from one exaggeration to another. Why not go back to the rudimentary stroke of the caveman? Is form less *spiritually* expressive in the works of the true Master because it obeys anatomy? What head emanates greater mystery than the *Mona Lisa*? What could better express the "triumph of the beautiful over the naturalist lie?" What head is more *sculpturally* constructed, more *perspectivally* modeled? The eye which does not perceive as much is abnormal.

Upon my word, the Byzantines, the precursors of Giotto and of Memling, distorted forms and used flat colors – *through ignorance*. They painted as men of their time – let us paint as men of ours; imperfections are affecting only in so far as the Divine shines forth in them, in so far as Faith has guided the hand that limned them; furthermore, to ape the incompetence of those who are less advanced than ourselves is tantamount to renouncing civilization – for what end? For the creation of an art which is inferior, since it bears no relation to our race and our modernity.

If Gauguin understands art as a savage does, haunted as he is by simplistic conceptions – or coarse ones, according to my own sensitivities –

This article in one of the leading Symbolist magazines of the 1890s was Alphonse Germain's response to the first exhibition of the Nabis held in August 1891. It was organized primarily by Maurice Denis in his home town of Saint Germain-en-Laye and included works by Bonnard, Denis, Ibels, Ranson, Verkade, Vuillard and Sérusier, whom Germain called "followers of Gauguin." He also associated Van Gogh and Cézanne with the stylistic features that he condemned.

"Neo-traditionism": the term coined by Maurice Denis (pseudonym "Pierre Louÿs") for his article in Art et Critique, August 30, 1890.

Saurias: a painter of ancient Greece thought to have been the inventor of the black silhouette profile.

Louis Anquetin (1861–1932), painter included in the "Impressionist and Synthetist" exhibition at the café Volpini in the champs de Mars in 1889.
Kakemono: a type of Japanese print.
John Ruskin (1819–1900), English art historian and critic.

Paul Gauguin photographed in his studio. Late 1893 or 1894. Larousse-Giraudon Archives.

at least he is sufficiently logical to go and paint in Tahiti; in a Latin land, the coloring of his successors jars and fails to strike home. The superiority of the scenes of Maurice Denis derives from the fact that they do indeed awaken a feeling of infinity; would they lose this power were they more correctly painted? Assuredly not. Neither naivety nor simplicity exclude knowledge; Fra Giovanni knew how to draw, and who subordinates his material to his ideal better than Puvis de Chavannes?

When the Hellenes combined the human form and the animal form in certain figures (head of Zeus with a lion's body, Heracles with a bull's neck, etc.), their distortion did not violate the harmonic Norm, because they were obeying the laws of nature. By setting out to distort in an anti-natural way, our young decorators become the interpreters of a nature that is on the decline, the portrayers of a degenerate race at its last gasp; they might as well depict foetuses, or illustrate works of teratology.

In a word, by painting with a technique fitted to stained glass or mosaic, they demonstrate a lack of deontological feeling. An artist cannot use every medium for every genre; the choice of material is of capital importance in art. Are missal illuminations or tailpieces done on canvas? Does Chéret paint in fresco? Can the figurines of vases be transposed into high relief? The mystic paintings by Maurice Denis are anagogical as were those of Angelico; looking at them, we no longer experience optical over-stimulation: we have the dream, the flight toward the beyond! But how

Jules Chéret (1836–1933), painter, lithographer and poster artist.

COLORPLATE 54. Vincent van Gogh. *Still Life of Oranges with Lemons and Blue Gloves.* 1889.
18³/₄ × 24¹/₂″ (47.6 × 62.2 cm). Paul Mellon Collection, Upperville, VA.

COLORPLATE 55. Vincent van Gogh. *Orchard in Bloom with Poplars*. 1889.
28³⁄₈ × 36¹⁄₄″ (72 × 92 cm). Bayerische Staatsgemäldesammlungen, Munich.

COLORPLATE 56. Vincent van Gogh. *Blossoming Chestnut Branches*. June 1890.
28¼ × 35¾″ (72 × 91 cm). E. G. Bührle Foundation, Zurich.

COLORPLATE 57. Paul Gauguin. *The Man with the Ax.* 1891. 36¼ × 27¼″ (92 × 69 cm).
Private Collection.

COLORPLATE 58. Paul Gauguin. *Aha oe feii? (What! Are you Jealous?).* 1892.
26 × 35″ (66 × 89 cm). Pushkin State Museum of Fine Arts, Moscow.

COLORPLATE 59. Paul Gauguin. *Vase of Flowers, after Delacroix*. 1894–97.
Watercolor, 6¾ × 4¾″ (17 × 12 cm). Frontispiece for MS of *Noa Noa*. Musée du Louvre, Paris.

COLORPLATE 60. Paul Gauguin. *Tahitian Figures. c.*1896/97.
Watercolor, 11¾ × 8½″ (30 × 22 cm). Folio 173 of the MS of *Noa Noa,* 1893/97.
Musée du Louvre, Paris.

COLORPLATE 61. Paul Gauguin. *Tahitian Woman with a Pig. c.*1893.
Pencil and watercolor, 2²⁄₅ × 6¹⁄₂″ (6 × 16.7 cm). Collection of Linda Rodgers Emory.

much better does paper lend itself to these archaisms! The *trouvailles* of an impetuous imagination, the fleeting nature of ecstatic transports, are sketched in by the pencil with an ease, rendered with a grace, that the paintbrush can never attain. Thus several of Denis' drawings inspired by Verlaine's *Sagesse* – which are simply *book illustrations* – are indeed intensely expressive.

In a word, if "traditionist" theory were truly to reflect the sensibilities of its adepts, they should have drawn inspiration from the Greek and Etruscan decorators; yet they took the Japanese as models – which was false reasoning. The most artistic synthesis in plastic art is to be found in the drawings of Ingres and Puvis de Chavannes; but our synthesis-loving distorters had recourse to prehistoric techniques; they were less interested in the painter of the *poor fisherman* than in Cézanne, Gauguin, Van Gogh, intensive temperaments all, but unbalanced and in no way Latin – again, false reasoning.

Cézanne labored painfully; Gauguin has the soul of an artist, but his mind is sick, or else his hand betrays his thought; Van Gogh, with his hypertrophizing vision, demonstrates irrefutably the pointlessness of painting without any knowledge of draftsmanship. The mistake made by their admirers was to deduce a theory from highly idiosyncratic exemplars; may they reflect upon this in the holy name of Art while they are as yet unformed. For, as long as they confuse the simple with the distorted, as long as they deviate from natural laws, all decorative beauty will elude them and, instead of giving birth to an original work, they are in danger of aborting.

An undistorted drawing, with the structure of its planes duly indicated without any detail detrimental to the whole – that is simplicity. But to prefer to imitate an earlier faltering! when they still have so much to learn! These cross-grained primitives remind me of those world-weary people who have experienced all previous ages, plumbed all deliquescences – all too soon . . . . To imitate an earlier faltering! What! To cease to respect form because art is not reality! So – are all the masterpieces created since the Renaissance mere magnificent aberrations?

The title poem of Verlaine's collection Sagesse *(1881) was printed on the same page as Germain's article in* La Plume *with an illustration by Maurice Denis.*

Jean-Auguste-Dominique Ingres (1780–1867).
Pierre Puvis de Chavannes, The Poor Fisherman, *1879, Musée d'Orsay, Paris.*

PAUL GAUGUIN

MERCURE DE FRANCE

"Armand Séguin"

February 1895

A gesture of deliberate sympathy: that, for me, is the whole meaning of a preface.

The desire to be judged by some and to gain insight into one's own strengths: for an artist, this is the only legitimate reason to hold an exhibition.

I am making this gesture, I am writing this preface, because, in my opinion, Séguin is an artist. This word frees me from all the current superlatives, for I use it in the proud and almost sacred way that Swedenborg did when he said: "Somewhere in the world there is a mysterious book where the eternal laws of the Beautiful are written. Only artists can decipher its meaning; and since God has chosen them to understand him, I shall call them the Chosen."

And Swedenborg was a man of learning!

Séguin is not a master. His faults are not yet sufficiently clearly established to earn him this title. But he knows how to read in the *Book* of

The Mercure de France *reprinted the introduction Gauguin had written for the catalogue of Séguin's exhibition on February 1 at Le Barc de Boutteville's gallery, 47 rue le Peletier. Armand Séguin (1869–1903) belonged to the "École de Pont-Aven" which gathered around Gauguin from 1886 to 1896 and formed the nucleus of early Symbolism/Synthetism. Séguin was a minor but devoted follower. Gauguin has used this catalogue preface to publicize aspects of his own thinking about the meaning of line and color.*

mystery, and he can speak its language. He has a personal conception of Beauty, he feels the need to forge his own way toward it.

Today he is showing us the results of his efforts, in order to hear the opinion of those whom he respects in the interests of his own development.

Thus on his part there is no sense of self-advertisement. That is why, for my part, I am not writing in any spirit of facile camaraderie, but only for the solemn pleasure of asking art-lovers to listen to me.

Here, a talented artist has brought together the fruits of his labors and his reveries.

To paint one's dreams is an act of sincerity.

It is to artists, his peers, that he is addressing himself. In offering him this gesture of solidarity, I am not contracting any obligation to put forward aesthetic theories, concerning either movements or the painter's craft: I am no art critic.

Suffice it for me to warn the visitor that Séguin is above all a cerebral painter – by which I do not, of course, mean a "literary" one – that he expresses not what he sees but what he thinks, through an original harmony of line and a draughtsmanship delicately communicated through the arabesque.

Manzana-Pissarro. *Gauguin at his Exhibition.* 1893. Caricature. Private Collection.

There is nothing of the "school" in his work; no conventional admiration translated through barren imitation. His is a sincere, robust and healthy temperament.

Séguin has studied nature fully. It was in Brittany, this year, that I first met him.

I painted that beautiful region myself in former days, I scanned its horizons, seeking some harmony between human life and plant and animal life in compositions where the great voice of the earth played a large part. Séguin, on the contrary, makes do with a restricted setting for his figures, achieving marvelous results.

Look at the Breton peasant woman in the large canvas without any horizon: she is stretched out, quite without dreaminess or affectation. She is resting. There is no literature here: everything is expressed through the arabesque of the lines which make up this figure, through the intertwining curves, some parallel to the frame. What skill in the deep tones of the bonnet, summing up a whiteness.

The black, too, I maintain, is a very beautiful color.

I would probably prefer a little more distinction in the use of his materials. Less insouciance, more craft, and the artist will surely prove master of his medium.

Conversely, craft is too evident in his etchings; there I could wish for greater artlessness. Yet here too Séguin has his own unusual way of understanding design.

Those of his etchings which will probably meet with most approval – the Parisian ones – are not those which most engaged my attention. It seems to me today that Paris, for Parisian painters, is a mere pretext for posters and caricatures, while I sometimes see the Mona Lisa at the Folies-Bergère . . . but I probably lack a *Parisian sense*.

After Brittany, I was glad to meet Séguin again, and his works, at the gallery of Le Barc de Boutteville, in a "petit monde" (as knowing schoolboys designate art's unofficial venues).

The spirit bloweth where it listeth, talent will out where it can. In my opinion it is sufficient unto itself as decoration, and can do without testimonials.

Furthermore, this "petit monde" will have a place in the art history of our time, indeed, has it not already? We shall remember it when we have forgotten all manner of fancy insults and childish admonishments.

MAURICE DENIS

LA PLUME

"On the Exhibition of Armand Séguin"
March 1, 1895

Those who have followed the development of those painters called successively Cloisonists (Dujardin, *Revue indépendante*, 1886), Synthetists (1889), Neo-traditionists (Pierre Louys, *Art et critique*, 1890), Ideists (Aurier, *Mercure*, 1891), Symbolists and Distorters (A. Germain) from their beginnings, will find Séguin's exhibition of particular interest. They will enjoy picking up certain forgotten aspects of the Exhibition at the Café Volpini, on the Champ-de-Mars in 1889; they will see echoes of successful formulae of the School of Pont-Aven.

Séguin is one of the few artists to have retained the methods of that period. He has made them his own, I hasten to acknowledge, and in particular he has made them serve his own very personal statements. With

Maurice Denis' review of Séguin's exhibition at Le Barc de Boutteville was an attempt to re-publicize the original principles of Symbolism/Synthetism which both he and Gauguin felt had become obscured through critical attack and misunderstanding. He particularly restates the formal emphasis on line and color as opposed to literary subject matter.

"Impressionists and Synthetists" at the café Volpini, 1889.

Maurice Denis. *Self-Portrait*. 1896. Charcoal drawing, 10½ × 8½″ (26 × 22 cm). Private Collection, France.

Charles Filiger (1863–1928).

more freedom than Filiger or Bernard, he persists in using black outlines and flat colors: as did Cloisonnism. But he should be admired for a very pure, I would say classical, conception of form: I love the discreet modeling he gives his figures, not in order to simulate relief but to emphasize the beauty of the outline. He has a very apt feeling for distortion, he knows how to obey the demands of his sensibility as well as those of decoration.

* * *

Thus it is as well, at the Séguin Exhibition, to enquire into what the synthetist or symbolist painters wanted to achieve.

We no longer know. Young men of letters, knowing schoolboys, as Gauguin calls them, have now extended their brief to painting, thereby confusing all notions: they call upon the Laws of nature and the Norm of Harmony. They will accuse Séguin of not knowing how to draw. . . .

Who remembers the Café Volpini I mentioned just now? There, we saw a collection of very beautiful works, some of which will endure. Since then we have rarely seen any affirmation of such simple, primitive methods, of any tendency that is so clearly artless.

At the exhibitions of Le Barc de Boutteville, from the end of '91 onward, flat color no longer appeared with such rigor; forms were no longer set within black lines, there was no longer an exclusive use of pure colors. This could be explained, I imagine, by the more or less complete abstention of Bernard and Gauguin; by Anquetin's evolution toward modeling; by the attitude of several newcomers, engaged upon more sentimental researches and more exquisite methods.

The art-loving public which has seen no symbolist Art other than the exhibitions since '91 will be unacquainted with its purely theoretical and speculative manifestations, those of the early days. It is thus that these literary newcomers are unaware of the fanaticism of the now defunct little reviews, the unheard-of inventions of the first decadents.

The public barely knows the part played, in this complex movement, by the Impressionism of Paul Gauguin, the idealism of Émile Bernard and the naturalism of Louis Anquetin. They know little of Van Gogh and the pioneer Cézanne. They do not sense the parallel influence of mystical theories, such as those of Bernard, and of scientific research such as that of Seurat.

This is because we have become accustomed to scan these paintings for poetic intentions, for literary expressions. How deplorable are the commentaries of certain critics! Symbolist art is not the art of neurosis and madness it is generally believed to be. This art is idealist in one sense and, in another, not at all, and this cannot be stressed often enough. . . .

The painters of whom I am talking believed that, before being a representation of nature or of a dream, a picture was essentially *a flat surface covered with colors arranged in a certain order.* They were painters first and foremost. They preferred expression through decoration, form, color, the material used expressively through the subject. What they were expressing was indeed their ideals, their vision of life, their emotion before objects, but they expressed this only through pictorial means. That was their virtue: they transposed their sensations into Beauty.

Denis frequently repeated this maxim from "The Definition of Neo-traditionism," Art et Critique, *August 30, 1890.*

And therefore – unconsciously, no doubt, like all Masters – they practiced what analysts have since called *subjective Distortion* (the old doctrine of *homo additus naturae,* nature seen through a temperament) for the purpose of greater sincerity – and *objective Distortion,* for the purpose of shaping their visions in accordance with the eternal laws of the decorative.

It was while they were defining these ideas, through more schematic research, that the young of ten years ago became particularly concerned to define the laws of the decorative and of expression. Some, with Bernard, found them in tradition, others, with Seurat, in the physical and mathematical sciences.

That was Symbolism.

And as reaction against the pervading mood had to be violent, these young painters decided to begin again from scratch. They believed that Art should be taken back to the artlessness of its beginnings, when its decorative purpose was still unchallenged. And their first attempts were instinct with an extraordinary awkwardness.

Denis defined as "subjective distortion" Zola's well-known formulation of naturalist and impressionist art, "nature seen through a temperament," that is, nature seen through the distorting lens of personal emotion. "Objective distortion," according to Denis, resulted from the artist's search for absolute laws of visual expression derived from the art of the past or from more recent visual research. Many of these ideas repeat what Albert Aurier had written in his articles on Van Gogh (1890) and Gauguin (1891).

They favored rustic scenes, landscapes, still lifes which revealed their methods, their efforts at synthesis at their most straightforward. Then they created a new style, by which I mean a logical body of decorative formulae, which were then put into practice.

It is above all for such artistic concerns that I congratulate Armand Séguin, for such concerns are rare. It is because of him, and several other good toilers in the vineyard, and despite so many clumsy, unintelligent, unhealthy imitations, that I still believe in Symbolism: in a theory which proclaims the possibility of the expression of human emotions and thoughts through aesthetic analogues, through equivalents in Beauty.

RENÉ MAURICE
NOUVELLE REVUE DE BRETAGNE
"Concerning Gauguin"
November–December 1953

Sometime during April 1894, just after receiving an inheritance from an uncle who died in Orléans, Gauguin arrived in Brittany with his friend Annah the Javanese, whom he had met several weeks earlier through Ambroise Vollard, an art dealer who thought she might be a good model for him. He was hoping to be able to set himself up again in Le Pouldu at Mlle. Henry's inn, but it had gone out of business in November 1893. He stayed for several weeks with the Polish painter Slevinsky, who had a villa near the large beaches, then he went down to Pont-Aven, to the inn at Gloanec. On 25 May 1894, accompanied by Annah and the painter Séguin and his wife, he went to visit Concarneau and its old port.

It would be curious to know how Gauguin was dressed, since, for some, his dress was part of the cause of the scene that took place that day. Several writers, notably Charles Kunstler, want to see him dressed up as a cabaret performer, with an astrakhan cap, blue coat with mother-of-pearl buttons, putty colored pants, white gloves on his hands, a sculpted cane with real pearl inlays, a gray, Buffalo Bill-style felt hat with a sky-blue band, and, to complete the character, a monkey perched on his shoulder. . . .

Nothing suggests that he was in the habit of dressing like this in Brittany. Only Etienne Port, under the name Careil, wrote in an article that appeared in *Fureteur Breton* in November 1919, 25 years after the event, that that afternoon the painter went for a stroll with his Negress and his "exotic bird" (a green parrot). For some, this "green parrot" has become a young monkey. . . .

All the photographs that I have seen of Gauguin in Brittany, which are in the possession of Emile Bernard, and some of which have been reproduced in his *Memories of Pont-Aven and Le Pouldu*, show the painter of *La Belle Angèle* dressed like a Breton fisherman: beret, blue wool sweater, clogs. It seems, in fact, that Gauguin liked to dress in the costume of each country he lived in, one after the other. Thus, he later dressed in the Maori style.

Ambroise Vollard (1868–1939), art dealer; he opened a gallery in Paris in 1893 which attracted the interest of avant-garde artists and patrons. Gauguin's business relations with him proved complicated and bitter.

Wladyslaw Slewinsky (1854–1918) met Gauguin in Paris in 1889 and painted with him in Le Pouldu.

Charles Kunstler (1887–1977), author of a biography of Gauguin published in 1934.

La Belle Angèle, *1889, Musée d'Orsay, Paris.*

Paul Gauguin with a cello, Annah the Javanese, Paul Sérusier (*back left*) and friends in Gauguin's studio, 6 rue Vercingétorix, Montparnasse. Photograph, 1894. Courtesy of Musée Gauguin, Papeari, Tahiti.

For the study of this "news item," I want to keep strictly to the stories in the Breton newspapers of the period, leaving aside all the captions and "images d'Epinal." What did they say? They all wrote his name with an *e* where the *i* should be: Gauguen, evidently a confusion due to the common Breton name Guéguen, as M. Waquel [sic] judiciously writes. There is no question of the artist's eccentricity in dress, nor of the presence of an "exotic animal," but only of the presence of "Madame Gauguen" who "is of the black race" and who, for that alone, could have been the unintentional cause of the row.

In the course of this afternoon of 25 May 1894, during the time when "these artists took a stroll on Quai Péneroff, accompanied by their ladies," some children, attracted by the presence of the Negress (undoubtedly they had never seen one in their lives), followed and threw stones at them. Séguin seized one of the rascals, the young Sauban, and pulled his ear. The people of the port immediately took the part of this scamp and began to insult the strangers grossly. A pilot from Concarneau, the child's father, René Sauban, ran toward them and punched Séguin in the face. He was so frightened that he dove into the water to escape his aggressor by swimming. Gauguin, intervening in turn to defend his friend, threw Sauban to the ground. But three fishermen who had been sitting at the tavern next door then came to the latter's aid. Gauguin defended himself courageously, but he was not able to avoid a blow that "fractured his right leg at the internal malleolus and dislocated his right foot." Mme. Séguin was also struck and suffered an "injured side."

Le Finistère related the events in the Saturday, 29 May 1894 edition of his paper, filed from Concarneau, on page 3 as follows:

A brutal assault, without reasonable motive, took place last Friday . . .

M. Paul Gauguen, a painter living in Pont-Aven, went to Concarneau accompanied by his wife and some friends. Mme. Gauguen is of the Negro race. Nothing more was needed for several children to feel they had the right to throw stones at her and at the same time those who accompanied her. M. Gauguen's friends pulled the ear of one of these poorly raised children. Immediately, several people at the scene began to insult the strangers in the grossest possible manner.

On the Quai Péneroff, an individual ran toward them and struck one of M. Gauguen's friends, M. Séguin, in the face. M. Gauguen, therefore, pushed the aggressor and threw him to the ground. But he got up. Three others joined him and, all together, attacked M. Gauguen. He defended himself energetically but he could not avoid a blow that fractured his leg at the internal malleolus and dislocated his right foot.

These savages also struck Mme. Séguin and injured her side.

The principal author of this unspeakable and ridiculous assault is someone named René Sauban, age 44, pilot, living in the rue Duguay-Trouin.

The other individuals who took part are as yet unknown. It is to be hoped that the police and the gendarmerie, who are uniting their efforts to find the accomplices of Sauban, are successful in their investigation.

And here is the article that appeared in *L'Union Agricole et Maritime* of Quimperlé, in the 30 May 1894 edition, page 3, in the local news:

CONCARNEAU (by our correspondent). Last Friday, following an altercation between fishermen and painters vacationing at Concarneau, blows were exchanged. One of these men, named Gauguen, suffered a broken leg; the doctor who was called to treat this poor man filed a certificate declaring that the malleolus of his right leg was fractured and his foot dislocated and that rest in a cast for 40 to 45 days was critical.

Our populace was very much struck by this act of brutality, committed by one called Sauban, a pilot who, furious that anyone should pull the ear of his son, wished to avenge himself.

Henri Waquet (b. 1887), author of many studies of Breton history and culture.

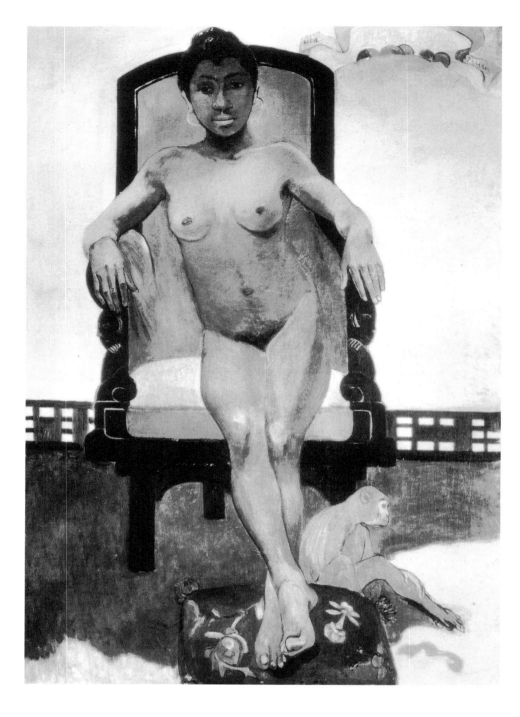

Paul Gauguin. *Annah the Javanese Girl.* 1893–94. 45½ × 31″ (116 × 81 cm). Private Collection.

Here is more or less what happened:

These artists were strolling on the Quai Péneroff, accompanied by their ladies, one of whom was a Negress; the color of this one attracted the children, who followed them throwing stones. One of the men, tired of the pursuit, and above all of the scheming, was able to surprise one of the stone throwers, grab him, and pull his ear. There began the altercation, during which one lady who was vacationing with her husband at Le Pouldu also received a punch that injured her left side.

We should point out just how much this aggression can be prejudicial to the interest of our city. The fortune of Concarneau is due largely to the affluence of strangers who are attracted to the beauty of our port and its surroundings as well as the affability they find here. Now, it could take an act of savagery such as the one of which we have just spoken to set against us strangers who, fearing that they will not be safe in our town, may hesitate to come to our locality. It was, it is true, an isolated incident and we are sure that nothing like it will happen again. But it is good to point out the harm that can result from such a thing, should it happen, for our city where, moreover, we have been unanimous in censuring Sauban's brutality.

During the fracas, Gauguin thus received a broken leg and the doctor who was called to treat him estimated that he would not be able to work for 40 to 45 days.

* * *

Following the investigation, two men from Concarneau, René-Yves Sauban, pilot, and Pierre-Joseph Monfort, fisherman, were served summonses to appear before the *Tribunal correctionel de Quimper*, in the session of August 23, 1894, to answer for having voluntarily struck and injured Paul Gauguen on May 25, 1894 with the result of malady or incapacity to work for more than twenty days.

PAUL GAUGUIN

CAHIER POUR ALINE

"Genesis of a Painting"

1893

A young Kanaka girl is lying on her stomach, showing a part of her frightened face. She lies on a bed decorated with a blue *paréo* and a clear, chromium-yellow sheet. A violet purple background, sown with flowers like electric sparks; a rather strange figure stands next to the bed.

Seduced by a shape, a movement, I paint them with hardly any other concern than to do a nude piece. As is, the nude study is a bit indecent, nevertheless I want to make a chaste painting out of it which would render the Kanaka spirit, character, and tradition.

The *paréo* being intimately linked to the existence of a Kanaka, I use it as a bedcover. The sheet, of a fabric made from tree bark, must be yellow because when it is this color it inspires something unexpected in the spectator, because it suggests the lighting from a lamp, which spares me having to make a lamp-light effect. I've got to have a background which is a bit frightening. Violet is everywhere. That's the musical part of the painting which has been built up. In this rather daring position, what can a young Kanaka girl be doing completely nude on a bed? Preparing herself

COLORPLATE 44

Paul Gauguin. Page from *Cahier pour Aline*, with sketch of *Manao Tupapau*. MS, Bibliothèque d'Art et d'Archéologie Fondation Jacques Doucet, Paris.

for love? All of this is in her character, but it's indecent and I don't want it. To sleep! The love-making still indecent, will have been finished. I see only fear. What kind of fear? Certainly not the fear of a Susanna surprised by the elders. That doesn't exist in Oceania.

The *tùpapaù* (Spirit of the Dead) is all that's needed. For the Kanakas, it's a constant fear. At night, a lamp is always lit. No one walks out in the streets when there is no moon, unless someone has a lantern, and even then they go out in groups.

Once my *tùpapaù* is found I attach myself to it completely, and I make it the theme of my painting. The nude is relegated to the background.

What could a ghost be for a Kanaka woman? She doesn't know theater, doesn't read novels, and, when she thinks of a dead person, she necessarily thinks of someone she has already seen. My ghost can only be a small and very ordinary woman. Her hand reaches out as though to seize a prey.

The sense of the decorative leads me to sow the background with flowers. They are flowers of *tùpapaù*, phosphorescences, a sign that the ghost is taking care of you. Tahitian beliefs.

The title, *Manao tùpapaù*, has two meanings; either she thinks about the ghost, or the ghost thinks about her.

To recapitulate. The musical part: horizontal, wavy lines; harmonies of orange and blue, linked together with yellows and violets – their derivatives – lit up with greenish sparks. The literary part: the Spirit of a living woman linked with the Spirit of the Dead. Night and Day.

This genesis is written for those who have always wanted to know the *whys* and *wherefores*.

Otherwise, it's simply a study of an Oceanian nude.

This painting was part of a group of recent Tahitian works sent to France in December 1892 for inclusion in an exhibition in Copenhagen due to open in March 1893. Gauguin described the painting many times: in letters to his wife (December 8, 1892) and to Daniel de Monfreid (February 1898), in the text of the Cahier pour Aline *(his daughter) and finally in* Noa Noa *(1897).*

ANDRÉ FONTAINAS

MERCURE DE FRANCE
"Modern Art – Gauguin"
January 1899

In January 1899 Vollard held an exhibition of Gauguin's recent work from Tahiti including Where Do We Come From? What Are We? Where Are We Going? *It was reviewed with mixed feelings for the Symbolist* Mercure de France *by the poet and critic André Fontainas (1865–1948) and elicited an explanatory letter from Gauguin (March 1899: see below).*

I do not like M. Paul Gauguin's painting very much. For a long time I was repelled by it and spoke of it slightingly, perhaps a little brusquely: I knew almost nothing about it. This time I examined with care his few recent canvases now on exhibition at Vollard's gallery in the rue Laffitte; and if my opinion of them has changed very little, at least I have become aware of a new and growing respect, solid and profound, for the serious, thoughtful, and sincere work of this painter. I have tried to understand it, I believe I have grasped some of his motives and impulses, I have caught myself discussing and criticizing them, becoming enthusiastic over some while disregarding others. Yet even after this careful study I have never been as moved or excited as I have been by certain other painters. I have sought for the causes of my indifference and believe I have found them.

I do not criticize M. Gauguin either for his drawing, so often disparaged, or for his exoticism; I should be more apt to praise him for them if, in truth, there were any need to do so. Indeed what other analysis of drawing should one accept than that of Balzac in the *Chef d'oeuvre inconnu*: "Line is the means by which the effect of light on an object makes itself manifest. Form is . . . an instrument for the dissemination of ideas, sensations; it is poetry. The mission of art is not to copy nature but to express it." Therefore I acknowledge M. Gauguin's right to express himself as he sees fit, on condition that he inspires in the mind of the spectator sensations, ideas, anything at all that will produce a vision similar to his own.

Honoré de Balzac, Le Chef d'oeuvre inconnu, *1831.*

In this respect, I admit, M. Gauguin is irreproachable. He has created his own drawing even though it may resemble that of van Gogh or Cézanne; his aggressive drawing, new and precise in pattern, has a positive effect; indeed it would be impossible to find fault with it.

The same holds true for his exoticism. Everyone is at liberty to choose either a commonplace or an unusual setting as he pleases. That in itself is of no importance. The essential – since I cannot see in these pictures an exact representation of scenes in Tahiti or in the Marquesas – is that the art of the painter must convey to us an image, true or false (it does not matter), of a tropic land, luxuriant and primitive, covered with gigantic dense jungle growth, a land of deep waters and violent contrasts of light and air, peopled by a dignified race, modest and unspoiled. That M. Gauguin should have abandoned the too artificial simplicity of Brittany for his oceanic mirages is yet another proof of his complete sincerity. Out there on his enchanted island he is no longer concerned with the absurd mania for playing at restoring the great archaic romance of Brittany, so tedious after all. He no longer need worry about his reputation among the literary aesthetes; he is alive in the midst of distant seas, and the pictures he sends to his friends from time to time continue to prove to us that he is working.

What impresses the beholder at once is the careful study of arrangement in his canvases, which are primarily decorative. The landscapes that compose their profound, subdued harmony are organized not so much for crude picturesque effect as for the purpose, almost always achieved, of creating warm, brooding wellsprings for the surging emotions. If the violent oppositions of such full and vibrant tones, which do not blend and never merge into one another through intermediate values, first distract and then rivet the attention, it must also be admitted that while they are often glowing, bold, and exultant, they sometimes lose their effect by monotonous repetition, by the juxtaposition, irritating in the long run, of a startling red and a vibrant green, identical in value and intensity. And yet it is undoubtedly the landscape that satisfies and even exalts one in M. Gauguin's painting. He has invented a new and broad method of painting landscapes by synthesis and, in the words that he himself wrote in the *Mercure de France*, by "seeking to express the harmony between human life and that of animals and plants in compositions in which I have allowed the deep voice of the earth to play an important part."

At Vollard's, hanging not far from an extremely delicate landscape painted some years ago, in which figures at the water's edge are watching the reflection of the sun sparkling on the waves, there is a purely decorative picture conceived in this manner and, I believe, very characteristic of the artist's personality. In the midst of the somber blues and greens, noble animal and vegetable forms intermingle, composing a pure pattern. Nothing more; a perfect harmony of form and color.

There is also a landscape of varied yellows spread out like a delicate curtain of thin golden rain. Here and there the green of some strange leaf, the repeated detail of bright red berries. A man in a sarong reaches toward the low branches of a tree. All this – the light, the graceful effort of the gesture, the grouping of objects and colors – compose a simple and exquisite picture.

If only M. Gauguin were always like that! Or if he would paint as he does when he shows us ceremonial dancers lingering under the trees amid thick undergrowth, or nude women bathing surrounded by gorgeous, strangely illumined vegetation. But too often the people of his dreams, dry, colorless, and rigid, vaguely represent forms poorly conceived by an imagination untrained in metaphysics, of which the meaning is doubtful and the expression is arbitrary. Such canvases leave no impression but that of deplorable error, for abstractions are not communicated through concrete images unless, in the artist's own mind, they have already taken shape in some natural allegory that gives them life. That is the lesson

Gauguin: Mercure de France, *"Préface à l'exposition d'oeuvres nouvelles d'Armand Séguin,"* February 1895.

taught by the noble example Puvis de Chavannes gives us through his art. To represent a philosophical ideal he creates harmonious groups of figures whose attitudes convey to us a dream analogous to his own. In the large picture exhibited by M. Gauguin, nothing – not even the two graceful and pensive figures standing so tranquilly and beautifully, or the masterful evocation of a mysterious idol – would reveal to us the meaning of the allegory, if he had not taken the trouble to write high up in a corner of the canvas: "Where do we come from? What are we? Where are we going?"

However, in spite of the outlandishness of these near-savages, to which one becomes accustomed, the interest is diverted from the naked woman crouching in the foreground and again becomes fixed wholly upon the charm of the setting in which the action takes place.

But if I point out the grace of a woman half-reclining on a sort of couch, magnificent and curious, in the open air, I prefer not to dwell on other paintings which show the persistent efforts of an obstinate innovator in all the willfulness, slightly brutal, of his struggle.

In other respects M. Gauguin is without doubt an unusually gifted painter, from whom the opportunity of displaying the vigorous energy of his temperament by the execution of an important decorative composition on the walls of a public edifice has been too long withheld. There we could see exactly what he is capable of doing, and if he would guard against a tendency toward abstraction, I am sure we should see powerful and truly harmonious creations produced by his hand.

COLORPLATE 64

Paul Gauguin. *Tahitian Woman.* c.1892/93. Chalk and pastel, 15⅓ × 11⅘" (39 × 20 cm). Metropolitan Museum of Art, New York (Bequest of Miss Adelaide Milton de Groot, 1967.187.13).

Landscape with hut in Tahiti.
Photograph. Roger-Viollet, Paris.

PAUL GAUGUIN

Letter to André Fontainas

March 1899

TAHITI

Un grand sommeil noir
Tombe sur ma vie
Dormez, tout espoir
Dormez, toute envie.

Verlaine

"A huge dark sleep/ Falls on my life/ Sleep, all hope/ Sleep, all desire."

Monsieur Fontainas,
In the January number of the *Mercure de France* you have two interesting articles, "Rembrandt" and "The Vollard Gallery." In the latter you mention me. In spite of your dislike you have tried to make an honest study of the art, or rather the work, of a painter who has no emotional effect upon you. A rare phenomenon among critics.

I have always felt that it was the duty of a painter never to answer criticisms, even hostile ones – especially hostile ones; nor flattering ones either, because those are often dictated by friendship.

This time, without departing from my habitual reserve, I have an irresistible desire to write to you, a caprice if you will, and – like all emotional people – I am not good at resisting. Since this is merely a personal letter, it is not a real answer but simply a chat on art; your article prompts and evokes it.

We painters, we who are condemned to penury, accept the material difficulties of life without complaining, but we suffer from them insofar as they constitute a hindrance to work. How much time we lose in seeking our daily bread! The most menial tasks, dilapidated studios, and a thousand other obstacles. All these create despondency, followed by impotence, rage, violence. Such things do not concern you at all, I mention them only to convince both of us that you have good reason to point out numerous defects, violence, monotony of tone, clashing colors, etc. Yes, all these probably exist, do exist. Sometimes, however, they are unintentional. Are not these repetitions of tones, these monotonous color harmonies (in the musical sense) analogous to oriental chants sung in a shrill voice to the accompaniment of pulsating notes which intensify them by contrast? Beethoven uses them frequently (as I understand it) in the *Sonata Pathétique*, for example. Delacroix, too, with his repeated harmonies of brown and dull velvet, a somber cloak suggesting tragedy. You often go to the Louvre; with what I have said in mind, look closely at Cimabue. Think also of the musical role color will henceforth play in modern painting. Color, which is vibration just as music is, is able to attain what is most universal yet at the same time most elusive in nature: its inner force.

Here near my cabin, in complete silence, amid the intoxicating perfumes of nature, I dream of violent harmonies. A delight enhanced by I know not what sacred horror I divine in the infinite. An aroma of long-vanished joy that I breathe in the present. Animal figures rigid as statues, with something indescribably solemn and religious in the rhythm of their pose, in their strange immobility. In eyes that dream, the troubled surface of an unfathomable enigma.

Night is here. All is at rest. My eyes close in order to see without actually understanding the dream that flees before me in infinite space; and I experience the languorous sensation produced by the mournful procession of my hopes.

In praise of certain pictures that I considered unimportant you exclaim, "If only Gauguin were always like that!" But I don't want to be always like that.

"In the large panel that Gauguin exhibits there is nothing that explains the meaning of the allegory." Yes, there is; my dream is intangible, it comprises no allegory; as Mallarmé said, "It is a musical poem, it needs no libretto." Consequently, the essence of a work, unsubstantial and out of reach, consists precisely of "that which is not expressed; it flows by implication from the lines without color or words; it is not a material structure."

Standing before one of my pictures of Tahiti, Mallarmé also remarked, "It is amazing that one can put so much mystery in so much brilliance."

To go back to the panel: the idol is there not as a literary symbol, but as a statue, yet perhaps less of a statue than the animal figures, less animal also, combining my dream before my cabin with all nature, dominating our primitive soul, the unearthly consolation of our sufferings to the extent that they are vague and incomprehensible before the mystery of our origin and of our future.

And all this sings with sadness in my soul and in my design while I paint and dream at the same time with no tangible allegory within my reach – due perhaps to a lack of literary education.

Awakening with my work finished, I ask myself, "Where do we come from? What are we? Where are we going?" A thought which no longer has

anything to do with the canvas, expressed in words quite apart on the wall that surrounds it. Not a title but a signature.

You see, although I understand very well the value of words – abstract and concrete – in the dictionary, I no longer grasp them in painting. I have tried to interpret my vision in an appropriate décor without recourse to literary means and with all the simplicity the medium permits: a difficult job. You may say that I have failed, but do not reproach me for having tried, nor should you advise me to change my goal, to dally with other ideas already accepted, sanctified. Puvis de Chavannes is the perfect example. Of course Puvis overwhelms me with his talent and experience, which I lack; I admire him as much as you do and more, but for entirely different reasons (and – don't be annoyed – with more understanding). Each of us belongs to his own period.

The government is right not to give me an order for a decoration for a public building which might clash with the ideas of the majority, and it would be even more reprehensible for me to accept it, since I should have no alternative but to cheat or lie to myself.

At my exhibition at Durand-Ruel's [in 1893] a young man who didn't understand my pictures asked Degas to explain them to him. Smiling, he recited a fable by La Fontaine. "You see," he said, "Gauguin is the thin wolf without the collar [that is, he prefers liberty with starvation to servitude with abundance]."

After fifteen years of struggle we are beginning to free ourselves from the influence of the Academy, from all this confusion of formulas apart from which there has been no hope of salvation, honor, or money: drawing, color, composition, sincerity in the presence of nature, and so on. Only yesterday some mathematician (Charles Henry) tried to prove to us that we should use unchangeable light and color.

Now the danger is past. Yes, we are free, and yet I see still another danger flickering on the horizon; I want to discuss it with you. This long and boring letter has been written with only that in view. Criticism of

Paul Gauguin. *The Universe is Created.* Winter 1893–94. Woodcut painted in black, ocher, orange, blue, green and yellow, 8 × 13¾″ (20.3 × 35.1 cm). © 1992 The Art Institute of Chicago (Clarence Buckingham Collection, 1948.259).

Gauguin showed 46 works at Durand-Ruel's gallery in November 1893.

today, when it is serious, intelligent, full of good intentions, tends to impose on us a method of thinking and dreaming which might become another bondage. Preoccupied with what concerns it particularly, its own field, literature, it will lose sight of what concerns us, painting. If that is true, I shall be impertinent enough to quote Mallarmé, "A critic is someone who meddles with something that is none of his business."

In his memory will you permit me to offer you this sketch of him, hastily dashed off, a vague recollection of a beautiful and beloved face, radiant even in the shadows. Not a gift, but an appeal for the indulgence I need for my foolishness and violence.

Very cordially
Paul Gauguin

PAUL GAUGUIN

Letter to Daniel de Monfreid

February 1898

TAHITI

I did not write you last month, I didn't have anything more to tell you that wasn't repetitive, then later I didn't feel up to it. As soon as the mail arrived, having received nothing from Chaudet, suddenly my health was almost restored; that is, with no risk any more of dying naturally, I wanted to kill myself. I went off to hide on the mountain where my corpse would have been devoured by the ants. I didn't have a gun, but I had some arsenic that I had hoarded when I was sick with eczema: whether the dose was too strong, or the vomiting nullified the action of the poison by expelling it, I don't know. Finally, after a night of terrible suffering, I went back to my lodgings. All during this month, I have been plagued by a pressure at the temples, then dizziness, and nausea at my tiny meals. This month I receive 700 francs from Chaudet and 150 francs from Mauffra [sic]: with that I pay the most relentless creditors, and continue to live as before, on troubles and shame, until May, when the bank will have seized and sold dirt-cheap my belongings, among other things my paintings. Well, we'll see then about starting over in some other way. I must tell you that my resolution was firmly made for December. At that time I wanted, before dying, to paint a great canvas that I had in mind, and for the whole month I worked day and night in an unprecedented fever. What! it's not a canvas done like a Puvis de Chavannes, with studies from nature, then preliminary cartoon, etc. It is all dashed off with the tip of the brush, on burlap full of knots and wrinkles, so that its appearance is terribly rough.

They will say it's slipshod . . . unfinished. It is true that one cannot judge oneself accurately but, nonetheless, I think that this canvas not only surpasses in merit all the preceding ones, but even that I will never do a better or a similar one. I put into it before dying all my energy, such a sorrowful passion in terrible circumstances, and so clear a vision without corrections, that all that is hasty disappears, and life rises up out of it. It doesn't stink of models, technique, and so-called rules – which I have always shaken off, though sometimes with fear.

It is a canvas 4.5 by 1.7 meters high. The two upper corners are chromium yellow with the inscription on the left and my signature on the right, like a fresco damaged in the corners and applied onto a gold wall. On the lower right, a sleeping baby, then three crouching women. Two

Georges-Alfred Chaudet (d. 1899), painter who agreed to act as an agent on Gauguin's behalf with responsibility for the sale of paintings he had left behind in France when he returned to Tahiti in 1895.

Maxime Maufra (1861–1918), painter who met Gauguin at Pont-Aven in 1890 and who received a number of Gauguin's paintings from Chaudet for which he owed money to the artist.

COLORPLATE 64

COLORPLATE 63. Paul Gauguin. *Oviri*. 1887–88. Glazed stoneware, ht 7⅛″ (18.2 cm).
Musée d'Orsay, Paris.

COLORPLATE 62. Paul Gauguin. *Te Po (The Night)*. *c*.1893–94. Woodcut, 8 × 14″ (20.5 × 35.5 cm).
© 1991 The Art Institute of Chicago (Clarence Buckingham Collection, 1948.253).

COLORPLATE 66. Paul Gauguin. *Vairumati*. 1897. 28¾ × 37″ (73 × 94 cm).
Musée d'Orsay, Paris.

COLORPLATE 64. Paul Gauguin.
Where Do We Come From? What Are We?
Where Are We Going? 1897.
54¾ × 147½″ (130.1 × 374.6 cm).
Museum of Fine Arts, Boston
(Tompkins Collection).

COLORPLATE 65. Paul Gauguin. *Fatata te Miti (By the Sea)*. 1892. 26¾ × 36″ (68 × 92 cm).
National Gallery of Art, Washington, D.C. (Chester Dale Collection).

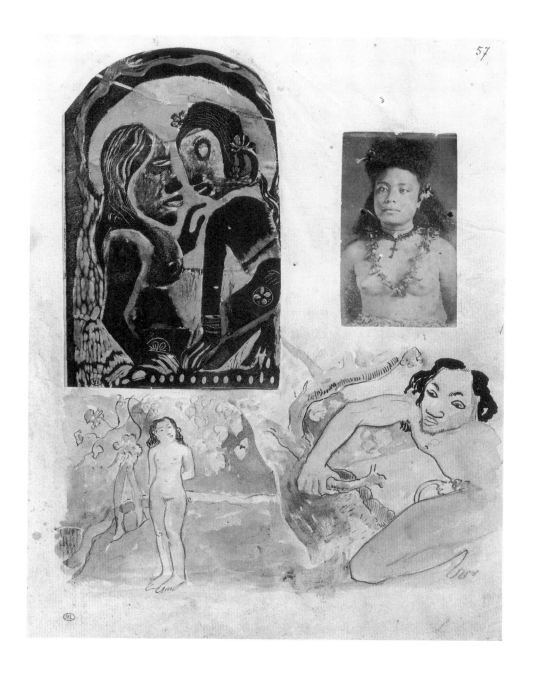

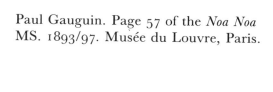

Paul Gauguin. Page 57 of the *Noa Noa* MS. 1893/97. Musée du Louvre, Paris.

figures dressed in purple confide their reflections to one another; an enormous figure crouched deliberately and not in perspective raises its arms in the air and looks, astonished, at the two personages who dare to think about their destiny. A figure in the middle picks a fruit. Two cats near a child. A white goat. The idol, its two arms raised mysteriously and rhythmically, seems to point to the hereafter. A crouching figure seems to listen to the idol; then, lastly, an old woman near death seems to accept, to resign herself to what she thinks and brings the legend to an end; at her feet a strange white bird holding a lizard in its foot represents the uselessness of idle words. Everything takes place on the bank of a stream in the woods. In the background, the sea, then the mountains of the neighboring island. Despite the gradations of color, the appearance of the landscape is consistently blue and Veronese green from end to end. Against that, all the nude figures stand out in bold orange. If one were to tell the students of the Beaux-Arts for the Rome competition, "The painting you are to do will represent: 'Where do we come from, what are we, where are we going?'" – what would they do? I have finished a philosophical piece of work on this theme comparable to the Gospel: I think it is good: if I have the strength to copy it, I will send it to you. . . .

The *"philosophical work"* is *"L'Esprit moderne et le catholicisme,"* which he illustrated with monotypes and woodcuts. The manuscript is in the St. Louis Art Museum.

VAN GOGH: IMPRESSIONISM AND EXPRESSION

VINCENT VAN GOGH

Letters to Theo

1883, 1885

THE HAGUE, EARLY AUGUST 1883

Dear Theo,

...While painting recently, I have felt a certain power of color awakening in me, stronger and different than what I have felt till now.

It may be that the nervousness of these days is related to a kind of revolution in my working methods, which I have been seeking, and which I have already been thinking of for a long time.

I have often tried to work less dryly, but it always turned out to be the same thing all over again. But now that a kind of weakness prevents me from working in my usual way, it seems to help rather than hinder, and now that I let myself go a little, and look more through the eyelashes, instead of staring at the joints and analyzing the structure of things, it leads me more directly to seeing things more like patches of color in mutual contrast.

* * *

Now you will understand that I am very eager for your coming, for if you too saw that there is a change, I shouldn't doubt but that we are on the right track. I dare not quite trust my own eyes as regards my own work. Those two studies, for instance, which I made while it was raining – a muddy road with a little figure – seem to me exactly the opposite of some other studies. When I look at them, I again find the atmosphere of that dreary rainy day; and a kind of life is in the figure, though it is nothing but a few patches of color – it's not summoned by the correctness of the drawing, for there is practically no drawing. What I mean to suggest is that in these studies I believe there is something of that mysteriousness one gets by looking at nature through the eyelashes, so that the outlines are simplified to blots of color.

* * *

NUENEN, JULY 1885

Dear Theo,

... The figures in the pictures of the old masters do not *work*. I am drudging just now on the figure of a woman whom I saw digging for carrots in the snow last winter.

Look here, Millet has done it, Lhermitte, and in general the painters of rural life in this century – Israëls for instance – they think it more beautiful than anything else.

But *even* in this century, how relatively few among the innumerable painters want the figure – yes, above all – for the figure's sake, that is to say for the sake of line and modeling, *but cannot imagine* it otherwise than in action, and want to do what the old masters avoided – even the old Dutch masters who clung to many conventional actions – and I repeat – want *to paint the action for the action's sake.*

This letter, written three years before Van Gogh came to Paris in 1886 and before he had any knowledge of Impressionism, anticipates the abstraction of technique ("patches of color in mutual contrast") of the new painting.

Photograph of Theo van Gogh. *c.*1888–90. Rijksmuseum Vincent van Gogh Foundation/Van Gogh Museum, Amsterdam.

Léon Augustin Lhermitte (1844–1925), painter of the rural countryside, close in spirit to Millet.

(*Opposite*) Vincent van Gogh. *Road with Poplars.* Neunen, March 1884. Rijksmuseum Vincent van Gogh Foundation/Van Gogh Museum, Amsterdam.

216

So that the picture or the drawing has to be a drawing of the figure for the sake of the figure and the inexpressibly harmonious form of the human body, but at the same time a digging of carrots in the snow. Do I express myself clearly? I hope so, and just tell this to Serret. I can say it in a few words: a nude by Cabanel, a lady by Jacquet and a peasant woman, *not by Bastien Lepage himself*, but a peasant woman by a Parisian who has learned his drawing at the academy, will always indicate the limbs and the structure of the body in one selfsame way, sometimes charming – correct in proportion and anatomy. But when Israëls, or when Daumier or Lhermitte, for instance, draws a figure, the shape of the figure will be felt much more, and yet – that's why I like to include Daumier – the proportions will sometimes be almost *arbitrary*, the anatomy and structure often quite wrong "in the eyes of the academician." But it will *live*. And especially Delacroix too.

It is not yet well expressed. Tell Serret that *I should be desperate if my figures were correct*, tell him that I do not want them to be academically correct, tell him that I mean: If one photographs a digger, *he certainly would not be digging then*. Tell him that I adore the figures by Michelangelo though the legs are undoubtedly too long, the hips and the backsides too large. Tell him that, for me, Millet and Lhermitte are the real artists for the very reason that they do not paint things as they are, traced in a dry analytical way, but as *they* – Millet, Lhermitte, Michelangelo – feel them. Tell him that my great longing is to learn to make those very incorrectnesses, those deviations, remodelings, changes in reality, so that they may become, yes, lies if you like – but truer than the literal truth.

VINCENT VAN GOGH

Letter to Émile Bernard

April 9, 1888

ARLES

My dear comrade Bernard,
Thanks for your kind letter and for the enclosed sketches of your decoration, which I think very funny. Sometimes I regret that I cannot make up my mind to work more at home and extempore. The imagination is certainly a faculty which we must develop, one which alone can lead us to the creation of a more exalting and consoling nature than the single brief glance at reality – which in our sight is ever changing, passing like a flash of lightning – can let us perceive.

A starry sky, for instance – look, that is something I should like to try to do, just as in the daytime I am going to try to paint a green meadow spangled with dandelions. So much in criticism of myself and in praise of you.

At the moment I am absorbed in the blooming fruit trees, pink peach trees, yellow-white pear trees. My brush stroke has no system at all. I hit the canvas with irregular touches of the brush, which I leave as they are. Patches of thickly laid-on color, spots of canvas left uncovered, here and there portions that are left absolutely unfinished, repetitions, savageries; in short, I am inclined to think that the result is so disquieting and irritating as to be a godsend to those people who have fixed preconceived ideas about technique.

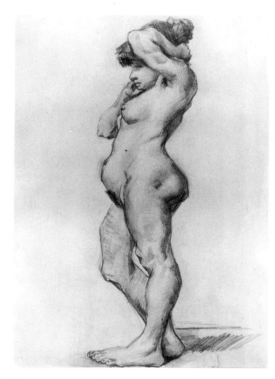

Vincent van Gogh. *Standing Female Nude*. 1886. Carpenter's pencil, $19^{2}/_{3} \times 15^{1}/_{2}"$ (50×39.5 cm). Rijksmuseum Vincent van Gogh Foundation/Van Gogh Museum, Amsterdam.

Photograph of the Yellow House in Arles, *c.*1940. Postcard. Rijksmuseum Vincent van Gogh Foundation/Van Gogh Museum, Amsterdam.

VINCENT VAN GOGH

Letters to Theo

1888, 1889

ARLES, SEPTEMBER 8, 1888

My dear Theo,

I have just mailed the sketch of the new picture, the "Night Café," as well as another that I did some time ago. I shall end perhaps by making some crépons.

Well now, yesterday I was busy furnishing the house. . . . Someday or other you shall have a picture of the little house itself in bright sunshine, or else with the window lit up, and a starry sky.

Henceforth you can feel that you have your country house in Arles. For I am very anxious to arrange it so that you will be pleased with it, and so that it will be a studio in an absolutely individual style; that way, if say a year from now you come here and to Marseilles for your vacation, it will be ready then, and the house, as I intend it, will be full of pictures from top to bottom.

The room you will have then, or Gauguin if he comes, will have white walls with a decoration of great yellow sunflowers. . . .

In my picture of the "Night Café" I have tried to express the idea that the café is a place where one can ruin oneself, go mad or commit a crime. So I have tried to express, as it were, the powers of darkness in a low public house, by soft Louis XV green and malachite, contrasting with yellow-green and harsh blue-greens, and all this in an atmosphere like a devil's furnace, of pale sulphur.

And all with an appearance of Japanese gaiety, and the good nature of Tartarin.

But what would Monsieur Tersteeg say about this picture when he said before a Sisley – Sisley, the most discreet and gentle of the impressionists – "I can't help thinking that the artist who painted that was a little tipsy." If he saw my picture, he would say that it was delirium tremens in full swing.

* * *

The Night Café, 1888, Yale University Art Gallery, New Haven.
Crépons: the special term Van Gogh used for Japanese drawings and prints, with reference to their slightly wrinkled surface.

Hermannus Tersteeg, director of the firm of dealers Goupil and Co. at The Hague when Van Gogh began work there in 1869, and a friend of the family.

219

Émile Bernard. *Self-Portrait "to his Pal Vincent."* 1888. 18⅛ × 21⅝" (46 × 55 cm). Rijksmuseum Vincent van Gogh Foundation/Van Gogh Museum, Amsterdam.

ARLES, SEPTEMBER 10, 1888

My dear Theo,

If Gauguin were working with me and if for his part he were fairly generous with pictures, doesn't it mean that you would be giving work to two artists who could do nothing without you? And while admitting that I think you are perfectly justified in saying that as far as money is concerned, you see no advantage in it, yet on the other hand you would be doing the same sort of thing as Durand Ruel, who bought pictures from Claude Monet in the days before anybody else had recognized his individuality. And Durand Ruel made nothing on it; at one time he was overloaded with the pictures and could not pass them on, but still, what he did remains well done, and now he can always say that he carried the day. If, however, I saw it would mean losing money, I wouldn't suggest it. But Gauguin must be loyal, and now that I see that his friend Laval's arrival has temporarily opened a new resource to him, I think that he is hesitating between Laval and us. . . .

I think now is a good opportunity for you to ask Gauguin bluntly when he writes to you, "Are you coming or not? If you have not made up your mind one way or the other, we shall not feel bound to carry out the scheme."

If the plan of a more serious combination cannot be carried out, all right, but then each should regain his freedom of action. I have sent off my letter to Gauguin; I asked them for an exchange. If they are willing, I would very much like to have here the portrait of Bernard by Gauguin and that of Gauguin by Bernard. . . .

Ideas for my work are coming to me in swarms, so that though I'm alone, I have no time to think or to feel, I go on painting like a steam engine. I think there will hardly ever be a standstill again. And my view is that you will never find a live studio ready-made, but that it is created from day to day by patient work and going on and on in one place.

I have a study of an old mill painted in broken tones like the oak tree on the rock, that study you were saying you had framed along with the "Sower."

The idea of the "Sower" continues to haunt me all the time. Exaggerated studies like the "Sower" and like this "Night Café" usually seem to me atrociously ugly and bad, but when I am moved by something, as now by this little article on Dostoievsky, then these are the only ones which appear to have any deep meaning.

* * *

Charles Laval (1862–94), painter who met Gauguin at Pont-Aven in 1886, became very influenced by him, and accompanied him to Panama and Martinique in 1887. Laval, who was one of the first painters to rejoin Gauguin in the summer of 1888 at Pont-Aven, was supported on a monthly stipend by an anonymous patron.

It was originally planned that Gauguin and Bernard should paint each other's portrait for Van Gogh. In the end they each painted self-portraits which included images of each other – Émile Bernard: Self-Portrait: dedicated to Vincent van Gogh, *1888, Rijksmuseum Vincent van Gogh, Amsterdam; Paul Gauguin:* Self-Portrait: "Les Misérables": dedicated to Vincent van Gogh, *1888, Rijksmuseum Vincent van Gogh, Amsterdam.*

The Sower, *June 1888, F422, Rijksmuseum Kröller-Müller, Otterlo, is the first of four versions of the subject (October: F494, Private Collection, Switzerland; November: F451, Rijksmuseum Vincent van Gogh, Amsterdam; F450, Bührle Collection, Zurich:* COLORPLATE 72*). It is one of the most documented paintings of the Arles period; there are four different descriptions of it in the letters.*

My dear Theo,

Only a few words to tell you that my health and my work are not progressing so badly.

It astonishes me already when I compare my condition today with what it was a month ago. Before that I knew well enough that one could fracture one's legs and arms and recover afterward, but I did not know that you could fracture the brain in your head and recover from that too.

I still have a sort of "what is the good of getting better?" feeling about me, even in the astonishment aroused in me by my getting well, which I hadn't dared hope for.

During your visit I think you must have noticed the two size 30 canvases of sunflowers in Gauguin's room. I have just put the finishing touches to copies, absolutely identical replicas of them. I think I have already told you that besides these I have a canvas of "La Berceuse" the very one I was working on when my illness interrupted me. I now have two copies of this one too.

I have just said to Gauguin about this picture that when he and I were talking about the fishermen of Iceland and of their mournful isolation, exposed to all dangers, alone on the sad sea – I have just said to Gauguin that following those intimate talks of ours the idea came to me to paint a picture in such a way that sailors, who are at once children and martyrs, seeing it in the cabin of their Icelandic fishing boat, would feel the old sense of being rocked come over them and remember their own lullabys.

Now, it may be said that it is like a chromolithograph from a cheap shop. A woman in green with orange hair standing out against a background of green with pink flowers. Now these discordant sharps of crude pink, crude orange, and crude green are softened by flats of red and green.

I picture to myself these same canvases between those of the sunflowers, which would thus form torches or candelabra beside them, the same size, and so the whole would be composed of seven or nine canvases. . . .

It is still beyond my powers to go into the details of this money question, and yet I want to do that very thing, and I am furiously at work from morning till night, to prove to you (unless my work is another hallucination), to prove to you that indeed and indeed we are following Monticelli's track, and what's more, that we have a light before our feet and a lamp upon our path in the powerful work of Brias of Montpellier, who did so much to create a school in the South. . . .

Ever yours, Vincent

After his breakdown on December 23, 1888, Van Gogh had been admitted to hospital, the Hôtel Dieu, where he was looked after by Dr. Félix Rey (1867–1932). Gauguin had left Arles almost immediately.

Van Gogh had begun a painting of Mme Roulin (the wife of the postman Roulin) in December 1888. He explained the title in a letter of January 23, 1889 to Arnold Hendrick Koning as "La Berceuse . . . [COLORPLATE 77] quite simply 'our lullaby or the woman rocking the cradle.'" In a letter to Gauguin he mentioned placing the portrait in an Icelandic fishing boat as "a consoling art for broken hearts." Like The Sower this is one of the important "ugly" paintings, of which there are five versions (F504–F508).

(Below) Vincent van Gogh. Sketch of projected triptych, La Berceuse flanked by Sunflowers. In letter to Theo. Late May 1889. Rijksmuseum Vincent van Gogh Foundation/Van Gogh Museum, Amsterdam.

Alfred Bruyas (1821–77), important patron of Delacroix and Courbet.

VINCENT VAN GOGH
Letter to Émile Bernard
Early December 1889

My dear friend Bernard,
Thanks for your letter and especially for the photographs, which give me an idea of your work.

My brother wrote to me about it the other day for that matter, and told me that he liked the harmony of the colors and a certain nobility in many of the figures very much.

Now look here, I am too charmed by the landscape in the "Adoration of the Magi" to venture to criticize, but it is nevertheless too much of an impossibility to imagine a confinement like that, right on the road, the mother starting to pray instead of giving suck; then there are those fat ecclesiastical frogs kneeling down as though in a fit of epilepsy, God knows how, and why!

No, I can't think such a thing sound, but personally, *if* I am capable of spiritual ecstasy, I adore Truth, the possible, and therefore I bow down before that study by Millet – powerful enough to make one tremble – of peasants carrying home to the farm a calf which has been born in the fields. Now this, my friend, all people have felt from France to America; and after that are you going to revive medieval tapestries for us? Now

Émile Bernard: Adoration of the Magi, *1889, Private Collection.*

Paul Gauguin. Sketch for *Christ in the Garden of Olives* in a letter to Van Gogh. November 1889. Watercolor. Rijksmuseum Vincent van Gogh Foundation/Van Gogh Museum, Amsterdam.

honestly, is this a sincere conviction? No! you can do better than that, and you know you must seek after the possible, the logical, the true, even if you should have to forget the Parisian things à la Baudelaire a little. How much I prefer Daumier to that gentleman!

An "Annunciation," of what? I see figures of angels – dear me, quite elegant – a terrace with two cypresses which I like very much; there is an enormous amount of air, of brightness in it; but, once this first impression is past, I ask myself whether it is a mystification, and those secondary figures no longer mean anything to me.

But it will be enough if you will just understand that I am yearning to know such things of yours as that picture which Gauguin has, those Breton women strolling in a meadow, so beautifully ordered, so naïvely distinguished in color. And you will trade this for what is – must I say the word? – counterfeit, affected!

Last year you did a picture – according to what Gauguin told me – which I think was something like this: on a grassy foreground a figure of a young girl in a blue or whitish dress, lying stretched out full length; on the second plane the edge of a beech wood, the ground covered with fallen red leaves, the verdigris-colored tree trunks forming a vertical barrier.

I suppose the hair is an accent of a color tone which is necessary as a color complementary to the pale dress, black if the dress is white, orange if it is blue. But what I said to myself was, what a simple subject, and how well he knows how to create elegance with nothing.

Gauguin told me about another subject, nothing but three trees, an effect of orange foliage against a blue sky; but then very clearly designed, and very categorically divided into planes of contrasting and candid colors – bravo!

And when I compare such a thing with that nightmare of a "Christ in the Garden of Olives," good Lord, I mourn over it, and so with the present letter I ask you again, roaring my loudest, and calling you all kinds of names with the full power of my lungs – to be so kind as to become your own self again a little.

The "Christ Carrying His Cross" is appalling. Are those patches of color in it harmonious? I won't forgive you the *spuriousness* – yes, certainly, spuriousness – in the composition.

As you know, once or twice, while Gauguin was in Arles, I gave myself free rein with abstractions, for instance in the "Woman Rocking," in the 'Woman Reading a Novel," black in a yellow library; and at the time abstraction seemed to me a charming path. But it is enchanted ground, old man, and one soon finds oneself up against a stone wall.

Émile Bernard: Annunciation, *1889, Private Collection, New York.*

Émile Bernard: Bretonnes dans la prairie verte, *1888, Collection Famille M. Denis, Saint-Germain-en-Laye, which Gauguin had brought with him to Arles, and of which Van Gogh made a watercolor copy.*

Émile Bernard: Madeleine dans le Bois d'Amour, *1888, Musée Nationale d'Art Moderne, Paris.*

Christ in the Garden of Olives, *1889, Private Collection;* Christ Carrying his Cross, *1889, formerly Collection Ambroise Vollard.*

"Abstractions": i.e. paintings from imagination.

G.-ALBERT AURIER

MERCURE DE FRANCE

"The Isolated Ones: Vincent van Gogh"

January 1890

Beneath skies, that sometimes dazzle like faceted sapphires or turquoises, that sometimes are molded of infernal, hot, noxious and blinding sulfurs; beneath skies like streams of molten metals and crystals, which, at times, expose radiating, torrid solar disks; beneath the incessant and formidable streaming of every conceivable effect of light, in heavy, flaming, burning atmospheres that seem to be exhaled from fantastic furnaces where gold and diamonds and singular gems are volatilized – there is the disquieting and disturbing display of a strange nature, that is at once entirely realistic

This was the first in a series of articles on "isolated" artists Aurier had planned for the newly-founded Symbolist magazine Mercure de France *in which he has attempted to recruit Van Gogh to the Symbolist cause. For Van Gogh's vehement reaction to Aurier's rejection of naturalism, see his letters on Aurier's article, pages 227–29.*

and yet almost supernatural, of an excessive nature where everything – beings and things, shadows and lights, forms and colors – rears and rises up with a raging will to howl its own essential song in the most intense and fiercely high-pitched timbre: Trees, twisted like giants in battle, proclaiming with the gestures of their gnarled menacing arms and with the tragic waving of their green manes their indomitable power, the pride of their musculature, their blood-hot sap, their eternal defiance of hurricane, lightning and malevolent Nature; cypresses which expose their nightmarish, flame-like, black silhouettes; mountains which arch their backs like mammoths or rhinoceroses; white and pink and golden orchards, like the idealizing dreams of virgins; squatting, passionately contorted houses, in a like manner to beings who exult, who suffer, who think; stones, terrains, bushes, grassy fields, gardens, and rivers that seem sculpted out of unknown minerals, polished, glimmering, iridescent, enchanted; flaming landscapes, like the effervescence of multicolored enamels in some alchemist's diabolical crucible; foliage that seems of ancient bronze, of new copper, of spun glass; flowerbeds that appear less like flowers than opulent jewelry fashioned from rubies, agates, onyx, emeralds, corundums, chrysoberyls, amethysts and chalcedonies; it is the universal, mad and blinding coruscation of things; it is matter and all of Nature frenetically contorted in paroxysms, raised to the heights of exacerbation; it is form, becoming nightmare; color, becoming flame, lava and precious stone; light turning into conflagration; life, into burning fever.

Such – and it is by no means an exaggeration, though one might think so – is the impression left upon the retina when it first views the strange, intense and feverish work of Vincent van Gogh, that compatriot and not unworthy descendant of the old Dutch masters.

Oh! how far we are – are we not? – from the beautiful, great traditional art, so healthy and very well-balanced, of the Dutch past. How far from the Gerard Dows, the Albert Cuyps, the Terburgs, the Metzus, the Peter de Hooghes, the Van der Meers, the Van der Heydens and from their charming canvases, a bit bourgeois, so patiently detailed, so phlegmatically over-finished, so scrupulously meticulous! How far from the handsome landscapes, so restrained, so well-balanced, so timelessly enveloped in soft tones, grays, and indistinct haze, those Van der Heydens, Berghems, Van Ostades, Potters, Van Goyens, Ruysdaëls, Hobbemas! How far from the somewhat cold elegance of Wouwermans; from Schalken's eternal candlelight; or from the fine brushwork and magnifying-glass vision of the good Pierre Slingelandt's timid myopia! How far from the delicate, always somewhat cloudy and somber colors of the northern countries and from the tireless exactitude of those wholesome artists of yore who painted "in their manner" with calm spirits, warm feet and bellies full of beer; and how far from that very honest, very conscientious, very scrupulous, very Protestant, very republican, very congenially banal art of those incomparable old masters whose only fault – if to them it was a fault – was that they were all family men and burgomasters! . . .

Seventeenth-century Dutch masters.

And yet, make no mistake, Vincent van Gogh has by no means transcended his heritage. He was subject to the effect of ineluctable atavistic laws. He is good and duly Dutch, of the sublime lineage of Franz Hals.

And foremost, like all his illustrious compatriots, he is, indeed, a realist, a realist in the fullest sense of the term. *Ars est homo, additus naturae*, Chancellor Bacon said, and M. Emile Zola defined naturalism as "nature seen through the temperament." Well, it is this "homo additus," this "through a temperament," or this molding of the objective unity into a subjective diversity that complicates the question and abolishes the possibility of any absolute criterion for gauging the degrees of the artist's sincerity. To determine this, the critic is thus inevitably reduced to more or less hypothetical, but always questionable, conclusions. Nevertheless, in the case of Vincent van Gogh, in my opinion, despite the sometimes

Francis Bacon (1561–1626), English philosopher.

misleading strangeness of his works, it is difficult, for an unprejudiced and knowledgeable viewer, to deny or question the naive truthfulness of his art, the ingenuousness of his vision. Indeed, independent of this indefinable aroma of good faith and of the truly-seen that all his paintings exude, the choice of subjects, the constant harmony between the most excessive color notes, the conscientious study of character, the continual search for the essential sign of each thing, a thousand significant details undeniably assert his profound and almost childlike sincerity, his great love for nature and for truth – his own personal truth.

Given this, we are thus able to infer legitimately from Vincent van Gogh's works themselves his temperament as a man, or rather, as an artist – an inference that I could, if I wished, corroborate with biographical facts. What characterizes his work as a whole is its excess, its excess of strength, of nervousness, its violence of expression. In his categorical affirmation of the character of things, in his often daring simplification of forms, in his insolence in confronting the sun head-on, in the vehement passion of his drawing and color, even to the smallest details of his technique, a powerful figure is revealed – a masculine, daring, very often brutal, and yet sometimes ingenuously delicate. Furthermore, as can be divined from the almost orgiastic extravagances of everything he painted, he is a fanatic, an enemy of the bourgeois sobriety and minutiae, a sort of drunken giant, more suited to disrupting mountains than to handling bric-a-brac on whatnots, a brain at its boiling point irresistibly pouring down its lava into all of the ravines of art, a terrible and demented genius, often sublime, sometimes grotesque, always at the brink of the pathological. Finally, and above all, he is a hyper-aesthetic, with clearly shown symptoms, who perceives with abnormal, perhaps even painful, intensities the imperceptible and secret characters of line and form, but still more the colors, the lights, the nuances invisible to healthy eyes, the magic iridescence of shadows. And hence, the personal realism of this neurotic, and likewise his sincerity and his truth are so different from the realism, the sincerity and the truth of those great *petit-bourgeois* of Holland, those so healthy of body, so well balanced of mind, who were his ancestors and his masters.

Yet, this respect and this love for the reality of things does not suffice alone to explain or to characterize the profound, complex, and quite distinctive art of Vincent van Gogh. No doubt, like all the painters of his race, he is very conscious of material reality, of its importance and its beauty, but even more often, he considers this enchantress only as a sort of marvelous language destined to translate the Idea. He is, almost always, a Symbolist. Not at all a Symbolist in the manner of the Italian primitives, those mystics who barely felt the necessity to materialize their dreams, but a Symbolist who feels the continual need to clothe his ideas in precise, ponderable, tangible forms, in intensely sensual and material exteriors. In almost all his canvases, beneath this morphic exterior, beneath this flesh that is very much flesh, beneath this matter that is very much matter, there lies, for the spirit that knows how to find it, a thought, an Idea, and this Idea, the essential substratum of the work, is, at the same time, its efficient and final cause. As for the brilliant and radiant symphonies of color and line, whatever may be their importance for the painter, in his work they are simply expressive *means*, simply *methods* of symbolization. Indeed, if we refuse to acknowledge the existence of these idealistic tendencies beneath this naturalist art, a large part of the body of work that we are studying would remain utterly incomprehensible. How would one explain, for example, *The Sower*, that august and disturbing sower, that rustic with his brutally brilliant forehead (bearing at times a distant resemblance to the artist himself), whose silhouette, gesture and labor have always obsessed Vincent van Gogh, and whom he painted and repainted so often, sometimes beneath skies rubescent at sunset, sometimes amid the golden dust of blazing noons – how could we explain

Photograph of G.-Albert Aurier in about 1890. Bibliothèque Nationale, Paris (Cabinet des Estampes).

COLORPLATE 72

The Sower without considering that *idée fixe* that haunts his brain about the necessary advent of a man, a messiah, sower of truth, who would regenerate the decrepitude of our art and perhaps of our imbecile and industrialist society? And how could we explain that obsessive passion for the solar disk that he loves to make shine forth from his emblazoned skies, and, at the same time, for that other sun, that vegetable-star, the sumptuous sunflower, which he repeats, tirelessly, monomaniacally if we refuse to accept his persistent preoccupation with some vague and glorious heliomythic allegory?

Vincent van Gogh, indeed, is not only a great painter, enthusiastic about his art, his palette and nature; he is, furthermore, a dreamer, a fanatical believer, a devourer of beautiful Utopias, living on ideas and dreams.

For a long time, he took pleasure in imagining a renovation of art, made possible by displacing the center of civilization: an art of the tropical regions, the natives imperiously demanding works corresponding to the newly inhabited surroundings; the painters finding themselves face-to-face with a hitherto unknown nature, radiant with light, at last admitting to themselves the impotence of the old academic tricks, and naively setting out to discover the direct translation of all these new sensations! . . . Wouldn't he, the intense and fantastic colorist, grinder of golds and of precious stones, have been the most well-suited painter, rather than the Guillaumets, the insipid Fromentins and the muddy Gérômes, of these countries of resplendence, of glowing sun and blinding colors?

Then, as a consequence of this conviction of the need to begin entirely from the beginning in art, he had long cherished the idea of inventing a very simple, popular, almost childlike sort of painting capable of moving the humble folk, who do not seek refinement, and of being understood by the most naive in spirit. The *Berceuse*, that gigantic and brilliant *image d'Epinal* that he repeated, with curious variations several times, the portrait of the phlegmatic and indescribably jubilant *Postmaster*, the *Drawbridge*, so crudely luminous and so exquisitely banal, the ingenuous *Young Girl with a Rose*, the *Zouave*, the *Provençal Woman*, all display with the greatest clarity this tendency toward the simplification of art, which one finds again more or less in all his work and which neither appears so absurd nor so negligible in these times of excessive complication, myopia and clumsy analysis.

All these theories, all these hopes of Vincent van Gogh, are they practicable? Are they not merely vain and beautiful chimeras? Who knows? In any case, I will not go into that here. It will suffice, in order to come to the end, to characterize somewhat further this curious spirit, so removed from all banal paths, by saying a few more words about his technique.

The external and material side of his painting is absolutely in keeping with his artistic temperament. In all his works, the execution is vigorous, exalted, brutal, intense. His drawing, excited, powerful, often clumsy and somewhat heavy-handed, exaggerates the character, simplifies, leaps – master and conqueror – over detail, attains a masterful synthesis and sometimes, but by no means always, great style.

We are already familiar with his color. It is unbelievably dazzling. He is, as far as I know, the only painter who perceives the coloring of things with such intensity, with such metallic, gemlike quality. His studies on the coloring of shadows, of the influences of one tone upon another, of the effect of full sunlight, are among the most curious. He is, however, not always able to avoid a certain disagreeable crudeness, disharmony, dissonance. . . . As for his actual technique, his approach to coloring the canvas is like everything else with him, passionate, very powerful and very nervous. He directs his brush with enormous dabs of impasto of pure color in sinuous trails broken by rectilinear strokes, . . . in sometimes awkward piles, of quite shining masonry, and all this gives to certain of his canvases the solid appearance of great dazzling walls made of crystal and sun.

Auguste Achille Guillaumet (1840–87), Eugène Fromentin (1820–76), Jean-Léon Gérôme (1824–1904), painters of oriental subjects.

COLORPLATE 77

This robust and true artist, a thoroughbred with the brutal hands of a giant, the nerves of a hysterical woman, the soul of a mystic, so original and so removed from the milieu of our pitiful art of today, will he one day know – anything is possible – the joys of rehabilitation, the repentant flatteries of fashion? Perhaps. But whatever happens, even if it became fashionable to buy his canvases – which is unlikely – at the prices of M. Meissonier's little infamies, I don't think that much sincerity could ever enter into that belated admiration of the general public. Vincent van Gogh is at once too simple and too subtle for the contemporary bourgeois spirit. He will never be fully understood except by his brothers, the true artists ... and by the fortunate among the little people, the lowest social level, who have, by chance, escaped the good-intentioned teachings of public education! . . .

VINCENT VAN GOGH
Letters on the Article by Aurier
February and April 1890

TO THEO, FEBRUARY 2, 1890

I was extremely surprised at the article on my pictures which you sent me. I needn't tell you that I hope to go on thinking that I do not paint like that, but I do see in it how I ought to paint. For the article is very right as far as indicating the gap to be filled, and I think that the writer really wrote it more to guide, not only me, but the other Impressionists as well, and even partly to make the breach at a good place. So he proposed an ideal collective ego to the others quite as much as to me; he simply tells me that there is something good, if you like, here and there in my work, which is at the same time so imperfect; and that is the comforting part of it which I appreciate and for which I hope to be grateful. Only it must be understood that my back is not broad enough to carry such an undertaking, and in concentrating the article on me, there's no need to tell you how immersed in flattery I feel, and in my opinion it is as exaggerated as what a certain article by Isaäcson said about you, namely that at present the artists had given up squabbling and that an important movement was silently being launched in the little shop on the Boulevard Montmartre. I admit that it is difficult to say what one wants, to express one's ideas differently – in the same way as you cannot paint things as you see them – and so I do not mean to criticize Isaäcson's or the other critic's daring, but as far as we are concerned, really, we are *posing* a bit for *the model*, and indeed that is a duty and a bit of one's job like any other. So if some sort of reputation comes to you and me, the thing is to try to keep some sort of calm and, if possible, clarity of mind.

Why not say what he said of my sunflowers, *with far more grounds*, of those magnificent and perfect hollyhocks of Quost's, and his yellow irises, and those splendid peonies of Jeannin's? And you will foresee, as I do, that such praise *must* have its opposite, the other side of the medal. But I am glad and grateful for the article, or rather "*le coeur à l'aise,*" as the song in the *Revue* has it, since one may need it, as one may really need a medal. Besides, an article like that has its own merit as a critical work of art; as such I think it is to be respected, and the writer *must* heighten the tones, synthesize his conclusions, etc. . . .

TO THEO, EARLY FEBRUARY 1890

And so Gauguin has returned to Paris. I am going to copy my reply to M. Aurier to send to him, and you must make him read this article in the *Mercure*, for really I think they ought to say things like that of Gauguin, and of me only very secondarily.

* * *

Joseph Jacob Isaacson (1859–1942), Dutch critic and artist who wrote a series of articles from 1887 to 1890 on young artists for De Portefeuille. *Van Gogh discouraged him from writing at any length about himself.*

Ernest Quost (1842–1931), Georges Jeannin (1841–1925), academic painters whose flower pieces were exhibited at the Salon.

Aurier's article would encourage me if I dared to let myself go, and venture even further, dropping reality and making a kind of music of tones with color, like some Monticellis. But it is so dear to me, this truth, *trying to make it true*, after all I think, I think, that I would still rather be a shoemaker than a musician in colors.

In any case, trying to remain true is perhaps a remedy in fighting the disease which still continues to disquiet me.

TO AURIER, EARLY FEBRUARY 1890

Many thanks for your article in the *Mercure de France*, which greatly surprised me. I like it very much as a work of art in itself, in my opinion your words produce color, in short, I rediscover my canvases in your article, but better than they are, richer, more full of meaning. However, I feel uneasy in my mind when I reflect that what you say is due to others rather than to myself. For example, Monticelli in particular. Saying as you do: "As far as I know, he is the only painter to perceive the chromatism of things with such intensity, with such a metallic, gemlike luster," be so kind as to go and see a certain bouquet by Monticelli at my brother's – a bouquet in white, forget-me-not blue and orange – then you will feel what I want to say. But the best, the most amazing Monticellis have long been in Scotland and England. In a museum in the North – the one in Lisle, I believe – there is said to be a very marvel, rich in another way and certainly no less French than Watteau's "Départ pour Cythère." At the moment M. Lauzet is engaged in reproducing some thirty works of Monticelli's.

Here you are; as far as I know, there is no colorist who is descended so straightly and directly from Delacroix, and yet I am of the opinion that Monticelli probably had Delacroix's color theories only at second hand; that is to say, that he got them more particularly from Diaz and Ziem. It seems to me that Monticelli's personal artistic temperament is exactly the same as that of the author of the *Decameron* – Boccaccio – a melancholic, somewhat resigned, unhappy man, who saw the wedding party of the world pass by, painting and analyzing the lovers of his time – he, the one who had been left out of things. Oh! he no more imitated Boccaccio than Henri Leys imitated the primitives. You see, what I mean to say is that it seems there are things which have found their way to my name, which you could better say of Monticelli, to whom I owe so much. And further, I owe much to Paul Gauguin, with whom I worked in Arles for some months, and whom I already knew in Paris, for that matter.

Gauguin, that curious artist, that alien whose mien and the look in whose eyes vaguely remind one of Rembrandt's "Portrait of a Man" in the Galerie Lacaze – this friend of mine likes to make one feel that a good picture is equivalent to a good deed; not that he says so, but it is difficult to be on intimate terms with him without being aware of a certain moral responsibility. A few days before parting company, when my disease forced me to go into a lunatic asylum, I tried to paint "his empty seat."

It is a study of his armchair of somber reddish-brown wood, the seat of greenish straw, and in the absent one's place a lighted torch and modern novels.

If an opportunity presents itself, be so kind as to have a look at this study, by way of a memento of him; it is done entirely in broken tones of green and red. Then you will perceive that your article would have been fairer, and consequently more powerful, I think, if, when discussing the question of the future of "tropical painting" and of colors, you had done justice to Gauguin and Monticelli before speaking of me. *For the part which is allotted to me, or will be allotted to me, will remain, I assure you, very secondary.*

And then there is another question I want to ask you. Suppose that the two pictures of sunflowers, which are now at the Les Vingt exhibition, have certain qualities of color, and that they also express an idea symbolizing "gratitude." Is this different from so many flower pieces, more skill-

Narcisse Virgile Diaz de la Peña (1807–76), Barbizon painter; Félix Ziem (1821–1911), painter of romantic views of Venice and the East.

Galerie Lacaze, in the Louvre.

fully painted, and which are not yet sufficiently appreciated, such as "Hollyhocks," "Yellow Irises" by Father Quost? The magnificent bouquets of peonies which Jeannin produces so abundantly? You see, it seems so difficult to me to make a distinction between Impressionism and other things; I do not see the use of so much sectarian spirit as we have seen these last years, *but I am afraid of the preposterousness of it.*

* * *

TO WIL, LATE FEBRUARY 1890

I thought the article by M. Aurier – leaving out of consideration whether I deserve what he says of me – very artistic and very curious in itself. But it is rather like this that I *ought to be*, instead of the sad reality of how I do feel. I wrote to tell him that in any case it seems to me that Monticelli and Gauguin are more like this – that it seems to me that the part which should be assigned to me is of a secondary, very secondary order.

The ideas he speaks of are not my property, for in general all the impressionists are like that, are under the same influence, and we are all of us more or less neurotic. This renders us very sensitive to colors and their particular language, the effects of complementary colors, of their contrasts and harmony. But when I had read that article I felt almost mournful, for I thought: I ought to be like that, and I feel so inferior. And pride, like drink, is intoxicating, when one is praised, and has drunk the praise up. It makes one sad, or rather – I don't know how to express it, I feel it – but it seems to me that the best work one can do is what is done in the privacy of one's home without praise. And then you do not always find a *sufficiently* friendly disposition among artists. Either they exaggerate a person's qualities, or else they neglect him too much. However, I should be pleased to be able to believe that justice is better done after all than appears to be the case.

TO THEO, LATE APRIL 1890

Please ask M. Aurier not to write any more articles on my painting, insist upon this, that to begin with he is mistaken about me, since I am too overwhelmed with grief to be able to face publicity. Making pictures distracts me, but if I hear them spoken of, it pains me more than he knows. . . .

ÉMILE BERNARD
LETTRES DE VINCENT VAN GOGH À ÉMILE BERNARD
Preface

1911

I answered Theo's letter affirmatively and went to his home on Saturday. The hanging was completed in no time. He left everything up to me. When it was finished, the rooms gave the impression of a series of galleries in a museum, because I'd not left a single empty space on the walls. I had taken great care to follow an idea that Vincent had often mentioned in his letters: to make one painting sing by placing it next to another; to place a color scale of yellow next to a scale of blue, a scale of green next to a red, etc. . . . There was the green *Berceuse*, which shone between the yellow and orange sunflowers like a village madonna between two gold candelabra. When everything was done, in order to block out the houses across the street and to create some intimacy in the gallery dedicated to the memory of my friend, I transformed the window into a stained-glass and painted a sylvan picture in the essence of *The Sower*, *The Shepherd*, and *Haystacks*, to summarize the rural affinities of Van Gogh.

After Vincent's funeral, Theo had solicited Bernard's help (letter, September 18, 1890) in organizing a show of Vincent's paintings in his Montmartre apartment.

But, alas! This repository was not up for long. We had hardly finished it when Theodorus, heartbroken over his brother's suicide, lost his reason and was struck down, paralyzed. The most assiduous care was given to him, but to no avail. He was taken to Holland, where he died six months later.

I had not given up on making Vincent known. Friends and artists whom I took to Pigalle, to brother Theo's apartment, recognized his merits as colorist, his originality, his passion, his painter's ardent nature. I took some photographs, which I distributed by subscription.

Mme. Van Gogh, in her haste to take her husband to Holland, had to abandon the Paris apartment.

She soon asked that all of the paintings be sent to her. I assumed the responsibility of supervising their packing. Because of feelings one could easily understand, she didn't want to return to France, to Paris, to the place where the cruelest tragedy had happened.

She retreated to Bussum, near Amsterdam, and opened a boarding-house. "It's a nice house," she wrote to me then, "where baby, the paintings, and myself will be better accommodated than in our Paris apartment where we, nonetheless, felt so at home and where I spent the happiest days of my life. Therefore, you shouldn't fear that the paintings are going to be put in the attic, or in dark cupboards. They'll decorate the whole house, and I hope that you'll come to Holland sometime to see what care I've taken of them." Mme. Van Gogh wanted very much to execute her husband's project; she pursued the idea of doing an exhibition of works by Vincent. To this effect, she gave me six hundred francs, but at the time the galleries were few and very expensive. I could afford nothing with this sum. I decided to do an exhibition at no expense at Lebarcq de Boutteville's, who was willing to lend me his gallery for a month for this purpose. In rough wood, I myself engraved the catalogue, which included fourteen sizable pieces.

What surprised me the most at the time was Paul Gauguin's attitude. He was a friend of the Van Goghs and had received many favors from them. He owed them his daily existence and, furthermore, he had been introduced to the collectors of Boussod & Valadon (today, Manzi-Joyant) by Theodorus.

COLORPLATE 67. Vincent van Gogh. *Landscape at Auvers in the Rain*. 1890. 19⅝ × 39⅜″ (50 × 100 cm). National Museum of Wales, Cardiff.

COLORPLATE 68. Paul Signac. *Quai de Clichy*. April–May 1887. 18¼ × 25¾″ (46.4 × 65.4 cm).
Baltimore Museum of Art (Gift of Frederick H. Gottlieb).

COLORPLATE 69. Vincent van Gogh. *Interior of a Restaurant*. Paris, summer 1887. 18 × 22¼″ (45.5 × 56.5 cm). Kröller-Müller Museum, Otterlo.

COLORPLATE 70. Vincent van Gogh. *Landscape near Montmajour with the Little Train from Arles to Orgon.*
Arles, mid-July 1888. Pen, reed pen and black chalk, 19¼ × 24″ (49 × 61 cm).
British Museum, London.

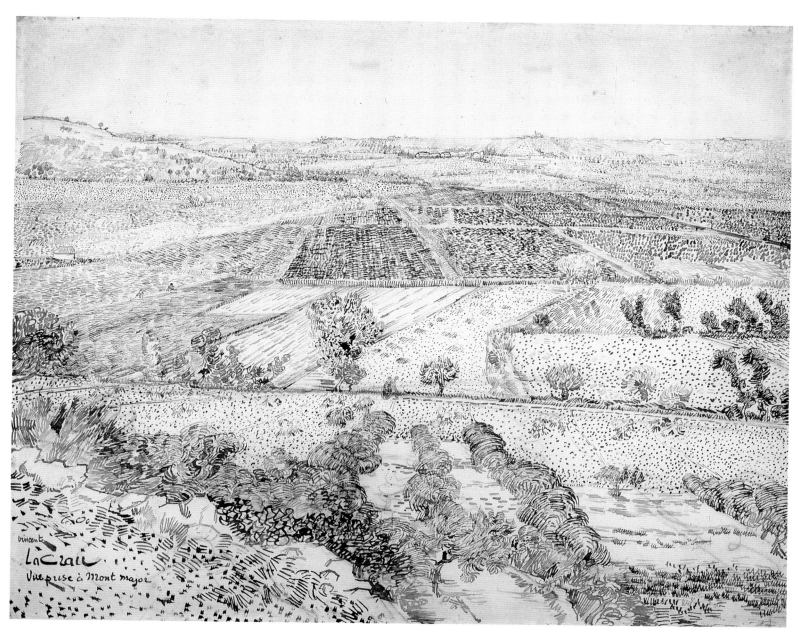

COLORPLATE 71. Vincent van Gogh. *La Crau seen from Montmajour.* Arles, mid-July 1888.
Black chalk, pen, reed pen, brown and black ink.
Rijksmuseum Vincent van Gogh Foundation/Van Gogh Museum, Amsterdam.

COLORPLATE 72. Vincent van Gogh. *The Sower*. Arles, autumn 1888.
Burlap on canvas, 28⅞ × 36¼″ (73.5 × 92 cm). E. G. Bührle Foundation, Zurich.

COLORPLATE 73. Vincent van Gogh. *Olive Trees*. St-Rémy, September–December 1889.
29¼ × 36½″ (74 × 93 cm). Konstmuseum, Göteborg.

COLORPLATE 74. Vincent van Gogh. *Olive Trees: Yellow Sky with Sun.*
St-Rémy, September–November 1889. 29 × 36½″(74 × 93 cm).
Minneapolis, Institute of Arts (William Hood Dunwoody Fund).

COLORPLATE 75. Vincent van Gogh. *Flowering Branch of Almond Tree.*
St-Rémy, February 1890. 28¾ × 36¼″ (73 × 92 cm).
Rijksmuseum Vincent van Gogh Foundation/Van Gogh Museum, Amsterdam.

COLORPLATE 76. Vincent van Gogh. *Still Life: Vase with Fifteen Sunflowers*. Arles, August 1888.
$36\frac{1}{2} \times 28\frac{3}{4}''$ (92.1 × 73 cm). National Gallery, London.

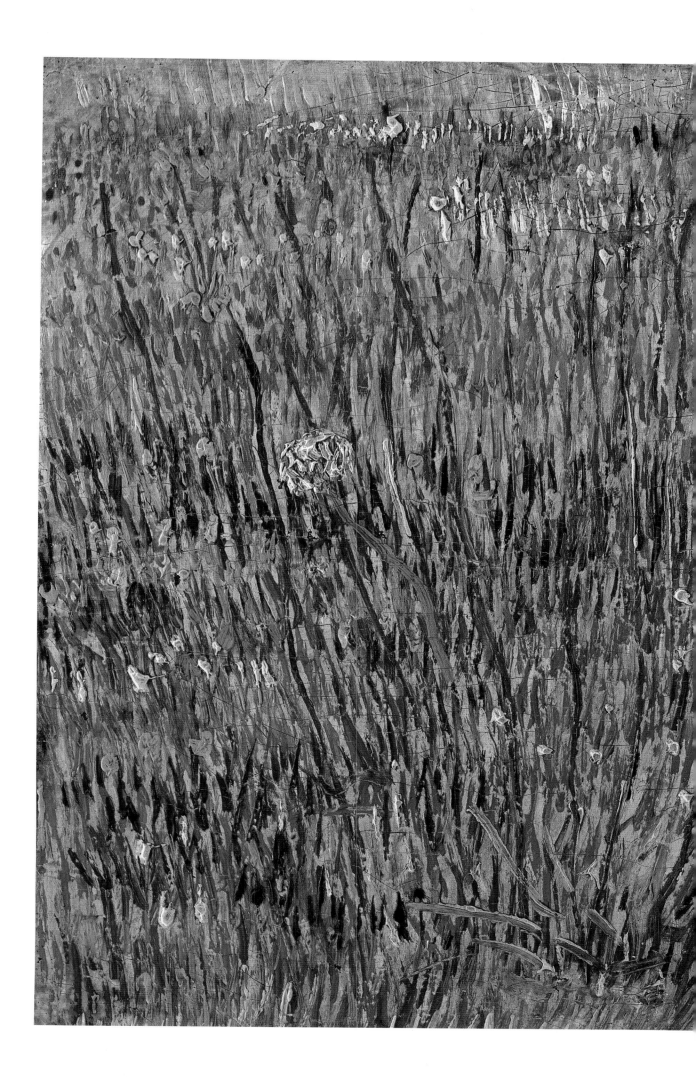

243

COLORPLATE 78. Vincent van Gogh. *Still Life with Twelve Sunflowers*. Arles, August 1888.
35¾ × 28″ (91 × 71 cm). Bayerische Staatsgemäldesammlungen, Munich.

COLORPLATE 77. Vincent van Gogh. *La Berceuse.* 1889. 36 × 28″ (91.4 × 71 cm).
© 1993 The Art Institute of Chicago (Helen Birch Bartlett Collection).

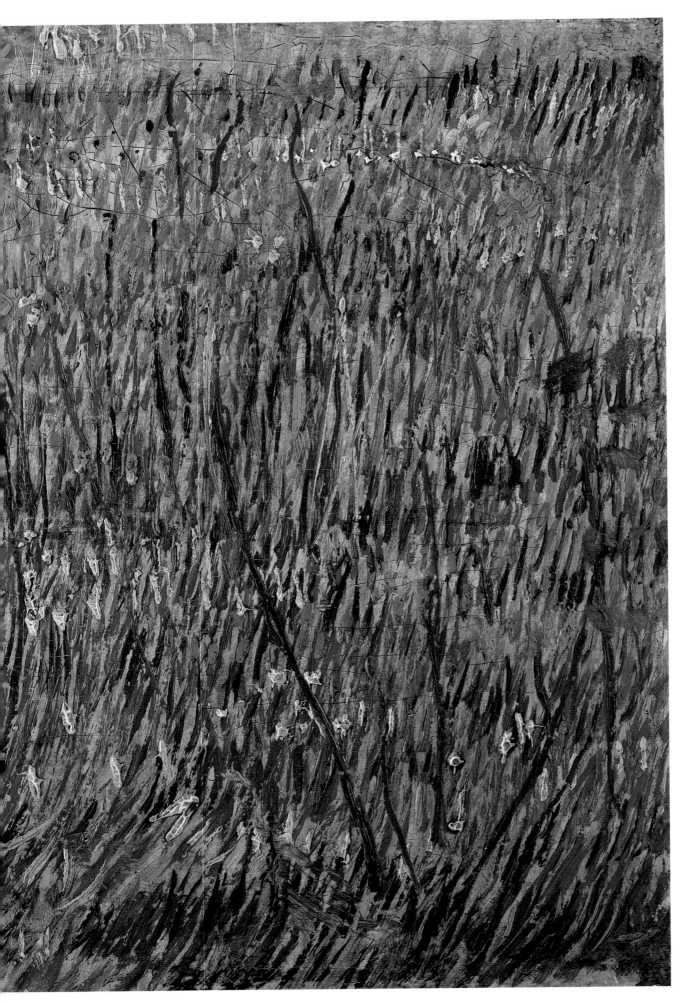

COLORPLATE 79. Vincent van Gogh. *Pasture in Bloom*. April–June 1887.
12⅝ × 16⅛″ (31.5 × 40.5 cm). Rijksmuseum Kröller-Müller, Otterlo.

PAUL GAUGUIN
Letter to Émile Bernard
January 1891

I just received one [a letter] from Sérusier telling me that you're organizing an exhibition of Vincent. How awkward!

You know that I like Vincent's art – but considering the public's stupidity, it's completely out of place to remember Vincent and his madness when his brother is in the same situation! Many people say that our painting is madness. That does us harm without doing any good to Vincent, etc. . . .

Anyway, go ahead – but it's IDIOTIC.

PAUL GAUGUIN
MERCURE DE FRANCE
"Avant et Après"
October 1903

For a long time I have wished to write about Van Gogh, and I will certainly do so one fine day when I am in the mood: for the moment, I intend to recount about him – or, better, about us – certain things that are apt to correct an error that has circulated in certain circles.

It is surely chance that in the course of my existence several men who have spent time in my company and with whom I've enjoyed discussions have gone mad.

This was the case with the two Van Gogh brothers, and some, from evil intentions, and others, from naiveté, have attributed their madness to my doing. Certainly, some people may have more or less of an influence over their friends, but that is a far cry from provoking madness. Well after the catastrophe, Vincent wrote me from the mental asylum where he was being treated:

"How fortunate you are to be in Paris! This is still where one can find the leading authorities, and certainly you should consult a specialist in order to cure you of madness." Aren't we all a little mad? The advice was good, that is why I did not follow it, from contrariness, no doubt.

The readers of the *Mercure* were able to see, in a letter of Vincent's published a few years ago, how insistent he was that I come to Arles to found, according to his idea, an atelier of which I would be the director.

I was working at the time at Pont-Aven, in Brittany, and whether because the studies I had undertaken bound me to that place, or because by some vague instinct I foresaw something abnormal, I resisted for a long time, until the day when, won over by Vincent's sincere flights of friendship, I set out.

I arrived at Arles toward the end of night and awaited daybreak in an all-night café. The owner looked at me and cried out: "It's you, his pal, I recognize you."

A self-portrait that I had sent to Vincent suffices to explain this proprietor's exclamation. While showing him my portrait, Vincent had explained that it was of a pal who was to arrive soon.

Neither too early, nor too late, I went to awaken Vincent. The day was devoted to my settling in, to much chatting, to a bit of strolling to admire the beauties of Arles and the Arlésiennes (for whom, incidentally, I was unable to work up any enthusiasm).

In February 1903, three months before his death, Gauguin submitted the manuscript of "Avant et Après" to the Mercure de France. *The sections concerning Van Gogh were included in the obituary article written by Charles Morice.*

More mercenary considerations entered into Gauguin's decision to go to Arles. After prolonged negotiations with Theo van Gogh it was agreed that Theo would pay his fares, provide 150 francs per month and free lodging in exchange for a painting each month. Gauguin's stay lasted from October 23 to December 26, 1888.

245

Beginning the following day, we were at work, he continuing, and I, starting fresh. You should know that I have never had the cerebral facility that others, without any trouble, find at the tip of their brushes. Those others get off the train, pick up their palette, and in no time at all set you down a sunlight effect. When it's dry, it goes to the Luxembourg and it's signed: Carolus Duran.

I do not admire such painting, but I admire the man: he so sure, so tranquil! – I so uncertain, so restless!

In every country, I need a period of incubation to learn each time the essence of the plants, the trees, of all of nature, in short – so varied and so capricious, never wanting to let itself be divined or revealed.

So it was several weeks before I clearly sensed the sharp flavor of Arles and its environs. That did not prevent our working steadily, especially Vincent. Between the two beings, he and I, the one entirely a volcano and the other, boiling as well, but inside. Some sort of struggle was bound to occur.

First of all, I was shocked to find a disorder everywhere and in every respect. His box of colors barely sufficed to contain all those squeezed tubes, which were never closed up, and despite all this disorder, all this mess, everything glowed on the canvas – and in his words as well. Daudet, de Goncourt, the Bible fueled the brain of this Dutchman. At Arles, the quays, the bridges, the boats, the whole Midi became another Holland for him. He even forgot how to write in Dutch and, as one could see from the publication of his letters to his brother, he always wrote in French only, and did so admirably, with no end of phrases like *tant que* and *quant à*.

Alphonse Daudet (1840–97), Provençal writer.

Van Gogh was trilingual in Dutch, French and English.

Despite all my efforts to disentangle from that disordered brain a logical reasoning behind his critical opinions, I could not explain to myself the complete contradiction between his painting and his opinions. So that, for example, he had an unlimited admiration for Meissonier and a profound hatred for Ingres. Degas was his despair and Cézanne was nothing but a fraud. When thinking of Monticelli, he wept.

What angered him was to be forced to admit that I had great intelligence, although my forehead was too small, a sign of imbecility. In the midst of all this, a great tenderness, or rather, the altruism of the Gospel.

From the very first month, I saw our common finances taking on the same appearance of disorder. What to do? The situation was delicate as the cash box being filled, only modestly, by his brother employed at Goupil's, and, for my part, through the exchange of paintings. I was obliged to speak, and to come up against that great sensitivity of his. It was thus only with many precautions and quite a bit of coaxing hardly compatible with my character that I approached the question. I must confess, I succeeded far more easily than I had supposed.

In a box, so much for nightly outings and hygiene, so much for tobacco, so much, too, for unforeseen expenses, including the rent. On top of it all, a piece of paper and a pencil to inscribe honestly what each took from this till. In another box, the balance of the sum, divided into four parts, for the cost of food each week. Our little restaurant was given up and, with the aid of a little gas stove, I did the cooking while Vincent, without going very far from the house, did the shopping. Once, however, Vincent wanted to make a soup, but I don't know how he mixed it – no doubt like the colors on his paintings – in any event, we couldn't eat it. And my Vincent exclaimed in laughter: "Tarascon! La casquet au père Daudet!"

On the wall, with chalk, he wrote:

Je suis Saint Esprit.
Je suis sain d'esprit!

How long did we remain together? I couldn't say, having entirely forgotten. Despite the rapidity with which the catastrophe arrived, despite the fever of working that had overtaken me, that whole time seemed like a century.

246

Without the public having any suspicion, two men had done there a colossal work, useful to them both – perhaps to others. Certain things bear fruit.

Vincent, at the moment when I arrived in Arles, was fully immersed in the Neo-Impressionist school, and he was floundering considerably, which caused him to suffer; the point is not that this school, like all schools, was bad, but that it did not correspond to his nature, which was so far from patient and so independent.

With all these yellows on violets, all this work in complementary colors – disordered work on his part – he only arrived at subdued, incomplete, and monotonous harmonies; the sound of the clarion was missing.

I undertook the task of enlightening him, which was easy for me, for I found a rich and fertile soil. Like all natures that are original and marked with the stamp of personality, Vincent had no fear of his neighbor and was not stubborn.

From that day on, my Van Gogh made astonishing progress: he seemed to catch a glimpse of all that was within him, and hence that whole series of suns on suns in full sunlight.

Have you seen the portrait of the poet?

1. The face and hair, chrome yellow.
2. The clothing chrome yellow.
3. The tie chrome yellow. With an emerald, green-emerald pin.
4. On a background of chrome yellow.

This is what an Italian painter said to me and he added:

"[Merde, merde], everything is yellow: I don't know what *painting* is any longer!"

It would be idle to go into details of technique here. This is said only to inform you that Van Gogh, without losing one inch of his originality, gained a fruitful lesson from me. And each day he would thank me for it. And that is what he means when he writes to M. Aurier that he owes much to Paul Gauguin.

See Van Gogh's letter to Aurier (page 228), a copy of which he sent to Gauguin.

When I arrived in Arles, Vincent was trying to find his way, whereas I, much older, was a mature man. I do owe something to Vincent; namely, in the awareness of having been useful to him, the *affirmation* of my earlier ideas about painting. Moreover, for the recollection at difficult moments that there are those unhappier than oneself.

Gauguin was in fact five years older than Van Gogh.

When I read this passage: "Gauguin's drawing somewhat recalls that of Van Gogh," I smile.

During the latter part of my stay, Vincent became excessively brusque and noisy, then silent. Several nights I surprised Vincent who, having risen was standing over my bed.

Gauguin is misquoting from Fontainas' article in Mercure de France, *January 1899.*

To what can I attribute my awakening just at that moment?

Invariably it sufficed for me to say to him very gravely:

"What's the matter, Vincent?" for him to go back to bed without a word and to fall into a deep sleep.

I came upon the idea of doing his portrait while he painted the still life that he so loved – some sunflowers. And, the portrait finished, he said to me: "That's me all right, but me gone mad."

That same evening, we went to the café: he took a light absinthe.

Suddenly he threw the glass and its contents at my head. I avoided the blow and, taking him bodily in my arms, left the café and crossed the Place Victor-Hugo; some minutes later, Vincent found himself in bed, where he fell asleep in a few seconds, not to awaken again until morning.

When he awoke, he said to me very calmly:

"My dear Gauguin, I have a vague memory of having offended you last evening."

"I gladly forgive you with all my heart, but yesterday's scene could happen again, and if I were struck I might lose control of myself and strangle you. So permit me to write your brother and announce my return."

My God, what a day!

Paul Gauguin. *Portrait of Vincent van Gogh painting Sunflowers.* 1888. 28³/₄ × 36¹/₄" (73 × 92 cm). Rijksmuseum Vincent van Gogh Foundation/Van Gogh Museum, Amsterdam.

When evening had arrived and I had quickly eaten my dinner, I felt the need to go out alone and take in the air, scented with flowering laurels. I had already almost crossed the Place Victor Hugo, when I heard behind me a familiar short footstep, rapid and irregular. I turned just at the moment when Vincent rushed towards me, an open razor in his hand. My look at that moment must have been powerful indeed, for he stopped, and lowering his head, took off running in the direction of the house.

In his account to Bernard six days after the incident no mention was made of a razor.

Was I lax at that moment, and oughtn't I to have disarmed him and sought to calm him down? Often I have questioned my conscience, but I do not reproach myself at all.

Let him who will cast the stone at me.

Only a short stretch, and I was in a good hotel in Arles, where, after asking the time, I took a room and went to bed. Very agitated, I could not fall asleep until about three in the morning, and I awoke rather late, about seven-thirty.

Upon arriving at the square, I saw a large crowd assembled. Near our house, some gendarmes and a little gentleman in a bowler hat, who was the police commissioner. Here is what had happened.

Van Gogh returned to the house and, immediately, cut off his ear close to the head. He must have taken some time in stopping the hemorrhage, for the next day there were many wet towels scattered about on the floor tiles of the two rooms downstairs.

In fact Van Gogh had cut only the bottom of the earlobe.

The blood had stained the two rooms and the little staircase that led up to our bedroom.

When he was in good enough condition to go out, his head covered up by a Basque beret pulled all the way down, he went straight to a house where, for want of a fellow-countrywoman, one can find a chance acquaintance, and gave the "sentry" his ear, carefully washed and enclosed in an envelope. "Here," he said, "a remembrance of me." Then he fled and returned home, where he went to bed and slept. He took the trouble, however, to close the shutters and to set a lighted lamp on a table near the window. Ten minutes later, the whole street given over to the *filles au joie* was in commotion and chattering about the event.

I had not the slightest inkling of all this when I appeared on the threshold of our house and the gentleman with the bowler hat said to me point-blank, in a more than severe tone:

"What have you done, sir, to your comrade?" – "I don't know." – "Oh, yes, . . . you know very well, . . . he is dead."

I would not wish anyone such a moment, and it took me a few long minutes to be able to think clearly and to repress the beating of my heart.

Anger, indignation, and grief as well, and the shame of all those gazes that were tearing my entire being to pieces suffocated me, and I stuttered when I said, "Alright, sir, let us go upstairs, and we can explain ourselves up there." In the bed, Vincent lay completely enveloped in the sheets, curled up like a gun hammer; he appeared lifeless. Gently, very gently, I touched the body, whose warmth surely announced life. For me it was as if I had regained all my powers of thought and energy.

Almost in a whisper, I said to the commissioner of police:

"Be so kind, sir, as to awaken this man with great care and, if he asks for me, tell him that I have left for Paris. The sight of me could be fatal to him."

I must avow that from this moment on the commissioner of police was as reasonable as possible and intelligently sent for a doctor and a carriage.

Once awake, Vincent asked for his comrade, his pipe, and his tobacco, and he even thought of asking for the box that was downstairs containing our money. A suspicion, without a doubt, that barely touched me, having already armed myself against all suffering.

Vincent was taken to the hospital where, upon arrival, his brain began to wander about again.

All the rest of it is known to everyone that it could be of interest to, and it would be useless to speak of it, were it not for the extreme suffering of a man who, cared for in a madhouse, at monthly intervals, regained his reason sufficiently to understand his condition and furiously paint the admirable paintings that we know.

The last letter that I had from him was dated from Auvers, near Pontoise. He told me that he had hoped to recover enough to come to visit me in Brittany, but that now he was obliged to recognize the impossibility of a cure.

"Dear master (the only time that he had used this word), after having known you and caused you pain, it is more dignified to die in a good state of mind than in a degraded state."

And he put a pistol shot in his stomach, and it was not until a few hours later, lying in his bed and smoking his pipe, that he died having complete lucidity of mind, with love for his art, and without hatred for others.

In *Les Monstres*, Jean Dolent writes:

"When Gauguin says 'Vincent,' his voice is gentle."

Without knowing it, but having guessed it, Jean Dolent is right.

One knows why. . . .

Jean Dolent, pseudonym of Antoine Fournier (1835–1909), author of Les Monstres, *1896.*

Vincent van Gogh's cell in the St-Paul-de-Mausole Asylum, St-Rémy. Photograph. Rijksmuseum Vincent van Gogh Foundation/Van Gogh Museum, Amsterdam.

JOACHIM GASQUET

CÉZANNE

"What He Told Me"

1921

Joachim Gasquet (1873–1921), the son of Cézanne's childhood friend Henri Gasquet, met the painter in April 1896 and remained on terms of close friendship with him for about four years. Gasquet, a writer and poet, wrote this account of his conversations with Cézanne in the exuberant style of his own writing, which has cast some considerable doubt on their value as a record of Cézanne's exact words. Scholars have come to regard Gasquet's Cézanne *as a mixture of the fanciful and the authentic. See Michael Doran's* Conversations avec Cézanne, *Paris, 1978.*

CÉZANNE. All right, look at this . . . (*He repeated his gesture, holding his hands apart, fingers spread wide, bringing them slowly, very slowly together again, then squeezing and contracting them until they were interlocked.*) That's what one needs to achieve . . . If one hand is too high, or too low, the whole thing is ruined. There mustn't be a single slack link, a single gap through which the emotion, the light, the truth can escape. I advance all of my canvas at one time, if you see what I mean. And in the same movement, with the same conviction, I approach all the scattered pieces . . . Everything we look at disperses and vanishes, doesn't it? Nature is always the same, and yet its appearance is always changing. It is our business as artists to convey the thrill of nature's permanence along with the elements and the appearance of all its changes. Painting must give us the flavour of nature's eternity. Everything, you understand. So I join together nature's straying hands . . . From all sides, here, there and everywhere, I select colours, tones and shades; I set them down, I bring them together . . . They make lines. They become objects – rocks, trees – without my thinking about them. They take on volume, value. If, as I perceive them, these volumes and values correspond on my canvas to the planes and patches of colour that lie before me, that appear to my eyes, well then, my canvas "joins hands." It holds firm. It aims neither too high nor too low. It's true, dense, full . . . But if there is the slightest distraction, the slightest hitch, above all if I interpret too much one day, if I'm carried away today by a theory which contradicts yesterday's, if I think while I'm painting, if I meddle, then whoosh!, everything goes to pieces.

MYSELF. What do you mean, if you meddle?

CÉZANNE. The artist is nothing more than a receptacle of sensations, a brain, a recording machine . . . A damned good machine, fragile and complex, above all in its relationship to other machines . . . But if he intervenes, if he dares to meddle voluntarily with what he ought merely to be translating, he introduces his own insignificance into it and the work is inferior.

MYSELF. In short, you consider the artist inferior to nature.

CÉZANNE. No, that's not what I'm saying. You're on the wrong track. Art has a harmony which parallels that of nature. The people who tell you that the painter is always inferior to nature are idiots! He is parallel to it. Unless, of course, he deliberately intervenes. His whole aim must be silence. He must silence all the voices of prejudice within him, he must forget, forget, be silent, become a perfect echo. And then the entire land-

Paul Cézanne. *Scene of Violence.* c.1869–72. Reed pen, ink and wash, $5^{1}/_{2} \times 7^{1}/_{6}''$ (14.1 × 18.2 cm). Öffentliche Kunstsammlung, Kupferstichkabinett, Basle.

scape will engrave itself on the sensitive plate of his being. After that, he will have to use his craft to fix it on canvas, to externalize it; but this craft, too, is always ready to obey, to translate automatically, familiar as it is with the language, with the text to be deciphered, with the two parallel texts, nature as it is seen and nature as it is felt, the nature that is there . . . (*he pointed towards the green and blue plain*) and the nature that is here (*he tapped his forehead*), both of which have to fuse in order to endure, to live that life, half-human and half-divine, which is the life of art or, if you will . . . the life of God. The landscape is reflected, humanized, rationalized within me. I objectivize it, project it, fix it on my canvas . . . You were talking to me the other day about Kant. It may sound like nonsense, but I would see myself as the subjective consciousness of that landscape, and my canvas as its objective consciousness. My canvas and the landscape are both outside me, but while the one is chaotic, transient, muddled, lacking in logic or rational coherence, the other is permanent, tangible, classifiable, forming part of the world, of the theatre of ideas . . . of their individuality. I know. I know . . . I am interpreting. I am no university professor. I would not dare to venture into these realms with Dumesnil . . . Good Lord, how I envy you your youth and its impetuousness! But time is pressing . . . Maybe I am wrong to run on like this . . . No more theories! Works . . . Theories are man's downfall! You need a powerful constitution and inexhaustible energy to withstand them. I ought to be more sedate, ought to realize that I am getting too old for these bursts of enthusiasm . . . that they will always be my ruin.

(*He had become gloomy. He was often depressed like this after an excited outburst. And it was no good trying to cheer him up. That only made him furious. He felt bad . . . There was a long silence. He picked up his brushes again, looking in turn at his canvas and his motif.*)

Paul Cézanne. *The Temptation of St Antony.* 1873–75. Drawing, 5¹⁄₈ × 8¹⁄₄″ (31 × 21 cm). Staatliche Museen, Kupferstichkabinett, Berlin-Dahlem.

Georges Dumesnil (1855–1916), philosopher, was Gasquet's teacher at the Lycée Mignet in Aix.

Paul Cézanne. *Hills with Houses and Trees*. *c*.1880/83. Pencil, 12⅓ × 18⅔″ (31.3 × 47.3 cm). Öffentliche Kunstsammlung, Kupferstichkabinett, Basle.

ÉMILE BERNARD

L'OCCIDENT

"Paul Cézanne"

July 1904

They [the Impressionists] have purified the vision of their eye and the logic of their spirit, that is why the work which they have accomplished has been excellent, and despite its simple documentary appearance, is of capital importance.

Paul Cézanne was not the first to enter upon this path. He gladly recognizes that it is to Monet and Pissarro that he owes his having set himself free from the over-preponderant influence of the museums to place himself under that of nature. Despite this proximity, his work does not show it. Only, however great they could have been with pleasure, the primitively sombre and rough canvases of Cézanne came down to restricted proportions, an exigency of working after nature. The master leaves his studio, goes morning and evening to his motif, follows the effect of the atmosphere on the forms and the locations, and analyzes, searches, finds. Soon it is no longer Pissarro who is advising him, it is he who is acting on the pictorial evolution of the latter. Thus he did not adopt Monet's or Pissarro's manner of working; he remained what he was, that is to say a painter with an eye which clarifies and educates itself, exalts itself before the sky and the mountains, in the presence of things and beings. According to his own expression, he has made a fresh optic for himself, for his was obliterated and led away by a limitless passion towards too many images, engravings, pictures. He wanted to see too much; his insatiable desire for beauty has made him search into the multiform volume of art too closely; henceforth he finds that it is necessary to restrict himself, to shut himself away in a conception and an ideal that are aesthetic; thus if he goes to the Louvre, if he concentrates his gaze for a long time on Veronese, this time it is to strip its appearances and scrutinize its laws; in it he learns the contrasts, the tonal oppositions and distills his taste, ennobling and elevating it. If he goes to look at Delacroix again, it is to follow in his work the

Émile Bernard (*1868–1941*), *a painter and art theorist trained in Pont-Aven in "the school of Gauguin," whom he also influenced, became one of Cézanne's earliest supporters and, after the artist's death, one of his principal detractors. This article, which incorporated witness accounts of Cézanne's practice as a painter and citations from Cézanne's letters, is significant for the information it provided for the first time to younger artists, such as Matisse, on Cézanne's theory of color. The overall tone of the article, however, characterizing Cézanne as "classicist" and "mystic," is governed by the theoretical outlook of Bernard himself.*

Paolo Veronese (1528–88), Venetian painter of the High Renaissance.

flowering of the effect in the colored sensation; for he declares: "Delacroix was, in regard to colors, imaginative and sensitive" – a most powerful and exceptional gift; in fact, the artist sometimes possesses a brain and not an eye, sometimes an eye and not a brain; and Cézanne immediately quotes Manet as an example: the nature of a painter, the intelligence of an artist, but mediocrely sensitive to color.

It was at Auvers, near to Pissarro, that Cézanne retired in order to disengage himself from all influence before nature after having painted grand and forceful works under the sway of Courbet; and it was at Auvers that he began his astonishing creations of an art sincere and so naively knowing that he has since developed. . . .

From the day when Paul Cézanne set himself face to face with nature with the firm resolution to *forget everything*, he began these discoveries which, being spread by superficial imitation from that time onwards, have had the finality of a revolution on contemporary comprehension.

But all this happened without his being aware of it, for heedless of glory, reputation, success, dissatisfied with himself, the painter plunged into the absolute of his art without ever wishing to listen to anything from the outside world, pursuing the occult deepening of his analysis, giving slowly

Cézanne painting in Aix-en-Provence. Photograph taken by Maurice Denis with Émile Bernard. January 1904. Collection Sirot-Angel, Paris.

253

and with reflexion and power the thrusts with his spade which would one day come in contact with the marvelous vein whence all splendour would emerge.

Such was his method of work: primarily, complete submission to the model; using care, establishing the setting, the search for the contours, the relations of proportions; then, in very meditative sessions, the exaltation of the sensations of colour, the elevation of the form towards a decorative conception; of colour towards the most musical pitch. Thus the more the artist works, the more remote his work becomes from the objective; the farther he removes himself from the opacity of the model serving him as his starting point, the more he enters into unalloyed, absolute painting, without any other purpose than itself; the more he abstracts his picture, the more he simplifies and amplifies it, after having brought it into being, narrow, conforming, hesitant.

Gradually the work has grown, has reached the result of a pure conception. In this attentive and patient procedure, every part is brought into operation simultaneously, accompanies the others, and it can be said that each day a more exasperated vision comes to superimpose itself on that of the day before, until the artist grows weary, feels his wings melting at the sun's approach, that is, leaves off at the highest point to which he has been able to raise his work; so that if he had taken as many canvases as he has spent sessions, there would result from his analysis a sum total of ascending visions, gradually living, singing, abstract, harmonious, the most *supernatural* of which would be the most definitive; but in taking only a single canvas for this slow and fervent elaboration, Paul Cézanne shows us that analysis is not his objective, that it is not his means, that he is using it as a pedestal, and that all he cares about is the destructive and conclusive synthesis. This method of working which is peculiar to him, he advocates as the only one which must lead to a serious result, and he condemns mercilessly any deliberate bias in favour of simplification which does not pass through submission to Nature, through thoughtful and progressive analysis. If a painter is satisfied with little, it is, according to Paul Cézanne, because his vision is mediocre, his temperament of poor value. . . .

"The destructive and conclusive 'synthesis'" is a term from Bernard's "symbolist/synthetist" vocabulary rather than Cézanne's.

The expressive syntheses of Cézanne are detailed and submissive studies. Taking nature as a focal point he conforms to the phenomena and transcribes them slowly and attentively until he has discovered the laws which produce them. Then, logically, he takes possession of them and completes his work by an imposing and living synthesis. His conclusion, in harmony with his southerner's expansive nature, is decorative; that is, free and exalted.

Madame de Staël wrote in her book on Germany: "The French consider external objects as the motive power of all ideas and the Germans, ideas as the motive power of all impressions." Paul Cézanne justifies this opinion of Madame de Staël on the French but he knows how to go to a depth of art which is not common to our contemporaries. As a good traditionalist, he maintains that Nature is our focal point, that one must draw nothing out, except from her alone, at the same time giving oneself liberty to improvise with what we borrow from her. . . .

Madame de Staël (Anne Louise Germaine Necker, 1766–1817), author of De L'Allemagne.

What the painter primarily needs, according to Cézanne, is a personal optic, and such an optic can only be obtained from persistent contact with the vision of the universe.

Of course it is essential to have frequented the Louvre, the museums – in order to realise the elevation of Nature to art. "The Louvre is a good book to consult, but it should not be more than an intermediary; the real and major study to be undertaken is the diversity of the picture of Nature."

Without the vision of Art, the copy of Nature would become a mere stupidity, that is obvious, but one must fear about limiting one's invention

Quoted from Cézanne (letter to Bernard, May 12, 1904).

to repetitions or pastiches, about losing one's foothold in abstractions or useless repetitions; it is essential to maintain oneself on the ground of analysis and observation, to forget the works already completed in order to create unforeseen ones, drawn from the heart of the work of God.

Paul Cézanne considers that there are two plastic arts, the one sculptural or linear, the other decorative or colorist. What he calls sculptural plasticity would be amply signified by the type of the Venus de Milo. What he calls decorative plasticity is linked with Michelangelo and Rubens: the one of these plasticities is servile, the other free; in the one the contour prevails, in the other the projection, colour, and fire. Ingres belongs to the first category, Delacroix to the second. . . .

Here are some opinions of Cézanne:

"Ingres is a pernicious classicist, and so in general are all those who deny nature or copy it with their minds made up and look for style in the imitation of the Greeks and Romans.

"Gothic art is deeply inspiring; it belongs to the same family as we do.

"Let us read nature; let us realize our sensations in an aesthetic that is at once personal and traditional. The strongest will be he who sees most deeply and realizes fully like the great Venetians.

"Painting from nature is not copying the objective, it is realizing one's sensations.

"There are two things in the painter, the eye and the mind; each of them should aid the other. It is necessary to work at their mutual development, in the eye by looking at nature, in the mind by the logic of organized sensations which provides the means of expression.

"To read nature is to see it, as if through a veil, in terms of an interpretation in patches of colour following one another according to a law of harmony. These major hues are thus analysed through modulations. Painting is classifying one's sensations of colour.

"There is no such thing as line or modeling; there are only contrasts. These are not contrasts of light and dark, but the contrasts given by the sensation of colour. Modelling is the outcome of the exact relationship of tones. When they are harmoniously juxtaposed and complete, the picture develops modelling of its own accord.

"One should not say model, one should say modulate.

"Shadow is a colour as light is, but less brilliant; light and shadow are only the relation of two tones.

"Everything in nature is modelled on the sphere, the cone and the cylinder. One must learn to paint from these simple forms; it will then be possible to do whatever one wishes.

"Drawing and colour are not separate at all; in so far as you paint, you draw. The more the colour harmonises, the more exact the drawing becomes. When the colour achieves richness, the form attains its plenitude. The contrasts and connections of tones – there you have the secret of drawing and modelling.

"The effect is what constitutes a picture. It unifies the picture and concentrates it. The effect must be based on the existence of a dominating patch.

"It is necessary to be workmanlike in art. To get to know one's way of realisation early. To paint in accordance with the qualities of painting itself. To use materials crude and pure.

"It is necessary to become again classical by way of nature, that is to say through sensation.

"It is all summed up in this: to possess sensations and to read nature.

"In our period there are no more true painters. Monet has given a vision. Renoir has made the woman of Paris. Pissarro was very close to nature. What follows doesn't count, composed only of bluffers who feel nothing, who do acrobatics. . . . Delacroix, Courbet, Manet made paintings.

"Work without regard for anyone, and become strong – that is the aim of the artist. . . .

"The artist must disregard opinion which isn't based on intelligent observation of character. One must eschew the literary spirit, which is so often divergent from the true voice of painting: the concrete study of nature in order not to get lost too long in intangible speculations.

"The painter must devote himself entirely to the study of nature and to try to produce pictures which can become a lesson. Causeries on art are almost useless. Work which realises its progress in its proper medium is a sufficient compensation for the incomprehension of imbeciles. The man of letters expresses himself in abstractions while the painter concretises his sensations, his perceptions by means of drawing and colour.

"One cannot be too scrupulous, too sincere, too submissive to nature, but one is more or less master of one's model, and above all one's means of expression. Penetrate that which is before you, and persevere to express it as logically as possible."

Such is Cézanne, such is the lesson of his art. As one can see, it is essentially differentiated from Impressionism, from which it derives but in which he could not imprison his nature. Far from being spontaneous, Cézanne is a man who reflects, his genius is a flash in depth. It thus follows that his typically painter's temperament has led him to new

256

decorative creations, to unexpected syntheses; and these syntheses have in truth been the greatest progress that has sprung from modern apperceptions; for they have overthrown the routine of the schools, maintained tradition and condemned the hasty fantasy of the excellent artists of whom I have spoken. In short, Cézanne, through the reasonableness of his works, has proved himself the only master on whom the art of the future could graft its fruition. Yet how little appreciated were his discoveries. Wrongly considered by some, because of their unfinished state, as research which has not come to fruition; by others as strange studies without a future, due to the unique fantasy of an unhealthy artist; by himself confronted with an ideal of the absolute as bad rather than good, doubtless with resentment at seeing himself betrayed (he destroyed a large number of his works and showed none), such as they are they constitute nevertheless the finest effort towards a pictorial and colourist renaissance that France has been able to see since Delacroix.

I do not hesitate to declare that Cézanne is a painter with a mystical temperament and one is mistaken to have always classified him in the deplorable school inaugurated by M. Zola, who, despite his blasphemies against nature, hyperbolically attributed to himself the title of naturalist. I say that Cézanne is a painter with a mystical temperament by reason of his purely abstract and aesthetic vision of things. Where others, to express themselves, are concerned with creating a subject, he is content with certain harmonies of lines and tones taken from just any objects, without troubling about these objects in themselves, like a musician who, disdainful of embellishing on a score, would be satisfied with making series of chords whose exquisite nature would infallibly plunge us into something beyond art, inaccessible to his skillful colleagues. Cézanne is a mystic precisely by this scorn for any subject, by the absence of a material vision, by a taste which his landscapes, his still-life, his portraits show to be the most noble and the highest style. And the very nature of his style confirms what I was saying by a quality of candour and grace that is wholly of Giotto, showing things in their essential beauty. Take any painting by the master, it is in its knowledge and truly superlative quality a sensitive and conscious lesson of interpretation. . . .

Thus, among the painters who are great, Paul Cézanne can be placed as a mystic, for that is the lesson of art which he gives us, he sees things not in themselves, but through their direct relationship with painting. That is to say, with the concrete expression of their beauty. He is contemplative, he regards aesthetically, not objectively; he expresses himself by sensibility, that is to say with an instinctive and conscious perception of relationships and affinities. And since his work is thus akin to music it can quite definitely be repeated that he is a mystic, this last means being the supreme one, that of heaven. Every art which becomes musical is on the way to its absolute perfection. In language it becomes poetry, in painting it becomes beauty.

This word "beauty" used about Paul Cézanne's work demands an explanation. In this case I should like it to be understood as follows: *Absolute expansion of the art used.* Certainly in his portraits, for instance, the master painter has scarcely troubled to choose a model. He has worked on the first person of good will whom he found near him, his wife, his son, and, more often than not, ordinary folk, a laborer, or a dairymaid, in preference to a dandy or some civilized person whom he abhors for his corrupt tastes and his worldly sham.

Here, of course, it is no longer a question of seeking beauty outside the means of painting; lines, values, colouring, brush-stroke style, presentation, character. We are certainly far from an agreed or material beauty and the work will only be beautiful for us to the extent that we possess a very high sensitivity, capable of making us lose sight of the thing represented, to enjoy it artistically. "It is indeed essential to see one's model, to perceive it very accurately, and even to express oneself with distinction

Quoted from Cézanne (letter to Bernard, May 12, 1904).

257

and force. Taste is the best judge. It is rare. Art is only addressed to an exceedingly limited number of individuals." These are the words of the master, corroborated by his work; they express his preoccupations. Taste is the special sense (so little and so badly cultivated, alas!) to which he addresses himself.

The master is pleased to appeal to tradition. He knows the Louvre better than any painter, he has even, according to his own view, looked at the old pictures too much. What he thinks should be asked of the ancients is their classical and serious fashion of organizing their work logically. Nature intervening in the artist's work will animate what reason would leave dead. He recommends above all to start from Nature.

Surely one should be a theorist to enter into possession of oneself and bring one's work to a successful conclusion, but one should be so in regard to one's feelings and not only in regard to the means. One's sensation demands that the means be constantly transformed, re-created, to express them in their intensity. One must thus not try to make the sensation enter into a pre-established means, but to put one's genius which is inventive of expression at the service of the sensation. On the one hand it would be the École des Beaux-Arts which would bring everything to a uniform mold, whereas on the other it is a constant renewal. Organize one's sensations, that is then the first precept of Cézanne's doctrine, doctrine which is not at all sensualist, but sensitive. The artist will then gain in logic without losing in expression; he will be able to produce the unforeseen while remaining classical in Nature. . . .

The impression of immediacy conveyed by Bernard's assertion that the piece was written in Aix in March – he dated it thus – is belied by quotations from Cézanne's letters to Bernard dated in May.

PAUL CÉZANNE

Letters

1904–06

TO ÉMILE BERNARD   AIX, JULY 25, 1904

My dear Bernard,
I have received the "*Revue Occidentale*". I can only thank you for what you wrote about me.

I am sorry that we cannot be side by side, for I don't want to be right in theory, but in front of nature. Ingres in spite of his "estyle" (Aixian pronunciation) and his admirers, is only a very small painter. The greatest, you know them better than I; the Venetians and the Spaniards.

Cézanne's response to Bernard's article, though affirmative, was cool.

In order to make progress, there is only nature, and the eye is trained through contact with her. It becomes concentric through looking and working. I mean to say that in an orange, an apple, a ball, a head, there is a culminating point; and this point is always – in spite of the tremendous effect; light and shade, colour sensations – the closest to our eye; the edges of the objects flee towards a centre on our horizon. With a small temperament one can be very much of a painter. One can do good things without being very much of a harmonist or a colourist. It is sufficient to have a sense of art – and this is without doubt the horror of the bourgeois, this sense. Therefore institutions, pensions, honours, can only be made for cretins, humbugs and rascals. Don't be an art critic, but paint, there lies salvation.

A warm handclasp from your old comrade

The words between dashes had been added by Cézanne on the margins of the letter.

P. Cézanne

My kind regards to Madame Bernard and love to the children.

* * *

My dear Bernard,

Your letters are precious to me for a double reason: The first being purely egoistic, because their arrival lifts me out of the monotony caused by the incessant pursuit of the sole and unique aim, which leads in moments of physical fatigue to a kind of intellectual exhaustion; and the second, allows me to reassess for you, undoubtedly rather too much, the obstinacy with which I pursue the realization of that part of nature, which, coming into our line of vision, gives us the picture. Now the theme to develop is that – whatever our temperament or form of strength face to face with nature may be – we must render the image of what we see, forgetting everything that existed before us. Which, I believe, must permit the artist to give his entire personality, whether great or small.

Now being old, nearly 70 years, the sensations of colour, which give the light, are for me the reason for the abstractions which do not allow me to cover my canvas entirely nor to pursue the delimitation of the objects where their points of contact are fine and delicate; from which it results that my image or picture is incomplete. On the other hand the planes fall one on top of the other, from whence neo-impressionism emerged, which circum-scribes the contours with a black line, a fault which must be fought at all costs. But nature, if consulted, gives us the means of attaining this end.

The black line to which Cézanne refers related not to Neo-Impressionism, but to the style formulated by Bernard himself which he called "cloisonism."

I remembered quite well that you were at Tonnerre but the difficulties of settling down in my house make me place myself entirely at the disposal of my family, who make use of this to seek their own comfort and neglect me a little. That's life; at my age I should have more experience and use it for the general good. I owe you the truth about painting and shall tell it to you.

Please give my kind regards to Madame Bernard; the children I must love, seeing that St. Vincent de Paul is the one to whom I must recom-mend myself most.

Your old

Paul Cézanne

A strong handshake and good courage.

Optics, which are developed in us by study, teach us to see.

My dear Paul,

It rained on Saturday and Sunday and there was a thunderstorm, the weather is much cooler – in fact it is not hot at all. You are quite right in saying that here we are deep in the provinces. I continue to work with difficulty, but in the end there is something. That is the important thing, I believe. As sensations form the basis of everything for me, I am, I believe, impervious. I shall, by the way, let the poor devil, you know who, imitate me as much as he likes, it is scarcely dangerous.

Give my regards, when you have the opportunity, to Monsieur and Madame Legoupil, who are kind enough to remember me. Do not forget Louis and his family either and my good father Guillaume. – Everything passes with frightening speed, I am not too bad. I take care of myself, I eat well.

I should like to ask you to order me two dozen marten-hair brushes, like the ones we ordered last year.

My dear Paul, in order to give you news as satisfactory as you would like, I would need to be 20 years younger. – I repeat, I eat well, and a little moral satisfaction – but work alone can give me that – would do me a lot of good. – All my compatriots are arseholes beside me.

I should have told you that I received the cocoa.

I embrace you and mamma, your old father,

Paul Cézanne

I think the young painters are much more intelligent than the others, the old ones see in me only a disastrous rival. Ever your father

P. Cézanne

I must say it again, Emile Bernard seems to me worthy of deep compassion for he has to look after his family.

CAMILLE PISSARRO

Letter to Lucien

November 21, 1895

PARIS

My dear Lucien,
Yesterday at Portier's I made the acquaintance of the English painter O'Kean, – I don't know whether I am spelling his name correctly. He is very intelligent and greatly admires the Impressionists, especially my work. He didn't know me by sight, and he was praising my *Sunset in Knocke*, a canvas of 25 × 21 inches, so highly that I was abashed. . . . He wanted to show me a canvas of his so that I could advise him, which I did scrupulously. His painting, like that of many English artists, is literature, which is not a defect in itself, but does result from a lack of painting content; his work is thin and hard and lacks values. It is, however, intelligent, a little like Chavannes, sentimental and feminine, but as I told him, it is not really painting. . . . Speaking of England, I asked him how it was that we were so little understood in a country that had had such fine painters. England is always late and moves in leaps. This is pretty much our own opinion.

On leaving Portier I had this thought: How rarely do you come across true painters, who know how to balance two tones. I was thinking of Hayet, who looks for noon at midnight, of Gauguin, who, however, has a good eye, of Signac, who also has something, all of them more or less paralyzed by theories. I also thought of Cézanne's show in which there were exquisite things, still lifes of irreproachable perfection, others *much worked on* and yet unfinished, of even greater beauty, landscapes, nudes and heads that are unfinished but yet grandiose, and so *painted*, so supple. . . . Why? Sensation is there!

On the way to Durand-Ruel's, I saw two paintings of Puvis de Chavannes. No, no! That sort of thing is cold and tiresome! A representation of natives of Picardy, and very well composed. But all the same, at bottom the whole thing is an anomaly, it can't be seen as a painting, no, a thousand times no! On a great stone wall it is admirable . . . but it is not painting. I am simply noting my immediate impressions.

Curiously enough, while I was admiring this strange, disconcerting aspect of Cézanne, familiar to me for many years, Renoir arrived. But my enthusiasm was nothing compared to Renoir's. Degas himself is seduced by the charm of this refined savage, Monet, all of us. . . . Are we mistaken? I don't think so. The only ones who are not subject to the charm of Cézanne are precisely those artists or collectors who have shown by their errors that their sensibilities are defective. They properly point out the faults we all see, which leap to the eye, but the charm – that they do not see. As Renoir said so well, these paintings have I do not know what quality like the things of Pompeii, so crude and so admirable! . . . Nothing of the *Académie Julian*! Degas and Monet have bought some marvelous Cézannes, I exchanged a poor sketch of Louveciennes for an admirable small canvas of bathers and one of his self-portraits.

Charles Samuel Keene (1823–91).

Vollard gave Cézanne his first one-man show, which opened in November 1895.

COLORPLATE 80. Paul Cézanne. *Vessels, Fruit and Cloth. c.*1879–80. 17¾ × 21¼″ (45 × 54 cm).
Hermitage, St Petersburg, Russia.

COLORPLATE 81. Paul Cézanne. *Carafe and Knife*. 1890–95. Watercolor, 8¼ × 10¾″ (21 × 28 cm).
Philadelphia, Museum of Art (A. E. Gallatin Collection).

COLORPLATE 82. Paul Cézanne. *Portrait of Madame Cézanne. c.*1885. 31¾ × 25½″ (81 × 65 cm).
Musée de l'Orangerie, Paris (Collection Walter–Guillaume).

COLORPLATE 83. Paul Cézanne. *Fruits, Napkin and Jug of Milk.* c.1880. 23½ × 28¾″ (60 × 73 cm).
Musée de l'Orangerie, Paris (Collection Walter–Guillaume).

COLORPLATE 84. Paul Cézanne. *View through Trees, L'Estaque.* c.1882–85. 9 × 23½″ (23 × 60 cm).
Private Collection, England (Photo courtesy The Trustees of the Fitzwilliam Museum, Cambridge).

COLORPLATE 85. Paul Cézanne. *Landscape in Provence (Mont Sainte-Victoire)*. 1885–87.
23 × 31¾″ (58.5 × 81 cm). Nasjonalgalleriet, Oslo.

COLORPLATE 86. Paul Cézanne. *Mont Sainte-Victoire seen beyond the Wall of the Jas de Bouffan.* 1885–88.
Watercolor, $18\frac{1}{2} \times 11\frac{3}{4}''$ (47 × 29.8 cm).
National Gallery of Art, Washington, D.C. (Mellon Collection).

COLORPLATE 87. Paul Cézanne. *The Village of Gardanne*. 1885–86. 36¼ × 29⅜″ (92 × 74 cm).
The Brooklyn Museum, New York (Ella C. Woodward Fund, A. T. White Memorial Fund).

R. P. RIVIÈRE AND J. F. SCHNERB

LA GRANDE REVUE

"Cézanne's Studio"

December 25, 1907

Jacques Félix Simon Schnerb (1879–1915), painter, printmaker and art critic, visited Cézanne in January 1905 with R. P. Rivière, who was also a printmaker, but about whom little else is known. Their account is a valuable record of the theory and practice of Cézanne's last years.

According to certain legends concerning Cézanne, he was a misanthrope, a sort of unapproachable bear. Long before his death, it was said that this painter had stopped painting, that he was most reluctant to show his earlier work. Even the best-informed could provide only the vaguest information about his place of residence and style of life. Even the hardest head might say that Cézanne was a mythical being without any real existence.

It may therefore be interesting to quote some of the painter's own remarks, based on notes taken during a visit. Indeed, Cézanne did intend to write down his thoughts on painting, though he probably never did so. Moreover, much nonsense has been spoken about his work; so few painters, even among those who drew inspiration from him, have understood the real implications of his work, that an attempt at a faithful account of the ideas of this pioneer painter will have its uses.

When you rang M. Cézanne's doorbell at No. 23 rue Boulegon, a peaceful road in Aix, you were received, Provençal fashion, with a bluff handshake, by a fellow-painter seeking news of the capital, who did not allow you to address him as "maître" and who would say, when questioned about his work: "I am an old man; I paint, what else could I do?"

So, he painted. He never took any care of his works, and canvases lay about in corners, rolled up or still on their stretchers. Those which were rolled up might be left on chairs and flattened. His studios, one on rue Boulegon and one on the chemin de l'Aubassane, outside the town, were in extreme and unaffected disorder. The walls were bare, and the light harsh. The table was strewn with half-empty tubes of paint, paintbrushes with bristles stiffened by colors which had long since dried out and the remains of meals in the process of becoming still lifes. In one corner was a whole collection of landscape-painters' umbrellas whose rough frames probably came from some local tradesman, their iron tips possibly from the neighboring blacksmith's; nearby lay game bags for taking provisions into the countryside.

L'Atelier des Lauves.

As visits were rare and Cézanne had almost no close friends to whom he could talk about painting in Aix, he would express himself in the elliptical and sometimes obscure language of those who are much alone. Some of his axioms were answers long sought to questions which the difficulties of his art had forced him to consider and which his interlocutor might never have thought of.

In order to clarify the ideas which Cézanne proffered more or less at random, it may be convenient to group together those concerning drawing, color and composition and, lastly ideas on art in general.

In connection with drawing as such, in so far as it can arbitrarily be regarded separately from color, Cézanne roundly declared his horror of the photographic eye, the kind of mechanically exact drawing as taught in the École des Beaux-Arts, to which he claimed to have attempted to gain admission twice, unsuccessfully. It was not that he justified the superficial incorrectness of his drawing, an incorrectness which is neither carelessness nor lack of ability, but which arises rather from an excessive sincerity – if that is not a paradox – from an excessive mistrust of purely manual dexterity, a distrust of any movement made with the eye guiding the hand without the intervention of reason. Thus Cézanne never pretended to be unaware of the asymmetry of his bottles, the faulty perspective of his plates. Showing me one of his watercolors, he used his fingernail to correct a bottle which was not vertical, and he said, as though excusing himself: 'I am a primitive, I have a lazy eye. I have twice tried to gain admission to the École des Beaux-Arts, but I do not concentrate on the work as a whole: if a head interests me particularly, I make it too big."

Thus, rightly or wrongly, Cézanne forbade himself the slightest insincerity; but though he regretted that his bottles were not vertical, he did not correct them; similarly, if parts of the canvas had been left bare as he painted it, he left them that way rather than add any tone at random.

Cézanne did not try to represent forms by lines. For him the outline existed only as the place where one form ended and another began. Look at his unfinished canvases; the objects on a nearer plane are often left white, with their outline indicated only by the background against which they stand. No outline as a matter of principle, a form exists only by virtue of neighboring forms. For Cézanne, the black strokes which often play a determining role in his paintings were not an element intended to be added to the color, but simply a way of summing up an overall form more easily through its outline before modeling it with color.

For color and modeling were inseparable for him; from the technical point of view, this was perhaps the aspect of his art which he has most strongly developed, and the one where his singleminded study had truly rendered him a master.

"What I want is to render the cylindrical aspect of objects," he would say. And one of his favorite axioms, which rang unforgettably in his Provençal accent, was: "Everything is spherical and cylindrical." This requires an explanation.

While pronouncing this formula, Cézanne would point either to an apple, to some clearly spherical or cylindrical object, or to a flat surface such as a wall or floor. Now look at his paintings: we can indeed see that one of the reasons for their solid appearance is the skill and knowledge

Photograph of Paul Cézanne's studio at Aix.

brought to the modeling of the flat surfaces, whether of a meadow or a table laden with fruit.

To complete the setting forth of this theory, it should be added that, in relation to the eye, conceived as motionless, the light rays coming from any surface, flat or otherwise, are such that the sum total of light which the eye receives is not identical for any of the points of the surface. A surface seems even in color and tone to us only because our eye moves to perceive it as a whole; and if the painter spread a monochrome layer of color on his canvas to represent it, this representation would be unconvincing.

"I am not a tonal painter," Cézanne would say, and indeed, he modeled rather through color than through tonal value. For him, oppositions of light and shade were above all oppositions in color which observation and reasoning allowed the painter to reproduce. The parts struck directly by the light and those which were lit only by reflected light are colored differently, but according to a uniform law whatever their local color might be. It is through the opposition of warm and cool that the colors disposed by the painter – colors with no absolute qualities of luminosity in themselves – nevertheless succeed in representing light and shade. The lightest color on the palette, white, for example, will emerge as shade if the painter can contrast it with a more luminous tone. That is why Cézanne was fond of saying: "You do not make light, you reproduce it." The painter merely reproduces its coloring effects.

Cézanne knew that Claude Monet possessed a unique eye as a colorist; to recall his friend's skill in coloring shadow, that is, the parts which, deprived of the direct light of the sun, received only a reflection from the sky, Cézanne would say: "The sky is blue, is it not? and it was Monet who discovered it."

Thus Cézanne saw contrasts of light and dark even on flat surfaces giving the appearance of unified tone. Certain of his watercolors, where his analytical procedures are particularly in evidence, looked like badly synchronized three-color exposures as obtained by isochromatic photography. In such proofs, where the mixture by superimposition is imperfect, one can see that each of the three basic colors is present in all the tones. Only the proportion differs.

Cézanne's whole manner is determined by this chromatic conception of modeling. If he mixed his pigments on the palette and laid them on the canvas simply by juxtaposing them, if he avoided blending two hues by the simple play of the brush, it was because he conceived of modeling as a succession of colors ranging from warm to cool, because for him the whole interest lay in determining each of these colors exactly and because to replace one of them by the mixture of two neighboring colors would have struck him as mindless. This was not an *a priori* approach used with the aim of giving his colors added freshness; and yet it is this freshness, this *éclat* (which is merely a by-product of his method) which his imitators tried to borrow from him, though without going back to its cause, from which more might have been learned, namely, logical observation substituted for empiricism.

Cézanne had acquired this knowledge of color through theoretical and practical research. "You must use your brain," he would say, "looking is not enough, you must use your brain." In a word, modeling through color, which was his language, forced the painter to use a close range of tones, in order to be able to observe the contrasts even in the half-tint, in order to avoid white lights and black shadows. Rivière was surprised to see Cézanne paint as green the gray-white wall which was behind his model. "The sensation of color," replied the artist, "must be developed through application and hard thought. Look at Veronese; his youthful work is gray; but later, with the *Pilgrims at Emmaus*, how warm it became!"

Thus Cézanne preferred to work when the sun, still low in the sky, lights up colors with a very warm light. He would stop painting after ten in the morning: "The light is going," he would say.

Yet he was less concerned with painting the violent contrasts made by full sunlight than the delicate gradations which model objects almost imperceptibly. He painted a light more general than the sun. For him, a painter who worked for several months on the same motif, a patch of sunlight or a reflection were rather irritating accidents, and of secondary importance. He pierces the atmosphere with his gaze, eager to seize the form and as it were the weight of things, and does not pause to contemplate its multiple variations, as the Impressionists did.

As to composition, one finds no care for that in the paintings of Cézanne, if by composition one means the premeditated bringing together of elements which will constitute the subject of the picture, and their arrangement in view of a harmonious collection of lines, tones and colors, whether the artist is working objectively before a motif which he will exploit by choosing a viewpoint, or whether his imagination provides him with this motif subjectively. But is this not arrangement rather than composition?

Composition, according to Cézanne, must be the result of work. Any motif copied precisely as it falls before the eye of the painter must become a perfectly balanced whole through study, not through choice, nor omissions inspired by decorative taste, but through the logic of the representation, through the study of the balance of luminous parts with those in shadow. It is here that the theory of the spherical nature of objects in relation to the eye found its full application, the motif being considered as a portion of nature embraced by the eye and hence becoming isolated, making a whole out of what is in fact a fragment. "The picture must be made from nature," Cézanne would say. Thus it is logic, for which observation can never be a complete substitute, which composes the picture, it is logic which concludes that two points of a single visual whole cannot, any more than two points of a single form, send back the same amount of light, and logic which uses reasoning to deduce the picture's maximum point of luminous intensity.

When Cézanne had thus discovered the laws which made him master of his subject, the rest might seem irrelevant to his research, which was mainly theoretical. Does not his entire *oeuvre* consist of analysis working towards a synthesis, observation trained upon a scientific rather than a decorative end? For this Provençal master, the canvas was nothing more than the blackboard on which a geometrician seeks the solutions to a problem, and the large number of paintings he left unfinished has perhaps as much to do with this conception of his work as with the lack of care he took to make them known.

For him, the condition indispensable for real work was to be able to achieve it without material worries. "Excuse me, have you independent means?" he would ask the young artists who came to seek his advice, "well, work, otherwise you'll have to live." To be sure, he regarded himself as a student all his life, and his modesty emerges in the lines he wrote to M. Roger Marx to thank him for the perceptive judgment the latter had devoted to him at the Salon d'Automne of 1904: "With a painter's temperament and an artistic ideal, that is to say, a conception of nature, sufficient powers of expression would have been necessary to be intelligible to the general public and to occupy a fitting position in the history of Art."

We have already seen how, after studying the masters in the museums, he wanted to go out and re-experience a direct vision of nature. "Pissarro," he would say, "used to claim that the Louvre should be burnt down; he was right, yet we mustn't do it!" and he would make a restraining gesture as though to ward off a misfortune which he would have been the first to deplore. This expressed both his hatred of the conventional *métier* and his love for the masters. Veronese was among those most in his mind towards the end of his life. He had a photograph of the *Bergers d'Arcadie* pinned up in his room, he was drawn by the beauty of the subject.

(*Opposite*) Cézanne in his Lauves studio, in front of his large composition of *Bathers*. Photograph by Émile Bernard, March 1904. 10³/₄ × 14³/₈″ (27.4 × 36.6 cm). Collection Sirot-Angel, Paris.

Poussin's painting in the Louvre from which Cézanne had made two drawings (Chappuis 1973 n. 1011 and 1012), now in Basle.

He loved Poussin, in whom facility is complemented by reason. Other preferences were more surprising: "What an admirable picture!" he would say, referring to the *Dropsical Woman* by Gerard Dou. He also had his dislikes: "I abhor Jules Lefèvre and those pupils of the École," he would say, and the blood would rush to his cheeks.

This particular visit dates from January 1905. At that time the atelier on the chemin de l'Aubassane contained a large painting of bathers with eight almost lifesize figures on which Cézanne was still working. "I hardly like to admit it," he said, "but I've been working on it since 1894. I wanted to lay on the paint as thickly as Courbet." He seemed no longer to feel his earlier admiration for the master from the Franche-Comté, whom he described as "a fine brute." Cézanne was also painting a portrait of a man, in profile, wearing a cap; he said that he always conducted the study from nature and the practice of painting side by side. He seemed to attach great importance to this painting: "If I succeed with this fellow," he said, "it will mean that my theory is right."

La Femme hydropique, *Gerard Dou (1613–75), Louvre. Jules-Joseph Lefebvre (1836–1911), academic painter successful at the Salon.*

The Great Bathers, *Barnes Foundation, Merion, PA.*

Possibly the portrait of Vallier called The Sailor, *1905–6, National Gallery of Art, Washington, D.C., or* The Gardener Vallier, *1905–6 (V 716), Private Collection, France. Letter of January 23, 1905, to Roger Marx (1859–1913), critic and collector, an early admirer of Cézanne.*

THE CRITICS' REACTION

LE FIGARO
"A New School"
September 14, 1891

In view of the dawning sense of the need for a new school, the *Romanitas* School is to be formed, which will maintain that our language has been dying since the day when, after Racine, it strayed from the Romance dialect, father of the French.

M. Jean Moréas, the author of *Cantilènes*, the inventor of Symbolism and of so many other surprising things, is the founder of this new School.

M. Jean Moréas told one of our friends that the Symbolists had done nothing but make mock of his idea for six years: "Today," he added, "they are apparently reduced to setting a dead man up against me: Jules Laforgue! Well, I will compromise myself no longer with these trivia! I am founding the École Romane Française, which will welcome all those in whom the love of the Greco-Latin language inspires the superb shoots of a literary and moral renaissance. Yes! I shall be joined by all those who understand that the French genius must be pure, and not daubed with northern impurities! . . . For details, turn to my prefaces, manifestos and interviews.

"As to those whom I shall be admitting into my company immediately, they are just three in number: MM. Raymond de la Tailhède, that marvelous poet to whom Jules Tellier addressed the exquisite rondel: *Raymond, give us divine verse* . . . Maurice du Plessys and Charles Maurras. Thus there are four of us in all.

"Others may join us if they wish, but I could never bring myself to admit any of those negligible symbolists who have dishonored me."

The repudiation of Symbolism by Jean Moréas, one of its founding fathers, the author of the "Symbolist Manifesto," was symptomatic of a new increasingly conservative mood in the art and criticism of the 1890s. The "call to order" demanded a return to "healthy," French classical principles, to clear forms and clear meanings.

Charles Maurras (1868–1952), Provençal poet who emerged in the 1890s as principal leader of the ultra-right-wing movement "Action Française."

CHARLES MERKI
MERCURE DE FRANCE
"Apologia for Painting"
June 1893

No real agreement has yet been reached, as far as I know, as to how the role of painting should be viewed. Should we require it to be an exclusively plastic art, or a literary art? Should painting conjure up ideas beyond colors and forms, or ideas at the expense of color and form? Should it be just a clever transposition of forms on to canvas, an arbitrary arrangement of nature, viewed, as the cliché has it, through a temperament? There is no shortage of opinions, rather the reverse. Some require painting to show forth life, others demand evocation, the dream; yet others, emotion, states of mind; others again, the photographic reproduction of objects, proving once and for all that truth and beauty, in art, are one and the same.

Such contradictory theories demand a scrutiny I shall not accord them here. I would simply like to point out that color and form have hitherto

Merki's ironical "apologia" for painting demonstrates the mood of reaction against Symbolism, deploring mysticism, primitivism, and the attempt to apply the formal principles of music or literature to painting. He particularly singled out for extended criticism the distortion of drawing and color in Van Gogh and Gauguin. He attacked the artists connected with Le Barc de Boutteville's gallery, which had held a fourth exhibition of "Les Peintres Impressionnistes et Symbolistes" in April 1893.

unanimously been considered as essentially important elements. Painting is first and foremost a plastic art. Whether the painter wants to depict life, tell us his dreams, capture emotional or psychic states of mind; whether he puts ideas or thoughts into his work, or strives for evocation, to convey the symbol, in every case, and whatever he is seeking – ideas, symbols, feelings, dreams – all is subordinate to pictorial expression, all is revealed only by this same expression, all is subject to this very humble matter of métier. Perception alone is not enough; and the best intentions in the world can never replace a degree of technical perfection, of learned knowledge, manual dexterity and felicitous "rendering," which are indispensable.

But here I would just like to call to mind one of the foremost precepts of the current aesthetic. Preached, professed, proclaimed, discussed in fifty articles, one of the errors it has engendered is the adoption of the symbolist literary method; on close examination, it is driving a whole group of painters towards the *illustration* of this same symbolism.

* * *

Ever since we learned of the resurrection of symbolism and the cult of veiled Beauty in literature, it has been acknowledged that every work must have a second meaning apart from its immediate one; granted, by virtue of this second, books now often no longer had a first one; most, unable to be profound, made do with being obscure; though this does not mean that the "sowers of ideas" are responsible for the damage they cause, and while admitting that literature, the theatre and painting itself have the right, as it were, to express themselves through the symbol – this is a matter of fashion and we must not bridle too overtly – I would like to point out that the means of expression available to an art are, despite everything, fairly limited. It has been claimed in vain, for instance, that the composers of this century have enabled us to enjoy literary or descriptive music, it is pure obligingness on our part when we declare that a phrase of such and such an orchestral suite depicts the appearance of a forest, a meadow, a calm sea, a fair sky, night or day; the tremolos expressing sunrise would be equally fitting for moonlight; the "wrath of the waves" is expressed through an uproar that would do equal duty for the outrage of a spurned heart or a fit of passionate jealousy; and this is so widely accepted that the audiences at our great concerts are frequently presented with programmes with advance explanations, whose sole aim is charitably to forewarn them of the composer's intentions. . . . Yet one more proof that music has no power to be specific. Indeed it can render only feelings, motifs of uncertain value; it reflects the general movements of the soul, impersonal emotions; we may hear allusions to anger and joy, pain, lust, love, anguish, terror and pride, all the passions and sensations which lie dormant within us, watch over us and struggle at our bedsides; music leads us gladly towards the dream, and at that point we care little what the composer wanted to express; music is the art of suggestion, of evocation par excellence; a sweet cheat, it offers us trickery, the illusion that it expresses the inexpressible; but, apart from some exceptional (and somewhat childish) examples, in seeking to incorporate descriptions and "pictures" and literature and painting into music, the composer is deceiving himself without deceiving anyone else.

On the other hand, compared to music, literature and painting may be considered precise arts, arts which are not suggestive by nature, which will "express" mysterious things beyond the written word, the outlined form, only as a result of hard work and the talent of the artist. Painting and literature show us the general only behind the particular. They have their own domains, they function differently and are quite separate, despite resemblances in theory and metaphors celebrating the page as a form of painting, or a painting as a form of speech.

* * *

JEAN MORÉAS

Émile Cohl. Drawing of Jean Moréas for *Les Hommes d'Aujourd'hui*, No. 268, 1886. Bibliothèque Nationale, Paris.

Let us go into the gallery of M. Le Barc, into the last room of the Indépendants, so judiciously baptized the Chamber of Horrors. Here we are presented with a prevailing love of the ugly, the ignoble inherited from the macaronic Samuel Johnson; here we have the final stages of lunacy, the work of a confraternity of madmen suddenly let loose in a paint shop. Frames, chalked over more often than not, harbor pink sheep, the mauve cows of Jaipur; green women, chicken-shit skies, braying trees; lurid greens, offensive blues and brick reds jostle, clash, yap and howl with the blatancy and brazenness of an *image d'Épinal*. The excuse of "meticulous research" and "merciless observation," and an avowed desire to study and combine various tones, has led to the exhibition of *pochades*, studio pranks, slatternly exposures, the pendulous breasts of a quadragenarian, the faces of bogeymen, houses and plots encircled with black, puppets clumsily imitated from the Japanese or in the hieratic manner of the primitives. . . . But I cannot contain myself with glee when I mention Van Gogh. He is a genius, a full-blooded colorist (as you may know, everyone is something of a genius now). He has not only admirers, but imitators. His lavish color, which may be several centimeters thick on occasion, has infatuated some. Yet how not to believe it is a practical joke? This man has positively fought with his canvases. He has stoned them with pellets of earth. He has taken a mortar to them and lashed out with all the relish of a man administering rough justice to a miscreant. Using whole trowelfuls of yellow, red, brown, green, orange, blue, and with all the panache of someone hurling a basket of eggs from a fifth-floor window, he has sprayed streams of paint on the whole affair, then blindly traced several lines with a finger dipped in ink. This, apparently, is representational; by pure chance, in all likelihood and, as gossip has it, one is not too sure as to "whether the carriage is a pair of shoes, or a pair of shoes the carriage."

This fairground painting, though none the better for it, takes a different turn with M. Gauguin. M. Gauguin represents *idéiste* or symbolist art, whichever you prefer. Here the color is not two inches thick, but its brutality is possibly even more disconcerting. It has been said that M. Gauguin was imitating stained glass. This opinion is as valid as another and harms no one. Hyperbolic landscapes, of a barbarity which no visual impairment can excuse, are dotted with gingerbread men. Plates of spinach, poor draftsmanship, grandiose ideas, scrawlings by Bob on the covers of his school books . . . M. Gauguin is currently devoting himself to painting on negresses. One fine morning we shall find him with a complete cargo of freaks, and that will be the time to discuss him further. What we can say without further ado of his *Jacob Wrestling with the Angel* is that if Jacob and the angel are distorted in the minds of Breton women, Breton women have been similarly distorted in the mind of the painter, for they are as ill-rendered as the rest.

COLORPLATE 24

"A Montmartre Donkey paints a Picture with its Tail for the Salon des Indépendants." Photograph at the Lapin Agile. *c.*1900.

GUSTAVE GEFFROY
LA VIE ARTISTIQUE
"Paul Cézanne"
1894

La Vie Artistique *was one of the first extensive studies of Impressionism within an historical context. The chapter on Cézanne exemplifies the problems critics were having with his painting in the 1890s, with what Geffroy describes as Cézanne's "incompleteness," "awkwardness," and "primitiveness."*

... In artistic circles, Cézanne's reputation has confirmed itself further, has visibly grown. Cézanne has become a kind of precursor to whom the Symbolists have referred, and it is quite certain, to stick to the facts, that there is a direct relation, a clearly established continuity, between the painting of Cézanne and that of Gauguin, Emile Bernard, etc. And likewise, with the art of Vincent van Gogh. From this point of view alone, Paul Cézanne deserves that his name be put into the place that is his. It is certain that, in the independent or Impressionist group, he revealed, in comparison with his companions, a special talent, an original nature, and there was a bifurcation developing from his work, a branch-road begun by him and continued by others. Whether this new road continues, ends up in magnificent spaces, or loses itself in bogs and swamps is not what is under investigation today. It is the secret of the future. Whatever happens, Cézanne will have been there as a signpost, and that is the point that must not be forgotten. The history of art is made with a laying out of broad paths and of ramifications, and Cézanne has at any rate had control over one of these latter.

It would be a different matter to state that there is an extremely marked intellectual bond between Cézanne and his successors, and that Cézanne has had the same theoretical and synthetic preoccupations as the symbolic artists. Today, if one really cares to, it is easy to create for oneself an idea of the series of efforts and of the total effect of Cézanne's work. In a few days, I had the opportunity of seeing about twenty characteristic paintings, through which the personality of the artist could be summarized as correctly as possible. However, the impression experienced with a growing strength, and which remains dominant, is that Cézanne does not approach nature with a program of art, with the despotic intention of submitting this nature to a law that he has conceived, of subjecting it to an ideal formula which is within himself. He is not, however, completely without program, law, and ideal, but they do not come to him from art, they come to him from the intensity of his curiosity, from his desire to possess the things that he sees and admires. He is a man who looks about him, near him, who experiences an intoxication from the spectacle displayed, and who would like to transfer the sensation of this intoxication onto the restricted space of a canvas. He goes to work and he seeks out the means for achieving this transposition as truthfully as possible.

This desire for truth, visible in all the canvases of Cézanne, is attested to by all those who have been his contemporaries, his friends.

* * *

It was an unforgettable sight, Renoir tells me, to see Cézanne installed at his easel, painting, looking at the countryside: he was truly alone in the world, intense, concentrated, attentive, respectful. He would come back the next day, and every day, he would accumulate his efforts, and at times would even go away in desperation, return without his canvas which he left abandoned on a rock or on the grass, at the mercy of the wind, the rain, the sun, absorbed by the earth, the painted landscape received back by surrounding nature.

One would not realize it, although the works of Cézanne state it openly, manifest the tension toward the real – that patience, that length of time, that nature of an upright artist, that conscience satisfied with such difficulty. It is obvious that the painter is frequently incomplete, that he has been unable to conquer the difficulty, that the obstacle to realization is

Paul Cézanne. *Trees leaning over Rocks.* c.1892. Watercolor, 16½ × 11⅘″ (42 × 30 cm). National Gallery of Art, Washington, D.C. (Mr and Mrs Paul Mellon Fund).

revealed to all eyes. It is a little bit, apart from the technique, like the touching efforts of the primitives. There are absences of atmosphere, of the fluidity through which the planes must be separated and the farthest depths be placed at their proper distance. The forms become awkward at times, the objects are blended together, the proportions are not always established with sufficient rigor.

But these remarks cannot be made before each canvas of Cézanne. He has laid out and completely materialized infinitely expressive pages. In these he unfolds animated skies, white and blue, he erects, within a limpid atmosphere, his dear hill of Sainte-Victoire, the straight trees which surround his Provençal home of the Jas de Bouffan, a hillock of colored and golden foliage, in the countryside near Aix, a weighty inlet of the sea in a rocky bay where the landscape is crushed beneath an atmosphere of heat.

The arbitrary distribution of light and shade which might otherwise be surprising is no longer noticeable. One is in the presence of a unified painting which seems all of a piece and which is executed over a long period of time, in thin layers, which has ended up by becoming compact, dense, velvety. The earth is solid, the carpet of grass is thick, of that green with bluish nuances which belongs so much to Cézanne, that he distributes in precise strokes in the mass of leafage, that he spreads out in large, grassy stretches on the ground, that he mingles with the mossy softness of tree trunks and rocks. His painting then takes on the muted beauty of tapestry, arrays itself in a strong, harmonious weft. Or else, as in the *Bathers*, coagulated and luminous, it assumes the aspect of a piece of richly decorated faïence.

I know another work by Cézanne, a portrait of a *Gardener* which belongs to Paul Alexis, a too large canvas, the clothing empty, but the head solid, well supported by the hand, burning eyes that really *look*. And finally, there are the famous apples that the painter has loved to paint and that he has painted so well. The backgrounds sometimes come forward, but the tablecloths, the napkins, are so pliant, the whites so nuanced, and the fruits are such naïvely beautiful things! Green, red, yellow, in little twopenny heaps, placed on dishes or poured from full baskets, the apples have the roundness, the firmness, the lively colours of nature that harmonize with each other. They are healthy, speak of rusticity, they suggest the good smell of fruit.

No matter what subject he takes up, there is true sincerity in Cézanne, the sometimes charming, sometimes painful sign of a will that either satisfies itself or fails completely. Often as well, an ingenuous grandeur, as in the *Gardener*, where the incorrect figures have such a proud look; that bather, for example, who rests a foot on a hillock, and who takes on, with his sad face, his long, muscular limbs, a sort of Michelangelesque appearance, certainly unsought for.

That Cézanne has not realized with the strength that he wanted the dream that invades him before the splendor of nature, that is certain, and that is his life and the life of many others. But it is also certain that his idea has revealed itself, and that the assemblage of his paintings would affirm a profound sensitivity, a rare unity of existence. Surely this man has lived and lives a beautiful interior novel, and the demon of art dwells within him.

Paul Cézanne. *Rocks at Château-Noir.* c.1900. Pencil and watercolor, 19 × 12¼″ (48 × 31.2 cm). Musée Granet, Aix-en-Provence.

279

Pierre Bonnard. *Portrait of Ambroise Vollard* (with Cézanne's *Four Bathers*, 1879–82, in background). 1904–05. 29$\frac{1}{8}$ × 36$\frac{3}{4}$″ (74 × 92.5 cm). Kunsthaus, Zurich.

GEORGES LECOMTE

LA REVUE D'ART

"Paul Cézanne"

December 9, 1899

Georges Lecomte (1867–1958), writer, critic and friend of Pissarro and Fénéon who shared their anarchist sympathies. He edited the Symbolist weekly La Cravache *to which Geffroy and Fénéon contributed. In this article Lecomte develops further the notion of Cézanne's "primitiveness," explaining that none of his "clumsiness" and "awkwardness" was deliberate, but was the result of the "naive sincerity" of a true primitive.*

The exhibition currently showing at the Vollard gallery will kindle the curiosity of art lovers and artists alike concerning this enigmatic, solitary, nomadic painter, so superbly instinctive, and who is something of a legendary figure for the men of our time.

For he is never seen. He roams the countryside of France. He prowls, observes, detects, parading his sensibility amidst the ever-shifting enchantments of nature, the radiant marvels of the sky. Has some landscape deeply moved him, or is he in the grip of a sudden fantasy?

He settles down before the subject that has ravished him, some corner of nature or some sweeping space. Sometimes it is the edge of a snowy wood, sometimes a valley dense with all the greenery and foliage of summer, sometimes a village with its roofs showing russet and golden amidst the plumes of the trees, and peasants, round-backed, seated at inn tables.

Wanderings of which the world was unaware. Only much later did we learn of these meanderings, these happy bursts of work, when discovering new motifs at the shop of the occasional dealer who had managed – through what wizardry? – to wrest two or three canvases from him. What regions do they depict, what climes? It is often very difficult to be precise. For Cézanne does not seek out aspects that are very revealing of their geographical locations. Provided he has grass, leaves, sky, some roofs, from which to conjure soft and simple harmonies, that is enough. Nor do we know what orchards have yielded up this beautiful, perfect fruit, bursting and heavy, which the artist strews with relish upon rumpled white cloths. And as the rare recent works are almost always exhibited amidst much older paintings, unearthed by chance, the mystery of this artist's life, rather than becoming clearer, becomes further confused.

* * *

Before 1894, canvases by Cézanne were seen only by chance, and infrequently, in the houses of friends. Newcomers to the world of art and literature know him only through personal accounts; an anecdote would arouse curiosity concerning the mysterious wanderer. A landscape of his was known to be at M. Zola's house, a painting of fruit at Paul Alexis', studies in the houses of MM. Duret and Huysmans. You learned, now and then, that a picture had made its way into Père Tanguy's shop on rue Clauzel, in Montmartre. You went there with a sense of pilgrimage; and had the pleasure of observing that legend had not exaggerated the talent of Cézanne and that he was a very good painter.

At that time, no critic talked of him. It was only in 1888 that a very modest literary journal, *La Cravache*, had the great honor of publishing an article by M. J.-K. Huysmans on this strange artist who had willingly taken refuge in oblivion. Then we personally had the opportunity to examine the *oeuvre* and influence of Cézanne in *L'Art impressionniste* (1892) and at a lecture given the same year at the Cercle des XX, in Brussels. M. Roger Marx defined the nature of his talent in his well-documented article in *Le Voltaire*. And M. Gustave Geffroy, after having devoted several eloquent essays to him in *La Justice*, published a complete and penetrating overall study in one of the volumes of his *Vie artistique* in 1894. This was more or less the moment when Paul Cézanne re-emerged from the shadows and came to Paris; and when dealers could stock up with his oil paintings and watercolors with some ease.

Reprinted in J.-K. Huysmans, Certains, *1889.*
Lecomte: "L'Art Impressionniste, d'après la collection privée de M. Durand-Ruel," Paris, 1892.

But now, Cézanne's work is well-known and much sought after. Aware of this, collectors fight over his canvases. They are to be found in the grandest galleries. Dealers, previously contemptuous, stockpile them. Frequent exhibitions are organized. Art reporters pay heed to them. Success at last.

Following the large retrospective of Cézanne's paintings in 1895, Vollard held a second exhibition in May and June 1898.

And Cézanne, heedless of all this trumpeting, continues to indulge in the pleasure of painting on the sites he holds so dear. But now that he knows the affection in which he is held, he has probably cured himself of his former carelessness, which caused him to leave unfinished paintings lying around in forests. Indeed, legend has it – to complete the portrait of this passionate and disinterested artist – that his family had often set out in search of canvases that had thus been left abandoned against some mossy trunk, amidst the lacy emerald ferns. A fine example of a man who works only for the pure joy of painting and, having had his pleasure, is no longer concerned with the result.

A strange character, into whom we may gain further insight through the superb etching by M. Camille Pissarro . . . A large nose, bespeaking strong will and passion, stands out in a rather wild face; beneath the beard, one can sense a strong, taut jawline. The eyes, at once alert and gentle, look out with a calm energy. The peasant's cap, well pulled down, and the ample waggoner's cloak, tell of a rough solitary life in the open air. Clearly, landscapes could not be perceived in a superficial manner by this penetrating gaze, nor reflected in banal images by this mind, that of a contemplative and observant man.

Indeed, every work by Cézanne is an affirmation of a most original talent. This unsociable being is marvelously instinctive. I do not know whether any teacher, at some point during his schooldays in Aix, ever gave him a vague feeling for line. Certain it is that no master ever taught him to draw and paint.

He paints as he walks, as he eats, for his temperament has thrust him towards the plastic reproduction of objects. He sensed the boundless grace and joy of nature. His deeply observant eye perceived harmonies of line and color. He felt the need to put them down on canvas. He persisted in this effort without teaching or formulae. And gradually, because he was gifted, he found very personal means of rendering his vision, which is delicate, subtle and grave. Incapable of imitation, he recalls no earlier master. He is strictly himself.

Of necessity, like all instinctive and self-made artists, at first his work was awkward and naive, and his compositions sometimes lacked balance. On occasions, the flesh of his female nudes was heavy and bulging to the point of distortion. His dishes seemed destined to topple over and the marvelous fruit to be scattered over the ground in a burst of radiant hail. But this clumsiness has its own savor. It is the final proof of the painter's fine sincerity. And anyway, what matter? Despite these excesses, this naked flesh does indeed have the rich softness of a woman's body, and if the fruit-dishes stand rakishly on the white cloths, the apples are as fresh as the cheeks of young peasant girls, as bright as full-blown sunlit mornings.

Cézanne has retained some of this awkwardness. He is not an even painter. He paints according to his mood. Are there not days when the man of the fields, too, digs and walks less vigorously? As Cézanne does not have the resources to make good his fortunate disposition by specialist knowledge, when he is not in good form, his ineptitude becomes more marked. It is at such times that his figures are in grave danger of falling apart, his bottles and jugs are askew, his fruit bowls teeter and his women's rumps are a little too heavy. Usually, however, Cézanne's painting has a healthy, serene energy and his compositions are well balanced.

In the heroic days of naturalism, it was these *gaucheries* which were praised the most. In the revolt against convention, the necessary laws of logic were even confused with hackneyed textbook formulae. In reaction against a correct and dreary academicism, Cézanne was praised above all for faults committed through ignorance, and which the artist himself would dearly have liked to avoid.

For it is certain that none of this maladroitness is intentional. Being a man of instinct, entirely self-reliant, Cézanne experienced the same difficulties as the Primitives once did. Separated by four centuries, they have certain things in common. This is very strange. Cézanne, of course, knows all about the great periods of art which preceded him. He would wish to be totally adept and knowledgeable, to have the means effortlessly to render what he sees, what he feels, but as he has no guide other than his sensibility, he trips and fumbles. He has the awkwardness and imperfections of a true Primitive. He paints landscapes? He captures their character, the color, the light. He conveys their intimacy, or their grandeur, but he has no skill in creating space between the planes, in giving the illusion of a sweep of distance. His meager knowledge plays him false. Cézanne does not have the means to render all that he sees. He does his best. Often he is saved by instinct and experience. But often, too, his spontaneous art is impotent. The studies from nature are frequently without depth. They give the impression of a sumptuous tapestry without a sense of distance. They are exquisite harmonies, of very close values, using very simple flat colors which increase the impression of softness and charm. But the various lines of the landscape create no sense of space in the atmosphere.

Not so long ago, amusingly enough, the following occurred. Just as, in the heady days of naturalism, people were captivated by Cézanne's hazardous constructions, similarly, in the halcyon days – so quickly over – of mystical symbolism, they were especially delighted by this absence of depth. It started a fashion. As it became the vogue systematically to take up the naiveties of the Primitives, Cézanne was hailed as a precursor. He was appreciated for his imperfections (which he himself did his utmost to avoid), as though he had deliberately accepted them. Thus on two occasions, Cézanne had the bizarre fate of being praised less for his qualities than for his failings. But symbolism found its own justification in these shortcomings.

Yet apart from these habitual faults, what great qualities his work has, what good advice is to be found there! What robust cause for joy and admiration! No art gives off more sincerity, passion, authority. It is an *oeuvre* well and truly created out of love. Think of the many landscapes

(*Opposite*) Pierre Bonnard. *Portrait of Ambroise Vollard. c.*1914? Etching, printed in black, 13^{15}/$_{16}$ × 9^{3}/$_{8}$″ (35.4 × 23.8 cm). Museum of Modern Art, New York (Purchase).

with their rich greenery, luxuriant foliage, soft curvings. Solemn harmonies in green beneath subtly shaded skies. The earth is rendered in all its fruitfulness. The laden branches of the trees hang over the lush meadows. The grassy valleys have the splendour of matt velvet. One might wish the planes more firmly established, for more feeling of space, more depth. But these calm and simple harmonies have all the rich softness of the tapestry.

We have mentioned the landscapes first, in reaction against a recent tendency, which would have it that Cézanne is above all a painter of still lifes. But his fruit is among the most beautiful ever painted by our French school. The full, heavy flesh, the lights and hollows, the dazzling bloom, were never better painted by Chardin at his finest. Apples, pears, peaches lie strewn among black bottles, the light reflecting on their necks, among stone jugs, on white cloths, their folds creating a play of light and shade. They are piled up on fruit bowls, in joyous pyramids. They are masterly. To the beauties we are accustomed to seeing in Chardin, Cézanne adds the marvels of a fresh, free, bold color which does justice to the fruit in all its splendor.

Despite excess and awkwardness, Cézanne's nudes also merit our affection, for they are studied with such naive sincerity; as are his portraits, so rough and severe. Beneath that lovely greenery, the darkish bodies of his women are almost shocking. But look at the soft weightiness of the line, the rich, heavy flesh. Finally, the portrait of an old man, the nut-brown, almost baked-looking head, with its crown of silvery hair and its white beard, is proof enough of the gravity with which Cézanne's art expresses the human face.

I would have welcomed the inclusion of some watercolors, for there Cézanne's painterly gifts emerge even more clearly.

But the thirty canvases hung in M. Vollard's gallery are sufficient to endear this robust, frank and lovely art to us. Rare imperfections scarcely count in an *oeuvre* which so strikingly and originally translates the happiness and emotion of a simple, admirably gifted man as he beholds earth's wonders ever new.

ÉMILE BERNARD

LA RÉNOVATION ESTHÉTIQUE
"Reflections on the Salon d'Automne"
December 1907

A retrospective of Cézanne was held at the Salon d'Automne in December 1907.

AND PEACE ON EARTH TO MEN OF GOODWILL

To cast a deep and advantageous light upon the Salon d'Automne (for this is not a review, nor a string of favorable mentions); that is, to deduce from it a fair assessment of the errors of our time, and to convince oneself of the absolute falsity of the paradoxes which inspire them and give them an appearance of truth through the subtle byways of rhetoric, I would like to divide it into three parts, namely: one inspired by modishness, including banal paintings wearing the emperor's new clothes of the palette of the moment; one of paradoxes; and one of a desire for self-advertisement.

I shall pass over the first category, since everyone can recognize it with ease; but I shall have much to say of the second and third.

After Courbet, a good traditionalist painter, and after Manet, a spirit already in thrall to theories conceived with objectivity rather than aes-

This article reflects Bernard's later disillusionment with Cézanne. He came to regard the abstraction in the late paintings, which he saw as resulting from Cézanne's emphasis on color as opposed to tone, as a sign of Cézanne's "impotence" and "failure."

COLORPLATE 88. Paul Cézanne. *Vase of Tulips. c.*1890–92. 23½ × 16⅝″ (59.6 × 42.3 cm).
© 1990 The Art Institute of Chicago (Mr and Mrs Lewis Larned Coburn Memorial Collection,
1933.423). All Rights Reserved.

COLORPLATE 89. Paul Cézanne. *Madame Cézanne in a Red Dress*. c.1890–94.
45⅞ × 35¼″ (116.5 × 89.5 cm).
Metropolitan Museum of Art, New York (Mr and Mrs Henry Ittleson, Jr. Fund, 1962.45).

COLORPLATE 90. Paul Cézanne. *Portrait of Joachim Gasquet.* 1896–97. 25³/₄ × 29″ (65.5 × 73.5 cm).
Narodni Gallery, Prague.

COLORPLATE 91. Paul Cézanne. *Self-Portrait in a Black Hat*. 1890–94. 23⅝ × 19⁵/₁₆″ (60 × 49 cm).
Bridgestone Museum of Art, Ishibashi Foundation, Tokyo.

COLORPLATE 92. Paul Cézanne. *Forest Path.* 1895–1900. 31¼ × 25⅜″ (79.5 × 64.5 cm).
Galerie Beyeler, Basle.

COLORPLATE 93. Paul Cézanne. *Château Noir*. 1904. 28¾ × 36¼" (73 × 92 cm).
Oskar Reinhart Collection, Winterthur.

COLORPLATE 94. Paul Cézanne. *Seven Bathers. c.*1900. 14¾ × 17⅞″ (37.5 × 45.5 cm). Galerie Beyeler, Basle.

COLORPLATE 95. Paul Cézanne. *Still Life with Apples, Pears and Pot (The Kitchen Table)*. 1900–04. Pencil and watercolor, 11 × 18¾″ (28.1 × 47.8 cm). Musée du Louvre, Paris (Cabinet des Dessins).

thetics (theories which came only from artists), the Impressionists marked the coming of an epoch. In comparison with the second category of painters in the Salon d'Automne (the *paradoxicals*) they seemed painters guided purely by sensation. Observing the brightness in nature, they simply bent their means of expression to the use of bright colors alone, those of the prism; and in Claude Monet, Pissarro, Renoir and Sisley, I see nothing other than the well-balanced pursuit of the true effect of sunlight, mist, morning and evening. They put color in the place of chiaroscuro. Cézanne, who is one of their pupils and who was a disciple of the Spanish painters and handled everything in terms of black and white before he came into contact with the Impressionists, embraced their ambition in his turn, but without restricting himself to their palette; and we see him, in the retrospective at the Salon d'Automne, starting from these early, sumptuous paintings with their use of chiaroscuro, solidly constructed in the fashion of Courbet, and arriving at a vision where blue, yellow and red predominate, in a harmony more decorative than lifelike and in a style characterized by a deliberate simplicity, and often by a naivety of form. His theory, for he has one, is limited to the following: *to have a sufficient amount of blueness to make the yellows and reds vibrate*. In the past this amount of blueness was represented solely by a sum of grays and blacks (for in the language of the colorist, blue is none other than black in relation to the other colors of the prism and above all to yellows and reds). Thus here we have a theory, that is, a convention. What is the result? Quite simply this: that the canvas will present objects on a flat surface rather than putting them into relief, for the very simple reason that black thrusts white forward; but that blue, if it does indeed make the yellow and red vibrate, cannot give them sufficient relief by producing white light. Color, or rather the absence of color, representing shadow, which is called black, being logically the only contrast possible to the absence of the color representing light, which is called *white*. To tone down black to the benefit of blue, that is, the colorless to the benefit of that which has color – acting in this way both for the dark and for the light – is to diminish contrasts and, ultimately, to make the picture flat. Cézanne had created this impasse for himself, and he suffered from it as a result. He did not realize that it was precisely this absence, increasingly constant, in his paintings, of black and white, which prevented the creation of relief and the establishing of planes. He was battling in a vicious circle: namely, to achieve his total effect of shadows, half-tints, and highlights through color alone – when it is primarily by shadows, half-tints and highlights that objects are visually established, and that it is only later that we see that they have color; sometimes, indeed, we are hesitant about these colors, when they are indecisive or plunged in transparent half-light.

Thus Cézanne, unlike the other Impressionists, his contemporaries, is not content with having the seven gradations of the prism on his palette and painting everything he sees with no further ado, with the superimposition of pure colors. He wants to regulate the color as the need arises, over the broadest scale, and in accordance with some absolute logic; he purges it of every intrusion alien to the color alone, he keeps the earth colors, the ochers, the lakes on his palette, but he fights off black and white in his paintings to the point of reducing them to blues, yellows and reds. He pursues a vision of what had hitherto been regarded as colorless or virtually so; and this is what causes him to reject the old masters, for their first principle was that everything must be done in black and white, and that color comes as a bonus. So did the old masters envisage drawing as coming first and color afterwards? If one bases oneself on the Roman school one might say yes; for Raphael and even Michelangelo drew *cartoons* before they painted; but the true painters, in the sense in which we understand the term today, that is, those who brought nature into their pictures with the striking aspect of relief through dark and light, through the effect of light and shade, have always proceeded, through black and

Photograph of Cézanne in his studio in Paris. On the easel: *The Apotheosis of Delacroix*.

white, broadly and directly, without lingering on the dry pursuit of the outline, but through a wide, generous and general establishing of the form through the gradation and distribution of light; one may say of them that they normally perceived forms through the light which falls upon them, as opposed to seeing the forms as forms, afterwards determining the fall of light, which is an abstract procedure. Cézanne, on the other hand, wanted to do without the general effect of white and black and to proceed even more as a colorist; thus he replaced the effect of chiaroscuro by the effect of color; and he replaced vibration through light and shadow, by vibration through blue – a cold tone – contrasting with reds and yellows – warm tones. He thus thrust himself into another abstraction from which he was unable to escape, for he did away with planes and obtained a sense of the roundness of objects only with great difficulty. In this way, without meaning to, he ended up with the results of the Primitives, who were equally unable to distribute gradation from light to dark, but in their case their starting-point derived from an earlier, decorative art, from which this effect had been *rightly* driven by taste.

It would greatly interest me to show to what degree, despite this awful error, Cézanne is nearer to art than to nature (ever invoked by him), how superior he is to the Impressionists by virtue of a constant need for style and, as it were, by an involuntary distancing from the very objectivity which is his goal. But from the point of view of style he has not merely run aground, he has capsized; for style can belong only to those who truly understand form; and Cézanne knows nothing of form at all. His style, in its turn, verges on distortion – and, I would hazard, unintentionally. He dares sublimely, but fails naively. He retains a special grace in this sincere downfall and earns one's affection nonetheless. If I had to take sides concerning his work, I would opt for his use of color rather than his style, since his color seems to me often to have achieved *harmony*; but his style only rarely reveals his taste and the knowledge required to justify some admiration. To be a stylist one must know one's language, and Cézanne, locked exclusively into research into color, knows very little about form. His portraits attest as much and his nudes proclaim it. The great stylists of all ages, the Egyptians, the Greeks, the Byzantines, the artists of the Middle Ages and Renaissance, had a perfect knowledge either of nature or of the established canon concerning nature, they could recreate the truth of the external world in the image of the truth which they perceived instinctively; their style reveals a harmony all their own as well as one perceived beneath the many-sidedness of appearance. But Cézanne has no knowledge of the human form and has deduced no laws from it; he carries on naively, forcing illogical forms into the fabric of his patient and logical brushstrokes – illogical because they are born of ignorance, and without foundation. I acknowledge that he obeys rules – his own, made up by him – concerning lines; but these lines remain lifeless because they are not the substratum of any reality, or the *parallel* representation of any objectivity. I see that Raphael is pursuing an architectural harmony even in his least drawing, and that, in his works, form is both reality and ideality; but all I see in Cézanne is a complete abandoning of this reality in the form, and indeed a formulation so naive that I am no longer moved by his style, which thus descends into artificiality.

And yet, this noble desire for style is what saves Cézanne from Impressionism (the pure imitation of nature/platitude) and what shows him to be an *artist*, that is, a painter concerned with art. In truth for the last thirty years have not all efforts been aimed at banishing art? Art is a convention, we are told. But is painting not one too? What seems to you to imitate nature so well, imitates it in your sight only by force of habit. The Chinese do not imitate it as we do, and their imitation (which seems to you false) seems to them more accurate than your own. Thus you see that painting itself is a convention, and I am looking no further than the last twenty years; for what has struck a previous generation as an abominable long-shot is considered by the present generation today as the sole correct vision of the world. Whence the European convention, the tradition of our race, of the Asiatic, African or Oceanic races. Whence the absurdity of adopting non-European art in Europe. Our eye does not see in a vacuum; it sees with our mentality, our sensations, our aspirations. Europe (the Greeks) saw things more *beautifully* than other peoples as a result of a higher culture of the mind and senses. The Greeks created aesthetics. They made life into art. Until the eighteenth century in France art bore the traces of its *intellectual* origin; a vain effort to return to this was made after the Revolution. In its own realm, the full empowering of the non-intellectual classes was to end in the same way. Hence the disciples of positivism, of reality, more or less skilful rivals of photography or the open window. All in all, the Salon des Artistes français, representing a professional routine, never had any other desideratum than that of the Impressionists, it aimed at the *non-intellectual* representation of modern life, if through a duller prism.

Would that be tantamount to saying that we see more with our eyes than with our intellects, today? No. We see according to our non-intellects, according to our spiritual weakness. Books, such as Zola's *L'Oeuvre*, Tolstoy's *What is art?*, are the ultimate catastrophe; here we have the non-intellectual anathematizing intelligence and genius. One would therefore have to conclude that we no longer have any real and positive point of view of what we call the *spectacle of nature*, and that we must rely far more upon our taste, upon aesthetics, than upon the *diversity of the tableau of nature*. Such a matter would lead us far from the present argument but with no possibility of resolving it, for it verges upon the absolute. The plastic world must have a healthy fear of the world of philosophical abstraction, just as it must distrust all science foreign to aesthetics. To build art upon itself – upon its past, upon its masters, its masterpieces, what we call tradition – is to seize the clue as to what guides the work of the painter towards its ideal goal. To stray from this engenders only fantastic, facile and spontaneous creation, as ephemeral as everything born of caprice. To base art on nature, to wish to make a painting an exact reproduction of the world, is to repudiate art, it is to enter into the anarchy of Beauty. Art has but one goal: ITSELF. Art lives by its own laws; it dies by their negation. Thus what still distinguishes Cézanne, and proclaims him an artist, is his final assent to style. Without this style – whatever its failings – he would be banal.

But I see that I have put Cézanne into the *Paradoxical* category. Does he deserve this classification? Indeed he does, for several reasons, and here they are: what is paradoxical in Cézanne is his theory of color, and the resulting failure to establish depth confirms it; nonetheless, his particular color has created harmonies and it is his chief merit; it is through color that he is Cézanne, and he resembles no one else. What is also paradoxical in Cézanne is his style, which is not built up from reality and which verges on naive ignorance. To conclude, I would simply like to say that I prefer the paradox of a man of genius to the formula of a dull man. But after Cézanne, where is painting going in the Salon d'Automne? It is going towards scholastic science and self-ignorance; it is going towards childish naivety, and deliberately so; for all these painters have talent and they sin only out of an incorrigible intellectual perversion.

Leo Tolstoy (1828–1910): What is Art?, *1896.*

"Failure to establish depth": literally "the impotence of his planes."

POST-IMPRESSIONISM DEFINED

ROGER FRY AND DESMOND MacCARTHY

THE POST-IMPRESSIONISTS

1910

The pictures collected together in the present Exhibition are the work of a group of artists who cannot be defined by any single term. The term "Synthesists," which has been applied to them by learned criticism, does indeed express a quality underlying their diversity; and it is the principal business of this introduction to expand the meaning of that word, which sounds too like the hiss of an angry gander to be a happy appellation. As a definition it has the drawback that this quality, common to all, is not always the one most impressive in each artist. In no school does individual temperament count for more. In fact, it is the boast of those who believe in this school, that its methods enable the individuality of the artist to find completer self-expression in his work than is possible to those who have committed themselves to representing objects more literally. This, indeed, is the first source of their quarrel with the Impressionists: the Post-Impressionists consider the Impressionists too naturalistic.

Yet their own connection with Impressionism is extremely close; Cézanne, Gauguin and Van Gogh all learnt in the Impressionist school. There are pictures on the walls by these three artists, painted in their earlier years, which at first strike the eye as being more Impressionist than anything else: but, nevertheless, the connection of these artists with the Impressionists is accidental rather than intrinsic.

By the year 1880 the Impressionists had practically won their battle; nor is it likely any group of artists will ever have to fight so hard a one again. They have conquered for future originality, if not the right of a respectful hearing, at least of a dubious attention. By 1880 they had convinced practically everybody whose opinion counted, that their methods and ideas were at any rate those of artists, not those of cranks and charlatans. About this date the reaction against Impressionism, which this Exhibition represents, began to be distinctly felt. The two groups had one characteristic in common: the resolve of each artist to express his own temperament, and never to permit contemporary ideals to dictate to him what was beautiful, significant, and worthy to be painted. But the main current of Impressionism lay along the line of recording hitherto unrecognised aspects of objects; they were interested in analysing the play of light and shadow into a multiplicity of distinct colours; they refined upon what was already illusive in nature. In the pictures of Seurat, Cross, and Signac here exhibited, this scientific interest in the representation of colour is still uppermost; what is new in these pictures is simply the method of representing the vibration of light by painting objects in dots and squares. The Post-Impressionists on the other hand were not concerned with recording impressions of colour or light. They were interested in the discoveries of the Impressionists only so far as these discoveries helped them to express emotions which the objects themselves evoked; their attitude towards nature was far more independent, not to say rebellious. It is true that from the earliest times artists have regarded nature as "the mistress of the masters"; but it is only in the nineteenth

The introductory essay to the catalogue of the exhibition "Manet and The Post-Impressionists" at the Grafton Galleries in London (November 1910–January 1911) is thought to have been a collaboration between the critic and art historian Roger Fry (1866–1934) and the secretary to the exhibition committee, Desmond MacCarthy. The term "Post-Impressionism" was their invention, which they characterized as a reaction against Impressionism led by Cézanne. Roger Fry's formalist aesthetics dominated the discussion of Cézanne between the wars.

Roger Fry (or Vanessa Bell?). *View of Second Post-Impressionist Exhibition, London, 1912.* Musée d'Orsay, Paris.

century that the close imitation of nature, without any conscious modification by the artist, has been proclaimed as a dogma. The Impressionists were artists, and their imitations of appearances were modified, consciously and unconsciously, in the direction of unity and harmony; being artists they were forced to select and arrange. But the receptive, passive attitude towards the appearances of things often hindered them from rendering their real significance. Impressionism encouraged an artist to paint a tree as it appeared to him at the moment under particular circumstances. It insisted so much upon the importance of his rendering this exact impression that his work often completely failed to express a tree at all; as transferred to canvas it was just so much shimmer and colour. The "treeness" of the tree was not rendered at all; all the emotion and associations such as trees may be made to convey in poetry were omitted.

This is the fundamental cause of difference between the Impressionists and the group of painters whose pictures hang on these walls. They said in effect to the Impressionists: "You have explored nature in every direction, and all honour to you; but your methods and principles have hindered artists from exploring and expressing that emotional significance which lies in things, and is the most important subject matter of art. There is much more of that significance in the work of earlier artists who had not a tenth part of your skill in representing appearance. We will aim at that;

though by our simplification of nature we shock and disconcert our contemporaries, whose eyes are now accustomed to your revelations, as much as you originally disconcerted your contemporaries by your subtleties and complications." And there is no denying that the work of the Post-Impressionists is sufficiently disconcerting. It may even appear ridiculous to those who do not recall the fact that a good rocking-horse often has more of the true horse about it than an instantaneous photograph of a Derby winner.

The artists who felt most the restraints which the Impressionist attitude towards nature imposed upon them, naturally looked to the mysterious and isolated figure of Cézanne as their deliverer. Cézanne himself had come in contact with Manet and his art is derived directly from him. Manet, it is true, is also regarded as the father of Impressionism. To him Impressionism owes much of its power, interest and importance. He was a revolutionary in the sense that he refused to accept the pictorial convention of his time. He went back to seventeenth-century Spain for his inspiration. Instead of accepting the convention of light and shade falling upon objects from the side, he chose what seemed an impossibly difficult method of painting, that of representing them with light falling full upon them. This led to a very great change in the method of modelling, and to a simplification of planes in his pictures which resulted in something closely akin to simple linear designs. He adopted, too, hitherto unknown oppositions of colour. In fact he endeavoured to get rid of chiaroscuro.

Regarded as a hopeless revolutionary, he was naturally drawn to other young artists, who found themselves in the same predicament; and through his connection with them and with Monet he gradually changed his severe, closely constructed style for one in which the shifting, elusive aspects of nature were accentuated. In this way he became one of the Impressionists and in his turn influenced them. Cézanne, however, seized upon precisely that side of Manet which Monet and the other Impressionists ignored. Cézanne, when rendering the novel aspects of nature to which Impressionism was drawing attention, aimed first at a design which should produce the coherent, architectural effect of the masterpieces of primitive art. Because Cézanne thus showed how it was possible to pass from the complexity of the appearance of things to the geometrical simplicity which design demands, his art has appealed enormously to later designers. They recognise in him a guide capable of leading them out of the *cul de sac* into which naturalism had led them. Cézanne himself did not use consciously his new-found method of expression to convey ideas and emotions. He appealed first and foremost to the eye, and to the eye alone. But the path he indicated was followed by two younger artists, Van Gogh and Gauguin with surprising results. Van Gogh's morbid temperament forced him to express in paint his strongest emotions, and in the methods of Cézanne he found a means of conveying the wildest and strangest visions conceived by any artist of our time. Yet he, too, accepts in the main the general appearance of nature; only before every scene and every object he searches first for the quality which originally made it appeal so strangely to him: *that* he is determined to record at any sacrifice.

Gauguin is more of a theorist. He felt that while modern art had opened up undiscovered aspects of nature, it had to a great extent neglected the fundamental laws of abstract form, and above all had failed to realise the power which abstract form and colour can exercise over the imagination of the spectator. He deliberately chose, therefore, to become a decorative painter, believing that this was the most direct way of impressing upon the imagination the emotion he wished to perpetuate. In his Tahitian pictures by extreme simplification he endeavoured to bring back into modern painting the significance of gesture and movement characteristic of primitive art.

The followers of these men are pushing their ideas further and further. In the work of Matisse, especially, this search for an abstract harmony of line, for rhythm, has been carried to lengths which often deprive the figure of all appearance of nature. The general effect of his pictures is that of a return to primitive, even perhaps of a return to barbaric, art. This is inevitably disconcerting; but before dismissing such pictures as violently absurd, it is fair to consider the nature of the problem which the artist who would use abstract design as his principle of expression, has to face. His relation to a modern public is peculiar. In the earliest ages of art the artist's public were able to share in each successive triumph of his skill, for every advance he made was also an advance towards a more obvious representation of things as they appeared to everybody. Primitive art, like the art of children, consists not so much in an attempt to represent what the eye perceives, as to put a line round a mental conception of the object. Like the work of the primitive artist, the pictures children draw are often extraordinarily expressive. But what delights them is to find they are acquiring more and more skill in producing a deceptive likeness of the object itself. Give them a year of drawing lessons and they will probably produce results which will give the greatest satisfaction to them and their relations; but to the critical eye the original expressiveness will have vanished completely from their work.

The development of primitive art (for here we are dealing with men and not children) is the gradual absorption of each newly observed detail into an already established system of design. Each new detail is hailed with delight by their public. But there comes a point when the accumulations of an increasing skill in mere representation begin to destroy the expressiveness of the design, and then, though a large section of the public continue to applaud, the artist grows uneasy. He begins to try to unload, to simplify the drawing and painting, by which natural objects are evoked, in order to recover the lost expressiveness and life. He aims at *synthesis* in design; that is to say, he is prepared to subordinate consciously his power of representing the parts of his picture as plausibly as possible, to the expressiveness of his whole design. But in this retrogressive movement he has the public, who have become accustomed to extremely plausible imitations of nature, against him at every step; and what is more, his own self-consciousness hampers him as well.

VIRGINIA WOOLF

ROGER FRY: A BIOGRAPHY

"The Post-Impressionists"

1940

Virginia Woolf (1882–1941) described the reaction to the 1910 exhibition in her biography of Fry.

There they stood upon chairs – the pictures that were to be shown at the Grafton Gallery – bold, bright, impudent almost, in contrast with the Watts portrait of a beautiful Victorian lady that hung on the wall behind them. And there was Roger Fry, gazing at them, plunging his eyes into them as if he were a humming-bird hawk-moth hanging over a flower, quivering yet still. And then drawing a deep breath of satisfaction, he would turn to whoever it might be, eager for sympathy. Were you puzzled? But why? And he would explain that it was quite easy to make the transition from Watts to Picasso; there was no break, only a continuation. They were only pushing things a little further. He demonstrated; he persuaded; he argued. The argument rose and soared. It vanished into the clouds. Then back it swooped to the picture.

George Frederick Watts (1817–1904), British painter of historical subjects and portraits.

* * *

It is difficult in 1939 to realise what violent emotions those pictures excited less than thirty years ago. The pictures are the same; it is the public that has changed. But there can be no doubt about the fact. The public in 1910 was thrown into paroxysms of rage and laughter. They went from Cézanne to Gauguin and from Gauguin to Van Gogh, they went from Picasso to Signac, and from Derain to Friesz, and they were infuriated. The pictures were a joke, and a joke at their expense. One great lady asked to have her name removed from the Committee. One gentleman, according to Desmond MacCarthy, laughed so loud at Cézanne's portrait of his wife that "he had to be taken out and walked up and down in the fresh air for five minutes. Fine ladies went into silvery trills of artificial laughter". The secretary had to provide a book in which the public wrote down their complaints. Never less than four hundred people visited the gallery daily. And they expressed their opinions not only to the secretary but in letters to the director himself. The pictures were outrageous, anarchistic and childish. They were an insult to the British public and the man who was responsible for the insult was either a fool, an impostor or a knave. Caricatures of a gentleman whose mouth was very wide open and whose hair was very untidy appeared in the papers. Parents sent him childish scribbles which they asserted were far superior to the works of Cézanne. The storm of abuse, Mr MacCarthy says, positively alarmed him.

The critics themselves were naturally more measured and temperate in their strictures, but they were dubious. Only one of the London critics, Sir Charles Holmes, according to Mr MacCarthy, came out on the side of the Post-Impressionists. The most influential and authoritative of them, the critic of *The Times*, wrote as follows:

> It is to be feared that when [Roger Fry] lends his authority to an exhibition of this kind, and gives it to be understood that he regards the work of Gauguin and Matisse as the last word in art, other writers of less sincerity will follow suit and try to persuade people that the Post-Impressionists are fine fellows, and that their art is the thing to be admired. They will even declare all who do not agree with them to be reactionaries of the worst type.

> It is lawful to anticipate these critics, and to declare our belief that this art is in itself a flagrant example of reaction. It professes to simplify, and to gain simplicity it throws away all that the long-developed skill of past artists had acquired and perpetuated. It begins all over again – and stops where a child would stop.... Really primitive art is attractive because it is unconscious; but this is deliberate – it is the rejection of all that civilisation has done, the good with the bad.... It is the old story of the days of Théophile Gautier – the aim of the artist should be "Épater le bourgeois" and by no means to please him! Such an aim is most completely realised by the painter Henri Matisse, from whose hand we have a landscape, a portrait, and a statue. We might have had more, but it is understood that nearly all his works belong to one rich family in Paris, who, we suppose, are so enamoured of them that they will not lend. Three are enough to enable us to judge the depth of the fall, in these strange productions, we will not say from the men of long ago, but from three idols of yesterday – from Claude Monet, from Manet, and from Rodin.

Finally *The Times* critic concluded by appealing to the verdict of Time – "le seul classificateur impeccable", which he assumed, somewhat rashly, would be given in his favour.

Among the artists themselves there was a great division of opinion. The elder artists, to judge from a letter written by Eric Gill to Sir William Rothenstein, were uneasy. "You are missing an awful excitement just now being provided for us in London," Eric Gill wrote to William Rothenstein in India, "to wit, the exhibition of Post-Impressionists now at the Grafton Galleries. All the critics are tearing one another's eyes out over it, and the

André Derain (1880–1954) and Émile Othon Friesz (1879–1949), Fauvist painters.

Sir Max Beerbohm. *A Law-Giver, Roger, First King of Bloomsbury.* c.1936. National Portrait Gallery, London.

Eric Gill (1882–1940), British sculptor and graphic artist. Sir William Rothenstein (1874–1945), British painter.

sheep and the goats are inextricably mixed up. The show", he continued, "quite obviously represents a reaction and transition, and so, if, like Fry, you are a factor in that reaction and transition, then you like the show. If, like MacColl and Robert Ross, you are too inseparably connected with the things reacted against and the generation from which it is a transition, then you don't like it. If, on the other hand, you are like me and John, McEvoy and Epstein, then, feeling yourself beyond the reaction and beyond the transition, you have a right to feel superior to Mr Henri Matisse (who is typical of the show – though Gauguin makes the biggest splash and Van Gogh the maddest) and you can say you don't like it. But have you seen Mr Matisse's sculpture? . . ." To which Sir William Rothenstein adds, "Yes, I had seen Matisse's sculpture in his studio in Paris. I could not pretend to like it." Nor did Mr Ricketts make any bones about his contempt for the pictures. "Why talk of the sincerity of all this rubbish?" he asked. And he proposed, ironically, to start a national subscription "to get Plymouth and Curzon painted by Matisse and Picasso"; and detected definite signs of insanity in the painters. Here he was supported by eminent doctors. Dr Hyslop lectured on the exhibition in Roger Fry's presence. He gave his opinion before an audience of artists and craftsmen that the pictures were the work of madmen. His conclusions were accepted with enthusiastic applause and Mr Selwyn Image expressed his agreement with Dr Hyslop in an appreciative little speech. Privately, Professor Tonks circulated caricatures in which Roger Fry, with his mouth very wide open and his hair flying wildly, proclaimed the religion of Cézannah, with Clive Bell in attendance as St Paul. And in his diary Wilfrid Blunt gave expression to the feelings of those who were not painters or critics but patrons and lovers of art:

> 15th Nov. – To the Grafton Gallery to look at what are called the Post-Impressionist pictures sent over from Paris. The exhibition is either an extremely bad joke or a swindle. I am inclined to think the latter, for there is no trace of humour in it. Still less is there a trace of sense or skill or taste, good or bad, or art or cleverness. Nothing but that gross puerility which scrawls indecencies on the walls of a privy. The drawing is on the level of that of an untaught child of seven or eight years old, the sense of colour that of a tea-tray painter, the method that of a schoolboy who wipes his fingers on a slate after spitting on them. . . . Apart from the frames, the whole collection should not be worth £5, and then only

Robert Ross: art critic for The Morning Post.

Augustus John (1878–1961), British painter. Arthur Ambrose McEvoy (1878–1927), British painter. Sir Jacob Epstein (1880–1959), British sculptor.

Henry Tonks (1862–1937), British painter, influential professor at the Slade School of Art from 1893. Clive Bell (1881–1964), British art critic whose most important book, Art, *1914, introduced the concept of "significant form." Wilfrid Blunt (1840–1922), British poet and traveller.*

Henry Tonks. *The Unknown God.* Exhibited 1923. Fry holds up a dead cat, a symbol of pure form, while Clive Bell rings a bell announcing the new creed, "Cézannah, Cézannah."

for the pleasure of making a bonfire of them. Yet two or three of our art critics have pronounced in their favour. Roger Fry, a critic of taste, has written an introduction to the catalogue, and Desmond MacCarthy acts as secretary to the show.... They are the works of idleness and impotent stupidity, a pornographic show.

* * *

Desmond MacCarthy records that in the midst of the uproar Roger Fry "remained strangely calm and 'did not give a single damn'". The pictures themselves, and all that they meant, were of absorbing interest to him, and much of the annoyance that he was causing his respectable colleagues passed over him unnoticed. He never realised, it is safe to say, how from this time onward he obsessed the mind of Professor Tonks, so that that gentleman could scarcely bear to hear his name mentioned and felt at his death that it was for English art "as if a Mussolini, a Hitler, or a Stalin had passed away". Professor Tonks did not obsess Roger Fry. He and other of his colleagues tended to recede into the background, and were rather to be pitied than abused for remaining in their little eddy of suburban life instead of risking themselves in the main stream of European art.

DESMOND MacCARTHY

THE LISTENER
"The Art-Quake of 1910"
February 1, 1945

But you will be wondering why *I* should be chosen by the B.B.C. to talk about painting. If I said that I knew nothing about art, it would be a modest lie, but if I said that there must surely be two or three thousand in England who know more about it than I do, though I hope that would still be a modest statement, it would be correct. The reason, however, is that I do know about that exhibition. I was secretary of it, and helped collect the pictures. Well, we all enjoy a little inside history, and that is what I can provide tonight about that famous Art-quake in 1910.

Again, you may well wonder why Roger Fry chose me to help him, for I had never seen the work of any of the artists exhibited. By the way, he himself had seen very few of their pictures. But he was a man of exploring sensibility, and those he had seen had impressed him. Well, when he proposed that I should go abroad and help assemble a representative exhibition of such pictures (incidentally he promised me a few days' bicycling in France) I don't think he chose me because he had special trust in my judgment. Of course he knew I was fond of pictures and that if confronted with one I could look at it with interest for more than two minutes – a faculty not so common as you might suppose. (Next time you are in a gallery you can verify this by timing people as they go round.) And then, though I could not generalise about artists, I did occasionally say something about a picture which would interest him, though it might be only "I'm almost sure that cow is too near the tree"; or "that crimson blob next her nose – of course, I see something of the kind is necessary and I didn't notice it at all at first; but now I have – it bothers me. Once it catches your eye, you can't overlook it; it is too shapeless and emphatic". Now that's the only kind of observation I ever contributed when we looked at pictures together, while he explained all sorts of things – aims, intentions, styles, about which I knew nothing....

Hearing that the Grafton Galleries had no show for the months between their usual London Season exhibition and the new year's, he proceeded to convince them that they might do worse than hold a stop-gap exhibition of modern foreign artists – also that Desmond MacCarthy was an excellent man of business which indeed, in my opinion (but of this you must judge for yourselves) he did turn out to be....

Of course, the first people we went to see were dealers who had modern pictures. If they could be persuaded to lend, then the London show would be representative. There was Vollard, of course, whom Roger Fry already knew – the man who had begun collecting Cézanne when his pictures only fetched a few hundred francs – and some could be got from the artist as gifts. And there was another small dealer whose name I have forgotten, and then an important one whose name I won't mention for a reason which you will presently discover to be discreet....

DEALING WITH THE DEALER

Now, though I was by way of being a man of affairs, when the big dealer asked me what percentage the Galleries wanted on sales, I confess I was floored. It was a point on which I had neglected to inform myself before starting. At a venture I murmured, "twenty per cent", and he replied, "*Parfaitement, Monsieur*". Then he went on, "If you get an offer for a picture, do not communicate at once with the artist, but with me first. He may accept less and then we can share the difference". Now the success of the exhibition largely depended on keeping on good terms with him. How would you have behaved? Well, I summoned up all the tact for which an aunt of mine had been famous, and replied: "I don't think I can agree to anything not down in black and white, but if you write to me...". He looked a little hard at me and then repeated, "*Parfaitement, Monsieur*". Of course, I never received that letter. We remained on excellent terms, and all was well.

On my return to London I reported that several hundred interesting pictures were available (transit insurance probably £150). I was told that expenses had to be kept down as the venture was a certain loss; still, one hundred pounds might be spent on advertising; *that* was satisfactory. I was about to leave when the director casually remarked: "I suppose you secured our usual percentage on sales?" Feebly, I murmured: "You never told me what it was". There was an oppressive pause. "Do you mean to say you didn't ask if you didn't know? What *did* you get?" "Twenty per cent". "Twenty? Why, we've *never* got more than eleven!" For several days after that I was convinced that I was cut out for a business career.

What was the exhibition to be called? That was the next question. Roger and I and a young journalist who was to help us with publicity, met to consider this; and it was at that meeting that a word which is now safely embedded in the English language – "post-impressionism" – was invented. Roger first suggested various terms like "expressionism", which aimed at distinguishing these artists from the impressionists; but the journalist wouldn't have that or any other of his alternatives. At last Roger, losing patience, said: "Oh, let's just call them post-impressionists; at any rate, they came after the impressionists".

Visitors to the Post-Impressionist Exhibition, 1910. Cartoon. "Some who are angry, some who point the finger of scorn . . ."

MATISSE, BRAQUE, AND BONNARD

HENRI MATISSE

"The Chapel of the Rosary"

1951

All my life I have been influenced by the opinion current at the time I first began to paint, when it was permissible only to render observations made from nature, when all that derived from the imagination or memory was called bogus and worthless for the construction of a plastic work. The teachers at the Beaux-Arts used to say to their pupils, "Copy nature stupidly".

Throughout my career I have reacted against this attitude to which I could not submit; and this struggle has been the source of the different stages along my route, in the course of which I have searched for means of expression beyond the literal copy – such as Divisionism and Fauvism.

These rebellions led me to study separately each element of construction: drawing, colour, values, composition; to explore how these elements could be combined into a synthesis without diminishing the eloquence of any one of them by the presence of the others, and to make constructions from these elements with their intrinsic qualities undiminished in combination; in other words, to respect the purity of the means.

Each generation of artists views the production of the previous generation differently. The paintings of the Impressionists, constructed with pure colours, made the next generation see that these colours, if they can be used to describe objects or natural phenomena, contain within them, independently of the objects that they serve to express, the power to affect the feelings of those who look at them.

Thus simple colours can act upon the inner feelings with more force, the simpler they are. A blue, for example, accompanied by the brilliance of its complementaries, acts upon the feelings like a sharp blow on a gong. The same with red and yellow; and the artist must be able to sound them when he needs to.

In this excerpt from the introduction he wrote for the book illustrating his designs for the Vence Chapel, Matisse reflects on construction with pure color and its expressive value as the legacy of Impressionism.

HENRI MATISSE INTERVIEWED BY E. TÉRIADE

MINOTAURE

"The Persistence of Fauvism"

October 15, 1936

When the means of expression have become so refined, so attenuated that their power of expression wears thin, it is necessary to return to the essential principles which made human language. They are, after all, the principles which "go back to the source," which relive, which give us life. Pictures which have become refinements, subtle gradations, dissolutions

Vincent van Gogh. *Haystacks*. Arles, June 1888. Pen, reed pen, sepia ink, 9⁹/₁₆ × 12⁹/₁₆" (24 × 31 cm). Formerly Collection Henri Matisse. Philadelphia Museum of Art (Samuel S. White III and Vera White Collection).

without energy, call for beautiful blues, reds, yellows – matter to stir the sensual depths in men. This is the starting point of Fauvism: the courage to return to the purity of the means.

Our senses have an age of development which does not come from the immediate surroundings, but from a moment in civilization. We are born with the sensibility of a given period of civilization. And that counts far more than all we can learn about a period. The arts have a development which comes not only from the individual, but also from an accumulated strength, the civilization which precedes us. One can't do just anything. A talented artist cannot do just as he likes. If he used only his talents, he would not exist. We are not the masters of what we produce. It is imposed on us.

In my latest paintings, I have united the acquisitions of the last twenty years to my essential core, to my very essence.

The reaction of each stage is as important as the subject. For this reaction comes from me and not from the subject. It is from the basis of my interpretation that I continually react until my work comes into harmony with me. Like someone writing a sentence, rewrites it, makes new discoveries . . . At each stage, I reach a balance, a conclusion. At the next sitting, if I find a weakness in the whole, I find my way back into the picture by means of the weakness – I re-enter through the breach – and reconceive the whole. Thus everything becomes fluid again and as each element is only one of the component forces (as in an orchestration), the whole can be changed in appearance but the feeling still remains the same. A black could very well replace a blue, since basically the expression derives from the relationships. One is not bound to a blue, to a green or to a red. You can change the relationships by modifying the quantity of the components without changing their nature. That is, the painting will still be composed of blue, yellow and green, in altered quantities. Or you can retain the relationships which form the expression of a picture, replacing a blue with a black, as in an orchestra a trumpet may be replaced by an oboe.

. . . At the final stage the painter finds himself freed and his emotion exists complete in his work. He himself, in any case, is relieved of it.

The "purity of means" to which Matisse refers as the origin of Fauvism recalls the issues raised in the early years of the twentieth century concerning the abstract as opposed to representational values of color and mark.

HENRI MATISSE

L'ART VIVANT

"Interview with Jacques Guenne"

September 15, 1925

Slowly I discovered the secret of my art. It consists of a meditation on nature, on the expression of a dream which is always inspired by reality. With more involvement and regularity, I learned to push each study in a certain direction. Little by little the notion that painting is a means of expression asserted itself, and that one can express the same thing in several ways. "Exactitude is not truth", Delacroix liked to say. Notice that the classics went on re-doing the same painting and always differently. After a certain time, Cézanne always painted the same canvas of the *Baigneuses*. Although the master of Aix ceaselessly redid the same painting, don't we come upon a new Cézanne with the greatest curiosity? Apropos of this, I am very surprised that anyone can wonder whether the lesson of the painter of the *Maison du pendu* and the *Joueurs de cartes* is good or bad. If you only knew the moral strength, the encouragement that his remarkable example gave me all my life! In moments of doubt, when I was still searching for myself, frightened sometimes by my discoveries, I thought: "If Cézanne is right, I am right"; because I knew that Cézanne had made no mistake. There are, you see, constructional laws in the work of Cézanne which are useful to a young painter. He had, among his great virtues, this merit of wanting the tones to be forces in a painting, giving the highest mission to his painting.

We shouldn't be surprised that Cézanne hesitated so long and so constantly. For my part, each time I stand before my canvas, it seems that I am painting for the first time. There were so many possibilities in Cézanne that, more than anyone else, he had to organize his brain. Cézanne, you see, is a sort of god of painting.

Photograph of Henri Matisse in his fourth-floor apartment, 11 place Charles-Félix, Nice, 1932. Detail of portrait by Albert Eugène Gallatin. © Philadelphia Museum of Art (A. E. Gallatin Collection).

ANDRÉ VERDET

XXe SIÈCLE

"Meeting with Georges Braque"

February 1962

. . . For me the ultimate goal is the picture in its final wholeness, and not in each of its details. You have to make a whole . . . In one of these *Ateliers*, the Bird just simply came to sit on top of the tree, in all its surprising whiteness.

It looks so real, isn't it rather too striking?

That's the surprise of song . . . I wanted everything to proceed from this bird. Like some star, sun or moon shining in another picture. At first, that's all you see . . . Then you begin to look around this light. The eye fits this star in of its own accord. The song of its light floods the picture. The picture becomes a song.

Your risk has become your freedom . . .

I can but repeat, this freedom no longer existed in the works of the Italian Renaissance. After Giotto, Masaccio, Piero della Francesca and Uccello, art usually became eloquence – magisterial eloquence, I agree.

Georges Braque photographed by Pablo Picasso in the latter's studio at 11 Boulevard de Clichy, 1909–10. At left, Cézanne's lithograph *Large Bathers*, V1157. Picasso Archives, Musée Picasso, Paris.

For too long painters poisoned our minds with their idea of mastery at any price . . . Ultimately, this kind of picture makes for boredom! The painters of the Renaissance were more concerned with representation than with the picture. Composition suffered as a result. When Veronese paints two apples, the result is beautiful, very beautiful if you wish, but for me it's all theater, pomposity. Where is the purity, the bold creative innocence, the sense of dazzlement! It took years, centuries, to get rid of that theatricality! As I have written, the Renaissance confused the *mise-en-scène* with composition, I mean in painting, of course. Then came Cézanne! He swept painting clean of the idea of mastery. Cézanne wasn't a rebel, but a revolutionary, one of the greatest – this can never be said often enough. He introduced us to the joy of taking risks. His personality is always at issue, his positive qualities together with his weaknesses. With Cézanne, decorum has been cast to the winds. He stakes his life upon his work, and his work upon his life.

* * *

AROUND CUBISM

Your new pictorial idea – Fauvism, which you make technically your own – really took off with the sudden burst of pictures you did at La Ciotat, near Toulon, in 1907. I particularly like *La Petite Baie à la Ciotat* where the radiant color becomes a blaze.

COLORPLATE 98

I bought that canvas back. After it had been sold, I felt a great sense of sadness and regret. I missed it, I thought of it sometimes as you do of someone you love who is far away.

It's pointillist in style . . .

But it's very atmospheric and flexible and harmonious. It is a *fauve* [literally *wild beast*] which doesn't roar. The violence of the colors is contained within subtle harmonies. But I needed to go further, to find essential tones, tones from nature as opposed to decorative ones.

Then you came under the influence of Cézanne? His entire *oeuvre* weighed . . .

Indeed it did, and afterwards I had to rid myself of it! Discovering Cézanne knocked me sideways. I had to rethink everything. I was not the only one to have this upsetting experience. A battle to free ourselves from a large part of our knowledge, what we tended to respect, admire or love. Cézanne's work did not represent just a new pictorial construction, but also, and people tend to overlook this, a new intellectual way of seeing space. I myself understood this only later.

So do you think that Cézanne's geometry first developed as a result of a sudden awareness, in a way of an inner crisis which was finally resolved in terms of a liberating mathematical order, an order made up of lines, forms and structures of color, which demanded a painting that would break completely with the customary methods of plastic creation?

I don't think so, I *know*. But nothing was built up into a dogma, it was more a perceptive foreknowledge of the period to come at the beginning of this century. But Cézanne had the right kind of temperament to sense such things: free and open, intelligent, of course, but also with a lot of flair – yes, that's the word, flair.

A real revolutionary!

I have described him as a revolutionary, but the term should be used with great caution. Cézanne brought a marvelous disorder into painting and he is a true innovator because he was able both to pose and to solve problems of plastic reconstruction. Many see him only as the theoretician of modern painting, whereas all his work tended to blank out the original theory, indeed to annul it entirely, to proceed as though this theory had never existed. Because, in fact, there had never really been any theory anyway. So Cézanne has been very widely exploited without anyone knowing precisely who he really was. He is still misunderstood.

JACQUES LASSAIGNE

XXe SIÈCLE

"A Conversation with Georges Braque"

December 1973

GB: Contact with Cézanne was of fundamental importance for me. It was more than an influence, it was an initiation. Cézanne was the first to break with scholarly, mechanical perspective as practised by artists for centuries and which had finally made all spontaneity impossible.

JL: Before the "legitimate" perspective of the Italians, had there not existed an earlier, empirical type of perspective, practised by the Flemish painters (the master of Flémalle, Van Eyck in his first works, *The Turin Hours*), in which the objects were represented not in relation to infinity, but in relation to the artist himself? A sort of lateral perspective, within arm's reach, in a way, which allowed objects to retain a tactile volume.

GB: Exactly. We wanted to keep the subject within arm's reach. In the same way the old measurements – the foot, the *pouce* [inch, literally *thumb*]

Le Maître de Flémalle, Robert Campin (1378/9–1444). Jan Van Eyck (1390–1441). The Turin Book of Hours, painted at the end of the fourteenth century, from the library of the Duc de Berry.

COLORPLATE 96. Georges Braque. *The Mast – The Port of Antwerp*. Summer 1906.
18⅛ × 15⅛″ (46 × 38.4 cm). Nathan and Marion Smooke Collection, Los Angeles.

COLORPLATE 97. Georges Braque. *Olive Trees, La Ciotat*. Summer 1907. 15 × 18³/₁₆″ (38.1 × 46.2 cm).
Worcester Art Museum, Worcester, Mass.
(Gift from the Estate of Mrs Aldus Chapin Higgins, Worcester, Mass.).

COLORPLATE 98. Georges Braque. *The Little Bay at La Ciotat.* 1907. 14 × 18¾″ (36 × 48 cm).
Musée Nationale d'Art Moderne, Centre Pompidou, Paris.

COLORPLATE 99. Henri Matisse. *Still Life against the Light.* 1899. 29½ × 36⅝″ (74.9 × 93 cm). Private Collection, Paris (Courtesy © Hériteurs Matisse).

COLORPLATE 100. Henri Matisse. *Luxe, Calme et Volupté.* 1904–05. 33⅞ × 45⅝″ (86 × 116 cm). Musée d'Orsay, Paris.

COLORPLATE 101. André Derain. *Portrait of Matisse*. 1905. 18 × 13¾″ (46 × 35 cm).
Tate Gallery, London.

COLORPLATE 102. Henri Matisse. *Portrait of Derain*. 1905.
15½ × 11½″ (39.5 × 29 cm). Tate Gallery, London.

COLORPLATE 103. Henri Matisse. *Woman Beside the Water (La Japonaise, Madame Matisse).*
Collioure, summer 1905. Oil and pencil on canvas. 13⅞ × 11⅛″ (35.2 × 28.2 cm).
Museum of Modern Art, New York (Purchase and partial anonymous gift).

(*Above*) Paul Cézanne. *Gardanne*. 1885–86. 31½ × 25¼″ (80 × 64.2 cm). Metropolitan Museum of Art, New York (Gift of Dr and Mrs Franz H. Hirschland, 1957.181).

(*Left*) Georges Braque. *La Roche-Guyon*. 1909. 29 × 23½″ (74 × 60 cm). Musée d'Art Moderne, Villeneuve d'Ascq (Gift of Geneviève and Jean Masurel).

as implied by a sense of measurement that was not abstract, but worked out by man in relation to the measurements of his body. Similarly, we wanted to bring the object nearer to the spectator, retaining its beauty and its concrete, physical feel.

Whereas the painters who used classical perspective subjected the object to it; ultimately, they were painting only in order to show off this perspective itself; some even gained assistance from specialists, "perspecteurs," to prepare their working diagrams: someone like Canaletto turned himself into a positive camera. Cézanne was the first to free himself from this false science and to restore a sense of freedom to the subject.

JL: And Gauguin?

GB: Yes, probably, but we didn't know about him.

JL: When you went to L'Estaque, was it because of Cézanne?

GB: Yes – and with some preconceived ideas, too. I could say that I'd worked out my first pictures done at L'Estaque even before I got there. Still, I did try to reconsider them, bearing in mind the light and the atmosphere and the effect of rain as it brightened the colors.

JL: Paulhan wrote that your lighter color was to reveal the first signs of the sharp strokes and angles that foreshadowed Cubism, and you said to Paulhan: "One day, I notice that I can return to the motif whatever the weather. I no longer need sun, I carry my light within me . . . On my next trip, to feel anything strongly, I would have to go as far as Senegal!"

Giovanni Antonio Canaletto (1697–1768).

Braque first went to L'Estaque to paint in October 1906.

Jean Paulhan: Braque le Patron, *Geneva and Paris, 1946.*

317

GB: These angles were the result of a new conception of space. I bade farewell to the vanishing point. Indeed, to avoid projection towards infinity, I put in planes superimposed at a short distance from one another, to make it understood that objects overlap in space instead of being divided. Cézanne had thought a great deal about that. One need only compare his landscapes with those of Corot, for instance, to see that there is no longer any distance, and that for Cézanne there is no infinity.

Instead of painting by beginning with the foreground, I put myself in the centre of the picture. Soon I actually inverted perspective – the pyramid of forms – so that it came towards me and ended at the spectator.

First I knew Picasso, then Kahnweiler. I was living in Montmartre, on rue d'Orcel. Soon Picasso and I were having daily discussions, trying out our ideas as they occurred, comparing our respective works. But it wouldn't be quite accurate to say that we worked jointly. Also, I worked from nature. Indeed, that is what led me towards still life, where I found something more objective than landscape. The discovery of tactile space, which set my arm in motion before a landscape, encouraged me to seek out ever closer physical contact. If a still life is not within arm's length, I find that it ceases to be a still life and no longer moves me.

Daniel-Henri Kahnweiler (1884–1979), German dealer who handled the work of all the leading Cubists.

At first our progress was fairly slow. From 1910 onwards, our desire for abstraction dominated the subject. In the search for a new space, we had more or less abandoned color. As I said to Paulhan, this actually constituted a danger, a tendency to slip into the *camaieu*. We had to make things appear as if a mist were rising. Previously we had modeled the objects, they were interpreted as spherical. This interpretation became Cubist when we began painting their various facets.

A form of monochrome painting popular in the eighteenth century.

JL: Cubism has been accused of being both dogmatic and empirical.
GB: Once you've found the way, you have the right to use all possible means to pursue it. The great invention was *papier collé*. One crucial problem remained: the introduction of color. It had to exist independently, in complete freedom, unconnected with form. You can think of it as music. An opera libretto can be set to various kinds of music.

To avoid confusion, for things to be quite clear, I have always linked colors to local visual forms.
JL: In this way Cubism led to abstraction. I don't think enough stress is laid on its abstract character.
GB: But one must make a distinction between Cubist painters and those who want to use abstraction as such. Cubism did not have abstraction as its goal, it proceeded by abstract phases. Also, to gain an idea of an abstraction, you have to start from or refer to elements of reality. The abstract does not exist *per se*. The influence of our work is still very much alive in painting. The separation of color and form is always a fruitful approach. Fairly soon, we stopped painting from nature. Unlike Cézanne. The painter thinks in form and color, and the object is in the poetics. First the painter thinks of a color, then he thinks about what the object will be: I don't think about painting a white napkin, I think of a patch of white which may become a napkin. It's like the story of Cézanne visiting Courbet, who was painting *L'homme aux fagots*: in the foreground of the canvas there was a vague brownish patch. In answer to a question of Cézanne's, Courbet said: 'I don't know what it is." And some days later, this brown patch had become a faggot. Painters are often influenced by colors in this way.

In poetry, a rigid form – the quatrain, the rondeau, the rhyme itself – pre-exists the content of the poem. I am sure that rhyme was invented to prune back the development of the normal, the routine, and to encourage other developments. In this way a new truth bursts forth.

ANGÈLE LAMOTTE
VERVE
"The Bouquet of Roses"
August 1947

On the table stands a fine round bouquet of roses. Bonnard speaks:

"I tried to paint them directly, scrupulously, I allowed myself to become caught up in the details, I abandoned myself to painting the roses. I realized that I was floundering, that I was stuck; I was beaten, I'd lost sight of my original idea, of the vision which had first seduced me, of my starting-point. I hope to be able to recapture it – by re-experiencing that first seduction.

"I see interesting things all around me, but for me to want to paint them, they must have a particular lure – what one might call beauty, I suppose. I paint them, trying not to lose control of the original idea; but I am weak and if I let myself go, as with the bunch of roses, after a moment, I no longer know where I'm going.

"The presence of the object, of the motif, is highly intrusive for the painter while he is actually painting – since the starting-point for a picture is an idea – if the object is directly before the artist while he is working, there is always a danger that he will allow himself to be side-tracked by the immediate appearance of things and lose his initial idea en route. And once this has happened, and the painter cannot recover his starting-point, he will be caught up in the accidental, he will depict the shadows that he sees in front of him, details which had not struck him at the beginning."

"So do you never work on the motif?"

"Yes, but I walk away from it, I have a look round, I go back to it some time later, I do not let myself become absorbed by the object itself. I paint alone in my studio, I do everything there. In a word, there is a conflict between the original idea, which is the right one, the painter's idea, and the variable and varied world of the object, of the motif which was the cause of the initial inspiration.

"Painters who have managed to approach the motif directly are very rare – and they usually have some kind of very personal defence. Cézanne had a firm idea of what he wanted from the motif, and took from nature only what was relevant to his idea. He would often sit around basking in the sun, without touching a paintbrush. He could wait for things to revert to being as he wanted them to be. He was the purest, most sincere painter, very powerfully armed in the face of nature.

"Renoir painted mainly Renoirs. He often had models with grayish skin, not pearly as he painted them. He used the model for a movement, for a form, but he didn't copy it, he never lost sight of what he could do. I was walking with him one day and he said: 'Bonnard, the painter has to make things more beautiful.' By which he meant that particular vital element the artist must put into his picture.

"Claude Monet painted on the motif, but for ten minutes. He did not allow things the time to take a hold on him. He would go back to work when the light corresponded to his original idea. He knew how to wait. He would work on several paintings at a time.

"The Impressionists painted on the motif, but they were better protected from the object than others by their formal means, their very technique. This is particularly evident with Pissarro, who would arrange things – system played an important part in his painting. Seurat only did some very small studies from nature, all the rest was done in the studio.

"You can see the difference between painters who know how to defend themselves against the object, and those who cannot, by comparing Titian and Velazquez in the Prado. Titian had total control in front of the motif, all

In one of his rare statements, recorded by Angèle Lamotte in 1943, Bonnard speaks of the conflict between the representational and formal demands of painting.

his pictures bear the mark of Titian, they were conceived in accordance with his initial idea. While for Velazquez, there are marked variations between the motifs which truly seduced him – the portraits of the Infantas – and his large academic compositions, where all we find are the models themselves, the objects themselves, without any sense of the initial inspiration.

"It is through seduction, or this initial idea, that the painter attains the universal. It is seduction which determines the choice of the motif, which corresponds exactly to the painting. If this seduction, this original idea, is lost, all that remains is the motif, the object, which takes over the painter and dominates him. From that moment onwards, the painter is no longer doing his own painting. With certain painters – including Titian – this seduction is so strong that it never deserts them, even if they are in contact with the object over a very long period. I myself am very weak, I find it hard to control myself before the object."

ANNETTE VAILLANT
BONNARD
"On Yellow"
1965

Between 1932 and 1938 he made repeated visits to Deauville and Trouville. Indifferent to the ugliness of the flowered wallpaper on which he pinned his canvases, he worked in anonymous hotel-rooms to re-compose the light of the Norman seaboard, orchestrating it with a gleam of brass. Ochreous at first, his yellow tints kindle the clouds, the houses, the hulls of the fishing-boats. Bonnard became so fascinated by yellow, after the blue Riviera, that he later bathed a nude in yellow light. Even the still waters of the Gulf of Saint-Tropez he paints yellow as the sun, under round, peony-red clouds.

One day Jacques Rodrigues had said of a picture by Signac, "There is a lot of yellow in it."

"One can't have too much," said Bonnard. Just before he died, when he was already too weak to hold the brush himself, it was a touch of yellow that he asked his nephew Charles to add to his last painting. "On the left, at the bottom, there on the ground under the almond tree."

Jacques Rodrigues, dealer and friend of Bonnard who showed the artist at the Galerie Rodrigues-Henriques, Paris, in November 1945.

CHARLES TERRASSE
"Bonnard's Almond Tree in Flower"
1964

Charles Terrasse is Pierre Bonnard's nephew.

The spring of 1946 was to be the last spring Bonnard was ever destined to witness. He was not strong at the time. He had been deeply affected by the death of his wife four years earlier, then of his friends Vuillard, Roussel and Maurice Denis, and the disasters that had befallen his country. He sought consolation in work, and he never stopped drawing and painting.

There was an almond tree in his garden, just under his bedroom window. It came into blossom at the end of winter. Above its black trunk the flowers rose up in a shower of dazzling white, against a sky that was often deep blue. He adored that almond tree: so much joyous purity rising from a patch of ground which the odd ray of early sun was already dashing with gold! He painted his almond tree in flower almost every year.

Never had the tree been clad in rayment more sumptuous than that spring, like some promise of days of reprieve. Bonnard painted it one last

320

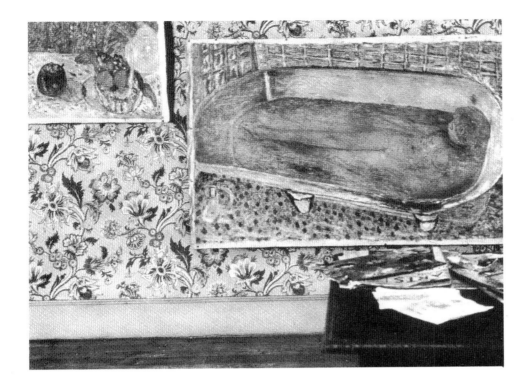

Photograph of the wall of a room in Deauville showing a partly finished *Nude in the Bath* by Bonnard. Photo Rogi André, 1937. Les Archives de la Kostrevy, Stockholm.

time – with passion, with enthusiasm. The very style of this painting is extraordinary. Never before had painting been so free and spontaneous. Bonnard, as we know, usually worked over his paintings many times. His painting, which could seem so easy, was in fact always done with difficulty, with revision and repainting, over whole months. "Paintbrush in one hand, rag in the other," he used to say. Here, the freedom of touch is total. One cannot fail to admire its verve, its sureness of execution.

Bonnard treated his *Almond Tree* as he did the rest of his works: he set it aside, then retouched it; finally, signed it. But he continued to think about it. He reconsidered it again – in January 1947. He was very weak at this point. At last he said: "The green on the patch of ground to the left is wrong. What it needs is yellow. . . ." He asked me to help him paint the bit of ground yellow, that is, gold. A few days later, Bonnard was dead.

The *Almond Tree in Flower* is his last painting. It is a small work; but, within its narrow confines, there are no limits to its breadth. This burst of whiteness, rising into the sky like a hymn, may be considered as the supreme declaration of love and gratitude offered by Bonnard to Nature.

COLORPLATE 119

GEORGES BESSON
Letter to Pierre Betz
January 1943

Georges Besson (1882–1971), critic, journalist, publisher and collector. He was the friend of many of the artists whose work he wrote about and collected, including Matisse and Bonnard.

My dear Betz,
You want memories? Thumbnail sketches? Anecdotes concerning Pierre Bonnard? Your readers will be disappointed: that man's life was utterly devoid of incident, let alone adventure. Though do you know of any adventure more absorbing than the constant development of this unique painter whose every finished work always held the promise of new conquests?

Unlike Van Gogh, Bonnard did not begin life as a reclaimer of fallen women. He did not cut off his ear. Unlike Lautrec, he did not spend his life you-know-where. He did not reheat Cézanne's "petite sensation" in the Maori fashion and did not use Beaujolais to find reasons to devote himself to St. Joan; his navel never acted as an advert on any beaches. He does not make claims for the rights of intelligence – he is far too intelligent – to provide dealers with a Montparnassian version of the dross of the museums. And if he sometimes affirms the blessings and powers of the imagination, it is always with the brush. He talks little, he explains little, he writes nothing.

* * *

You will have met people who claim to take pleasure in those casual remarks wrested from certain painters which are then repeated, embellished, crystalized and subsequently regarded as their credos, for instance those attributed to Rodin and expressed by Bourdelle, that Offenbach god. I hate eloquence, and therefore I prefer something more human, certain stifled groans from Delacroix or a confession made by Jules Renard, Corot or Bonnard:

> Our life here is fairly lonely and organized as best we can – today is a bad day. It snowed again this morning and the housekeeper is ill. The electricity is off and the milk probably won't be delivered this evening. Apart from that all is well, Mme la Marquise.

A touching note; for such "bad days" were to recur often, over thirty years – at Grasse, at St-Tropez, one winter at La Baule, at Arcachon, at Trouville. . . . Marthe Bonnard's poor health required these journeyings. They resulted in the most unlikely conditions for work. Bonnard has, probably always had, the studio in Montmartre. It resembles an empty barn, a disused warehouse. But his real studio was elsewhere and everywhere, in indescribable hotel rooms or furnished villas. Old-fashioned hanging lamps on the ceilings, flowered wallpaper on the walls, gradually concealed by tacked-up canvases. One, too tall, came below the skirting board, another, larger still, covered the floor. And Bonnard, bending over, his dog Ubu or Poucette between his legs, one foot on the painting, would scumble a color, stand up smiling, and admit that his work was "improved."

Bonnard liked to return to his old paintings. In the museum in Grenoble, then of the Luxembourg, he would sometimes wait for the guard to go to the next room, then take out a little box containing two or three tubes of paint and a small brush, and put a few "improving" touches to some detail that was worrying him. Having achieved his aim, he would walk off, as radiant as a schoolboy after writing a vengeful comment on the blackboard.

But what might I say next, my dear Betz, if I don't stop this chatter? I prefer to tell you that Bonnard is in perfect health. As for his work, in his own words, "I am torn between *intimisme* and decoration; you can't teach an old dog new tricks."

Photograph of Pierre and Marthe Bonnard at Vernon. 1912. © Antoine Terrasse/SPADEM.

JOHN BERGER

THE MOMENT OF CUBISM

"Bonnard"

1966

John Berger (b. 1926), novelist and critic.

Since his death in 1947 at the age of eighty, Pierre Bonnard's reputation has grown fairly steadily, and in the last five years or so quite dramatically. Some now claim that he is *the* greatest painter of the century. Twenty years ago he was considered a minor master.

This change in his reputation coincides with a general retreat among certain intellectuals from political realities and confidence. There is very little of the post-1914 world in Bonnard's work. There is very little to disturb – except perhaps the unnatural peacefulness of it all. His art is intimate, contemplative, privileged, secluded. It is an art about cultivating one's own garden.

It is necessary to say this so that the more extreme recent claims for Bonnard can be placed in an historical context. Bonnard was essentially a conservative artist – although an original one. The fact that he is praised as "a pure painter" underlines this. The purity consisted in his being able to accept the world as he found it. Was Bonnard a greater artist than Brancusi – not to mention Picasso, or Giacometti? Each period assesses all surviving artists according to its own needs. What is more interesting is why Bonnard will undoubtedly survive. The conventional answer, which begs the question, is that he was a great colourist. What was his colour for?

Constantin Brancusi (1876–1957), Romanian sculptor who worked in Paris from 1904. Alberto Giacometti (1901–66), sculptor and painter who worked in Paris from 1927.

Bonnard painted landscapes, still-lifes, occasional portraits, very occasional mythological pieces, interiors, meals and nudes. The nudes seem to me to be far and away the best pictures.

In all his works after about 1911 Bonnard used colours in a roughly similar way. Before then – with the help of the examples of Renoir, Degas, Gauguin – he was still discovering himself as a colourist; after 1911 he by no means stopped developing, but it was a development along an already established line. The typical mature Bonnard bias of colour – towards marble whites, magenta, pale cadmium yellow, ceramic blues, terracotta reds, silver greys, stained purple, all unified like reflections on the inside of an oyster – this bias tends in the landscapes to make them look mythical, even faery; in the still-lifes it tends to give the fruit or the glasses or the napkins a silken glamour, as though they were part of a legendary tapestry woven from threads whose colours are too intense, too glossy; but in the nudes the same bias seems only to add conviction. It is the means of seeing the women through Bonnard's eyes. The colours confirm the woman.

Then what does it mean to see a woman through Bonnard's eyes? In a canvas painted in 1899, long before he was painting with typical Bonnard colours, a young woman sprawls across a low bed. One of her legs trails off the bed on to the floor: otherwise, she is lying very flat on her back. It is called *L'Indolente: Femme assoupie sur un lit*.

The title, the pose and the *art-nouveau* shapes of the folds and shadows all suggest a cultivated *fin-de-siècle* form of eroticism very different from the frankness of Bonnard's later works; yet this picture – perhaps just because it doesn't engage us – offers us a clear clue.

Continue to look at the picture and the woman begins to disappear – or at least her presence becomes ambiguous. The shadow down her near side and flank becomes almost indistinguishable from the cast shadow on the bed. The light falling on her stomach and far leg marries them to the golden-lit bed. The shadows which reveal the form of a calf pressed against a thigh, of her sex as it curves down and round to become the separation between her buttocks, of an arm thrown across her breasts – these eddy and flow in exactly the same rhythm as the folds of the sheet and counterpane. The picture, remaining a fairly conventional one, does not actually belie its title: the woman continues to exist. But it is easy to see how the painting is pulling towards a very different image: the image of the imprint of a woman on an *empty* bed. Yeats:

> . . . the mountain grass
> Cannot but keep the form
> Where the mountain hare has lain.

Alternatively one might describe the same state of affairs in terms of the opposite process: the image of a woman losing her physical limits, over-flowing, overlapping every surface until she is no less and no more than the *genius loci* of the whole room.

Pierre Bonnard. *Séguidille*. Lithograph illustration for *Parallèlement* by Paul Verlaine, page 27. 12 × 9⁷/₈″ (30.5 × 25 cm). Bibliothèque Nationale, Paris.

Before I saw the Bonnard exhibition at the Royal Academy in London in January 1966, I was vaguely aware of this ambiguity in Bonnard's work between presence and absence, and I explained it to myself in terms of his being a predominantly nostalgic artist: as though the picture was all he could ever save of the subject from the sweep of time passing. Now this seems far too crude an explanation. Nor is there anything nostalgic about *Femme assoupie sur un lit*, painted at the age of thirty-two. We must go further.

The risk of loss in Bonnard's work does not appear to be a factor of distance. The far-away always looks benign. One has only to compare his seascapes with those of Courbet to appreciate the difference. It is proximity which leads to dissolution with Bonnard. Features are lost, not in distance, but, as it were, in the near. Nor is this an optical question of something being too close for the eye to focus. The closeness also has to be measured in emotional terms of tenderness and intimacy. Thus *loss* becomes the wrong word, and nostalgia the wrong category. What happens is that the body which is very near – in every sense of the word – becomes the axis of everything that is seen: everything that is visible relates to it: it acquires a domain to inhabit: but by the same token it has to lose the precision of its own fixed position in time and space.

The process may sound complex, but in fact it is related to the common experience of falling in love. Bonnard's important nudes are the visual expressions of something very close to Stendhal's famous definition of the process of "crystallization" in love:

> A man takes pleasure in adorning with a thousand perfections the woman of whose love he is certain; he recites to himself, with infinite complacency, every item that makes up his happiness. It is like exaggerating the attractions of a superb property that has just fallen into our hands, which is still unknown, but of the possession of which we are assured . . . In the salt mines of Salzburg they throw into the abandoned depths of a mine a branch of a tree stripped of its leaves by winter; two or three months later they draw it out, covered with sparkling crystallizations: the smallest twigs, those which are no larger than the foot of a titmouse, are covered with an infinity of diamonds, shifting and dazzling; it is impossible any longer to recognize the original branch.

Berger's translation from Stendhal, De L'Amour *(Paris: Editions de Cluny, 1938, p. 43).*

Many other painters have of course idealized women whom they have painted. But straightforward idealization becomes in effect indistinguishable from flattery or pure fantasy. It in no way does justice to the energy involved in the psychological state of being in love. What makes Bonnard's contribution unique is the way that he shows in pictorial terms how the image of the beloved emanates *outwards from her* with such dominance that finally her actual physical presence becomes curiously incidental and in itself indefinable. (If it could be defined, it would become banal.)

Bonnard said something similar himself.

> By the seduction of the first idea the painter attains to the universal. It is the seduction which determines the choice of the motif and which corresponds exactly to the painting. If this seduction, if the first idea vanishes all that remains . . . is the object which invades and dominates the painter . . .

Everything about the nudes Bonnard painted between the two World Wars confirms this interpretation of their meaning, confirms it visually, not sentimentally. In the bath nudes, in which the woman lying in her bath is seen from above as through a skylight, the surface of the water serves two pictorial functions simultaneously. First it diffuses the image of her whole body, which, whilst remaining recognizable, sexual, female, becomes as varied and changeable and large as a sunset or an aurora borealis; secondly, it seals off the body from us. Only the light from it comes through the water to reflect off the bathroom walls. Thus she is potentially everywhere, except specifically here. She is lost in the near. Meanwhile what structurally pins down these paintings to prevent their presence becoming as ambiguous as hers is the geometric patterning of the surrounding tiles or linoleum or towelling.

In other paintings of standing nudes, the actual surface of the picture serves a similar function to the surface of the water. Now it is as though a large part or almost all of her body had been left unpainted and was simply the brown cardboardy colour of the original canvas. (In fact this is not the case: but it is the deliberate effect achieved by very careful colour and tonal planning.) All the objects around her – curtains, discarded clothes, a basin, a lamp, chairs, her dog – frame her in light and colour as the sea frames an island. In doing so, they break forward towards us, and draw back into depth. But she remains fixed to the surface of the canvas, simultaneously an absence and a presence. Every mark of colour is related to her, and yet she is no more than a shadow against the colours.

In a beautiful painting of 1916–19 she stands upright on tip-toe. It is a very tall painting. A rectangular bar of light falls down the length of her body. Parallel to this bar, just beside it and similar in colour, is a rectangular strip of wall-papered wall. On the wall-paper are pinkish flowers. On the bar of light is her nipple, the shadow of a rib, the slight shade like a petal under her knee. Once again the surface of that bar of light holds her back, makes her less than present: but also once again, she is ubiquitous: the designs on the wall-paper are the flowers of her body.

In the *Grand Nu Bleu* of 1924, she almost fills the canvas as she bends to dry a foot. This time no surface or bar of light imposes on her. But the extremism of the painting of her body itself dissolves her. The painting is, as always, tender: its extremism lies in its rendering of what is near and what is far. The distance between her near raised thigh and the inside of the far thigh of the leg on which she is standing – the distance of the caress of one hand underneath her – is made by the force of colour to be felt as a landscape distance: just as the degree to which the calf of that standing leg swells towards us is made to seem like the emerging of a near white hill from the blue recession of a plain running to the horizon. Her body is her habitation – the whole world in which she and the painter live; and at the same time it is immeasurable.

It would be easy to quote other examples: paintings with mirrors, paintings with landscapes into which her face flows away like a sound, paintings in which her body is seen like a sleeve turned inside out. All of them establish with all of Bonnard's artfulness and skill as a draughtsman and colourist how her image emanates outwards from her until she is to be found everywhere except within the limits of her physical presence.

And now we come to the harsh paradox which I believe is the pivot of Bonnard's art. Most of his nudes are directly or indirectly of a girl whom he met when she was sixteen and with whom he spent the rest of his life until she died at the age of sixty-two. The girl became a tragically neurasthenic woman: a frightened recluse, beside herself, and with an obsession about constantly washing and bathing. Bonnard remained loyal to her.

Thus the starting point for these nudes was an unhappy woman, obsessed with her toilet, excessively demanding and half "absent" as a personality. Accepting this as a fact, Bonnard, by the strength of his devotion to her or by his cunning as an artist or perhaps by both, was able to transform the literal into a far deeper and more general truth: the woman who was only half present into the image of the ardently beloved.

It is a classic example of how art is born of conflict. In art, Bonnard said, *il faut mentir*. The trouble with the landscapes and still-lifes and meals – the weakness expressed through their colour – is that in them the surrounding world conflicts are still ignored and the personal tragedy is temporarily put aside. It may sound callous, but it seems probable that his tragedy, by forcing Bonnard to express and marvellously celebrate a common experience, ensured his survival as an artist.

(*Top*) *Nude in Tub*. Photograph by Pierre Bonnard, *c*.1908. Musée d'Orsay, Paris.

(*Above*) Pierre Bonnard. *Woman in a Tub* 1922. Pencil, 9 × 7⅛″ (22.9 × 18.1 cm). Musée du Louvre, Paris (Gift of Georges Besson).

TWENTIETH-CENTURY VIEWS OF POST-IMPRESSIONISM

RAINER MARIA RILKE

LETTERS ON CÉZANNE

October 1907

Rainer Maria Rilke (1875–1926), German poet and novelist. These letters to his wife were written in response to the Cézanne memorial exhibition at the Salon d'Automne in 1907 which showed fifty-six works.

OCTOBER 9

... Today I wanted to tell you a little about Cézanne. With regard to his work habits, he claimed to have lived as a Bohemian until his fortieth year. Only then, through his acquaintance with Pissarro, did he develop a taste for work. But then to such an extent that for the next thirty years he did nothing *but* work. Actually without joy, it seems, in a constant rage, in conflict with every single one of his paintings, none of which seemed to achieve what he considered to be the most indispensable thing. *La réalisation*, he called it, and he found it in the Venetians whom he had seen over and over again in the Louvre and to whom he had given his unreserved recognition. To achieve the conviction and substantiality of things, a reality intensified and potentiated to the point of indestructibility by his experience of the object, this seemed to him to be the purpose of his innermost work; old, sick, exhausted every evening to the point of collapse by the regular course of the day's work (often he would go to bed at six, before dark, after a senselessly ingested meal), angry, mistrustful, ridiculed and mocked and mistreated each time he went to his studio, – but celebrating Sunday, attending Mass and Vespers as he had in his childhood, and very politely requesting some slightly better food from Madame Brémond, his housekeeper – : hoping nevertheless from day to day that he might reach that achievement which he felt was the only thing that mattered. And all the while (assuming one can trust the testimony of a not very likable painter who associated with everyone for a while) he exacerbated the difficulty of his work in the most willful manner. While painting a landscape or a still life, he would conscientiously persevere in front of the object, but approach it only by very complicated detours. Beginning with the darkest tones, he would cover their depth with a layer of color that led a little beyond them, and keep going, expanding outward from color to color, until gradually he reached another, contrasting pictorial element, where, beginning at a new center, he would proceed in a similar way. I think there was a conflict, a mutual struggle between the two procedures of, first, looking and confidently receiving, and then of appropriating and making personal use of what has been received; that the two, perhaps as a result of becoming conscious, would immediately start opposing each other, talking out loud, as it were, and go on perpetually interrupting and contradicting each other. And the old man endured their discord, ran back and forth in his studio, which was badly lit because the builder had not found it necessary to pay attention to this strange old bird whom the people of Aix had agreed not to take seriously. He ran back and forth in his studio with green apples scattered about, or went out into his garden in despair and sat. And before him lay the small town, unsuspecting, with its cathedral; a town for decent and modest burghers, while he – just as his father, who was a hat maker, had foreseen – had become different: a

Written at 29, rue Cassette, Paris VIe.

A reference to Émile Bernard whose "Souvenirs sur Cézanne" had just appeared in the Mercure de France *in September/October 1907.*

Bohemian: that's how his father saw it and what he himself believed. This father, knowing that Bohemians live and die in misery, had determined to work for the son, had become a kind of small banker to whom people brought their money ("because he was honest," as Cézanne said), and it was thanks to these financial precautions that Cézanne later had the means to continue painting without interruption. Perhaps he went to his father's funeral; he loved his mother too, but when she was buried, he wasn't there. He was engaged "sur le motif," as he called it. That's how important work was for him already, and he couldn't afford to make an exception, not even this one, which surely must have commended itself to his piety and simplicity as an important occasion.

He became well known in Paris, and gradually his fame grew. But he had nothing but mistrust for any progress that wasn't of his own making (that others had made for him, quite aside from the question of *how* they had made it); he remembered only too well how thoroughly Zola (a fellow Provençal, like himself, and a close acquaintance since early childhood) had misinterpreted his fate and his aspirations in *L'Oeuvre*. From then on, any kind of scribbling about himself and his art was *out*, as far as he was concerned: "Travailler sans le souci de personne et devenir fort – " he once shouted at a visitor. But when the latter, in the middle of a meal, described the novella about the Chef d'Oeuvre inconnu (I told you about it once), where Balzac, with unbelievable foresight of future developments, invented a painter named Frenhofer who is destroyed by the discovery that there really are no contours but only oscillating transitions – destroyed, that is, by an impossible problem – , the old man, hearing this, stands up, despite Madame Brémond, who surely did not appreciate this kind of irregularity, and, voiceless with agitation, points his finger, clearly, again and again, at himself, himself, himself, painful though that may have been. Zola had understood nothing; it was Balzac who had foreseen or forefelt that in painting you can suddenly come upon something so huge that no one can deal with it.

* * *

OCTOBER 21

... There's something else I wanted to say about Cézanne: that no one before him ever demonstrated so clearly the extent to which painting is something that takes place among the colors, and how one has to leave them alone completely, so that they can settle the matter among themselves. Their intercourse: this is the whole of painting. Whoever meddles, arranges, injects his human deliberation, his wit, his advocacy, his intellectual agility in any way, is already disturbing and clouding their activity. Ideally a painter (and, generally, an artist) should not become conscious of his insights: without taking the detours through his reflective processes, and incomprehensibly to himself, all his progress should enter so swiftly into the work that he is unable to recognize them in the moment of transition. Alas, the artist who waits in ambush there, watching, detaining them, will find them transformed like the beautiful gold in the fairy tale which cannot remain gold because some small detail was not taken care of. That van Gogh's letters are so readable, that they are so rich, basically argues against him, just as it argues against a painter (holding up Cézanne for comparison) that he wanted or knew or experienced this and that; that blue called for orange and green for red: that, secretly listening in his eye's interior, he had heard such things spoken, the inquisitive one. And so he painted pictures on the strength of a single contradiction, thinking, at the same time, of the Japanese simplification of color, where separate planes are added or subtracted on a gradient of tones combining into a sum total; leading, again, to the drawn and explicit (i.e., invented) contour of the Japanese as a frame for the coordinate planes; leading, in other words, to a great deal of intentionality and arbitrariness – in short, to decoration. Cézanne, too, was provoked by the letters of a writing painter – who,

Zola's novel L'Oeuvre *("The Masterpiece") (1886) put an end to the lifelong friendship of Cézanne and Zola.*

Photograph of Paul Cézanne working near Aix-en-Provence. 1904.

Rilke had been reading a German translation of Van Gogh's letters on his trip from Munich to Naples, November 28, 1906.

Émile Bernard.

accordingly, wasn't really a painter – to make some pronouncements about painting; but when you see the few letters the old man wrote: how awkward this effort at self-explication remains, and how extremely repugnant it was to him. He was almost incapable of saying anything. The sentences in which he attempted it became long and convoluted, they balk and bristle, get knotted up, and finally he drops them, beside himself with rage. On the other hand, he manages to write very clearly: "I believe the best thing is work." Or: "I'm making progress every day, although very slowly." Or: "I am almost seventy years old." Or: "I will answer you through pictures." Or: "L'humble et colossal Pissarro – " (who taught him how to work), or: after some thrashing about (one senses with what relief, in beautiful script): the signature, unabbreviated: Pictor Paul Cézanne. And in the last letter (of September 21, 1905), after complaining about his bad health, simply: Je continue donc mes études. And the wish which was literally fulfilled: Je me suis juré de mourir en peignant. Just like in an old picture of the dance of death, that's the way death seized his hand from behind, painting the last stroke himself, quivering with pleasure; his shadow had been lying on the palette for a while, and he had had time to select from among the open round sequence of colors the particular one he liked most; as soon as that color would get into the brush, he would reach in and paint . . . there it was; he took the hand and made his stroke, the only one he was capable of.

*   *   *

OCTOBER 23

. . . I wondered last night whether my attempt to give you an impression of the woman in the red armchair was at all successful. . . . For a moment it seemed easier to talk about the self-portrait . . . In this case . . . the object itself is more tangible, and the words, which feel so unhappy when made to denote purely painterly facts, are only too eager to return to themselves in the description of the man portrayed, for here's where their proper domain begins. His right profile is turned by a quarter in the direction of the viewer, looking. The dense dark hair is bunched together on the back of the head and lies above the ears, in such a way that the whole contour of the skull is exposed; it is drawn with eminent assurance, hard and yet round, the brow sloping down and of one piece, its firmness prevailing even where, dissolved into form and surface, it is merely the outermost contour containing a thousand others. The strong structure of this skull which seems hammered and sculpted from within is reinforced by the ridges of the eyebrows; but from there, pushed forward toward the bottom, shoed out, as it were, by the closely bearded chin, hangs the face, hangs as if every feature had been suspended individually, unbelievably intensified and yet reduced to utter primitivity, yielding that expression of uncontrolled amazement in which children and country people can lose themselves, – except that the gazeless stupor of their absorption has been replaced by an animal alertness which entertains an untiring, objective wakefulness in the unblinking eyes. How great this watching of his was and how unimpeachably accurate, is almost touchingly confirmed by the fact that, without even remotely interpreting his expression or presuming himself superior to it, he reproduced himself with so much humble objectivity, with the unquestioning, matter-of-fact interest of a dog who sees himself in a mirror and thinks: there's another dog.

Farewell . . . for now; perhaps you can see in all this a little of the old man, who deserves the epithet he applied to Pissarro: humble et colossal. Today is the anniversary of his death . . .

"I am continuing my studies"
"I have sworn to die painting"

Cézanne was found unconscious on the road to Lauves and died two days later, October 23, 1906.

Mme Cézanne in a Red Armchair, *1877, Museum of Fine Arts, Boston.* Self-Portrait, *1873–76, Pellerin Collection, Paris.*

HÉLÈNE PARMELIN

PICASSO SAYS . . .

"Cézanne and Tintoretto"

1969

The main thing about modern painting is this. A painter like Tintoretto,
for example, begins work on a canvas, and afterward he goes on and,
finally, when he has filled it and worked it all over, then only is it finished.
Now, if you take a painting by Cézanne (and this is even more clearly
visible in the watercolors), the moment he begins to place a stroke of paint
on it, the painting is already there.

CHRISTIAN ZERVOS

CAHIERS D'ART

"Conversation with Picasso"

1935

It's not what the artist *does* that counts, but what he *is*. Cézanne would
never have interested me a bit if he had lived and thought like Jacques
Émile Blanche, even if the apple he painted had been ten times as beautiful. What forces our interest is Cézanne's anxiety – that's Cézanne's
lesson; the torments of Van Gogh – that is the actual drama of the man.
The rest is a sham.

MAURICE MERLEAU-PONTY

FONTAINE

"Cézanne's Doubt"

December 1945

Maurice Merleau-Ponty (1907–61),
philosopher and phenomenologist of the
postwar period.

The result of these procedures [of the Impressionists] is that the canvas –
which no longer corresponds point by point to nature – affords a generally
true impression through the action of the separate parts upon one another.
But at the same time, depicting the atmosphere and breaking up the tones
submerges the object and causes it to lose its proper weight. . . .

One must therefore say that Cézanne wished to return to the object
without abandoning the Impressionist aesthetic which takes nature as its
model. Emile Bernard reminded him that, for the classical artists, painting
demanded outline, composition, and distribution of light. Cézanne
replied: "They created pictures; we are attempting a piece of nature." He
said of the old masters that they "replaced reality by imagination and by
the abstraction which accompanies it." Of nature, he said that "the artist
must conform to this perfect work of art. Everything comes to us from
nature; we exist through it; nothing else is worth remembering." He stated
that he wanted to make of Impressionism "something solid, like the art in
the museums." His painting was paradoxical: he was pursuing reality
without giving up the sensuous surface, with no other guide than the
immediate impression of nature, without following the contours, with no

Émile Bernard's conversations with
Cézanne, "Souvenirs sur Paul Cézanne,"
were published in the Mercure de
France, *October 1907, and reprinted 1912,*
1921, 1925–26.

330

Paul Cézanne. *The Green Jar*. 1885–87. Pencil and watercolor. Musée du Louvre, Paris (Cabinet des Dessins).

outline to enclose the color, with no perspectival or pictorial arrangement. This is what Bernard called Cézanne's suicide: aiming for reality while denying himself the means to attain it. This is the reason for his difficulties and for the distortions one finds in his pictures between 1870 and 1890. Cups and saucers on a table seen from the side should be elliptical, but Cézanne paints the two ends of the ellipse swollen and expanded. The work table in his portrait of Gustave Geffroy stretches, contrary to the laws of perspective, into the lower part of the picture. In giving up the outline Cézanne was abandoning himself to the chaos of sensations, which would upset the objects and constantly suggest illusions, as, for example, the illusion we have when we move our head that objects themselves are moving – if our judgment did not constantly set these appearances straight. According to Bernard, Cézanne "submerged his painting in ignorance and his mind in shadows." But one cannot really judge his painting in this way except by closing one's mind to half of what he said and one's eyes to what he painted.

It is clear from his conversations with Emile Bernard that Cézanne was always seeking to avoid the ready-made alternatives suggested to him: sensation versus judgment; the painter who sees against the painter who thinks; nature versus composition; primitivism as opposed to tradition. "We have to develop an optics," said Cézanne, "by which I mean a logical vision – that is, one with no element of the absurd." "Are you speaking of our nature?" asked Bernard. Cézanne: "It has to do with both." "But aren't nature and art different?" "I want to make them the same. Art is a personal apperception, which I embody in sensations and which I ask the understanding to organize into a painting." But even these formulas put too much emphasis on the ordinary notions of "sensitivity" or "sensations" and "understanding" – which is why Cézanne could not convince by his arguments and preferred to paint instead. Rather than apply to his work dichotomies more appropriate to those who sustain traditions than to those men, philosophers or painters, who initiate these traditions, he preferred to search for the true meaning of painting, which is continually to question tradition. Cézanne did not think he had to choose between feeling and thought, between order and chaos. He did not want to separate the stable things which we see and the shifting way in which they appear; he wanted to depict matter as it takes on form, the birth of order through spontaneous organization. He makes a basic distinction not between "the senses" and "the understanding" but rather between the spontaneous organization of the things we perceive and the human organization of ideas and sciences. We see things; we agree about them; we are anchored in them; and it is with "nature" as our base that we construct our sciences. Cézanne wanted to paint this primordial world, and his pictures therefore seem to show nature pure, while photographs of the same landscapes suggest man's works, conveniences, and imminent presence. Cézanne never wished to "paint like a savage." He wanted to put intelligence, ideas, sciences, perspective, and tradition back in touch with the world of nature which they must comprehend. He wished, as he said, to confront the sciences with the nature "from which they came."

By remaining faithful to the phenomena in his investigations of perspective, Cézanne discovered what recent psychologists have come to formulate: the lived perspective, that which we actually perceive, is not a geometric or photographic one. The objects we see close at hand appear smaller, those far away seem larger than they do in a photograph. (This can be seen in a movie, where a train approaches and gets bigger much faster than a real train would under the same circumstances.) To say that a circle seen obliquely is seen as an ellipse is to substitute for our actual perception what we would see if we were cameras: in reality we see a form which oscillates around the ellipse without being an ellipse. In a portrait of Mme Cézanne, the border of the wallpaper on one side of her body does not form a straight line with that on the other: and indeed it is known that if a line passes beneath a wide strip of paper, the two visible segments appear dislocated. Gustave Geffroy's table stretches into the bottom of the picture, and indeed, when our eye runs over a large surface, the images it successively receives are taken from different points of view, and the whole surface is warped. It is true that I freeze these distortions in repainting them on the canvas; I stop the spontaneous movement in which they pile up in perception and in which they tend toward the geometric perspective. This is also what happens with colors. Pink upon gray paper colors the background green. Academic painting shows the background as gray, assuming that the picture will produce the same effect of contrast as the real object. Impressionist painting uses green in the background in order to achieve a contrast as brilliant as that of objects in nature. Doesn't this falsify the color relationship? It would if it stopped there, but the painter's task is to modify all the other colors in the picture so that they take away from the green background its characteristics of a real color. Similarly, it is Cézanne's genius that when the over-all composition of the picture is seen globally, perspectival distortions are no longer visible in their own right but rather contribute, as they do in natural vision, to the impression of an emerging order, of an object in the act of appearing, organizing itself before our eyes. In the same way, the contour of an object conceived as a line encircling the object belongs not to the visible world but to geometry. If one outlines the shape of an apple with a continuous line, one makes an object of the shape, whereas the contour is rather the ideal limit toward which the sides of the apple recede in depth. Not to indicate any shape would be to deprive the objects of their identity. To trace just a single outline sacrifices depth – that is, the dimension in which the thing is presented not as spread out before us but as an inexhaustible reality full of reserves. That is why Cézanne follows the swelling of the object in modulated colors and indicates *several* outlines in blue. Rebounding among these, one's glance captures a shape that emerges from among them all, just as it does in perception. Nothing could be less arbitrary than these famous distortions which, moreover, Cézanne abandoned in his last period, after 1890, when he no longer filled his canvases with colors and when he gave up the closely-woven texture of his still lifes.

COLORPLATE 104. Paul Cézanne. *Mont Sainte-Victoire*. 1902–06. 25⅝ × 31⅞″ (65 × 81 cm).
Collection Mrs H. Anda-Bührle, Zurich.

COLORPLATE 105. Paul Cézanne. *Le Château Noir*. 1904–06. Oil on canvas. 29 × 36¾″ (73.6 × 93.2 cm).
The Museum of Modern Art, New York (Gift of Mrs David M. Levy).

COLORPLATE 106. Paul Cézanne. *Mont Sainte-Victoire seen from Les Lauves*. 1904–06.
23⅝ × 28⅜″ (60 × 72 cm). Öffentliche Kunstsammlung, Kunstmuseum, Basle.

COLORPLATE 107. Paul Cézanne. *Provençal Landscape near Les Lauves.* c.1904–06.
25¾ × 31⅞" (65.4 × 80.9 cm). Phillips Collection, Washington, D.C.

COLORPLATE 108. Paul Cézanne. *Women Bathing*. 1902/06.
29 × 36″ (73.5 × 92.5 cm). Feilchenfeldt Collection, Zurich.

COLORPLATE 109. Paul Cézanne. *Bathers*. 1900–06. 51¼ × 76¾″ (130 × 195 cm).
National Gallery, London.

COLORPLATE 110. André Derain. *Landscape at Collioure*. Summer 1905. 15 × 17¾″ (36.2 × 44.4 cm).
Joanne and Ira Kirshbaum Collection, Los Angeles.

COLORPLATE 111. André Derain. *Bacchic Dance*. 1906. Watercolor and pencil, 19½ × 25½″ (49.5 × 64.8 cm). Museum of Modern Art, New York (Gift of Abby Aldrich Rockefeller).

The outline should therefore be a result of the colors if the world is to be given in its true density. For the world is a mass without gaps, a system of colors across which the receding perspective, the outlines, angles, and curves are inscribed like lines of force; the spatial structure vibrates as it is formed. "The outline and the colors are no longer distinct from each other. To the extent that one paints, one outlines; the more the colors harmonize, the more the outline becomes precise. . . . When the color is at its richest, the form has reached plenitude." Cézanne does not try to use color to *suggest* the tactile sensations which would give shape and depth. These distinctions between touch and sight are unknown in primordial perception. It is only as a result of a science of the human body that we finally learn to distinguish between our senses. The lived object is not rediscovered or constructed on the basis of the contributions of the senses; rather, it presents itself to us from the start as the center from which these contributions radiate. We *see* the depth, the smoothness, the softness, the hardness of objects; Cézanne even claimed that we see their odor. If the painter is to express the world, the arrangement of his colors must carry with it this indivisible whole, or else his picture will only hint at things and will not give them in the imperious unity, the presence, the insurpassable plenitude which is for us the definition of the real. That is why each brushstroke must satisfy an infinite number of conditions. Cézanne sometimes pondered hours at a time before putting down a certain stroke, for, as Bernard said, each stroke must "contain the air, the light, the object, the composition, the character, the outline, and the style." Expressing what *exists* is an endless task.

Nor did Cézanne neglect the physiognomy of objects and faces: he simply wanted to capture it emerging from the color. Painting a face "as an object" is not to strip it of its "thought." "I realize that the painter interprets it," said Cézanne. "The painter is not an imbecile." But this interpretation should not be a reflection distinct from the act of seeing. "If I paint all the little blues and all the little maroons, I capture and convey his glance. Who gives a damn if they want to dispute how one can sadden a mouth or make a cheek smile by wedding a shaded green to a red." One's personality is seen and grasped in one's glance, which is, however, no more than a combination of colors. Other minds are given to us only as incarnate, as belonging to faces and gestures. Countering with the distinctions of soul and body, thought and vision is of no use here, for Cézanne returns to just that primordial experience from which these notions are derived and in which they are inseparable. The painter who conceptualizes and seeks the expression first misses the mystery – renewed every time we look at someone – of a person's appearing in nature. In *La Peau de chagrin* Balzac describes a "tablecloth white as a layer of newly fallen snow, upon which the place-settings rise symmetrically, crowned with blond rolls." "All through youth," said Cézanne, "I wanted to paint that, that tablecloth of new snow. . . . Now I know that one must will only to paint the place-settings rising symmetrically and the blond rolls. If I paint 'crowned' I've had it, you understand? But if I really balance and shade my place-settings and rolls as they are in nature, then you can be sure that the crowns, the snow, and all the excitement will be there too."

We live in the midst of man-made objects, among tools, in houses, streets, cities, and most of the time we see them only through the human actions which put them to use. We become used to thinking that all of this exists necessarily and unshakeably. Cézanne's painting suspends these habits of thought and reveals the base of inhuman nature upon which man has installed himself. This is why Cézanne's people are strange, as if viewed by a creature of another species. Nature itself is stripped of the attributes which make it ready for animistic communions: there is no wind in the landscape, no movement on the Lac d'Annecy; the frozen objects hesitate as at the beginning of the world. It is an unfamiliar world in which one is uncomfortable and which forbids all human effusiveness. If one looks at the work of other painters after seeing Cézanne's paintings, one feels somehow relaxed, just as conversations resumed after a period of mourning mask the absolute change and give back to the survivors their solidity. But indeed only a human being is capable of such a vision which penetrates right to the root of things beneath the imposed order of humanity. Everything indicates that animals cannot *look at* things, cannot penetrate them in expectation of nothing but the truth. Emile Bernard's statement that a realistic painter is only an ape is therefore precisely the opposite of the truth, and one sees how Cézanne was able to revive the classical definition of art: man added to nature. . . .

The task before him was, first to forget all he had ever learned from science and, second *through* these sciences to recapture the structure of the landscape as an emerging organism. To do this, all the partial views one catches sight of must be welded together; all that the eye's versatility disperses must be reunited; one must, as Gasquet put it, "join the wandering hands of nature." "A minute of the world is going by which must be painted in its full reality." His meditation would suddenly be consummated: "I have my *motif*," Cézanne would say, and he would explain that the landscape had to be centered neither too high nor too low, caught alive in a net which would let nothing escape. Then he began to paint all parts of the painting at the same time, using patches of color to surround his original charcoal sketch of the geological skeleton. The picture took on fullness and density; it grew in structure and balance; it came to maturity all at once. "The landscape thinks itself in me," he said, "and I am its consciousness." Nothing could be farther from naturalism than this intuitive science. Art is not imitation, nor is it something manufactured according to the wishes of instinct or good taste. It is a process of expressing. Just as the function of words is to name – that is, to grasp the nature of what appears to us in a confused way and to place it before us as a recognizable object – so it is up to the painter, said Gasquet, to "objectify," "project," and "arrest." Words do not *look like* the things they designate; and a picture is not a *trompe-l'oeil*. Cézanne, in his own words, "wrote in painting what had never yet been painted, and turned it into painting once and for all." Forgetting the viscous, equivocal appearances, we go through them straight to the things they present. The painter recaptures and converts into visible objects what would, without him, remain walled up in the separate life of each consciousness: the vibration of appearances which is the cradle of things. Only one emotion is possible for this painter – the feeling of strangeness – and only one lyricism – that of the continual rebirth of existence.

Leonardo da Vinci's motto was persistent rigor, and all the classical works on the art of poetry tell us that the creation of art is no easy matter. Cézanne's difficulties – like those of Balzac or Mallarmé – are of a different nature. Balzac (probably taking Delacroix for his model) imagined a painter who wants to express life through the use of color alone and who keeps his masterpiece hidden. When Frenhofer dies, his friends find nothing but a chaos of colors and elusive lines, a wall of painting. Cézanne was moved to tears when he read *Le Chef-d'oeuvre inconnu* and declared that he himself was Frenhofer. The effort made by Balzac, himself obsessed with "realization," sheds light on Cézanne's.

*   *   *

There is thus no art for pleasure's sake alone. One can invent pleasurable objects by linking old ideas in a new way and by presenting forms that have been seen before. This way of painting or speaking at second hand is what is generally meant by culture. Cézanne's or Balzac's artist is not satisfied to be a cultured animal but assimilates the culture down to its very foundations and gives it a new structure: he speaks as the first man spoke and paints as if no one had ever painted before. What he expresses cannot, therefore, be the translation of a clearly defined thought, since such clear thoughts are those which have already been uttered by ourselves or by others. "Conception" cannot precede "execution." There is nothing but a vague fever before the act of artistic expression, and only the work itself, completed and understood, is proof that there was *something* rather than *nothing* to be said. Because he returns to the source of silent and solitary experience on which culture and the exchange of ideas have been built in order to know it, the artist launches his work just as a man once launched the first word, not knowing whether it will be anything more than a shout, whether it can detach itself from the flow of individual life in which it originates and give the independent existence of an identifiable *meaning* either to the future of that same individual life or to the monads coexisting with it or to the open community of future monads. The meaning of what the artist is going to say *does not exist* anywhere – not in things, which as yet have no meaning, nor in the artist himself, in his unformulated life. It summons one away from the already constituted reason in which "cultured men" are content to shut themselves, toward a reason which contains its own origins.

CLEMENT GREENBERG
PARTISAN REVIEW
"Cézanne and the Unity of Modern Art"
May–June 1951

Clement Greenberg (b. 1909), American writer on art and one of the most influential critics of art since the war. His advocacy of New York artists in the 1950s established the reputation of Abstract Expressionism against the dominance of the School of Paris and contributed to current definitions of Modernism.

Cézanne's art may no longer be the overflowing source of modernity it was thirty years back, but it endures in its newness and in what can even be called its stylishness. There remains something indescribably racy and sudden for all its familiarity by now, in the way his crisp blue line can separate the contour of an object from its mass. Yet how distrustful Cézanne himself was of bravura, speed – all the apparent concomitants of stylishness. And how unsure at bottom of where he was going.

He was on the verge of middle age when he had the crucial revelation of his artist's mission. Yet what he *thought* was revealed was largely inconsistent with the means he had already developed to meet and fulfill his revelation, and the problematic quality of his art – the source perhaps of its unfading modernity – came from the ultimate necessity of revising his intentions under the pressure of a method that evolved as if in opposition to them. He was making the first pondered and conscious attempt to save the key principle of Western painting – its concern for an ample and literal rendition of stereometric space – from the effects of Impressionist color. He had noted the Impressionists' inadvertent silting up of pictorial depth; and it was because he tried so hard to reexcavate that space without abandoning Impressionist color, and because this effort, while vain, was so profoundly conceived, that his art became the discovery and turning point it did. Like Manet, and with almost as little real appetite for the role of a revolutionary, he changed the direction of painting in the very effort to return it by new paths to its old ways.

Cézanne accepted his notion of pictorial unity, of the realized, final effect of a picture, from the Old Masters. When he said that he wanted to redo Poussin after nature and "make Impressionism something solid and durable like the Old Masters," he meant apparently that he wanted to impose a composition and design like that of the High Renaissance on the "raw" chromatic material provided by the Impressionist registration of visual experience. The parts, the atomic units, were still to be supplied by the Impressionist method, which was held to be truer to nature; but these were to be organized into a whole on more traditional principles.

The Impressionists, as consistent in their naturalism as they knew how to be, had let nature dictate the over-all design and unity of the picture along with its component parts, refusing in theory to interfere consciously with their optical impressions. For all that, their pictures did not lack structure; insofar as any single Impressionist picture was successful, it achieved an appropriate and satisfying unity, as must any successful work of art. (The overestimation by Roger Fry and others of Cézanne's success in doing exactly what he said he wanted to do is responsible for the cant about the Impressionist lack of structure. What is missed is geometrical, diagrammatic and sculptural structure; in its stead, the Impressionists achieved structure by the accentuation and modulation of points and areas of color and value, a kind of "composition" which is not inherently inferior to or less "structural" than the other kind.) Committed though he was to the motif in nature in all its givenness, Cézanne still felt that it could not of its own accord provide a sufficient basis for pictorial unity; what he wanted had to be more emphatic, more tangible in its articulation and therefore, supposedly, more "permanent." And it had to be *read* into nature.

The Old Masters had assumed that the members and joints of pictorial design should be as clear as those of architecture. The eye was to be led through a rhythmically organized system of convexities and concavities in which manifold gradations of dark and light, indicating recession and salience, were marshaled around points of interest. To accommodate the weightless, flattened shapes produced by the flat touches of Impressionist color to such a system was obviously impossible. Seurat demonstrated this in his *Sunday Afternoon on Grand Jatte Island*, as well as in most of his other completed group compositions, where the stepped-back planes upon which he set his figures serve – as Sir Kenneth Clark has noted – to give them the quality of cardboard silhouettes. Seurat's pointillist, hyper-Impressionist method of filling color in could manage a plausible illusion of deep space, but not of mass or volume within it. Cézanne reversed the terms of this problem and sought – more like the Florentines than like the Venetians he cherished – to achieve mass and volume first, and deep space as their by-product, which he thought he could do by converting the Impressionist method of registering variations of light into a way of indi-cating the variations in planar direction of solid surfaces. For traditional modeling in dark and light, he substituted modeling with the supposedly more natural – and Impressionist – differences of warm and cool.

Recording with a separate pat of paint each larger shift of direction by which the surface of an object defined the shape of the volume it enclosed, he began in his late thirties to cover his canvases with a mosaic of brush-strokes that called just as much attention to the physical picture plane as the rougher dabs or "commas" of Monet, Pissarro and Sisley did. The flatness of that plane was only further emphasized by the distortions of Cézanne's drawing, which started out by being temperamental (Cézanne was never able to master a sculptural *line*) but turned into a method, new in extent rather than in kind, of anchoring fictive volumes and spaces to the surface pattern. The result was a kind of pictorial tension the like of which had not been seen in the West since Late Roman mosaic art. The overlapping little rectangles of pigment, laid on with no attempt to fuse their edges, brought depicted form toward the surface; at the same time, the modeling and shaping performed by these same rectangles drew it back into illusionist depth. A vibration, infinite in its terms, was set up between the literal paint surface of the picture and the "content" established behind it, a vibration in which lay the essence of the Cézan-nian "revolution."

The Old Masters always took into account the tension between surface and illusion, between the physical facts of the medium and its figurative content – but in their need to conceal art with art, the last thing they had wanted was to make an explicit point of this tension. Cézanne, in spite of

COLORPLATE 21

himself, had been forced to make the tension explicit in his desire to rescue tradition from – and at the same time with – Impressionist means. Impressionist color, no matter how handled, gave the picture surface its due as a physical entity to a much greater extent than had traditional practice.

Cézanne was one of the most intelligent painters about painting whose observations have been recorded. (That he could be rather intelligent about many other things has been obscured by his eccentricity and the profound and self-protective irony with which he tried, in the latter part of his life, to seem the conformist in matters apart from art.) But intelligence does not guarantee the artist a precise awareness of what he is doing or really wants to do. Cézanne overestimated the degree to which a conception could precipitate itself in, and control, works of art. Consciously, he was after the most exact communication of his optical sensations of nature, but these were to be ordered according to certain precepts for the sake of art as an end in itself – an end to which naturalistic truth was but a means.

To communicate his optical sensations exactly meant transcribing, however he could, the distance from his eye of every part of the motif, down to the smallest facet-plane into which he could analyze it. It also meant suppressing the texture, the smoothness or roughness, the hardness or softness, the tactile associations of surfaces; it meant seeing prismatic color as the exclusive determinant of spatial position – and of spatial position above and beyond local color or transient effects of light. The end in view was a *sculptural* Impressionism.

Cézanne's habits of seeing – his way, for instance, of telescoping middle-ground and foreground, and of tilting forward everything in the subject that lay above eye level – were as inappropriate to the cavernous architectural schemes of the Old Masters as were Monet's habits of seeing. The Old Masters elided and glided as they traveled through space, which they treated as the loosely articulated continuum that common sense finds it to be. Their aim in the end was to create space as a theater; Cézanne's was to give space itself a theater.

His focus was more intense and at the same time more uniform than the Old Masters'. Once "human interest" had been excluded, every visual sensation produced by the subject became equally important. Both the picture as picture, and space as space, became tighter and tauter – distended, in a manner of speaking. One effect of this distention was to push the weight of the entire picture forward, squeezing its convexities and concavities together and threatening to fuse the heterogeneous content of the surface into a single image or form whose shape coincided with that of the canvas itself. Thus Cézanne's effort to turn Impressionism toward the sculptural was shifted, in its fulfillment, from the structure of the pictorial illusion to the configuration of the picture itself as an object, as a flat surface. Cézanne got "solidity," all right; but it is as much a two-dimensional, literal solidity as a representational one.

The real problem would seem to have been, not how to do Poussin over according to nature, but how to relate – more carefully and explicitly than Poussin had – every part of the illusion in depth to a surface pattern endowed with even superior pictorial rights. The firmer binding of the three-dimensional illusion to a decorative surface effect, the integration of plasticity and decoration – this was Cézanne's true object, whether he said so or not. And here critics like Roger Fry read him correctly. But here, too, his expressed theory contradicted his practice most. As far as I know, not once in his recorded remarks does Cézanne show any concern with the decorative factor except – and the words are the more revelatory because they seem offhand – to refer to two of his favorite Old Masters, Rubens and Veronese, as "the decorative masters."

No wonder he complained till his last day of his inability to "realize." The effect toward which his means urged was not the one he had conceived in his desire for the organized maximum of an illusion of solidity and depth. Every brush-stroke that followed a fictive plane into fictive depth harked back – by reason of its abiding, unequivocal character as a mark made by a brush – to the physical fact of the medium; and the shape and placing of that mark recalled the shape and position of the flat rectangle which was being covered with pigment that came from tubes. (Cézanne wanted an "elevated" art, if anyone ever did, but he made no bones about the tangibility of the medium. "One has to be a painter through the very qualities of painting," he said. "One has to use coarse materials.")

For a long while he overpacked his canvases as he groped along, afraid to betray his sensations by omission, afraid to be inexact because incomplete. Many of his reputed masterpieces of the later 1870s and the 1880s (I leave to one side the proto-expressionist feats of his youth, some of which are both magnificent and prophetic) are redundant, too cramped, lacking in unity because lacking in modulation. The parts are felt, the execution is often exact, but often there is too little of the kind of feeling that precipitates itself in an instantaneous whole. (No wonder so many of his unfinished paintings are among his best.) Only in the last ten or fifteen years of Cézanne's life do pictures whose power is complete as well as striking and original come from his easel with real frequency. Then the means at last fulfills itself. The illusion of depth is constructed with the surface plane more vividly, more obsessively in mind; the facet-planes may jump back and forth between the surface and the images they create, yet they are one with both surface and image. Distinct yet summarily applied, the square pats of paint vibrate and dilate in a rhythm that embraces the illusion as well as the flat pattern. The artist seems to relax his demand for exactness of hue in passing from contour to background, and neither his brushstrokes nor his facet-planes remain as closely bunched as before. More air and light circulate through the imagined space. Monumentality is no longer secured at the price of a dry airlessness. As Cézanne digs deeper behind his broken contours with ultramarine, the whole picture seems to unsheathe and then re-envelop itself. Repeating its rectangular enclosing shape in every part of itself, it seems also to strain to burst the dimensions of that shape.

Had Cézanne died in 1890, he would still be enormous, but more so in innovation than in realization. The full, triumphant unity that crowns the painter's vision, the unity offered like a single sound made by many voices and instruments – a single sound of instantaneous yet infinite variety – this kind of unity comes for Cézanne far more often in the last years of his life.

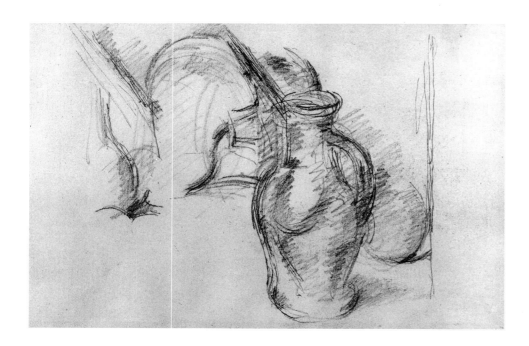

Paul Cézanne. *Still Life with Pitcher*, after Chardin. 1887–91. Pencil, 4³/₄ × 8″ (12.2 × 20.8 cm). Öffentliche Kunstsammlung, Kupferstichkabinett, Basle.

Then, certainly, his art does something quite different from what he said he wanted it to do. Though he may think as much as before about its problems, he thinks much less into its execution. Having attracted young admirers, he expands a little, has his remarks taken down and writes letters about his "method." But if he did not then confuse Emile Bernard, Joachim Gasquet and others among his listeners, he confuses us today, who can only read what he had to say. I prefer, however, to think with Erle Loran (to whose *Cézanne's Composition* I am indebted for more than a few insights into the essential importance of Cézanne's drawing) that the master himself was more than a little confused in his theorizing about his art. But did he not complain that Bernard, with his appetite for theories, forced him to theorize unduly? (Bernard, in his turn, criticized Cézanne for painting *too much* by theory.)

Erle Loran, Cézanne's Composition, *1943*.

To the end, he continued to harp on the necessity of modeling, and of completeness and exactness in reporting one's "sensations." He stated his ideal, with more than ordinary self-awareness, as a marriage between *trompe-l'oeil* and the laws of the medium, and lamented his failure to achieve it. In the same month in which he died, he still complained of his inability to "realize." Actually, one is more surprised, in view of the gathering abstractness of his last great paintings, to hear Cézanne say that he had made a "little progress." He condemned Gauguin and Van Gogh for painting "flat" pictures: "I have never wanted and will never accept the lack of modeling or gradation: it's an absurdity. Gauguin was not a painter; he only made Chinese pictures." Bernard reports him as indifferent to the art of the primitives of the Renaissance; they, too, apparently, were too flat. Yet the path of which Cézanne said he was the primitive, and by following which he hoped to rescue Western tradition's pledge to the three-dimensional from both Impressionist haze and Gauguinesque decoration, led straight, within five or six years after his death, to a kind of painting as flat as any the West had seen since the Middle Ages.

The Cubism of Picasso, Braque and Léger completed what Cézanne had begun. Its success divested his means of whatever might have remained problematical about them. Because he had exhausted so few of his insights, Cézanne could offer the Cubists all the resources of a new discovery; they needed to expend little effort of their own in either discovery or rediscovery. This was the Cubists' luck, which helps explain why Picasso, Léger and Braque, between 1909 and 1914, were able to turn out a well-nigh uninterrupted succession of "realizations," classical in the sufficiency of their strength, in the adjustment of their means to their ends.

Cézanne's honesty and steadfastness are exemplary. Great painting, he says in effect, ought to be produced the way it was by Rubens, Velasquez, Veronese and Delacroix; but my own sensations and capacities don't correspond to theirs, and I can feel and paint only the way I must. And so he went at it for forty years, day in and out, with his clean, careful *métier*, dipping his brush in turpentine between strokes to wash it, and then depositing each little load of paint in its determined place. It was a more heroic artist's life than Gauguin's or Van Gogh's, for all its material ease. Think of the effort of abstraction and of eyesight necessary to analyze every part of every motif into its smallest negotiable plane.

Then there were the crises of confidence that overtook Cézanne almost every other day (he was also a forerunner in his paranoia). Yet he did not go altogether crazy: he stuck it out at his own sedentary pace, and his absorption in work rewarded him for premature old age, diabetes, obscurity and the crabbed emptiness of his life away from art. He considered himself a weakling, a "bohemian," frightened by the routine difficulties of life. But he had a temperament, and he sought out the most redoubtable challenges the art of painting could offer him in his time.

ADRIAN STOKES
BRITISH JOURNAL OF AESTHETICS
"The Image in Form – A Lecture"
July 1966

Adrian Stokes (1902–72), British painter and poet whose writings on art have combined his own sensibilities as an artist with the psychoanalytic theory of Melanie Klein.

Often in a talk about art we get at least a partial division of formal attributes from representation. We say the formal relationships organize the representation, the images, on view. That's the traditional approach. On the other hand, in the theory of Significant Form, form is isolated from imagery, from the construction of likenesses in visual terms.

I am going to argue that formal relationships themselves entail a representation or imagery of their own though these likenesses are not as explicit as the images we obtain from what we call the subject matter. When later I shall refer to Cézanne's *Bathers* in the National Gallery, I shall suggest that there is far more imagery in this picture than the imagery of nudes in a landscape, a more generalized imagery, with references to all sorts of experiences, which proceeds from the formal treatment. Now I think one can say that that's obvious and indeed that it is presumed in the work of all the best writers today on current art; but it doesn't seem to have given rise to a really wide investigation of what is involved. I am going to make some suggestions about this.

* * *

Formal arrangements can sometimes transmit a durable image. That is not merely to say that they are expressive. There is a sense in which every object of the outside world is expressive since we tend to endow natural things, any piece of the environment, with our associations to it, thereby constructing an identity additional to the one generally recognized. At heightened moments anything can gain the aura of a personage. But in art it should not be we who do all the imaginative work in this way. The better we understand art the less of the content we impose, the more becomes communicated. In adopting an aesthetic viewpoint – this, indeed, is a necessary contribution on our part – which we have learned from study in many works of art, we discover that to a considerable extent our attention is confined to the relationship of formal attributes and of their image-creating relevance to the subject matter. The work of art should be to some extent a strait-jacket in regard to the eventual images that it is most likely to induce. Obviously any mode of feeling can be communicated by art, perhaps even by abstract art. Nevertheless the personification of that message in the terms of aesthetic form constructs a simulacrum, a presence that qualifies the image of the paramount feeling expressed. That feeling takes to itself as a crowning attribute more general images of experience. Form, then, ultimately constructs an image or figure of which, in art, the expression of particular feeling avails itself. A simple instance lies with Bonnard, with the shape of hats in his time that approximated to the shape of the head and indeed of the breast. He seems to co-ordinate experience largely through an unenvious and loving attitude to this form. He is equally interested in a concave rounded shape. Again, when we know well an artist and his work we may feel that among the characteristic forms he makes some at least are tied to an image of his own physique or of a personal aspect in his physical responses. This also would be an instance of form as an agent which, through the means of the artist's personality as an evident first step in substantiation, allows him to construct from psychical and emotional as well as physical concatenations a thing that we tend to read as we read a face. A face records more experience than its attention at the moment we look at it.

Perhaps all we demand of a work of art is that it should be as a face in this sense. But form in the widest sense of all, as the attempted organiza-

Paul Cézanne. *Bathers*. 1900–06. $51\frac{1}{4} \times 76\frac{3}{4}''$ (130 × 195 cm). National Gallery, London (see COLORPLATE 109).

348

tion that rules every experience, must obviously give rise to a strong and compelling imagery so generalized that it can hardly be absent from a consciousness in working order though ordinarily present in nothing like the aesthetic strength, since were it otherwise refreshment and encouragement that we gain from art would not be necessary. Form must possess the character of a compelling apparition, and it is easy to realize that it is the icon of co-ordination.

Integration or co-ordination of what? it will be asked. Some aspect, I have argued elsewhere, of the integration of experience, of the self, with which is bound up the integrity of other people and of other things as separate, even though the artist has identified an aspect of himself with the object, has transfixed the object with his own compulsion, though not to the extent of utterly overpowering its otherness. These perceptions of relationship that are the basis of a minimum sanity demand reinforcement. Outwardness, a physical or concrete adaptation of relationship, spells out enlargement, means certainty.

It must appear a strange suggestion that art is in any way bent upon constructing an image for sanity, however minimal, in view of the wild unbalanced strains of feeling that have so often been inseparably employed in making this image. But surely if art allows not only the extremity of expressiveness but the most conclusive mode, if it constructs of expressiveness an enduring thing, that mode must incorporate an element to transcend or ennoble a particular expressiveness of which otherwise we should soon tire. We are encouraged to experience a many-sided apprehension in art. Expressiveness – it may be infantile – becomes valuable in evolving the mature embrace by form.

* * *

But first Cézanne and the other very great painting that we have of late welcomed to this country, *Les Baigneuses*, in the National Gallery. At first sight these figures could suggest a quorum of naked tramps camped on top of railway carriages as the landscape roars by from left to right; except, of course, that studied, monumental, they altogether refuse the character of silhouettes. They absorb, and in absorbing rule, the environment. Beyond the long seal-like woman who regards the depths of the background, the standing, studious, twin-like girls with backs to us lean across towards the trees and clouds as if to be those upright trees. All the same the stretching across the picture plane is more intense, the stretching of these governing bodies that now seem poised on the easy rack of a level moving staircase. But movement to the left is blocked by the striding figures on that side, and since movement is braked at the other end as well it is as if shunted trucks were held between two engines. The tall, contemplative figure on the further bank remembers for us the stretching movement that, in effect, has crammed the centre where the two groups of bathers meet. Rich with dynamic suggestions, the movements coalesce into a momentary composure so that even within the crowd there appears to be airiness and space. It is now that we contemplate the broad back, laid out like a map, of the sitting woman with black hair on the left. Only in art, in an image, in a concrete realization of emotional bents, such powers with their reconciliation are found perfected.

Another image comes to us in terms of the heads of hair of walnut and stained oak. It speaks to us of the strength of the trees in those women and of the tawny arena on which the bodies lie and, by contrast, it includes the circumambient blue, the knife-like blue day that these nudes have crowded to inhabit. They feed on the blue, on the distance at which the seal-woman exclaims. The close, clumsy yet heroic flesh sips the sky. These nudes are blue-consuming objects and blue is the only colour almost entirely absent from all the varieties of nourishment. The dissociation invites us to examine them more for their sculptural value, to grasp the monumentality not only of the group but of the knife-sharp, simplified faces without mouths, the alternations between astounding bulk and summary, distorted sharpness that both underwrite the compositional move-

Bathers, *1900–06, was acquired by the National Gallery, London, in 1964.*

ments and, from a faceted flatness, heighten the picture plane. The sky too is faceted, spread thick like butter.

The distorted angularity of many shoulders, the insistence upon angle and strength of line, oppose with ferocity a facile mingling of these bodies, in order to rejoin them sharply; with the result that our apprehension of the bulky, answering V shapes is a startled apprehension, as if experienced by means of the extreme flare of a forked lightning flash. Coupled with the contrasting monumentality, this sharpness persists in the impression however long we gaze. Another reconciliation is between the sheet-lightning of the enwrapping towels and the slow swathes of blue daylight that dwell on ochre-tinted flesh and ochre hair and the ochreous strand.

For me the blue embrace is the final impression, withstanding a hurricane-like flattening of the light-toned foliage and a suggestion in the shape of the right-hand bathers' group of a petal-shaped volcanic orifice erupting into a steamy cloud beyond. But the group as a whole does not appear settled or rooted to the ground. The figures almost slide on it. We sense the possibility of fresh forms burrowing up from the ground's lightness to meet the blue embrace. This sense of lightness and fruitfulness balances yet enhances both monumentality and angularity.

The left-hand group is pyramidal; incline of the tree-trunks is an important element of the design, in the arrest and, on the right, in the reversal of movement. But especially in regard to so great and complex a picture I am the more unwilling to speak in the plainer functional terms of composition and design. I prefer to insist that the formal elements not only enrich but enlarge the subject matter. The fact that you do not agree with every image that I have associated with this picture does not invalidate my point. The emotive arrangements carry a number of such interpretations. Form is the container for a sum of meanings while it is from a concatenation of meanings that form is constructed, meanings that have been translated into terms of spatial significance. Without appreciation of spatial value, of empathy with bodies in space, there can be no understanding of the emotive images that form conveys. I believe that there is a nexus of meaning that we all recognize however various our explanations; it is composed from experiences otherwise divergent. The experiences will be largely individual but the power of an integrated communion between trends in concrete or corporeal terms is palpable. Let us agree that the material for creating this nexus is drawn from the artist's experiences and intentions, particularly, of course, his aims in regard to art. There are also broader limitations upon the realization of form without which we have no licence to conceive of art, matters of style, of the moment in the history of art and of the culture it mirrors, the many-sided limitations that are the concern of art history. But here, too, proper understanding depends upon an acceptance that cultural aim has been translated by all art, even sometimes without the help of iconography, into the concrete terms of the senses and within the range of our long memory for sensory experiences wherein traces of the first and primary objects are preserved. One more word about *The Bathers*. Some of the faces particularly are conceived as a series of ledges or blocks, wooden, primitive, strong. The tendency exists throughout Cézanne's development from the seventies. I believe this aspect of his work, especially in the last compositions of Bathers, is the first of his influences upon the evolution of Cubism. This same aspect of his influence is far more obvious upon *Les Demoiselles d'Avignon* and upon all those works that were so soon to forge the easiest of links with Negro sculpture. I cannot help speculating in the most far-fetched manner whether one day it will be possible to claim for *The Bathers* that it is among the first and perhaps the greatest works of a deeply founded cosmopolitan art which was to pre-figure the eventual evolution of a multi-racial society. That would indeed be to specify a very pregnant image implicit in form, the compulsions of which in the Industrial Age had substantiated out of the inner life a compulsion even of a history to be.

Picasso: Les Demoiselles d'Avignon, *1907, Museum of Modern Art, New York.*

Georges Seurat. *Promenade. c.*1882/87. Pen and ink, 11⁵/₇ × 8⁴/₅″ (29.8 × 22.4 cm). Von der Heydt Museum, Wuppertal.

BRIDGET RILEY
MODERN PAINTERS
"The Artist's Eye: Seurat"
Summer 1991

Bridget Riley (b. 1931), British painter on whose early work Seurat was an important influence.

Visiting the centennial exhibition of Seurat's work at the Grand Palais in Paris is an extraordinary experience for several reasons. Firstly, despite the fact that he left the smallest body of work of any great nineteenth century painter, the impression given by the exhibition is that it is huge, if not colossal. Secondly, it is extraordinary for the rigour of the discipline, and the delicacy of the sensibility which was a tool of that discipline; and thirdly for the nature of Seurat's aims, as distinct from the nature of his achievement. The contradictions are startling, and all the more so because they not only coexist but seem to be dependent one upon another. As a result, the works excite and surprise, are beautiful and mysterious. . . .

What is the mysterious presence which recurs so insistently? Curiously enough, although its treatment may differ from subject to subject or from manifestation to manifestation, one has an unmistakeable sense of the mystery being singular and constant. Superficially it can be explained to some extent by what is depicted, by the choice of solitary figures, empty landscapes, desolate buildings, low light, or darkness itself. But the heart of this mystery, it seems to me, lies more in its employment of our powers of perception. We cannot *quite* see. Within the myriad, subtle distinctions of close tones, or through the magic weaving of conté marks, we cannot sometimes be sure of the identity or even of the actual forms of what it is we are looking at. To put it another way, by confronting us with an experience just beyond our visual grasp, with something unfathomable, the *imperceptible* in short, Seurat asks: what is it that we are looking at?

There is no mystification. He takes the opposite approach, that of clarity and force of will. Nothing is fudged or evaded. Every tonal differentiation, every formal limit, every spatial position in these extraordinary areas has been exactly organised – and the mystery only deepens. Through precisely constructing the unfathomable, he brings the question to the forefront of our attention: what is it that we are looking at? Seurat is walking a tight-rope. Only an artist of his delicacy and determination, and fired by a sense of intellectual adventure, can hope to keep his head.

And it is little short of thrilling to realise that so sure is Seurat of what he is doing that he *can* eliminate all that is not essential. (It is not difficult to imagine how any other artist would have grasped at this or that incidental in such a situation.) At the same time he is *adding*, creating a richer if more exacting field from which he can fabricate even more complex mysteries with greater precision. Take *Forest at Poutaubent*: there he uses only tonal colour and simple gradation. Close up, the painting seems to be quite flat, a little curtain of sparkles drawn across a dense formlessness. But, to one's surprise, from further away another dimension appears. Hidden depths open up, soft volumes emerge.

Le forêt au Poutaubent, 1881–82, Metropolitan Museum of Art, New York.

This new importance of viewing distance increases Seurat's scope. At a few feet from *Le Petit Paysan en Bleu*, for instance, a vertical field of green brushstrokes rises straight up the canvas. The blue strokes for the jacket occupy the same plane as does the almost blank circular face. But step back a little, and slowly the space of the painting reveals itself. The body takes on volume, the figure emerges from its ground, the head becomes round, features appear. Suddenly a monumental image is there.

Le Petit Paysan en Bleu, 1881–82, Musée d'Orsay.

* * *

This elastic pictorial space produced by the scrupulously organised colour and the variable viewing distances is crucial. It facilitates a relationship between two extremes – the amorphous fabric and the monumental space it can generate. The Divisionist method breaks down and absorbs familiar distinctions of form and identity. By this it provides a conduit through which Seurat's particular and enigmatic sense of form and volume can be evoked.

But it is obviously an extremely delicate process and one which can only happen where a perfect correspondence has been achieved. Whenever these extremes of Seurat's vision are brought into open conflict the entire structure which he is fabricating becomes jumbled, and jars. Where they are well ordered perceptually, then there is a beautiful flow between the two which provides both a unity and a context in which his vision can unfold.

* * *

In *La Grande Jatte*. . . . Seurat develops the spatial organisation of *Peasants at Work* into a coherent system. '*La méthode*', as he called it, is now formulated. The basic principle is contrast, and this is applied to all the elements. He differentiates between the additive and subtractive colour-mixtures, that is to say between colour in light and colour in pigment, and chooses the former as his guide.

COLORPLATE 21

Seurat uses the three primaries of light: red-orange, green, and blue-violet for his canvas. Such honeing-in demanded a greater precision in colour application, and so the tiny pointilliste touch arrives. The preparatory work, which stands in for the great painting itself (now in the Art Institute of Chicago), makes it quite easy to follow the evolution from the freely hatched brush-stroke (still used to lay in the ground work) to the dot, that uninflected and non-referential mark. It is easy to see that the manner in which it draws attention to itself while carrying out a task discreetly would have appealed to Seurat.

COLORPLATES 17, 18, 19

* * *

The general direction of his preparatory work shows that it is no longer exclusively devoted to the study of nature, and that it increasingly serves as a body of material amenable to his purpose. And what is his purpose? According to Signac it was, in Seurat's own words: "To start anew what they have done". In no way could the Impressionist preoccupation with light and colour, with all its attendant ramifications of reflected light and ambient colour, possibly be at fault. It was the accidental, instinctual, restless ebb and flow of visual experience with which the Impressionist insights were associated that posed the problem. Seurat certainly did not imagine that the elusive or fugitive could ever be separated from phenomena, but it was rather more part of his programme that these should be understood on their own terms and reconstituted as pictorial elements.

The law of simultaneous contrast implicitly accepts the instantaneous. . . by its very definition. So in the final analysis one could say that it was in the attitude to perception that the divergence came. For Monet perception was the essential vehicle and supreme arbitrator of his art. He accepted its complexities unhesitatingly, even without reflection, and went along with it.

For Seurat's purpose perception itself had to be examined, methodically analysed and built up into a *technique*. However, it is a limitation of examination *per se* that it only examines that which it *can* examine. For an artist those fleeting sensations which pass unrecognised by the intellect are just as important as those which become conscious. They intermingle and operate together. . . . As with the drawings earlier, it is once again the *technicalities of nothing* which provides the clue. By the time Seurat is painting *La Grande Jatte*, these have evolved to an extraordinary degree. Penetration turns into a veil. Nothing appears to be hidden. It is four o'clock in the afternoon. The sun floods the island, there are pools and bars of shadow, but it is undeniably broad day and everything is seen. What a grand moment to choose for mystery – with the eyes wide open.

It is as though Seurat has turned a searchlight on nothing, and exposed it – not as a fraud but as a fact. There it is. But what is it? Every corner of the canvas has been weighed, judged and accounted for. Our eyes travel with ease over the precisely constructed surfaces and planes, over the huge expanses of brightnesses and darknesses, sensing volume and depth. Interval follows event; measure, rhythm and cadence all play their part faultlessly in Seurat's grand structure. But the more we can penetrate, the more we wonder what it is that eludes us. Our reason can, for the main part, identify all the objects in the picture. There may be a few curiosities, like the shape of the edge of a red umbrella against sunlit grass behind the tall lady standing on the right, or our actual disbelief in the size of the little man in the top hat sitting with his cane in the shade towards the left of the painting, but these simple oddities are trifling in comparison with the compelling quality of mystery which pervades the painting.

The achievement defies the intention. This is the stupefying greatness of *La Grande Jatte*. Seurat concentrates all his efforts on organising, in the full light of consciousness, a coherent perceptual structure, and as a consequence he extracts and focuses upon precisely that which normally escapes attention. The elusive is made present. The fugitive caught and stilled. But in so doing he simply arouses the somnambulist side of perception. Instead of enlisting the services of our sight as they are habitually balanced, he draws out the unknown on a radical, more profound level. Such an intent scrutiny of phenomena, and the painting out, step by step, of perception, as though it had been mapped, build up a perfect hallucination. The unfathomable appears in the guise of total visibility. His achievement is to have demonstrated the enigma of reality as it is available to us.

But, if so, why is this same paradox not felt in the work of Monet? It could be because Monet goes *with* perception, looking along its sightlines as it were, whereas Seurat looks *into* perception and shows it to be the activity which produces what it sees. He fabricates the answer to the question What is it that we are looking at? by holding up a sort of mirror; and what we see is ourselves looking.

PAUL KLEE

DIARIES

Van Gogh

1908, 1911

The spring Sezession exhibition is making a real effort. One can now see the latest art from Paris, which jibes with Herr Meier-Gräfe's views. Bonnard, no doubt cultivated, but very small and tight, very narrow. There is something to be learned from his economical way of selecting his values. He is so restrained that the bright accents, for all their quietness, can give a triumphant effect. Vuillard is weaker still, even though he strives to achieve a style that transcends the European. By Roussel, a beautiful still life with flowers.

The strongest is Vallotton, but a very unpleasant manner of painting. Not painting, and yet appetite for painting. But somehow he is quite a man.

Also, a large collection of drawings by Liebermann – "which Liebermann?" they asked in Solln. For people out there, there are two Liebermanns. Also etchings by the same artist. Long-familiar, well-assimilated things!

I stand on the kitchen balcony myself and hunt with some luck for children playing.

Two more exhibitions, quite important ones! Van Gogh at Brakl's and Van Gogh again at Zimmermann's on Maximilianstrasse. At Brakl's, a great deal; at Zimmermann's, the very famous pieces, like "L'Arlésienne," and many others. His pathos is alien to me, especially in my current phase, but he is certainly a genius. Pathetic to the point of being pathological, this endangered man can endanger one who does not see through him. Here a brain is consumed by the fire of a star. It frees itself in its work just before the catastrophe. Deepest tragedy takes place here, real tragedy, natural tragedy, exemplary tragedy.

Permit me to be terrified!

* * *

The longer my production moves in a definite direction, the less gaily it progresses. But just now something new seems to be happening to the stream: it is broadening into a lake. I hope it will not lack a corresponding depth. I was the faithful image of a part of art history; I moved toward Impressionism and beyond it. I don't want to say that I grew out of it; I hope this is not so. It was not dilettantism that made this small-scale replica out of me, but modesty: I wanted to know all these things, so as not to bypass any out of ignorance, and to assimilate some parts, no matter how small, of each domain that was to be given up.

At present, I begin to understand many things about Van Gogh. I develop more and more confidence in him, partly because of his letters of which I own a selection. He was able to reach deep, very deep into his own heart.

It cannot be easy, in fact, for anyone to hurry by such a landmark, for the historical clock moves more harshly in the present than in the meditation of art history. It never stops though; it only seems to, on foggy days.

Perhaps he did not say all he had to, so that a few others might still be called upon to complete the revelation?

It is particularly tempting to view Van Gogh in historical retrospect – how he came without a break from Impressionism and yet created novelty.

His line is new and yet very old, and happily not a purely European affair. It is more a question of reform than of revolution.

The diaries kept by Paul Klee (1879–1940) between 1898 and 1918, which chart the development of his early concerns as an artist, were first published in Cologne in 1957.

In the 1890s in Munich, Berlin and Vienna, Secessionist groups of avant-garde artists broke away from existing institutions for exhibiting. Together with Les XX *in Brussels, they were the first to hold large exhibitions of modern French art outside Paris. Julius Meier-Graefe (1867–1935), German art historian whose studies of Cézanne, Van Gogh and the development of modern art helped to introduce Impressionism and Post-Impressionism to Germany.*

Max Liebermann (1847–1935), German Impressionist painter.

The realization that there exists a line that benefits from Impressionism and at the same time conquers it has a truly electrifying effect on me. "Progress possible in the line!"

The possibility ripened in me of harmonizing my swarming scribbles with firmly restraining linear boundaries. And this will bear for me a further fruit: the line that eats and digests scribbles. Assimilation. The spaces still look a bit empty, but not for much longer!

In lucid moments, I now have a clear view of twelve years of the history of my inner self. First the cramped self, that self with the big blinkers, then the disappearance of the blinkers and the self, now gradually the reëmergence of a self without blinkers.

It is good that one didn't know this in advance.

GEORGES BATAILLE

VERVE

"Van Gogh as Prometheus"

December 1937

Georges Bataille (1897–1962), novelist, poet and philosopher associated with the Surrealist movement.

How is it that towering figures, reassuring in their power of persuasion, emerge among us? How is it that within the chaos of infinite possibility certain forms take shape, radiating a sudden brilliance, a force of conviction that excludes doubt? This would seem to happen independently of the crowd. It is quite generally agreed that once one stops to linger in contemplation of a painting, its significance in no way depends upon anyone else's assent.

This view stands, of course, as a denial of everything that obviously transpires in front of canvases placed on exhibition; the visitor goes not in search of his own pleasure, but rather the judgments expected of him by others. There is, however, little point in stressing the poverty of most viewers and readers. Beyond the absurd limits of present custom and even through the rash confusion that surrounds the paintings and the name of Van Gogh, a world can open – a world in which one no longer spitefully waves the crowd aside, but our own world, the world in which, at the arrival of spring, a human being discards, with a joyous gesture, his heavy, musty winter coat.

Such a person, coatless, drifting with the crowd – more in innocence than in contempt – cannot look without terror upon the tragic canvases as so many painful signs, as the perceptible trace of Vincent Van Gogh's existence. That person may, however, then feel the greatness that he represents, not in himself alone: he stumbles still at every moment under the weight of shared misery – not in himself alone, but insofar as he is, in his nakedness, the bearer of untold hopes for all those who desire life and who desire, as well, to rid the earth, if necessary, of the power of that which bears no resemblance to him. Imbued with this wholly future greatness, the terror felt by such a man would become laughable – laughable, even, the ear, the brothel, and "Vincent's" suicide; did he not make human tragedy the sole object of his entire life, whether in cries, laughter, love, or even struggle?

He must perforce marvel to the point of laughter at that powerful magic for which savages would, no doubt, require an entire drunken crowd, sustained clamor, and the beating of many drums. For it was no mere bloody ear that Van Gogh detached from his own head bearing it off to that "House" (the troubling, crude, and childish image of the world we represent to others). Van Gogh, who decided by 1882 that it was better to be Prometheus than Jupiter, tore from within himself rather than an ear, nothing less than a SUN.

Above all, human existence requires stability, the permanence of things. The result is an ambivalence with respect to all great and violent expenditure of strength; such expenditure, whether in nature or in man, represents the strongest possible threat. The feelings of admiration and of ecstasy induced by them thus mean that we are concerned to admire them from afar. The sun corresponds most conveniently to that prudent concern. It is all *radiance*, gigantic loss of heat and of light, *flame, explosion*; but remote from men, who can enjoy in safety and quiet the fruits of this great cataclysm. To the earth belongs the solidity which sustains houses of stone and the steps of men (at least on its surface, for buried within the depths of the earth is the incandescence of lava).

Given the foregoing, it must be said that after the night of December '88, when, in the house to which it came, his ear met a fate which remains unknown (one can only dimly imagine the laughter and discomfort which preceded some unknown decision), Van Gogh began to give to the sun a meaning which it had not yet had. He did not introduce it into his canvases as part of a decor, but rather like the sorcerer whose dance slowly rouses the crowd, transporting it in its movement. At that moment all of his painting finally became *radiation, explosion, flame*, and himself, lost in ecstasy before a source of *radiant* life, *exploding, inflamed*. When this solar dance began, all at once nature itself was shaken, plants burst into flame, and the earth rippled like a swift sea, or burst; of the stability at the foundation of things nothing remained. Death appeared in a sort of transparency, like the sun through the blood of a living hand, in the interstices of the bones outlined in the darkness. The flowers, bright or faded, the face of depressingly haggard radiance, the Van Gogh "sunflower" – disquiet? domination? – put an end to all the power of immutable law, of foundations, of all that confers on (many) faces their repugnant aspect of defensive closure.

This singular election of the sun must not, however, induce absurd error; Van Gogh's canvases do not – any more than Prometheus's flight – form a tribute to the remote sovereign of the sky, and the sun is dominant insofar as it is captured. Far from recognizing the *distant* power of the heavenly cataclysm (as though only an extension of its monotonous surface, safe from change, had been required), the earth, like a daughter suddenly dazzled and perverted by her father's debauchery, in turn luxuriates in cataclysm, in explosive loss and brilliance.

It is this that accounts for the great, festive quality of Van Gogh's painting. This painter, more than any other, had that sense of flowers which also represent, on earth, intoxication, joyous perversion – flowers which burst, beam, and dart their flaming heads into the very rays of that sun which will wither them. There is in this deep birth such disturbance that it induces laughter; how can we ignore that chain of knots which so surely links ear, asylum, sun, the feast, and death? With the stroke of a razor Van Gogh cut off his ear; he then brought it to a brothel he knew. Madness incited him, as a violent dance sustains a shared ecstasy. He painted his finest canvases. He remained for a while confined within an asylum, and a year and a half after cutting off his ear, he killed himself.

When all has happened thus, what meaning remains for art or criticism? Can we even maintain that in these conditions, art alone will explain the sound of crowds within the exhibition halls? Vincent Van Gogh belongs not to art history, but to the bloody myth of our existence as humans. He is of that rare company who, in a world spellbound by stability, by sleep, suddenly reached the terrible "boiling point" without which all that claims to endure becomes insipid, intolerable, declines. For this "boiling point" has meaning not only for him who attains it, but for *all*, even though *all* may *not yet* perceive that which binds man's savage destiny to *radiance*, to *explosion*, to *flame*, and only thereby to power.

COLORPLATE 112. Henri Matisse. *Open Window, Collioure*. 1905. 21³/₄ × 18¹/₈″ (55.2 × 46.1 cm).
Private Collection (Courtesy © Hériteurs Matisse).

COLORPLATE 113. Henri Matisse. *Landscape at Collioure*. Summer 1905. 18⅛ × 21⅝″ (46 × 55 cm). Statensmuseum for Kunst, Copenhagen (J. Rump Collection).

COLORPLATE 114. Pierre Bonnard. *The Open Window*. 1921. 46½ × 37¾″ (118 × 96 cm).
Phillips Collection, Washington, D.C.

COLORPLATE 115. Pierre Bonnard. *Woman with Basket of Fruit.* 1915–18. 26¾ × 15⅝″
(69.2 × 40 cm). Baltimore Museum of Art (Bequest of Miss Etta Cone,
from the Collection of Frederick W. Cone).

COLORPLATE 116. Pierre Bonnard. *Studio with Mimosa*. 1939–46. 49¼ × 49¼″ (125 × 125 cm).
Musée National d'Art Moderne, Centre Pompidou, Paris.

COLORPLATE I I 7. Pierre Bonnard. *Red Poppies*. 1926. $29\frac{1}{8} \times 16\frac{1}{2}''$ (74 × 41.9 cm).
The Jacques and Natasha Gelman Collection, on loan to the Metropolitan Museum of Art,
New York.

COLORPLATE 118. Pierre Bonnard. *La Toilette: Nude at the Mirror.* 1931. 60½ × 41″ (153.5 × 104 cm).
Museo d'Arte Moderna Ca' Pesaro, Venice.

COLORPLATE 119. Pierre Bonnard. *Almond Tree in Flower*. 1947. 21⅝ × 14¾″ (55 × 37.5 cm).
Musée National d'Art Moderne, Centre Pompidou, Paris.

RENÉ MAGRITTE
CAHIER DE NEVELVLEK-VAN GOGH
"Van Gogh and Freedom"
May–June 1955

René Magritte (1898–1967), Belgian Surrealist artist.

It has often been said that the Impressionist painters discovered a new sensibility – a sort of ingenuous happiness, of light intoxication – in a nature that was no longer regimented by more or less rational conventions. This sensibility did not pose any problems in a world without interruption: the painter no longer distinguished himself from *what he saw*, his consciousness was entirely *in sympathy*. To be sure, this sensibility only achieved purity when the painters abandoned their theories or their originality, for this purity has never been the property of one particular art. Certain chords in a Debussy suite give a blue sensation, a certain nude by Renoir causes us to hear happiness. But this new sensibility, which appeared with Impressionism, is not to be confused with, for example, Jean-Jacques Rousseau's love of nature, for that love was accompanied by a concern for "seeing clearly." It should be noted that the public and most critics or art historians have not perceived the sentiment revealed by the Impressionists. The public and exegetes "explain" something that is only a question of love.

Severe illumination, which oriented Classical painting, had been put into question and absolutely abandoned by the Impressionist painters. Various techniques inaugurated by them were employed by Van Gogh. But the uncertainty, the fever, and the violence of Van Gogh's explorations have left a painful mark on them. The twisted trees, the swirling clouds, the contrasts of acid tones do not suffice to fully express Van Gogh's great anguish. He even went so far as to try to express himself with a razor – and cut off an ear. With him, we are far from the atmosphere of freshness and enchantment that bestowed a new youth to the world the Impressionists represented. Van Gogh's delirious painting and his actions "keep" to a plane alien to Impressionism.

With Van Gogh, a domain opens in which artistic expression is subject to psychological and psychiatric examination. Aesthetics quit philosophy to be treated by so-called more "exact" sciences. Thanks to the interest of such scholars in artistic expression, the "art" of the inmates of lunatic asylums or prisons is the object of doctoral studies; "Sunday" painters, such as le douanier Rousseau, are more attentively observed than Leonardo da Vinci or Courbet; finally – so that nothing mediocre may be overlooked – the drawings and writings of schoolchildren are solemnly exhibited before a respectful procession of sentimental adults. It should be noted that a Gérard de Nerval, for example, escaped to this world from which poetry flees.

Henri Julien Félix Rousseau (1844–1910), naive painter who took up painting full-time in 1893 when he retired from the Civil Service as a customs official ("le Douanier") and was adopted by the French avant-garde.
Gérard de Nerval, pseudonym of Gérard Labrunie (1808–55), poet and novelist. The writings which recorded his mental states during the last years before his suicide were of particular interest to the Symbolists and the Surrealists.

The question posed by the "artistic" phenomenon under discussion and by Van Gogh, who is involuntarily responsible for it, is that of freedom. The Impressionists had bestowed on freedom a sense of truth, for they tried to achieve purity. To do this they needed a love of truth and intelligence that allowed them to free themselves from the problems to which the so-called "traditional" artists had consecrated themselves. Can one say that Van Gogh was liberated? It is scarcely possible. He subjected himself to passions that gave him a blind force in exchange for his submission. It is this blind force that Van Gogh brings to mind above all, and I cannot assign to it a value that commands admiration or love. I am of the opinion that violent sentiments reduce the world to something rather vulgar. When I look at what remains of Van Gogh's furious activity, I find in it the memory of a delirious life, a life without freedom.

W. H. AUDEN

ENCOUNTER

"Calm even in the Catastrophe"

April 1959

Wystan Hugh Auden (1907–73), British poet.

The great masters of letter-writing as an art have probably been more concerned with entertaining their friends than disclosing their innermost thoughts and feelings; their epistolary style is characterized by speed, high spirits, wit, and fantasy. Van Gogh's letters are not art in this sense, but human documents; what makes them great letters is the absolute self-honesty and nobility of the writer.

The nineteenth century created the myth of the Artist as Hero, the man who sacrifices his health and happiness to his art and in compensation claims exemption from all social responsibilities and norms of behavior.

At first sight Van Gogh seems to fit the myth exactly. He dresses and lives like a tramp, he expects to be supported by others, he works at his painting like a fiend, he goes mad. Yet the more one reads these letters, the less like the myth he becomes.

He knows he is neurotic and difficult but he does not regard this as a sign of superiority, but as an illness like heart disease, and hopes that the great painters of the future will be as healthy as the Old Masters.

> But this painter who is to come – I can't imagine him living in little cafés, working away with a lot of false teeth, and going to the Zouaves' brothels, as I do.

He sees the age in which he is living as one of transition rather than fulfillment, and is extremely modest about his own achievements.

> Giotto and Cimabue, as well as Holbein and Van Dyck, lived in an obeliscal solidly-framed society, architecturally constructed, in which each individual was a stone and all the stones clung together, forming a monumental society.... But, you know, we are in the midst of down-right *laisser-aller* and anarchy. We artists who love order and symmetry isolate ourselves and are working to define *only one thing....* We *can* paint an atom of the chaos, a horse, a portrait, your grandmother, apples, a landscape....
>
> We do not feel that we are dying, but we do feel the truth that we are of small account, and that we are paying a hard price to be a link in the chain of artists, in health, in youth, in liberty, none of which we enjoy, any more than the cab-horse that hauls a coachful of people out to enjoy the spring.

Furthermore, though he never wavers in his belief that painting is a vocation, he does not claim that painters are superior to other folk.

It was Richepin who said somewhere,

> *L'amour de l'art fait perdre l'amour vrai.*

I think that is terribly true, but on the other hand real love makes you disgusted with art....

> The rather superstitious ideas they have here about painting sometimes depress me more than I can tell you, because basically it is really fairly true that a painter as a man is too absorbed in what his eyes see, and is not sufficiently master of the rest of his life.

It is true that Van Gogh did not earn his living but was supported all his life by his brother who was by no means a rich man. But when one compares his attitude towards money with that of say, Wagner, or Baudelaire, how immeasurably more decent and self-respecting Van Gogh appears.

No artist ever asked less of a patron – a laborer's standard of living and enough over to buy paints and canvases. He even worries about his right to the paints and wonders whether he ought not to stick to the cheaper medium of drawing. When, occasionally, he gets angry with his brother, his complaint is not that Theo is stingy but that he is cold; it is more intimacy he craves for, not more cash.

> . . . against my person, my manners, clothes, world, you, like so many others, seem to think it necessary to raise so many objections – weighty enough and at the same time obviously without redress – that they have caused our personal brotherly intercourse to wither and die off gradually in the course of the years.
>
> This is the dark side of your character – I think you are mean in this respect – but the bright side is your reliability in money matters.
>
> Ergo conclusion – I acknowledge being under an obligation to you with the greatest pleasure. Only – lacking relations with you, with Teersteg [sic], and with whomever I knew in the past – I want *something else*. . . .
>
> There are people, as you know, who support painters during the time when they do not yet earn anything. But how often doesn't it happen that it ends miserably, wretchedly for both parties, partly because the protector is annoyed about the money, which is or at least seems quite thrown away, whereas, on the other hand, the painter feels entitled to more confidence, more patience and interest than is given him? But in most cases the misunderstandings arise from carelessness on both sides.

Few painters read books and fewer can express in words what they are up to. Van Gogh is a notable exception: he read voraciously and with understanding, he had considerable literary talent of his own, and he loved to talk about what he was doing and why. If I understood the meaning of the word *literary* as a pejorative adjective when applied to painting, those who use it are asserting that the world of pictures and the world of phenomenal nature are totally distinct so that one must never be judged by reference to the other. To ask if a picture is "like" any natural object – it makes no difference whether one means a "photographic" or a platonically "real" likeness – or to ask if one "subject" for a picture is humanly more important than another, is irrelevant. The painter creates his own pictorial world and the value of a painting can only be assessed by comparison with other paintings. If that is indeed what critics mean, then Van Gogh must be classified as a literary painter. Like Millet, whom all his life he acknowledged as his master, and like some of his contemporary French novelists, Flaubert, the Goncourts, Zola, he believed that the truly human subject for art in his day was the life of the poor. Hence his quarrel with the art-schools.

> As far as I know there isn't a single academy where one learns to draw and paint a digger, a sower, a woman putting the kettle over the fire or a seamstress. But in every city of some importance there is an academy with a choice of models for historical, Arabic, Louis XV, in short, *all really* non-existent figures. . . . All academic figures are put together in the same way and, let's say, *on ne peut mieux*. Irreproachable, *faultless*. You will guess what I am driving at, they do not reveal anything new. I think that, however correctly academic a figure may be, it will be superfluous, though it were by Ingres himself, when it lacks the essential modern note, the intimate character, the real *action*. Perhaps you will ask: When will a figure not be superfluous? . . . When the digger digs, when the peasant is a peasant and the peasant woman a peasant woman. . . . I ask you, do you know a single digger, a single sower in the old Dutch school? Did they ever try to paint "a labourer"? Did Velasquez try it in his water-carrier or types from the people? No. The figures in the pictures of the old master do not *work*.

It was this same moral preference for the naturally real to the ideally beautiful which led him, during his brief stay at an art-school in Antwerp, when he was set to copy a cast of the Venus de Milo, to make alterations in her figure and roar at the shocked professor: "So you don't know what a young woman is like, God damn you! A woman must have hips and buttocks and a pelvis in which she can hold a child."

Where he differs from most of his French contemporaries is that he never shared their belief that the artist should suppress his own emotions and view his material with clinical detachment. On the contrary, he writes:

> . . . whoever wants to do figures must first have what is printed on the Christmas number of *Punch*: "Good Will to all" – and this to a high degree. One must have a warm sympathy with human beings, and go on having it, or the drawings will remain cold and insipid. I consider it very necessary for us to watch ourselves and to take care that we do not become disenchanted in this respect.

and how opposed to any doctrine of "pure" art is this remark written only two months before his death.

> Instead of grandiose exhibitions, it would have been better to address oneself to the people and work so that each could have in his home some pictures or reproductions which would be lessons, like the work of Millet.

Vincent van Gogh. *Grove of Cypresses*. St-Rémy, June 1889. Pen, reed pen and ink, 24½ × 18¼" (62.5 × 46.5 cm). © 1990 The Art Institute of Chicago (Gift of Robert Allerton, 1927.543).

Here he sounds like Tolstoy, just as he sounds like Dostoevsky when he says:

> It always strikes me, and it is very peculiar, that whenever we see the image of indescribable and unutterable desolation – of loneliness, poverty and misery, the end and extreme of all things, the thought of God comes into one's mind.

When he talks of the poor, indeed, Van Gogh sounds more honest and natural than either Tolstoy or Dostoevsky. As a physical and intellectual human being Tolstoy was a king, a superior person; in addition he was a count, a socially superior person. However hard he tried, he could never think of a peasant as an equal; he could only, partly out of a sense of guilt at his own moral shortcomings, admire him as his superior. Dostoevsky was not an aristocrat and he was ugly, but it was with the criminal poor rather than the poor as such that he felt in sympathy. But Van Gogh preferred the life and company of the poor, not in theory but in fact. Tolstoy and Dostoevsky were, as writers, successful in their lifetime with the educated; what the peasants thought of them as men we do not know. Van Gogh was not recognized as an artist in his lifetime; on the other hand, we have records of the personal impression he made upon the coal-miners of the Borinage.

> People still talk of the miner whom he went to see after the accident in the Marcasse mine. The man was a habitual drinker, "an unbeliever and blasphemer," according to the people who told me the story. When Vincent entered his house to help and comfort him, he was received with a volley of abuse. He was called especially a *mâcheux d'capelots* (rosary chewer) as if he had been a Roman Catholic priest. But Van Gogh's evangelical tenderness converted the man. . . . People still tell how, at the time of the *tirage au sort*, the drawing of lots for conscription, women begged the holy man to show them a passage in the Holy Scripture which would serve as a talisman for their sons and ensure their drawing a good number and being exempted from service in the barracks. . . . A strike broke out; the mutinous miners would no longer listen to anyone except "*l'pasteur Vincent*" whom they trusted.

Both as a man and as a painter Van Gogh was passionately Christian in feeling though, no doubt, a bit heterodox in doctrine. "Resignation," he declared, "is only for those who *can* be resigned, and religious belief is for those who *can* believe. My friends, let us love what we love. The man who damn well refuses to love what he loves dooms himself." Perhaps the best label for him as a painter would be Religious Realist. A realist because he attached supreme importance to the incessant study of nature and never composed pictures "out of his head"; religious because he regarded nature as the sacramental visible sign of a spiritual grace which it was his aim as a painter to reveal to others. "I want," he said once, "to paint men and women with that something of the eternal which the halo used to symbolise, and which we seek to convey by the actual radiance and vibration of our colouring." He is the first painter, so far as I know, to have consciously attempted to produce a painting which should be religious and yet contain no traditional religious iconography, something which one might call "A Parable for the Eye."

> Here is a description of a canvas which is in front of me at the moment. A view of the park of the asylum where I am staying; on the right a grey terrace and a side wall of a house. Some deflowered rose bushes, on the left a stretch of the park – red ochre – the soil scorched by the sun, covered with fallen pine needles. This edge of the park is planted with large pine trees, whose trunks and branches are red-ochre, the foliage green gloomed over by an admixture of black. These high trees stand out against the evening sky with violet stripes on a yellow ground,

which higher up turns into pink, into green. A wall – also red-ochre – shuts off the view, and is topped only by a violet and yellow-ochre hill. Now the nearest tree is an enormous trunk, struck by lightning and sawed off. But one side branch shoots up very high and lets fall an avalanche of dark green pine needles. This sombre giant – like a defeated proud man – contrasts, when considered in the nature of a living creature, with the pale smile of a last rose on the fading bush in front of him. Underneath the trees, empty stone benches, sullen box trees; the sky is mirrored – yellow – in a puddle left by the rain. A sunbeam, the last ray of daylight, raises the sombre ochre almost to orange. Here and there small black figures wander among the tree trunks.

You will realise that this combination of red-ochre, of green gloomed over by grey, the black streaks surrounding the contours, produces something of the sensation of anguish, called "rouge-noir," from which certain of my companions in misfortune frequently suffer. Moreover, the motif of the great tree struck by lightning, the sickly green-pink smile of the last flower of autumn serve to confirm this impression.

I am telling you (about this canvas) to remind you that one can try to give an impression of anguish without aiming straight at the historic Garden of Gethsemane.

Evidently, what Van Gogh is trying to do is to substitute for a historic iconography, which has to be learned before it can be recognized, an iconography of color and form relations which reveals itself instantaneously to the senses, and is therefore impossible to misinterpret. The possibility of such an iconography depends upon whether or not color-form relations and their impact upon the human mind are governed by universal laws. Van Gogh certainly believed that they were and that, by study, any painter could discover these laws.

The *laws* of the colours are unutterably beautiful, just because they are not *accidental*. In the same way that people nowadays no longer believe in a God who capriciously and despotically flies from one thing to another, but begin to feel more respect and admiration for faith in nature – in the same way, and for the same reasons, I think that in art, the old-fashioned idea of innate genius, inspiration, etc., I do not say must be put aside, but thoroughly reconsidered, verified – and greatly modified.

In another letter he gives Fatality as another name for God, and defines Him by the image – "Who is the White Ray of Light, He in Whose eyes even the Black Ray will have no plausible meaning."

Van Gogh had very little fun, he never knew the satisfaction of good food, glory, or the love of women, and he ended in the bin, but, after reading his correspondence, it is impossible to think of him as the romantic *artiste maudit*, or even as tragic hero; in spite of everything, the final impression is one of triumph. In his last letter to Theo, found on him after his death, he says, with a grateful satisfaction in which there is no trace of vanity:

I tell you again that I shall always consider you to be something more than a simple dealer in Corots, that through my mediation you have your part in the actual production of some canvases, which will retain their calm even in the catastrophe.

What we mean when we speak of a work of art as "great" has, surely, never been better defined than by the concluding relative clause.

Vincent van Gogh. *A Pair of Shoes.*
Paris, late 1886. 14¾ × 18″ (37.5 ×
45.5 cm). Rijksmuseum Vincent van
Gogh Foundation/Van Gogh Museum,
Amsterdam.

MEYER SCHAPIRO

THE REACH OF MIND

"The Still Life as a Personal Object – A Note on Heidegger and Van Gogh"

1968

*Meyer Schapiro (b. 1904), American art
historian and art critic; Martin Heidegger
(1889–1976), modern existentialist
philosopher concerned with consciousness and
its objects, and the notion of "Being."*

*The dialogue conducted here with Heidegger
about object and meaning was continued by
the post-structuralist philosopher Jacques
Derrida in* The Truth in Painting
(1978).

*Heidegger first presented "The Origin of the
Work of Art" as a lecture in November
1935. It has been reprinted in* Poetry,
Language, Thought, *New York, 1971.*

Vincent van Gogh: A Pair of Shoes,
*1886, Rijksmuseum Vincent van Gogh,
Amsterdam.*

In his essay on *The Origin of the Work of Art*, Martin Heidegger interprets a painting by van Gogh to illustrate the nature of art as a disclosure of truth.

He comes to this picture in the course of distinguishing three modes of being: of useful artifacts, of natural things, and of works of fine art. He proposes to describe first, "without any philosophical theory . . . a familiar sort of equipment – a pair of peasant shoes"; and "to facilitate the visual realization of them" he chooses "a well-known painting by van Gogh, who painted such shoes several times." But to grasp "the equipmental being of equipment," we must know "how shoes actually serve." For the peasant woman they serve without her thinking about them or even looking at them. Standing and walking in the shoes, the peasant woman knows the serviceability in which "the equipmental being of equipment consists." But we,

> as long as we only imagine a pair of shoes in general, or simply look at the empty, unused shoes as they merely stand there in the picture, we shall never discover what the equipmental being of equipment in truth is. In van Gogh's painting we cannot even tell where these shoes stand. There is nothing surrounding this pair of peasant shoes in or to which they might belong, only an undefined space. There are not even clods from the soil of the field or the path through it sticking to them, which might at least hint at their employment. A pair of peasant shoes and nothing more. And yet.

From the dark opening of the worn insides of the shoes the toilsome tread of the worker stands forth. In the stiffly solid heaviness of the shoes there is the accumulated tenacity of her slow trudge through the far-spreading and ever-uniform furrows of the field, swept by a raw wind. On the leather there lies the dampness and saturation of the soil. Under the soles there slides the loneliness of the field-path as the evening declines. In the shoes there vibrates the silent call of the earth, its quiet gift of the ripening corn and its enigmatic self-refusal in the fallow desolation of the wintry field. This equipment is pervaded by uncomplaining anxiety about the certainty of bread, the wordless joy of having once more withstood want, the trembling before the advent of birth and shivering at the surrounding menace of death. This equipment belongs to the *earth* and it is protected in the *world* of the peasant woman. From out of this protected belonging the equipment itself rises to its resting-in-self.

Schapiro adds in a note another reference made by Heidegger to Van Gogh in a lecture of 1935: "Speaking of Dasein (being-there or 'essent') he points to a painting by Van Gogh. 'A pair of rough peasant shoes, nothing else. Actually the painting represents nothing. But as to what is in that picture, you are immediately alone with it as though you yourself were making your way wearily homeward with your hoe on an evening in late fall after the last potato fires have died down. What is here? The canvas? The brush strokes? The spots of colour?'"

Professor Heidegger is aware that van Gogh painted such shoes several times, but he does not identify the picture he has in mind, as if the different versions are interchangeable, all presenting the same truth. A reader who wishes to compare this account with the original picture or its photograph will have some difficulty in deciding which one to select. Eight paintings of shoes by van Gogh are recorded by de la Faille in his catalogue of all the canvases by the artist that had been exhibited at the time Heidegger wrote his essay. Of these only three show the "dark openings of the worn insides" which speak so distinctly to the philosopher. They are clearly pictures of the artist's own shoes, not the shoes of a peasant. They might be shoes he had worn in Holland, but the pictures were painted during van Gogh's stay in Paris in 1886–87; one of them bears the date: "87". From the time before 1886 when he painted Dutch peasants are two pictures of shoes – a pair of clean wooden clogs set on a table beside other objects. Later in Arles he represented, as he wrote in a letter of August 1888 to his brother, "une paire de vieux souliers" which are evidently his own. A second still life of "vieux souliers de paysan" is mentioned in a letter of September 1888 to the painter Émile Bernard, but it lacks the characteristic worn surface and dark insides of Heidegger's description.

In reply to my question, Professor Heidegger has kindly written me that the picture to which he referred is one that he saw in a show at Amsterdam in March 1930. This is clearly de la Faille's no. 255; there was also exhibited at the same time a painting with three pairs of shoes, and it is possible that the exposed sole of a shoe in this picture inspired the reference to the sole in the philosopher's account. But from neither of these pictures, nor from any of the others, could one properly say that a painting of shoes by van Gogh expresses the being or essence of a peasant woman's shoes and her relation to nature and work. They are the shoes of the artist, by that time a man of the town and city.

Heidegger has written: "The art-work told us what shoes are in truth. It would be the worst self-deception if we were to think that our description, as a subjective action, first imagined everything thus and then projected it into the painting. If anything is questionable here, it is rather that we experienced too little in contact with the work and that we expressed the experience too crudely and too literally. But above all, the work does not, as might first appear, serve merely for a better visualization of what a piece of equipment is. Rather, the equipmental being of equipment first arrives at its explicit appearance through and only in the work.

"What happens here? What is at work in the work? Van Gogh's painting is the disclosure of what the equipment, the pair of peasants' shoes, *is* in truth".

Alas for him, the philosopher has indeed deceived himself. He has retained from his encounter with van Gogh's canvas a moving set of associations with peasants and the soil, which are not sustained by the

J. B. de La Faille: L'Oeuvre de Vincent van Gogh, catalogue raisonné, *Paris, 1939 (no. 54, Fig. 60; no. 63, Fig. 64; no. 255, Fig. 248; no. 331, Fig. 249; no. 332, Fig. 250; no. 333, Fig. 251; no. 461, Fig. 488; no. 607, Fig. 597). The three showing "dark openings" are nos. 255, 332, 333. No. 333 is signed "Vincent 87".*
Nos. 54 and 63.
Vincent van Gogh: Verzamelde brieven van Vincent van Gogh, *Amsterdam, 1952–54 (Vol III, Letter no. 529; no. 461; Vol. IV, p. 227; no. 607).*
In a personal communication to the author, letter of May 6, 1965.

picture itself but are grounded rather in his own social outlook with its heavy pathos of the primordial and earthy. He has indeed "imagined everything and projected it into the painting." He has experienced both too little and too much in his contact with the work.

The error lies not only in his projection which replaces a close and true attention to the work of art. For even if he had seen a picture of a peasant woman's shoes, as he describes them, it would be a mistake to suppose that the truth he uncovered in the painting – the being of the shoes – is something given here once and for all and is unavailable to our perception of shoes outside the painting. I find nothing in Heidegger's fanciful description of the shoes represented by van Gogh that could not have been imagined in looking at a real pair of peasants' shoes. Though he credits to art the power of giving to a represented pair of shoes that explicit appearance in which their being is disclosed – indeed "the universal essence of things", "world and earth in their counterplay" – this concept of the metaphysical power of art remains here a theoretical idea. The example on which he elaborates with strong conviction does not support that idea.

Is Heidegger's mistake simply that he chose a wrong example? Let us imagine a painting of a peasant-woman's shoes by van Gogh. Would it not have made manifest just those qualities and that sphere of being described by Heidegger with such pathos?

Heidegger would still have missed an important aspect of the painting: the artist's presence in the work. In his account of the picture he has overlooked the personal and physiognomic in the shoes which made them so absorbing a subject for the artist (not to speak of the intimate connection with the peculiar tones, forms, and brush-made surface of the picture as a painted work). When van Gogh depicted the peasant's wooden sabots, he gave them a clear, unworn shape and surface like the smooth still life object he had set beside them on the same table: the bowl, the bottles, etc. In the later picture of a peasant's leather slippers he has turned them with their backs to the viewer. His own shoes he has isolated on the floor and he has rendered them as if facing us, and so individual and wrinkled in appearance that we can speak of them as veridical portraits of aging shoes.

We come closer, I think, to van Gogh's feeling for these shoes in a paragraph written by Knut Hamsun in the 1880's in his novel *Hunger*, describing his own shoes:

> As I had never seen my shoes before, I set myself to study their looks, their characteristics, and when I stir my foot, their shapes and their worn uppers. I discover that their creases and white seams give them expression – impart a physiognomy to them. Something of my own nature had gone over into these shoes; they affected me, like a ghost of my other I – a breathing portion of my very self.

In comparing van Gogh's painting with Hamsun's text, we are interpreting the painting in a different way from Heidegger's. The philosopher finds in the picture of the shoes a truth about the world as it is lived by the peasant without reflection; Hamsun sees the real shoes as experienced by the self-conscious contemplating wearer who is also the writer. Hamsun's personage, a brooding, self-observant drifter, is closer to van Gogh's situation than to the peasant's. Yet van Gogh is in some ways like the peasant; as an artist he works, he is stubbornly occupied in a persistent task that is for him his inescapable calling, his life. Of course, van Gogh, like Hamsun, has also an exceptional gift of representation; he is able to transpose to the canvas with a singular power the forms and qualities of things; but they are things that have touched him deeply, in this case his own shoes – things inseparable from his body and memorable to his reacting self-awareness. They are not less objectively rendered for being seen as if endowed with his feelings and revery about himself. In isolating his own

Schapiro adds further to this quotation from Heidegger: "Truth happens in Van Gogh's painting. This does not mean that something is rightly portrayed, but rather that in the revelation of the equipmental being of the shoes, that which is as a whole – world and earth in their counterplay – attains to unconcealment . . . the more simply and essentially the shoes appear in their essence . . . the more directly and fascinatingly does all that is attain to a greater degree of being along with them."

No. 607, Fig. 597.

373

worn shoes on a canvas, he turns them to the spectator; he makes of them a piece from a self-portrait, that part of the costume with which we tread the earth and in which we locate the strains of movement, fatigue, pressure, heaviness – the burden of the erect body in its contact with the ground. They mark our inescapable position on the earth. To "be in someone's shoes" is to be in his predicament or his station in life. For a painter to represent his worn shoes as the main subject of a picture is for him to express a concern with the fatalities of his social being. Not the shoes as an instrument of use, though the landscape painter as a worker in the fields shares something of the peasant's life outdoors, but the shoes as "a portion of the self" (in Hamsun's words) are van Gogh's revealing theme.

Gauguin, who shared van Gogh's quarters in Arles in 1888, sensed a personal history behind his friend's painting of a pair of shoes. He has told in his reminiscences of van Gogh a deeply affecting story linked with van Gogh's shoes.

"In the studio was a pair of big hob-nailed shoes, all worn and spotted with mud; he made of it a remarkable still life painting. I do not know why I suspected that there was a story behind this old relic, and I ventured one day to ask him if he had some reason for preserving with respect what one ordinarily throws out for the rag-picker's basket.

"'My father,' he said, 'was a pastor, and at his urging I pursued theological studies in order to prepare for my future vocation. As a young pastor I left for Belgium one fine morning, without telling my family, to preach the gospel in the factories, not as I had been taught but as I understood it myself. These shoes, as you see, have bravely endured the fatigue of that trip.'

"Preaching to the miners in the Borinage, Vincent undertook to nurse a victim of a fire in the mine. The man was so badly burned and mutilated that the doctor had no hope for his recovery. Only a miracle, he thought, could save him. Van Gogh tended him forty days with loving care and saved the miner's life.

"Before leaving Belgium I had, in the presence of this man who bore on his brow a series of scars, a vision of the crown of thorns, a vision of the resurrected Christ."

Gauguin continues: "And Vincent took up his palette again; silently he worked. Beside him was a white canvas. I began his portrait. I too had the vision of a Jesus preaching kindness and humility."

Quoted from J. de Rotonchamp: Paul Gauguin 1848–1903, *Paris, 1925, p. 53.*

It is not clear which of the paintings with a single pair of shoes Gauguin had seen at Arles. He described it as violet in tone in contrast to the yellow walls of the studio. It does not matter. Though written some years later, and with some literary affectations, Gauguin's story confirms the essential fact that for van Gogh the shoes were a piece of his own life.

INDEX

Page numbers in *italics* refer to illustrations within the text; page numbers in **bold** refer to Colorplates; n indicates margin note.